KEEP SMILING AND NEVER GIVE UP!

By

Daniel R. Williams

© 2002 by Daniel R. Williams. All rights reserved.

No part of this book may be reproduced, stored in a retrieval system, or transmitted by any means, electronic, mechanical, photocopying, recording, or otherwise, without written permission from the author.

ISBN: 1-4033-2988-5 (e-book)
ISBN: 1-4033-2989-3 (Paperback)
ISBN: 1-4033-2990-7 (Dustjacket)
ISBN: 1-4033-2991-5 (Rocket Book)

Library of Congress Control Number: 2002105731

This book is printed on acid free paper.

Printed in the United States of America
Bloomington, IN

1st Books - rev. 08/30/02

FOREWORD

Written by Rev. C. A. Kerschner

I write memories of a person who has been admired, and for many years was hindered from activities that required bodily function due to Polio. He was able to participate only mentally, able to think with a determination, and fellowship in a fashion that allowed him to join anyone willing to enter into a discussion of most current events; very able to carry his opinions and thoughts in a very clear manner.

My relationship with Dan Williams began one Sunday. As his parents came to Sunday School they told me that Danny was not able to be at church that day due to a terrible cold and some other problems. They were going home to see about him, and the next information I had was about 2:00 AM, when his mother called to tell me that Danny had been diagnosed as having Polio and that he was losing the ability to move his arms and legs. They were taking him to Riley Hospital for Children in Indianapolis immediately.

I went to the hospital on Tuesday to see him. He was fully encased in an iron lung with all the breathing being done with the equipment that pertained to his condition. To describe his mental attitude is fully stated in a prayer of an older Saint, "Lord grant me the serenity to accept the things I cannot change, the courage to change the things I can change, and the wisdom to know the difference".

I remember what Danny said to me as I called on him one day. After greeting me he said that he had been praying and talking to God about his situation. "I told the Lord that I was willing to spend the rest of my life in this iron lung, or whatever was the Lord's will for me, and I would love Him and serve Him with all that I had to do with." After he had said this to me he smiled and said, "I have given my whole life to Jesus" and his smile was like a ray of sunshine, bright and beautiful.

Later I would come to his house and show him how to play Chess. He decided what pieces he wanted moved and I would move them. He got so good that he was a tough competitor. His mental ability became very sharp. His memory was amazing. One of the things Danny was ever ready for was our time of prayer. He was totally given over to the Lord Jesus, and for me that was an inspiration. As I prayed for his family he always added his "amen".

Danny was in several Polio hospitals, each of them helping him in various ways. Danny married and I marvel at the many things that God, the Creator of the Universe is able to arrange. I praise God for this union and for what it has meant to Danny. This again manifests the fact that all the answers to every problem are found by allowing God to have His way.

Now that Danny has gone to be with the Lord Jesus Christ, the memories will be even more precious. I thank the Lord for my time that I had the privilege to be a friend of such a worthy young man and his family and loved ones.

INTRODUCTION

Keep Smiling and Never Give Up! is a compilation of 17 years of people, facts, and events in my life following the onset of Polio in 1957. The years 1967 through 1974 reveal a divinely directed acquaintance, courtship, and marriage to Kaye Williams. I began my story with ten years of struggle, humor, love, and demanded acceptance of a problem requiring myriad adjustments.

Man is innately endowed with courage from God to attain mental, physical, and spiritual heights, but His gift to all is manifested only through one's choices. Transforming what appear to be enormous obstacles into glorious opportunities is a privilege, the results of which can be fulfilling or frightening. Experience assures successfully confronting overwhelming odds and promises enduring hope when valleys of despair diminish, as afflictions become blessings.

I've required life-saving capabilities of respirators/ventilators twenty-four hours daily since surviving acute Poliomyelitis. Expertise at Polio Rehabilitation Centers (Respo Centers) allowed me to graduate from confinement in an iron lung to portable respirators after several months of intensive therapy, willpower, and God's grace. Eventually I progressed to oral positive pressure; rocking bed; cuirass or chest shell; and pneumobelt. Following experimentation with a pulmowrap respirator, I rejected the portability it provided because of confinement and discomfort. My ability to frog (glossopharyngeal) breathe supplemented mechanical respiration and assured me emergency support if necessary. Many Polios and other para/quadriplegics benefit from varied respiratory enhancements, some, the skill of frog breathing.

When first adjusting to respirator/ventilator cycling, speech is difficult to emote and understand. Throughout my book I endeavor to demonstrate this terrifying reliance upon life-support systems by adding appropriate gulps, dots, and spaces. Readers must strive to regulate their breathing in accordance with these strategically placed realistic aids so they may gain a semblance of second-hand experience. Those able-bodied people (AB's) who've conversed with individuals using respirator/ventilator support immediately discern our distinctive speech patterns. When participating in dialogue I personally verbalize in short, crisp sentences, maximizing monosyllabic words. Utilizing this format I strive to help readers understand the humbling world of we who benefit from total dependency on respirators and others aids for our next breath of life-sustaining air. I hope all will be cognizant of my flowing elucidation in later chapters, compensation derived from practice and longevity.

Conversely, writing provides me great panoramic avenues to compose picturesque prose. Total paralysis has ensured I view life from confinement to wheelchair or bed. Although my body remains tethered to the respirator; mind, thoughts, and captive spirit soar above clouds of heavenly aspiration, a zenith affording me precious moments of ecstatic freedom. While a resident at Columbus, Ohio's Respo Center, Mickey, an Occupational Therapist and dear friend advised, "Danny, creatively written words paint pictures for the mind."

Only direct personal or family involvement perpetuates true understanding of the complicated and divergent ramifications accompanying a challenging or debilitating disability. One must never forget the compassionate understanding and loving care exemplified by family, friends, and professionals. All importantly, each of us must remember the many considerate, devoted AB's struggling to comprehend seemingly implausible harsh requirements for we, who by necessity, must attempt to follow the beat of a different drummer.

I began this book as a callow youth, stumbling through adolescence, maturing to manhood, culminating after years of enduring adversity, strengthened by grace and love. People, places, and events are factual. Attempts to protect privacy and prevent recriminations have compelled me to eliminate or change names in some parts of the text. Introduction of all personalities in this limited space would be an exercise in futility. Suffice to say, doctors, nurses, ministers, male/female attendants, therapists, dietary staff, fellow Polios, and residents/patients, were part of my life. Prominently involved in this book are my family and friends.

Keep Smiling and Never Give Up! realistically portrays seventeen years of my life, striving for balance between the agony of defeat; mountain peaks of hope; monotonous plateaus of indifference; shadows of death; and grace unsurpassed. I will, God willing, write other books recounting Kaye's and my life together, travels, and residing in Florida where I confront an insidious repeat of Polio's devastation forcing our return to Indiana. Unfortunately my miraculous cure in Indianapolis meant disaster for Kaye.

In the seventeen years of my life following Polio I was a patient/resident at two Respo Centers, five hospitals, and four nursing homes. The presence of God accompanied me even when I chose to ignore His precepts, ascertaining protection and comfort through doubt, tribulation, and accomplishment. I sincerely trust the words and examples in my memoirs will enable readers to formulate a more enlightened awareness of terrifying, humbling, and seemingly hopeless situations. We must never surrender to self-pity where the enemy's weapons of choice are fear and discouragement.

Steadfast courageous reactions to pleasant or traumatic events ensure indwelling joy in one's heart.

Dedication

To Dad and Mom

and my wife

Kaye

Without whom these words would never have been written

WE ARE

Blessed with unconditional love from God the Father

Redeemed and saved by the grace of Jesus the Son

Comforted in spirit by the Holy Ghost

Holy Bible Scriptures quoted from King James Version

ACKNOWLEDGMENTS

Special honors to my parents, Ray and Velma and my brothers and sisters. Also to Rev. C. A. Kerschner, pastor, teacher, and friend.

Seventeen years after Polio God blessed me with my wife Kaye, her parents, brothers and sisters.

A multitude of doctors have participated in saving my life and sight. Allow me to recognize those most intimately involved. Drs. William C. Heilman Sr. (deceased), William C. Heilman Jr., Dwain N. Walcher (deceased), Ernest W. Johnson, Thomas K. Oliver, David G. Dickinson, Donita B. Sullivan, Arthur C. Burnett, and George W. Rector. These men and woman have my gratitude and unwavering respect.

I'm grateful to Henry County Memorial Hospital; Indiana University Medical Center; James Whitcomb Riley Children's Hospital; Ohio State University Respo Center of Children's Hospital, Columbus, OH; University of Michigan Respo Center, University Hospital, Ann Arbor, MI; IUMC's Robert Long and University Hospitals, Indianapolis, IN. Methodist Hospital, Indianapolis, IN; Heritage House Convalescent Center, New Castle, IN; and Northwest Manor Health Care Center, Indianapolis, IN.

National Foundation for Infantile Paralysis, March of Dimes; Ruth Lyons Club; Red Ball Moving Van; Indiana National Guard; New Castle Police Department and First Aid Unit.

Thousands of Polio survivors and their families will forever be grateful to valiantly tireless efforts exemplified by scores of doctors, nurses, and researchers. The National Foundation for Infantile Paralysis, funded through mother's March of Dimes campaigns, is forever a legacy to President Franklin D. Roosevelt. Basil O'Connor was appointed to direct the foundation providing much needed financial assistance for research to Dr. Jonas Salk and Dr. Albert Sabin.

Lisa E. Bayne, Archivist, Eli Lilly and Co. Indianapolis, IN, Nancy L. Eckerman, Special Collections Librarian, IUMC, Judy Hatfield, Special Collections Asst., IUMC, Eric Pumroy, Campus Archives, IUMC.

Love and thanks for handwriting and typing manuscripts to my sisters Vivian, Judy, and Anita; and friends Sharon, Jean, Linda, and Lisa.

These acknowledgments are sadly inadequate attempts to recognize and thank people so important in my life. Without question my best friend, supporter, confidant, incentive for living, sunshine of each day, starlight of every night, the person who keeps me smiling, will never let me give up, and never lose faith in me or us, is my dearest wife Kaye.

TABLE OF CONTENTS

INTRODUCTION v

PART ONE: ACCEPTANCE
    1   CHOSEN 1
    2.   POLIO 9
    3   CONSEQUENCES 15
    4   CINDY 23
    5   CHALLENGED 29
    6   GRACE 38
    7   COFFEE BREAK 46
    8   HOME FOR CHRISTMAS 54
    9   OVERWHELMED 62

PART TWO: ADJUSTMENT
    10   SELLERS EAST 72
    11   ROCKING 'N ROLLING 82
    12   PROMISES 93
    13   CHOICES 108
    14   HERE WE GO AGAIN 121
    15   MOTIVATE OR VEGETATE 133
    16   THE PENTHOUSE 148
    17   NEW HORIZONS 158
    18   SHADOWS UNEXPECTED 171
    19   CHANGES 187

PART THREE: ANGUISH
    20   REALITY 199
    21   TWILIGHT TO DAWN 212
    22   BURNING BRIDGES 231
    23   SOWING THE WIND 245
    24   QUICKSAND OF EVIL 256
    25   REAPING THE WHIRLWIND 265

PART FOUR: SERENDIPITY
    26   HERITAGE HOUSE 278
    27   OASIS 288
    28   HOPE DEFERRED 296
    29   BE PATIENT 309

| 30 | FEAR TO JOY | 318 |
| 31 | MTY/LTT FAITH and LOVE | 329 |

1
CHOSEN

Throughout life we each confront situations requiring creative solutions to solve complex problems. A toddler learning to talk and walk; a youngster's first school day; a young adult leaving home for the first time; or a child's first night alone in a hospital. All are traumatic moments demanding a courageously personal response. The same intestinal fortitude blended with hope must be utilized in accepting and adjusting to a handicap. At some time in everyone's life he or she must contend with physical problems. Whether they be minor sight disorders requiring glasses, or severe physical debilitation, a most crucial and decisive ingredient in our response is **choice**. Obstacles must be viewed as opportunities, encouraging one to discover life's purpose, striving for a life of fulfillment; or we may concede a defeatist attitude, refuse to adjust, yield to a meaningless existence, and suffer an eventual senseless death.

True joy and contentment in life can only be achieved when one's potential capabilities are utilized within the scope of one's limitations. To quote a famous author, "all life is a stage". In this context my story is presented, its success will be determined by audience approval. The curtain rises on October 7, 1957 with center stage occupied by me, Daniel Williams. My supporting cast includes medical staff, ancillary personnel, friends, and most of all family. The writer of this script is circumstance directed by God, with surrounding people my audience.

Participating in high school band day at Ball State Teacher's College (now University), Muncie, Indiana on a frigid, blustery September day, I caught a cold that refused all home remedies. Unknown to everyone, during the ensuing two weeks my strength was being stolen by an insidious, vicious germ bent on slowly destroying health, and possibly, my life.

The October 4th weekend began a series of events that forever changed my family, friends, and me. As a result of a fractured clavicle, playing football was no longer optional for me this year, so I became instrumental in the New Castle High School band. During musical presentations at varsity football half-time I attempted to emote mellow sounds from my cornet. Friday was another unseasonably cold October evening and our band uniforms were not designed to protect us from thirty-degree temperatures or blowing, freezing wet snow. I huddled in misery as strong, bitter winds cut through a thin uniform, my hands and face throbbing from cold weather. I looked longingly at the fur coat in front of me, decrying my stupidity in not wearing additional clothing. Unable to contain myself any longer, I pleaded to Kathy, a fellow band member wearing this coat, "Please let me press my cold hands against your fur collar."

Kathy, older and wiser by two years, replied, "OK, but watch the hands. I hope Judi understands. I guess if you're careful, I might even let you warm your face."

After the game a group of us gathered at a local teen hangout for sodas. I drank hot chocolate. Midway through the hot drink I became nauseated. "Judi," I choked to my girlfriend, "I'm sick. Let's go." Fortunately her house was on the way home because my legs were becoming unsteady. After escorting Judi home I continued the long trek to my house, forcing one foot in front of the other. Within a block of my house, reality slapped me in the face, "Oh No! I forgot my horn at the athletic field. I just can't walk that distance again," I thought, "but if I don't, it will be stolen and Dad will be MILDLY upset." I stumbled back to the field, cursing my stupidity with each step. The security guard was locking the fence gate when I trudged up and told him my dilemma. Grimacing, he told me, "Be quick. It's cold out here." I retrieved my cornet and resumed the arduous journey that had now doubled in length. Taking an hour and a half to walk nineteen blocks, I finally collapsed in one of our living room chairs. At last, I was safely home.

Saturday morning I weakly arose from bed, descending the steps groaning, "Dad I feel terrible."

"Come on in here and eat breakfast, you'll feel better. You're probably just hungry after your late night." he said. "You know we don't approve of you staying out after curfew."

"Here Danny, drink this orange juice. I'm fixing your breakfast now." Mom said. "Ray, doesn't he look pale this morning? Here night owl, let me take your temperature."

"Please don't mention food! I'm gonna barf and my head is pounding. I can't eat anything! After the game I almost didn't get home. I forgot my horn, and had to walk all the way back to the ball field. I got there just as the guard was locking the gate."

"Close your mouth and hold this thermometer. I knew you shouldn't have been out last night in that cold weather. Ray!" Mom exclaimed. "His temperature is 102°."

Dad said, "I'll phone Dr.Heilman. It's still early; maybe he'll give us a morning appointment. Danny is there anything else I should tell him?"

"I can't eat. I'm weak. My head is killing me, and my back hurts. Dad," I whispered embarrassed, "I can't pee or the other."

A couple hours later we were sitting in The Clinic's waiting room. Dr.Heilman prepared to leave town for a brief medical convention and I was his last appointment. Dr. Heilman Jr. would assume patient coverage in his absence. My eyes scanned the waiting room walls, which were covered by pertinent information. The March of Dimes' picture posters portrayed young adults on crutches, small children with tiny deformed legs, and babies being carried by fearful parents. The words on these emotionally compelling placards pleaded: "POLIO, the number one crippler of young people! Have you had your shots?" Reading those words and staring at the sad pictures I thought, "Get ready Williams, you're next."

After an examination, Dr.Heilman diagnosed a bad cold, gave me antibiotics, pain pills, and said, "Go home Danny. With this medicine and rest, you'll be well in a few days." Saturday I took my pills and slept fitfully, still unable to eat or go to the bathroom.

"Danny, it's time for Sunday School. Dad and I won't force you to attend, but you know how important we consider church in your life." Mom declared.

"I'm sick to my stomach and hurting too much Mom." I answered. "Besides, those people don't want this flu."

"You stay warm in bed." Dad instructed. "I'll be home after Sunday School and take you to the doctor."

On my second visit to The Clinic Dr.Heilman Jr. agreed with his father's diagnosis of a bad cold repeating these instructions, "This medicine, combined with time and rest will solve your problems."

Sunday afternoon my condition worsened. The pain in my back and head increased, and weakness overpowered me. Judy, one of my sisters, and her husband Norman visited us Sunday evening, bringing their movie camera and brilliant lights to film family activities. Millie, our little sister, held my cornet during the filming, and Andy, my baby brother, not only held the instrument, but also unwittingly blew through the contaminated mouthpiece I had used at half-time festivities. Screaming silently while blinding camera lights, and shrill piercing sounds from the cornet unmercifully attacked my senses, I covered my head with a pillow to shut out all the invading sights and sounds. No longer able to endure these mind-numbing events, I tried moving from our living room to a quiet place. My arms and legs barely worked, and a most terrifying weakness began descending over my body. Trying to get up from the couch, my mind cried in desperation when my body would no longer function on command. Frantically I struggled to twist off the couch onto my knees, attempting to stand. "Will one of you help me?" I screamed. "My legs won't work!" Fear blanketed Dad and Norman's faces as they grasped my arms, helping me to stand. Once on my feet the intolerable weight of each step became unbearably heavy, but I was afraid to sit down again.

Dad immediately called Dr.Heilman Jr. at his home to inform him of the situation. The doctor said, "Continue all antibiotics. I'll order a new pain medication, the present one might be too strong."

Dad and Norman prepared to leave for the pharmacy, but before going they said, "Sit down on this kitchen chair and don't move until we get back." I sat down. Judy placed my arms on the table, and my head fell forward, remaining there until they returned with new medicine.

"Here Danny, maybe these new pills will help you feel a little better." said Dad. Mom supported my weakened neck as I swallowed the pills between gags.

"Dad help me to the couch, I gotta lie down. No, on second thought," I said, "maybe you better help me upstairs to bed. I'll never get up from that couch again." Nearly carrying me, Dad helped me upstairs to my room. I couldn't go to the bathroom, but everyone's primary focus was fever, cold, and pain. I watched my body continue to die with ever-determined speed, numbing fear permeating every thought.

Mom rubbed my arms, legs and spastic, quivering muscles with liniment hoping to soothe the pain. I begged them to turn me onto my stomach and rub my back. "My muscles feel like I'm being cut open, my head hurts so bad, and I'm too weak to cough. Why can't I go to the bathroom? I feel so full, and my back hurts so bad."

About midnight Mom took my temperature once more, and said, "Ray call the doctor again. It's now 104°, and he's having trouble breathing. I'm worried."

Dr.Heilman Jr. arrived at our home and performed the few tests possible. "Ray," he said, "without further tests I can't make any preliminary statements. Danny needs blood tests and a spinal tap, these require hospitalization."

"Oh no! Please, no!" cried Mom. "I lost my baby girl after a spinal tap. Isn't there some other way?"

Dr.Heilman Jr. declared, "If you would prefer another doctor, I will make the arrangements. Believe me, there is simply no other way."

"Mom, I'll be all right." I said. "I need help now."

Two emergency attendants arrived and carried me down the stairs to a stretcher, taking me from my home. Thoughts and emotions combined with fear and dread as the stretcher was being lifted into a waiting vehicle. My eyes searched the early Monday morning sky for signs of a new day. There were no stars and moonlight was absent, a dense blanket of clouds covered the heavens.

My ambulance moved away from the curb taking me into a struggle of life or death. Waiting for me at Henry County Memorial Hospital (HCMH), was the beginning of an unknown ordeal destined to test not just my physical endurance, but reserve strength, courage, and trust.

After arriving at HCMH I was put through examinations and tests I never knew existed. Thermometers were stuck in my mouth, lights shined in

Keep Smiling and Never Give Up!

my eyes, and swabs jabbed down my throat. My body was pierced with needles at both ends, and I became acquainted with a procedure called lumbar puncture (spinal tap). Dr.Heilman Jr. and Dr.Fisher entered the room attired in gowns, masks, and gloves. "Danny this test will hurt a little, but it's necessary for an accurate diagnosis. Don't let our appearance frighten you, we just don't want to spread any unknown germs around." they mumbled fearfully, as Dr.Heilman Jr. proceeded to twist me into a fetal position so Dr.Fisher could prep me and insert a needle into my spine.

"Hey Doc, your hands are like ice! I'm the one in pain but you guys sound scared to death. What gives? By the way man," I groaned, "I haven't used the bathroom for two days. Don't hold me so tight. Oh no! I'm going to..." gag, gag, "be sick to my stomach."

"Just a few more minutes Danny," said Dr.Fisher, "then the nurse will get some medicine to help you feel better."

"OK." I said. "Could somebody do something about this pain in my back and head? Why can't I go to the bathroom?"

They finished with the exam, and after probing, poking, and testing what was left of my reflexes, they instructed the nurse to bring me a shot for pain.

I was just beginning to calm down when in walked a shy, young man in a white uniform whom I recognized from church. "Dave, why are you here?" Thinking I had been through just about everything, I discovered they had saved a big surprise for last. Smiling and joking trying not to further increase my anxiety, Dave quietly uncovered the tray he was carrying. I scanned the instruments assembled for this task, observing they were neatly arranged in order: cotton, soap, basin, and a rubber tube. Then I spotted it - a glass jar fastened to a gigantic needle. Seeing this I quickly debated calling for help. Dave, sensing my desperation said, "Don't worry, the syringe and needle are equipment necessary for this part of the procedure. It isn't for your body." About fifteen minutes later he offered me his prayers, a pat on the arm, and left the room. My bladder was about two quarts emptier and I no longer needed the bathroom. Mission accomplished.

Hovering between sedation and delirium, my mind flooded with memories. The preceding weekend had been filled with many experiences; some satisfying, some humorous, but most were terrifying. I watched strength and life drain from my body like sand trickling through an hourglass - slowly, but with ever increasing amounts.

About 5:30 A.M. Dad came into my room with an ominous look on his face. "Danny, are you all right?" he asked.

"Yes Dad, I'm all right, just thinking and trying to understand what's happening to me. Dad, what have I done?"

I realized Dad was going to talk about my condition. With tears in his eyes he walked over to my bed, took a deep breath and said, "Son, the preliminary tests suggest Polio. Shortly you must be moved to Riley Children's Hospital in Indianapolis."

"Yes Dad, I know it's Polio. I've known since seeing a March of Dimes poster at The Clinic. Maybe the shots would have been a good idea after all." This was a sudden shock to Dad, Mom, and my family, but I had been preparing myself to accept this reality for the last two days. With Polio virus sapping strength from my body the thought of dying was utmost on my mind. Maybe the premonition isn't explainable, but it was fact. My family though, failed to realize what was happening until informed by Dr. Heilman Jr. At this moment my sorrow for other people became greater than for self.

About 6:30 A.M. on the morning of October 7th, nurses and an orderly brought a stretcher into my room. I was snugly wrapped in a sheet and blanket, and then gently lifted from my bed to a stretcher. Everyone wore gloves, gowns, masks, and all speech was hushed. New Castle, Indiana's first case of suspected Polio in many years had just been discovered, and I was considered highly contagious. I was treated with great kindness, but felt unappreciated. Dave and the nurses moved my stretcher quickly through corridors to the elevator and the ambulance entrance. Outside the hospital, I looked upward at the breaking dawn. The sky was still cloudy, but now rain fell; prophetically, heaven was crying for me.

Waiting to begin my journey, I looked through ambulance windows at the people watching my departure. Mom, Judy, and Norman looked through tear-stained eyes with disbelief and fear covering their faces. Millie and Andy also had looks of frightened bewilderment in their eyes, not understanding anything happening to Danny, their big brother. Seeing my family upset broke my heart and tears began flowing onto my pillow. How could anyone understand what was happening? None of us could comprehend the innumerable events that had taken place within seventy-two hours.

Leaving home the night before became indelibly etched in my mind. I was beginning my second trip in an ambulance bound for a second hospital admission in hours. My hometown faded into the background as we sped away. Telephone poles, fences, and houses flashed by while I listened to rhythmic tires on the pavement. Every passing mile took me farther from the only life I had ever known with my family and close friends. Traveling along the highway I thought, "I'm only fourteen, will I ever see my home again?"

"Riley Hospital." I wondered drowsily, "What's it like? Bet I'm really in for it, guess I must be awful sick. Well, what's a few days anyway? Can't figure out what happened, maybe this is just a dream. Dream? Ha!! I just wish I'd wake up from this nightmare! It'll be better tomorrow."

There was a screech of brakes and the ambulance veered to one side, avoiding an oncoming car. The sudden movement brought me back to reality and I mused, "Man, I'm gonna be in another wreck before I get to the hospital! I thought people were supposed to move over for red lights and siren."

The ambulance's swerving abruptly reminded me of a recent occurrence in my life when innocent fun nearly had deadly consequences. Judi, Linda, Marilyn, and I were walking home from the "Y" one evening when Jerry, Linda's older brother, drove up in his new car. "Hey you guys!" he shouted. "Wanna take a spin? My Chevy has a souped up engine and believe me, it really moves!"

Enthusiastically we jumped at the chance to ride in his beautiful blue '57 two-door dream on wheels. Confining city streets restricted display of this vehicle's talents, so we detoured out of town on our way home. Zipping along on a paved country road the trees and fence posts whipped by in blurred motion. As we entered a curve the pavement suddenly changed to gravel and the car whirled wildly out of control, plunging us into a field, mowing down a row of fence posts. Trying desperately to brace myself with an elbow against the open window frame, gravity's force kept it there as a rusty nail lacerated my arm. Spinning back onto the road, Jerry tried vainly to regain control of his car, but loose gravel proved an unwelcome foe. Following one more wild rotation the car screeched onto the road and crashed into a concrete bridge, then fell from the roadbed. Screams, groans, and cries of, "Is everybody OK?" pierced the air as those who could climbed from the car. We were shaking, bruised, cut, bleeding everywhere, and some had broken bones or dislocated joints, but we were alive. I limped from the stream where we'd landed to hear Jerry moan, "OH NO! My car! I didn't have a chance to buy insurance." Jerry wasn't physically injured, but he was not very happy. From inside the car someone cried out, "Will somebody please help me, I can't walk!"

Jerry scrambled to what was left of the back door to find his sister Linda bleeding, her leg badly lacerated and difficult to move. "Sis, I'm sorry." Jerry blubbered. "Do you believe this, you're bleeding and my car's a wreck! I just know Mom's gonna kill me."

I aroused from my thoughts as Mr. Bowser, my ambulance driver, turned slowly onto a tree-lined boulevard, entering Indiana University Medical Center (IUMC). Nearing a brick building hiding behind strands of green ivy, I spotted a barely visible sign reading, Riley Hospital for Children. The area bustled with activity as people hurried from one place to another. The ambulance backed up to the emergency room entrance, the doors were jerked open, and my stretcher was moved quickly to an awaiting world of impending anguish.

Prior to my weekend of horror I had been only vaguely aware of the hospital, staff, or their purposes in life. I knew their presence and knowledge had been instrumental in saving the lives of relatives and friends, but this time I found myself the center of attention. I sought reassurance from the smiles, touches, and words of encouragement directed to me by the emergency room staff. I closed my eyes and begged quietly for relief as sheets and clothing were stripped away and doctors and nurses confidently began searching for the vicious attacker killing my body. Dimly recalling stories about Polio and its effects I wondered, "Will I have to walk with crutches and braces? Oh God, don't let me die." As I faded away in thought I cried, "No! I'll get better!"

The following were Newspaper Ad Mats, Courtesy: Eli Lilly and Company Archives,
Indianapolis, Indiana.

"POLIO CLAIMS 1600 VICTIMS!

During the first nine months of 1957, there were 1600 cases of paralytic polio – many died, others were left permanently paralyzed. This is a tragedy indeed... The vaccine protects only those who receive it. Don't gamble with your health or that of a loved one. See your physician! Be immunized!"

"POLIO STILL A THREAT!

Polio strikes without warning. Epidemics spread quickly. No section of the country is immune because the virus is still widespread... Unfortunately, the vaccine cannot wipe out the disease. It simply protects those who receive it. Don't take chances with your health or that of your loved ones. See your physician! Be immunized now!"

2
POLIO

Nurses pushed my stretcher through long, busy corridors to X-Ray and another procedure. Overhead I observed a maze of steel pipes conveying heat, water, and oxygen. Although looking much the same, each fulfilled a uniquely different purpose in the functioning of Riley Hospital. I was quickly learning each person also had a distinctive reason for being part of my life.

Eventually arriving at the treatment room, people who'd been assigned to provide care needed for my recovery during illness sprang into action. With hushed conversation they moved me from the stretcher to a cold hard table, assuring the examinations to follow would be ugly. Momentarily the staff stepped outside my presence and I was left alone where probably a few minutes seemed like hours. Unable to move, having trouble breathing, and giving rise to fear surging inside I thought, "Maybe they left me in the wrong room." I shuddered as pain wracked my body because I'd been informed until a diagnosis was more certain I couldn't be given any more pain medicine. Delirium from high fever increased times of panic and I wanted to just RUN AWAY! What am I thinking, I can't even scratch my nose let alone run! Scanning the room for a friendly sight, my eyes centered on objects destined to intensify anyone's insecurity. I saw glass-doored chests of bottled medicine, syringes with long needles, and oxygen tanks. There were hooks fastened to chains hanging from the ceiling and tubes extending from a wall full of gauges. The brilliance of overhead lights blinded me and the room reeked of alcohol. I tried to sigh in resignation, but breathing deeply proved impossible. Fearful images raced through my mind and I silently pleaded, "Please God, let me wake up!"

Modesty was quickly becoming a thing of the past. Upon admission to HCMH in New Castle, bed sheets had been my only protection from the outside world. During many examinations from doctors and nurses even these meager covers didn't stay on my body very long. I consoled myself by deciding, "These people are just doing their job," but it was still difficult lying naked while strangers established a traffic pattern in my area. Reasonable thoughts were few and far between, "If only the waiting would end, my worries might be over."

In walked a stocky muscular man sporting a crew cut and wearing a white lab coat with stethoscope draped around his neck. Smiling while extinguishing his cigarette, he said, "Hi, I'm Dr.Shoptaugh. How are you really feeling right now? Your dad informed me about a number of problems."

"I feel awful! My head hurts, there are knives in my back, and I can't move. Oh yeah, I can't, I can't. Oh you know, the bathroom."

Observing me warily, his examination followed a routine I was getting used to, checking eyes, ears, etc. Finally he began poking and probing, testing for nonexistent reflexes. Nearly an hour later the only thing not hurting was my hair. At last this ordeal was over and Dr.Shoptaugh confirmed the obvious, "Well Danny, you are very ill. The way it appears you will be our guest for a while so we may as well transfer you to your new room."

"Dr.Shoptaugh," I questioned, "New Castle doctors told Dad I might have Polio. Is this why I can't move?"

"Danny, I can only say we are doing everything possible to make you feel better." Continuing he said, "Stay patient and try not to be afraid. Right now let's introduce you to your new home, then someone will assist you in emptying your bladder." Following these words he called the nurse telling her, "Miss Beck, please make arrangements for this patient's move to the isolation ward."

While waiting to be transferred, my ambulance driver Mr. Bowser, stopped by to wish me good luck before leaving. He said, "You have to stay strong. Don't let Polio win."

"I'll try to remember your words." I said. "Thank you for the safe trip from New Castle to Indianapolis."

A student nurse and male attendant then transported me to the isolation unit. A small room with one tiny window to the outside and glass partitions for walls became my home. My strength and the Williams family's resiliency would be stretched to the breaking point by this strange new world. Upon entering my new room one of the first things I noticed was an ordinary hospital bed with an overused mattress. I had been lying paralyzed on stretchers or examination tables for several hours, so anything resembling a mattress looked not only comfortable, but very inviting. I really should have known they wouldn't let me get overly relaxed. I was just entertaining thoughts of rest and comfort, when a hospital equipment man assisted by an aide, trotted into the room with two sheets of plywood which they eagerly inserted under the waiting mattress. For hours I'd prepared myself for the worst, and it was happening as nurses and aides transferred me from my stretcher to bed. Softness is in the back of the beholder, but I guess it was better than tables and stretchers. To be honest, it only made me more homesick for my bed at home; I hoped it was not a part of my life never to be revisited.

Keep Smiling and Never Give Up!

Efficiently performing their duties, nurses monitored blood pressure, temperature, pulse, and respiration rate. "Danny, would you enjoy watching TV?" asked the head nurse.

"Sure." I replied. "The World Series is being played and my team, the Milwaukee Braves, is going to win." Since the television couldn't be moved inside isolation, it sat on a stand outside my door. Added to the TV's bad location, my eyes were blurred by fever and medicine, making it even more difficult to see. Anyway, the pain in my back and head was so intense I couldn't concentrate on baseball.

Dr. Shoptaugh came into my room wearing a gown and mask remarking, "I see you're in bed, but don't get comfortable. We need some more X-rays and they will take you by stretcher to a treatment room for another spinal tap. We both know this test is uncomfortable, but it's necessary to determine the magnitude of infection."

"What makes the difference," I muttered, "get it over with. I was wondering, are you afraid of me?"

"No Danny. You don't frighten us. These clothes are worn to prevent spreading germs. Most of us are married and have children too."

"How many kids do you have?" I asked. "You live here in town?"

"Danny I live in Colorado. I'm an Air Force Major on temporary duty receiving additional education in pediatrics. As for my children, I have eight boys and girls."

"Eight!" I exclaimed.

The next few hours were very hectic to say the least. I was taken to X-ray, endured another spinal tap, numerous blood tests, and various medical treatments from doctors, nurses and technicians. With help, I emptied my bladder again. Many people had taken part in my initial treatments, but at last I met the doctor destined to perform the leading role in saving my life. As Dr. Walcher walked into my room I immediately became aware of his importance, he commanded respect from all hospital staff members. Conducting another examination, I understood their reasons for obvious admiration shown to this man. Through methods he employed and the air of confidence he exuded, it was apparent he knew precisely what procedures to follow in determining the problems. Intently following every action, medical students closely listened to instructions and their facial expressions revealed thoughts of, "Maybe someday, I too will have this great ability as a doctor."

By this time I was well accustomed to the routine of a physical exam, but I didn't understand his words as he spoke about anticipated breathing difficulties. "In order to stay alive, you will require respiratory assistance."

A few minutes after Dr. Walcher left, Dad walked in with two magazines. Holding them out to me he said, "I know you can't see well enough to read right now, but I thought you might enjoy looking at the pictures." Trying to reach for a magazine, the shock of reality suddenly hit me - I couldn't move my arms! Dad too, became instantly aware as he turned away with tears in his eyes, tossing both magazines against the wall. The uncharacteristic anger and shakiness in his voice revealed what must have been Dad's initial, unnerving impact of my situation.

"Dad, what's happening in the ball game, why is there so much cheering?" I asked.

"Your Braves are leading the Yankees four-to-nothing in the seventh inning and Milwaukee's fans are going crazy!" Hearing Dad speak, I twisted my head toward the television, trying desperately to focus on the picture. My vision was blurred, like looking through water. I satisfied myself by just listening to Mel Allen, the play-by play-announcer.

"This is just great!" I lamented. "My Braves are ahead four-to-nothing. The World Series no less, and I'm stuck in a hospital and can't see them win."

Approximately 3:45 P.M. Monday, October 7, 1957, a very important saga of events began in my life. Entering my room Dr. Walcher shook hands with Dad, and said, "Forgive me for interrupting the ball game, but it's important I examine Danny, and explain necessary changes in the immediate future."

"No problem." said Dad. "I'll leave."

"No, I would rather you stay and listen to my words." said Dr. Walcher. "What happens in the next few days must be understood and it's imperative your family is prepared. Danny, you are aware breathing has become labored, and I think it necessary to place you in a respirator now." I didn't realize how his ominous words would radically alter my life.

He signaled to a team of waiting doctors and nurses, who pushed an iron lung into my room. At first glance it resembled a big yellow oil drum on wheels with an accordion at the foot. "This piece of equipment weighs eight hundred pounds, so it takes a number of people to move it around." explained Dr. Walcher. "As you can see, at the foot is a devise called a bellows operated by an electric motor. Your neck will be surrounded by a padded collar of foam rubber containing a circular opening, through which your head will protrude. On each side of the iron lung are hand openings for our personnel, allowing them to give you required hygiene and medical treatments. These openings are called portholes, sealed against air seepage by foam-insulated steel doors. Inserting one's arm inside to provide assistance, pressure loss is prevented and breathing is uninterrupted if people coordinate their movements with the respirator's cycle. The large door at the rear is for placement of equipment and supplies inside the iron lung." Releasing fastening clamps he pulled out a mattress covered tray. "The bed in an iron lung is essentially a stretcher without wheels at one end.

Keep Smiling and Never Give Up!

The front part with wheels rolls and the foot end glides inward on rails. Once you're inside, bellows extract all air from the iron lung. The vacuum thus created pulls air into one's lungs via your mouth and nose. You see, at this point your head and neck provide the seal. When the bellows relax, the vacuum is replaced by positive pressure, forcing you to exhale." Dr. Walcher completed his discourse about my new environment.

I interrupted. "That hole doesn't look big enough for my head."

Dr. Walcher smiled as he informed me of procedures used to place me in the respirator. "Danny there are five straps used to make the collar opening large enough for your head to be pushed through, hopefully without removing your nose. Whether or not this is successful remains to be seen. Ha!" Quickly my nearly six-foot, one hundred eighty pound body was lifted from hospital bed to iron lung, and they gently shoved my head through the collar. "Danny," instructed Dr. Walcher, "when I close the respirator I want you to relax. Try not to resist and let the iron lung do all the work."

At first I thought this would be very difficult because after release of the straps, tightness of the collar along with my fear and difficulty breathing, created a suffocating reaction. I knew immediately, becoming used to an iron lung would require time. They closed me inside and turned on the motor. My initial instinct was to struggle for air, but my lungs received the first deep breath of air in many long hours. I had been battling to breathe for quite some time, and only when the iron lung assumed control, did I realize the extent of my exhaustion. Acquainting myself with breathing methods of a respirator, I instantly became sleepy. I told Dr. Walcher this and he said, "Danny before you go to sleep I want to open the respirator one more time to assess what breathing capability you have remaining."

Only fifteen minutes in the iron lung and my diaphragm had become totally relaxed. He opened the iron lung's door, and immediately realized I could no longer breathe on my own. From the neck down, I was totally paralyzed.

Dr. Walcher, aware that I couldn't breathe without some assistance, closed the respirator and said, "Don't worry now everything is under control." Touching my head in assurance he commented, "Rest and sleep. I'll see you later."

Exhaustion, relaxation from fear, and replenishment for my oxygen-starved body induced moments of unconsciousness. Only nurses monitoring my unstable blood pressure and increasing temperature interrupted my rest. Loss of fluid presented a dangerous situation and the nurses frequently encouraged, "Danny, please take a few sips of ice water, you need liquids."

"I'm...sick...to my...stomach," I complained, "if I...drink...they will...put that...catheter...in me...again. I...still...can't do...anything...by myself."

Daniel R. Williams

Startled awake after a couple hours of sleep, it took a few frightful minutes to comprehend my situation. The iron lung was sitting facing the door, but since I could only see from side to side it was difficult to view my surroundings. I looked to one side and saw Dad standing by me watching for visitors in the hallway.

"Daadd." I moaned. "Who won... the game... today?"

Answering my feeble question he remarked, "Milwaukee."

Just as I started to say something, my mother and Judy stepped through the doorway. I heard Dad say, "Hello, don't worry Velma, it's helping him breathe."

Struggling to see, I twisted my head backwards. Judy had fear in her eyes, a shocked expression on her face, and her lips quivered. Mom was unable to control herself any longer. With tears streaming down her face she cried out, "Oh Danny!"

With these words ringing in my ears and visions of my family's horror, I drifted into an uncomprehending fog.

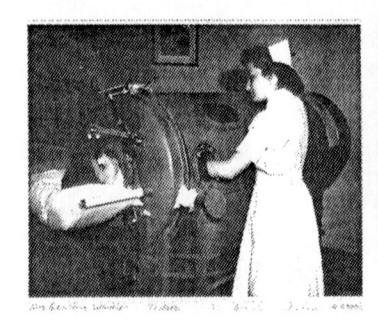

Photo courtesy: Special Collections and Archives Indiana University – Purdue University at Indianapolis, Indiana.

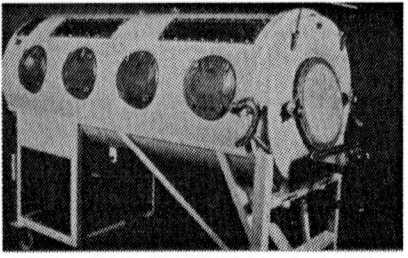

Iron lung "yellow tin can on wheels". Photo Courtesy of LIFECARE®, Lafayette, CO.

3
CONSEQUENCES

Numerous moments of delirium from an elevated temp and pain medicine prevent me from lucidly recounting the first few days at Riley Hospital. However, probing discussions with the people directly involved and review of my medical records allow me to present credible information. Intense, though obviously brief, I hope you will gain insight into the confusing days of my fight to survive and the doctor's refusal to accommodate death. As with all people surviving despite overwhelming adversity, I'm convinced God has a mission for my life.

Being semi-conscious, I was unable to fully comprehend the gravity of my situation, or understand actions of people around me while they performed needed medical treatments. I vaguely remember X-rays, numerous blood tests, and endless examinations by multiple doctors. An incident was seared in my mind from the pain and fear of what had recently become a daily test. One day, in my confusion, I strained to remain attentive as Dr.Walcher explained to residents and interns the reason I needed another spinal tap. He instructed, "We must be cognizant of the level his paralysis is progressing, and prepare for any further complications. I am unable to delay attending an urgent meeting, so monitor him closely until I return."

Dr.Shoptaugh was absent, so a substitute resident came in his place. Referred to herein as Dr.Savage, he entered the room with several colleagues and stated, "I'll proceed with the LP." Oxygen tanks and a mask were provided for me as Dr.Savage instructed an intern, "Hold the mask tightly over his face. Be sure he's breathing while outside the iron lung."

Obviously plans for this procedure were discussed prior to entering my room, and everyone apparently understood his responsibilities. Without further comment Dr.Savage opened the iron lung and pulled my bed out. Turning my body to one side, a nurse and intern attempted to bend my knees up into a fetal position. Two previous spinal taps in as many days were painful, but well tolerated, nothing comparable to the agony I now experienced. A bed in an iron lung won't fully extend, creating limited space in which to perform medical procedures. Restrictive confines prevented them bending my knees up as necessary and pain from muscles and raw nerves, a result of acute Polio, was excruciating. Frighteningly, a bad situation was worsened by inexperienced people who, when turning me, failed to expand the neck collar preventing any opportunity for adequate breathing assistance from my oxygen mask. I tried to gasp, scream, or twist my head, anything to signal a problem, but the intern in his effort to provide oxygen, simply forced the mask harder against my face. "It isn't working!" he yelled. "Please hurry!"

"Don't worry." said Dr.Savage. "As long as he keeps on struggling, he's all right. Hold him tight so I can remove the needle!"

"Hurry!" cried the intern, "He's cyanotic!"

"Just a minute!" growled Dr.Savage. "The needle must be stuck in a bone."

By this time pain, fear and my awareness of surrounding people began fading away. I heard someone yell, "For Pete's sake, don't break it off!"

When I awakened later with the iron lung closed, I saw Dr.Walcher standing at my head, his face blanketed by deep concern. "Danny, I'm sorry that procedure went so badly. I promise we'll do better next time. You realize of course, we must perform this test again."

"Oh no!...Not again!" I pleaded. "Please!"

"Listen Danny. Do you trust me?" he asked.

"Yes." I replied.

Dr.Walcher explained the plan step by step; assuring me previous mistakes would not be repeated. "First a securely fitted mask will be established to ensure your breathing. I will open your iron lung and enlarge the neck collar, and then you will be turned as painlessly as possible. When we are certain you're comfortable and breathing properly I will, at that time, proceed with the test."

The iron lung was opened, and my bed fully extended. An adequate airway was established with an oxygen mask, then he opened the collar and they turned me, maximally flexing my knees. It was still impossible to bend my body into a fetal position because of the narrow bed and confining iron lung. An injection of pain medication before the procedure helped control muscle spasms caused by positioning required for the spinal tap, and this time I received a local numbing agent. Even though painful, I could breathe and felt secure knowing Dr.Walcher was in charge.

In conversations with relatives I discovered my illness was not the only emotional anguish exhausting our family. A mild case of suspected Polio had affected my seven-year old sister Millie, who fortunately didn't retain any long-term maladies. Most people had expected Andy, only three years old, to become ill since he'd placed my horn's contaminated mouthpiece to his lips. Millie didn't touch the instrument. Only God can answer the mystery of why some people, but not others are afflicted by the Poliovirus.

The uncertainty of my condition prompted Dr.Walcher to advise relatives, "Remain in contact with Riley Hospital." Dad and Mom were emotionally torn between my bedside during initial critical stages of Polio, and providing a secure and calm environment for Millie. The frightful dilemma facing my parents required courage and wisdom for solution to this situation.

Once while peering through a drug-induced haze, staring at my parents standing beside the iron lung I mumbled, "Dad, I…really…like…that …shirt."

"It's a comfortable shirt," he said, "and I really like wearing it because it goes with all my other clothes."

"Oh really?" voiced Mom. "What other clothes?"

"Velma!" exclaimed Dad, frowning.

Not understanding their conversation or body language, I smiled, floating back into my fog. Since then members of my family have informed me upon admission to Riley, Dad had rented sleeping quarters near the hospital. Unfortunately, he never saw inside that room. Despite willingness of other family members to stay with me he refused to leave, resting as best he could in chairs or couches, sleeping occasionally in the lobby. My dad stayed at the hospital with me twenty-four hours a day.

Andy and Millie required supervision and care, so Mom was obligated to remain home. Seeking comfort for heartache and increasing emotional tension, she prayed and kept busy. Fearing the worst at any moment she furiously cleaned house, did laundry, and vacuumed or dusted. In battling to retain any semblance of normalcy in a situation that was perilously spinning out of control, she incessantly uttered prayers for deliverance from this tragedy in her family.

God, medicine, and ice packs surrounded me in the iron lung, forcing partial stabilization of my temperature, pulse, and equilibrium. Perhaps it was medicine or the incubation period of the virus, but my and Millie's temperature simultaneously decreased. I personally believe it was the hand of God, encouraged by sibling telepathy. With this new situation, demand for Mom's presence at home eased, enabling her to spend more time near me at the hospital.

Intermittently, doctors and nurses would open the tank to perform necessary examinations and treatments. Denied my source of life-giving support, even though semi-conscious, I gasped for air, positively terrified. My memory and family have told me that I frequently screamed, crying out in agony every time my body was repositioned. Severe, constant pain intensified when nurses taking care of me were required to perform life-saving treatments. I quickly learned from any touch, acute Poliomyelitis attacked the nerves and muscles, causing searing pain at all times. The application of even slight pressure produced unbearable spasms and cramps.

Somewhere, amidst swimming visions of strangers and my family, confession became good for the soul. "Dad…can I …talk? Remember when…Mark's car…was totaled? I uh,…well, I…was behind…the wheel.

Mark was... sick and...couldn't drive. It was...OK until...a big ...tractor and...farm wagon...wouldn't move...over. I'm lucky...the trailer...didn't hit...the windshield. Don't worry...I worked...off the...debt."

"Danny don't fret about that now," said Dad, "I'll pay for whatever is left of the expense."

"No...No!" I sleepily protested. "It's paid."

"OK son. Just get well." whispered Dad.

Periodic news releases appeared in *The Courier-Times*, and *The News Republican* following my onset of Polio. Daily prayers were broadcast via the public address system at New Castle High School, along with announcements concerning my condition. Stories updating the situation resulted in cards and letters from many concerned, caring people. Many prayer services were held at churches throughout the city. School friends and New Castle citizens became my most ardent, loyal supporters. A frequent visitor in my hospital room was our minister from the Wesleyan Methodist Church, Rev. Kerschner.

Adherence to strictly enforced hospital isolation kept visitation limited to immediate family and minister during this period of acute illness. Consequently, the halls and lobbies provided space for Williams supporters. One problem occurred, many friends were not permitted to see me. Since I was only fourteen most of them were also under the age of sixteen, a requirement for visiting at the hospital.

As the crisis of acute Polio resolved, Dad and Mom were informed my survival, without additional complications, was miraculous. Searching for a logical answer some people kept asking, "Why Danny? Why this family?" Devastating illness intertwined with days of horror faded, only to be replaced by a black cloud of despair. The reality of my body's death asserted itself and I too started asking, "Why, why me?"

The first agonizing week of Polio was behind me now and it was obvious I'd survived by God's grace and the knowledge He had bestowed upon my doctors and nurses. Staying alive was now dependent upon my faith, determination, and common sense approaches in coping with consequences of a dreadfully vile disease. Confusion reigned in my life, but I hoped the struggle ahead would be easier than overcoming this crisis. Monday morning not only began a second week of illness, but also initiated a new era in my life.

Attempting to force liquids and nutrition into my body, the nurse brought a breakfast tray to my room. It consisted of an "appetizing" meal of Jello, buttered toast, orange juice, and milk. Oops I forgot, delicious tapioca pudding! Between my gags and refusal to eat, in strolled Dr.Walcher followed by his entourage of residents, interns, medical students, and a lone head nurse. Most of these people were acquainted with me from previous

Keep Smiling and Never Give Up!

days. I recognized few of them. Searching for the face of Dr.Savage, he was strangely absent. "Who can tell?" I hoped, "Maybe all of this is a bad dream."

Dr.Walcher smiled, asking, "How do you feel today? Hmm look at this." Scanning my breakfast tray and observing the shaking of my nurse's head, he added solemnly, "Do you see all these people standing here? Have you thought about your family and friends? Don't you want to eat some more of this food? We will continue our rounds, returning momentarily to your room. I'm sure this will give you sufficient time for mastering the art of swallowing."

"Shall we continue?" asked the nurse with a smug look on her face. Trying to control the welling of tears in my eyes, an awful feeling in my stomach, and lump in my throat, I gagged, then swallowed a bite of tapioca pudding.

Returning later, Dr.Walcher looked at my breakfast tray and commented, "Well Danny, a little is better than nothing. Meet Mrs. Hunky Dory, your day shift private nurse. I have made arrangements for extended special nursing on each shift beginning now. Mrs. Hunky Dory meet Danny, your new patient who's apparently intent on starving himself."

"Hello Danny it's good to meet you." she said. "We'll get along just fine. Don't you worry everything is going to be hunky-dory."

"Oh brother!" I thought. "Now I have another reason to get well!"

Amidst Dr.Walcher's examination he said, "Danny, I have planned some activities for your immediate future. Shortly, Occupational Therapy (OT) will be here to position a mirror on your iron lung. It isn't designed for your vanity, but to help you see the activities and people in your room. The adjustable mirror fastens in these brackets on the front of your tank. Perhaps this will lessen feelings of isolation, allowing you to interact with your surroundings. Within the hour a physical therapist (PT) will begin administering some treatments commonly referred to as hot packs. The therapist will explain in detail, but basically they consist of moist, heated blankets. It is important to begin movement of your limbs, preventing muscular contractions occurring during any immobility - especially after the onset of Polio. Various treatments will be quite painful I'm sure, but bite your lip and have courage. They are imperative for your recovery."

Except for the warning about more pain, this was good news. The monotony of lying still would at last be broken. I had been paralyzed a week, and almost any movement would be a welcome change. An attractive young lady walked into my room, the image of fragile femininity.

Smiling at me she greeted, "Hello, I'm Miss Nash, your physical therapist. You must be weary of telling people how you feel, let me just assume you are anxious to escape the confines of this iron lung. Dr.Walcher told me he explained the basics of these treatments to you, but left the details for our first encounter. Danny, the hot packs he mentioned are simply wool blankets heated in a steam machine, placed on your limbs and body, covered with plastic insulation."

"Miss Nash." I interrupted. "I'm allergic...to wool. And I can't...breathe by...myself."

"That's okay," she said, "we can substitute bath towels for the wool blankets. I will put them inside the iron lung so your breathing won't be interrupted."

Finishing her explanation of the treatments with a look of anticipated pleasure upon her innocent face, she began my therapy program. The hot pack machine of wet, steaming, and odorous towels made my room smell like the gym. Fortunately the hot flannel blankets were placed inside the tank, thereby eliminating some of the odor. Nearly scalding my skin, they provided temporary relief from muscle spasms. The soothing effect disappeared much too soon as my hot packs cooled and became miserably cold, wet, and very uncomfortable. Inside the iron lung droplets of water condensation formed around rectangular side windows of the tank and moisture soaked my sheets. Miss Nash removed the hot packs then proceeded to begin PT, which she referred to as an exercise program.

After emitting several "Oh No's", groans, and feeling a cold, heavy covering of sweat on my body I concluded PT was short for "physical torture". The exercises relaxed me for one simple reason - I felt so good when the pain stopped.

Smiling with satisfaction Miss Nash said, "Today I was just testing. Tomorrow I begin the real treatments."

Contrary to beliefs of medical personnel, exercising or stretching muscles are not the most important factors in PT. We Polios and other qualified recipients of this diabolical treatment insist the true incentive for recovery is a desire to evade aggressive physical therapy. Acknowledging their procedures do inflict substantial pain, compassionate yet determined people are essential to this profession. Therapists are often rewarded when patients whom they have grown to love experience improved mobility and health. Paralysis became a blessing in disguise, after PT I was much too sore to move anyway. Fear, pain, and resentment soon replaced my initial enthusiasm; I dreaded Miss Nash's appearance.

With each passing day my understanding of Dr. Walcher's words increased. "Learn to adjust." he counseled. "Accept from the beginning, you must adapt to a new way of living."

I wondered, "Is he saying acceptance, adjustment, and adapting will be essential for the rest of my life?"

The iron lung had been my home for over a week. It was beginning to pose a heavy burden on thoughts and emotions. Sedation and fever had previously diminished the effects of my surroundings, but as they decreased I was becoming more aware of reality. Traumatized by my present situation and frightened of the future, numbing anxiety blanketed me with a maze of inner turmoil as I contemplated life's prospects.

The claustrophobic enclosure of my tank and suffocating pressure of this tiny room were fast becoming a prison. I panicked, awaking each morning to the torment of drab green walls separated by glass partitions, decorated by my cards. One event I eagerly anticipated each day was mail delivery. Relatives and friends mailed hundreds of get well greetings. Impressive to me were love and best wishes sent from totally uninvolved strangers. The compassion exhibited by all these wonderful people instilled a desire to answer every card and letter, but increasing correspondence, made it an impossible feat. With this book, I humbly thank you! Each word carried with it encouragement I desperately needed to continue my struggle.

The days passed slowly with ever-increasing emptiness providing little distinction between day and night. My only association with calendar or clock became changes of nurse's shifts and the different names of daily meals. Never-ending monotony and rigid routine comprised each twenty-four hours, sadly obliterating any semblance of rest or sleep. On one bad afternoon I could no longer contain my feelings. With lips quivering, tears gushing from my eyes, and twisting my head from side to side, I cried out, "I can't...stand it! I can't...take it...any more! Oh God!...I'm not... real bad...why is...this happening...to me?" Unknown to me, Dr.Walcher had been standing outside my door.

Entering my room he placed his hand on my forehead and said, "It's okay, Danny, get it out of your system. I can't think of anyone right now who has more reason."

"Dr.Walcher," I sobbed, "sometimes these...feelings of...anger and...hurt just...build up...in me...until I...feel like...exploding! I can't...run from ...my thoughts...or escape...the pain. Listen to...me talk...I can't...even do...that any...more...This tank...makes me...feel sick. Sometimes...I think ...what's the...use?"

"Danny." he consoled. "Let it out. The respirator's cycling is responsible for your broken speech and that will change once you develop a rhythmic response to its actions. You could eliminate many of these frustrations and terrible moments by thinking about the good things left in life for you to enjoy."

"That's just...it...Dr.Walcher." I cried. "I can't...have most...of those...good things...ever again, ...so why...think about...them?"

The nurse assisting Dr. Walcher interrupted, "May I say something? Danny, think about all the wonderful family you have at home; think about friends that write to you and are anxiously awaiting your return; think about Rev. Kerschner; think about your doctors and nurses; but most of all, think about the Lord who is protecting your every moment. You've told us about fishing trips, ball games, and your dreams of becoming a Marine. These are all good thoughts."

"Of course…I think…about my…family and…friends." I replied. "I never…want to…hurt my…loved ones…by giving…up. I also…think a…lot about…those other…things you…mentioned. The way…my body…is now…I can…only be…a fan…at ball…games. Watch other…people fish…and read…about Marines. I need a…reason for…living! I'm so…lost! Oh God…why is…this happening?"

Dr. Walcher continued, "Each day you must look upward to the compass of all our lives. Believe, and you'll never be lost. God has a reason for everything. Danny, paralysis is incomprehensible to any of us, but never doubt tomorrow, keep faith, patience, and hope. One day you will learn there is a reason for your Polio. Some day that reason will help you understand why God is polishing you at this time."

"What do…you mean…God is…polishing me?"

Dr. Walcher explained, "If He didn't consider you strong enough for the job, you would not have been chosen. Jagged rough edges of your life are being smoothed like a diamond. You are being polished for something of importance. Do not disappoint Him! Danny, do you enjoy listening to radio? I am sure if your family brought one to the hospital it could be placed on a chair outside your door. The television was not a good idea, but at least you could listen to music. If you're interested ask your parents. Mrs. Hunky Dory, isn't it time for this young man's therapy? I'll see you later."

Moments after Miss Nash completed my PT for the day, in walked Rev. Kerschner. Wiping tears of pain from my cheeks, he whispered, "It will get better, let's pray for strength."

Following his words of prayer and encouragement, I said to him, "I can't…talk. It hurts…and I'm…sick."

Rev. Kerschner, both in his role as a man of God and a friend, comforted me by saying, "Danny, miracles do happen."

Keep Smiling and Never Give Up!

4
CINDY

One morning a new iron lung was wheeled through my door and the room became smaller. "Mrs. Hunky Dory,...is that for...me? Am I being...moved to...another tank?"

"No Danny. You're getting a roommate," she said, "and I'm getting a new patient. Staff nurses will provide most of her initial care, but I will be available if needed. You two should get along fabulously. She's a blue-eyed doll with blonde hair, and her name is Cindy."

"Wow, this is great!" I thought. "Imagine my roommate, a blue-eyed blonde. Will the guys ever be impressed when I tell this news! Of course Judi probably won't be happy." I awaited Cindy's arrival with eager anticipation.

Momentarily, a little girl was brought into my room and drab surroundings became brighter. Watching nurses transfer this six year old from stretcher to iron lung reminded me of recent experiences. Cindy cried out in pain, "Please don't hurt me any more!" Terrorizing fear clouded her eyes as all these unfamiliar surroundings magnified lonely agony. Obviously, my new roommate was a very sick little girl.

The doctors gathered around Cindy, probing, poking, and pushing on her body asking where she hurt most. Emotionally, I observed many exhausting and necessary exams, reminiscent of my initiation into hospital life. When doctors finished, the nurses continued monitoring physical changes, employing motherly and sisterly persuasion, encouraging cooperation in her treatments. Cindy choked while trying to drink liquids needed for nourishment, so an aspirator was again moved to our room. Nurses performed multiple treatments, injections of antibiotics and pain medication, constant blood pressure monitoring, and efforts to control a raging fever. Another furiously intensive struggle to save a human life had begun. This time it was Cindy.

My routine continued with one exception. I personally was aware of Cindy's fight for life, the pain and agony she was experiencing demanded more than ordinary compassion from one person to another. This critically ill young girl could easily have been Millie. Thankfully, Rev. Kerschner entered our room as visiting hours began.

"Good afternoon Danny." he said, looking toward the new patient. "Well I see you have company."

"Hi. Good to...see you...today." I said. "Meet my...new roommate. Cindy isn't...speaking. She doesn't ...feel well...I think...she's justa...bit shy."

"Hi Cindy." he said, turning to her. "You remind me of my daughters when they were little. Do you have brothers or sisters?" Without speaking, she barely moved her head from side to side.

"Why does God...let people...suffer from...pain? Why are there...so many...diseases...Rev.Kerschner?" I whispered. I haltingly told him about my outburst and Dr. Walcher's comments about being polished.

"Those words and thoughts are important and true." He replied. "Doctors, nurses, and medicines can provide only a limited amount of healing, one also requires faith. Think about Dr.Walcher's words and what he was telling you. When a diamond is mined it is just a piece of rock with roughened edges and no shape. A man first strikes the stone breaking it apart, grinding the edges into a smoother form. Lastly, he begins the polishing. This requires great perseverance and patience by the craftsman, but also strength within the stone. We are all born with rough edges."

Puzzled, I asked, "What do you...mean Rev.Kerschner?"

"We all experience polishing in our lives." Continuing he said, "Our response reveals the true essence of courage. Displaying honesty, resolve, and inner strength will ensure you an excellent witness for His word. Through our faith in God, the answer to your question awaits us in heaven."

"Rev.Kerschner." I asked. "When you offer...prayers for me...please also...mention Cindy...and Cathy...her mother. She is very...upset and...so far I...have not met...her husband. No one has been...here with her today. No family or...friends. Maybe they are...busy. Anyway...she seems very...lonely."

"By all means." replied Rev.Kerschner. "Let's have a word of prayer."

Passing hours indicated a worsening condition for Cindy and her battle for life. As I listened to doctors discuss various possible causes of her illness, it became obvious a preliminary diagnosis was Poliomyelitis. In an attempt to distract Cindy's thoughts, I tried communicating with little success. From her few nods I learned she enjoyed toy dolls who cry and dirty their diapers, a topic of conversation not my forte. Since I was unfamiliar with this subject, I began talking about something else. "Cindy...would you try... some water? A cold...fizzy drink...always tasted... good to me...when I felt...so bad. A 7 UP...might be great." I received a very weak affirmative nod from her, so I asked Mrs. Hunky Dory our nurse if Cindy could have some soda. She filled a drinking glass, then held the straw to Cindy's lips. After only a few small sips she choked, and refused any more liquids. Throughout the night, nurses and aides provided

Keep Smiling and Never Give Up!

non-stop care, giving medicine and begging, "Cindy honey, please try to drink."

Many of these nurses were mothers themselves, which led me to wonder, "Where did they find strength to care for all these sick and dying children? Fighting a never-ending war against disease and death must be terribly depressing." In a calmer moment I expressed my thoughts to one of my nurses, "Mrs. Farrell...do you ever...want to stop...working at...the hospital? Do you want...to leave and...never come back? I sure would...go home if...I could."

"Sure Danny, I hate seeing people sick, but these are my kids." she replied. "I return to work each day knowing if my help and love saves only one child, it's worth all the effort. I go home to my children after work confident I've given another mother and father's baby the best possible care. Further reward isn't necessary for me to continue this job."

Over night Cindy's health deteriorated and Dr. Walcher's presence was requested early next morning. Reading charts and giving her thorough examinations, he beckoned the nurses aside for a hushed conference. Shortly, a new doctor walked into the room instructing the nurse to push a privacy screen between Cindy and me. Intense activity surrounded her iron lung and smells of alcohol disinfectant permeated the air. Certainly, something unpleasant was occurring.

After the privacy screen was removed I could see a wire-like metal frame in front of Cindy's neck. Curious, I asked Mrs. Hunky Dory, "What happened? What's that...metal frame around...Cindy's neck? Why does she...have bandages...on her throat?"

"Cindy needed help breathing." she answered. A surgeon inserted an artificial airway into her throat."

With a shocked whisper I asked, "You mean they...cut her throat?...I'm glad they...never did that...to me! Why did the...doctor do that...to her?"

Mrs. Hunky Dory quickly placed her hand over my mouth, leaning down she whispered in my ear, "Shush! She can hear what you're saying. Thank God, Polio did not involve your neck. Cindy's Polio involves her throat along with the rest of her body. The surgeon performed what is called a 'trach' or tracheotomy. This operation establishes a new opening in her throat so we can give her oxygen and help when she gets something caught as she swallows. Remember? We used this machine on you. It's called an aspirator. With this tube we can remove obstacles from her throat if she gets choked, and suction mucus from her lungs."

Amazed, I kept asking questions. "The tank collar...fits so tight...on our neck,...how does it...work?"

"Danny, see the wire frame around Cindy's neck? It's called a trach retainer. This metal device securely holds the collar below her tracheotomy opening." Mrs. Hunky Dory explained. "She's resting and breathing better, so let's try eating some of our breakfast."

Doctor's rounds, as usual, were timed perfectly for the middle of breakfast. Again studying her chart and speaking to other doctors, concern for Cindy was obvious. Looking at me Dr. Walcher asked, "Do you like your new roommate?"

"Yes sir." I replied. "She reminds me...of my little ...sister. Not long ago...I was that...sick. I think Cindy...is in worse...condition."

"Yes Danny, you're right. Perhaps some company will be beneficial to both of you." he said, continuing his rounds.

Mrs. Hunky Dory had just finished feeding me the rest of my breakfast, when in rushed Cathy, Cindy's mother "What happened? I got here as soon as possible. Oh No! My poor baby!"

Mrs. Hunky Dory firmly asserted, "Walk with me down the hall while I return this tray and I'll explain. Danny, I'll be back in a few minutes."

Later, I listened to Cathy as she tearfully recounted her situation. "I shouldn't be burdening you with this, but I have no one and I just need someone to listen." The words literally spewed forth from her soul, releasing many months of buried emotions. Overwhelming grief became evident. She rapidly continued, "Cindy was born when I was just sixteen, only months after we eloped. Last year Cindy's father was killed in an automobile accident, and two months ago my mom died from cancer. My family is gone. I don't have anyone. Cindy has to get well."

"Oh man!. .I thought...things were...bad for me. Try not to...worry. As they...told me...it will... be all right. See," I said, "she's...sleeping now."

"No it won't!" Cathy sobbed. "The doctors told me she might not live through the night." Tears streaming down her cheeks, Cathy fled from the room.

My little roommate was sleeping soundly when one of the aides stepped inside our room. "Hi Danny." said Ruth. "How are you feeling today?" Unable to speak, I nodded Okay. In less than forty-eight hours I became emotionally attached to my new friend and her mother. News of this tragic situation and the frightening report about Cindy created a large lump in my throat. I was learning first-hand what so many people had been telling me, "There are many people who are in worse condition than you".

Turning my head toward Cindy I watched while she opened her eyes in fear. "Hi there." I said. "Would you like... the nurse to...get you a drink?" She just stared, moving her head side to side indicating no. I remembered terrible pain from acute Polio. It was obvious, the tight iron lung collar needed for adequate breathing pressure combined with fear and discomfort from both Polio and the tracheotomy had absolutely terrorized my friend. Understanding how a small child could endure so much agony without

Keep Smiling and Never Give Up!

uttering a cry, or shedding one tear was bewildering. Cindy set an excellent example for everyone who entered our room. Watching Cindy tolerate so much pain without complaint would forever make an impression in my life. From now on, I'm fine.

Evidence of the doctor's earlier words to Cathy became apparent as nurses began making preparations to move Cindy to the room next door. I was watching for my parents when I heard a sob. Looking in the direction of the sound, Cindy was crying. This was only the second time I heard her voice and the first time I had seen her tears. The nurse had left the room for a moment so I asked, "Cindy do you…want me to…call for help?"

Through tear-stained eyes and quivering lips she cried out, "Oohhh!…I…hurt…so…bad!…Please… help…me!…Please…help!"

I will never forget those words. I felt powerless to help, and it wasn't because of Polio. With tears stinging my eyes I thought, "Dear God! What can I do? Are there any words that will comfort her at this moment?" The bitterness that had engulfed me for many days melted away as I silently prayed for Cindy and her mother. "Dear Jesus. I know you love all little children. Please help her get well. Give her mother strength. Most of all, relieve Cindy's pain."

Doctors and nurses moved Cindy to the room next door; and a mind-numbing stillness permeated the air. Entering the room my parents asked, "Where is Cindy?"

With tears in my eyes I replied, "They moved her… next door."

Sensing a desire not to discuss this subject, Mom wiped my tears and changed the conversation. "Anything new? Tell us about your day. Then one of us will leave and let Kenny and your sister visit with you. Vivian brought a newspaper article about you that appeared in *The Courier-Times*."

I told them quickly about different activities of the day and remarked, "If you don't…mind, I'm not…in a talkative…mood this…evening."

Mom kissed my forehead and said, "I'll exchange places with Kenny in the waiting room."

Through glass partitions between the rooms we observed doctors and nurses working feverishly, trying to save Cindy's life. Shortly a privacy screen was placed against the transparent wall, and my heart sank. Soon I heard a cry and the words, "Oh please God. NO!" as Cathy stumbled down the hall, supported by a nurse. Cindy was dead!!!

Dad and Kenny left saying, "We'll send Vivian and your Mom in to say goodbye."

"Danny, your dad told us about Cindy," Mom said, "so I know you can't talk anymore tonight. We'll just stay for a few minutes."

"Hi Danny, how are you feeling hon?" asked Vivian. "I guess this wasn't a very good evening to visit. We want you to know our thoughts and prayers are with you always. I'll save this story for another time. We won't stay long. Hon, you should see the long lines for Polio shots in New Castle, my phone never stops ringing with everyone asking if you're getting better. It's a shame your friends can't visit."

Mom said, "Vivian, I think maybe we should leave." She motioned with her head toward Cindy's room. They blew me a kiss, and quietly left the room.

At first I wondered why God had not answered my prayer for Cindy, but after a few days I realized perhaps He did. Cindy's agonizing pain was gone, and she was safely in the arms of Jesus. Thinking about this tragedy I realized, God needs sweet little girls in heaven for angels.

5
CHALLENGED

The following days were punctuated with loneliness and depression. I was weary from restless turmoil. Thoughts of Cindy's death were fresh in my mind. Time had passed slowly since my onset of Polio with no apparent improvement, recent heartaches making the situation even more disconsolate. My unassisted breathing time was zero, muscles spasmed, nerves screamed, and privacy for bodily functions proved impossible. Bluntly, all my control of life's challenges had vanished before the aggression of a minute virus labeled Polio. Pain of daily physical therapy promised scheduled suffering, and eagerly anticipating a new day was all but impossible when dreading its planned activities. I asked myself inevitable questions, "Will I ever get better, or will it ever end?" I became sullen and irritable. Ofttimes well-meaning people offered unsolicited opinions and I thought, "Patience".

Passive indifference to everything and everyone became increasingly apparent as my spirits spiraled perilously into the depths of despair. My first confrontation between life and death had been successfully passed. Fourteen years old, totally paralyzed from Polio, I now faced life encased in an iron lung. "Imagine," I thought, "'think of good times'. Ha!"

"Hello Danny, is it all right if I visit now?" inquired Rev.Kerschner, entering my room. "I attended a meeting in Indianapolis today, thus this early visit. If my being here is inconvenient just tell me to leave."

Dreading the anticipated arrival of Miss Nash in a few minutes, I sarcastically remarked, "It's just time…for my daily…stretch and scream. When my therapist…gets here…you both can…pray and leave. Sorry,…I'm in a…bad mood."

"Other than the obvious?" he observed. "What's wrong? Is there something I can help with, or anything I can say?"

"To be honest? I'm not sure." I mumbled. "Living this way…is disgusting. It's not worth…all this effort. Searching for…courage to fight…each day,…hoping my…determination to…handle the pain…and what's …becoming…hell on earth…just never ends. Living has ended. Now I just…exist."

"Danny," said Rev.Kerschner, "none of us can understand these questions now, but there's a purpose for this terrible illness. In the struggle facing you there will be many days of despair. When problems appear insurmountable, just close your eyes and pray. Remember, God listens."

"Rev.Kerschner!" I exclaimed. "What reason can…my life have? What's left? Fishing trips…with Norman are …over, sports are out. Working with Mark…delivering Chesty's…or Pepsi…is over. No more…paper route. I can't attend…school without…a forklift. I can't …play my…cornet again. I can't lift…300 pounds …anymore. Someone must…brush my teeth,…comb my hair,…scratch my nose,…give me the…urinal, and wipe…my rear. My faith is…getting weak…and any future…as a teenage boy…stinks!"

"Listen Danny," instructed Rev.Kerschner, "God says,'My grace is sufficient for thee; My strength is made perfect in weakness.' Man's words are useless in these circumstances. God's word will strengthen your faith, grant you courage to confront all problems, give rest to your soul, and peace to your spirit. You need only to believe."

"Hi Danny, are you ready for therapy again?" asked Miss Nash, entering the room. "Oops, excuse me, I didn't realize you had company."

"Miss Nash, meet…Rev.Kerschner, my…minister." I said. "Would you join us…for a few…words of prayer, …before he leaves?"

"I'm not sure," chuckled Rev.Kerschner, "but I think he just encouraged me to leave."

"Please don't think me atheist," she replied, "but I'll wait in the hall for a few minutes, providing you privacy."

"Danny, she's a breath of fresh air. From your vivid portrayal I expected an ogre." he whispered. "Let's pray."

Alone later, I begged for relief from the iron lung's constant, loud whooshing in my ears, thinking of this predicament, and the suffocating cage of a small room. In my naïveté, I assumed after the initial illness my fight for regained strength and health would be relatively easy. These appalling conditions paralleled times of desperation and sadness preceding one of the more frightening experiences in my life. Drowning in a sea of misery I cried, "Oh God,…I wish I…were dead! I can't…live like…this without…a good reason. I will never…get better. I'm no use…to anyone!" The words were barely spit out of my mouth when I heard, **Bang**! My breathing abruptly stopped and pressure vanished from the iron lung. Panic-stricken because no one was in my room, I could only make clicking noises with my tongue. Unable to take a breath, I couldn't call for help. Alone in the room, I knew unless someone walked by my door, these ineffectively weak efforts would be futile. Attempting to gasp for air, I was stricken by smothering sensations. Perspiration formed over face and body, with pounding, throbbing, blows echoing through my head. In previous discussions, Dr.Walcher said, "Don't panic! You can survive four minutes without oxygen."

Keep Smiling and Never Give Up!

It already seemed like an eternity! Searing my memory were the words I had just uttered. A thought sped through my mind - was this planned? Mrs. Hunky Dory had momentarily departed the room and an alarm situated on my respirator's pressure gauge failed to alert anyone. If this was a divine message, I thought, "Okay God, I got it! Please help me!"

Surprisingly, numerous thoughts flash before one's eyes when life is threatened. I thought of family and friends, hardships, worries, terrors of this illness, and everybody's fear of tomorrow. Perhaps my death would be better for all concerned. "Then," I thought, "if I'm dead the devoted love shown me in my short life could never be repaid. Maybe life wouldn't be so difficult watching other people work, fish, or play ball. At least my brain still functions. If only I could taste sweet air again. Somebody please help!" my mind screamed, "I'm really in trouble." The minutes elapsed since last taking a breath were incalculable, but I knew my life was quickly ebbing away.

Exhausted from clicking, I twisted my head while gasping for air; my eyes felt ready to explode from their sockets; and dizziness blurred my vision when I tried focusing on the now fading door. Weakly I attempted to click my tongue again, but my mouth was drawn so tightly, movement of tongue or lip was impossible. Pain in my chest and lungs developed into a raging inferno. Another chance at life seemed to be waning. Consciousness slipped away, and drab room surroundings began swirling. I begged, "Please God don't let me die." Swiftly passing into oblivion, I heard the words, "Help! Danny's in trouble." Someone slammed the porthole door. Pressure then returned to the tank and I drew my first breath of wonderful life-giving oxygen. Blackness descended and I fainted.

I regained consciousness to find numerous people around me, an intern monitoring the situation. After temporarily increasing the iron lung's pressure to elevate my oxygen I slowly stabilized, and he documented my return to normalcy. Happiness and smiles of relief shown on staff member's faces as they welcomed me back to consciousness. Shame flooded my soul, memories of my impatient outburst brought repentance.

Mrs. Hunky Dory pressed a cold cloth to my forehead and said, "Ruth saved your life with her quick action. Danny do you realize I'm getting too old for this sort of thing?"

Ruth had been one of my aides since admission to Riley isolation, but possibilities for real friendship between us were minimized because Mrs. Hunky Dory provided most of my daytime care. "Mrs. Hunky. .Dory please. .ask Ruth. .if she . .will step. .over here. .by me." I asked. "The tank. .is breathing. .me so. .fast I. .can't speak. .well."

"I'm here Danny, just relax." Ruth directed.

"Ruth thanks. .a lot." I sighed softly. "If only. .I could. .hug you."

Still nervous from the recent events Ruth said, "Daniel you gave me quite a scare! Thankfully I walked by your room at just the right time."

"Ruth I. .know your. .shift is. .ending, but. .can you . .stay for. .a few. .minutes and. .talk?" I asked.

"Sure Danny I can stay." she said. "Your nurses are in the middle of shift change right now, so I'll keep an eye on you just to be sure you won't do this again today."

"Thanks for. .staying Ruth. .I heard. .a loud. .noise I . .couldn't breathe. .I clicked. .for help. .no one. .came. My nurse. .was gone. .panicked. .I prayed. .What happened?"

Ruth answered, "We found out your failure alarm didn't sound when the equipment porthole mysteriously fell open and you suffered a total loss of pressure in the iron lung. We aren't exactly sure how long you went without breathing, but your face was blue when I walked into the room. Believe me, my friend, my color black is much prettier than your blue!"

I jabbered incessantly pouring out raw emotions, which I had concealed for three weeks. Knowing Ruth's compassionate character, I explained my thoughts immediately preceding the recent excitement. "Ruth I. .wished myself. .dead. When my . .iron lung. .failed I. .quickly changed. .my mind. Guess everybody. .makes mistakes." I quipped.

Looking at me with a frown on her face Ruth challenged, "Danny boy, I'm going to say some things that will hurt your feelings, but it's time you heard these words. You're not the first person to be handicapped in life and I think it's safe to say you won't be the last. There are many thousands of people handicapped each year. Only three weeks after you had Polio, and you've already given up! I think it's about time you stopped wallowing in self-pity and accept your life as it is, then start fighting back with some courage. Leave your mark on everyone you meet and then you'll give meaning to your presence in this world. Sure you don't know why you had Polio, none of us do, but some day you'll understand and this pain and heartache will be worth it all. Just remember one thing, don't quit and never again give up! Solving this problem will take a whole lot of determination, courage, and faith, but you can do it. Well Danny, I've listened to your problems and told you off in the same visit, now it's time I went home. See you tomorrow."

As Ruth left my room Dr. Laskee, an intern, returned to reset the pressure in my iron lung. Once again I could say three words in one breath instead of two. My ears stinging from Ruth's words I thought, "You don't understand. Think of all I've lost, I'll never by happy like other people. Oh boy, she's supposed to be my friend! How could she say such things to me? Ha, imagine accusing me of wallowing in self-pity!" Her comments kept echoing, "Could she be right? Am I just giving up? No! No! I have a

Keep Smiling and Never Give Up!

reason." Later in the evening I had some visitors whose vision of faith, healing, and religious fervor, along with the day's events, brought forth a personal unpleasant reaction. I couldn't believe they thought my weak faith was responsible for the slow recovery. Talking to Miss Bergenstout, my night shift private nurse, I sought comfort in her support of my arguments, but she said, "Danny, it pains me to say this, but Ruth is correct! Don't you realize how much it hurt her to say what she did? Maybe closing the porthole isn't the only time she tried to save your life. Better think about it."

Sleep didn't come easily as I couldn't clear my mind of Ruth's words. As light began filtering through the one tiny window in my room I realized how compassionate her lecture had really been. Maybe someday the wisdom she imparted will direct me in search of better days.

The isolation ward became solitary confinement when Dr. Walcher informed me no one except Dad, Mom, and my minister would be given visiting privileges. "Why?" I demanded, "The two things…most important…in my life…are letters and…visitors. Dr.Walcher,…must I lose…even more of…my life?"

"Danny, this time of the year is an excellent breeding season for communicable diseases." Dr.Walcher said "There are many outbreaks of cold and influenza viruses this year. Either would be detrimental to your health."

Determined to maintain control I pleaded, "Dr.Walcher! Maybe you could…sterilize them."

Chuckling he replied, "I've also been told you recently were visited by certain people who caused unnecessary stress in your recovery. Despite objections, please trust me."

Grudgingly I replied, "Of course I…trust you. Most people are…just interested in…my getting well. They want me…healthy, but on…their terms. Please don't …misunderstand. I don't know…how to explain…but I think…some people are…more interested in…being involved with…instant miracles…than witnessing…a miraculous recovery. Hopefully this…doesn't sound…mean because…I like these…fine people. My mind is…being healed and…with time my…body will follow. Stopping diseases…is understandable…but are you…sure limiting…my visitors…isn't just another…way to get me…fighting mad?"

"Danny, I think you are becoming wise to our tactics." he said, smiling as he left.

Regardless the reason, it worked. Visibly slow, steady progress became evident in my daily routine. I continued to loathe physical therapy, but at least my nose refrained from complaining about the pungent odor of steaming hot packs. I surprised my nurses by swallowing the many medicines without argument. Smiling when I submitted to various uncomfortable treatments, they nearly went into shock. Loneliness almost overpowered me during daily visiting hours. As I watched many people walk through the hallway to other rooms I wondered if my trust had been misplaced. Considering improvements in my health, I decided the situation was changing. Sloowly!

One morning about 3:00 A.M., stifling heat and humidity inside my tank combined with the room's temperature, giving me one more cross to bear. Since there was no thermostat on these iron lungs I asked Miss Bergenstout (Miss B), "Please open the…tank for a…few minutes. It's hot…and I need …some cool air."

This was the first time I ever requested time outside the tank and I should have realized the shock it would be to my nurse. The scenario that followed could have been taken from a comedy show. Miss B. was a plump, jovial, middle age Hungarian woman who seldom had an irritable word for anyone.

"Surely, surely." she said. "Let me get an assistant." Reaching the doorway she stopped in her tracks, standing in one spot a few seconds. Turning and slowly walking back to me she said with a non-believing giggle, "I must be sleepy Danny, or else it's the heat. Did you just ask to be taken out of the iron lung?"

"That's right…Miss B." I replied. "It's so…hot in here! I need cool…air. Didn't you say…the tank …temperature could…not be changed? Well, I am…changing it! Please open…my iron lung…a minute."

Muttering to herself and shaking her head in disbelief, Miss B. said, "It must be the night duty! OK Mr. Dan! Here we go. Remember, this was your idea." Raising the sealing clamps, she released pressure and pulled me from the tank.

I took a deep breath, determined to hold it as long as possible. Watching me warily, Miss B. asked, "Danny are you breathing? Why is your face getting so red?"

Shaking my head no, I felt my face beginning to flush. "Try taking at least one breath on your own." she coaxed. I ignored her instructions and she pushed on my chest, forcing the previously stored air from my lungs. "Now, try taking a breath." I panicked! Fearing suffocation I violently shook my head sideways gasping for air. She closed me back inside the iron lung, my steel cocoon of safety.

Smugly I asked, "Well, how long…was I out? Nearly two minutes?…You kept time…didn't you?"

Miss B. replied with a satisfied smile, "Actually, you held your breath for a long ten seconds. You've just begun, don't be discouraged."

Dr. Walcher walked into my room on rounds next morning and announced with a smile, "I have a big surprise for you Danny. I've arranged

Keep Smiling and Never Give Up!

for your transfer from this room to Ward C in the near future. You will have been in isolation one month Thursday. Acute Poliomyelitis has resolved, your fever is gone, and I think it is time you become a regular patient."

"This is great!" I exclaimed. "at last I'm...getting out of jail,...my birthday is...November 10th...what a wonderful...present. One favor please...Dr.Walcher. Don't say anything...to my parents. I want to...pull a double...surprise party. Before reading...my chart...I also have...a big surprise...for you. Last night...it was so hot...I asked to be...taken out of...my tank and...Miss Bergenstout...described it...as a long...time. I tried to...breathe by myself."

Dr.Walcher and his colleagues became totally speechless listening to my good news. Obviously, any similar shocking announcements of progress would require more tact to ensure continuation of physical stability among the medical staff. Satisfied facial expressions appeared on all the doctors and nurses, revealing pride for a job well done. At last, I saw a future filled with hope.

"Danny, reiterating my previous advice, just progress a little more each day." said Dr.Walcher. "Humm, according to this chart you held your breath for ten seconds. Presumably you don't anticipate traveling any long distances, such as from here to Ward C for your birthday. Seriously, you must learn to breathe normally again. The next time you're taken aback by an impulse of bravery, you must begin retraining your diaphragm. Any returned strength to your abdominal and intercostal muscles will rest largely on avid determination. When next you try breathing on your own outside the tank, go for twenty, then thirty seconds, and so on. That ten-second interlude will develop into an hour and before you know what is happening you will be sleeping in a regular hospital bed. You played football Danny; you know it is risky to chance everything on an end run. Sometimes when a quick gain is attempted, an irrecoverable loss ensues. Just keep pounding out the yards each day, one at a time." With these words of encouragement and a goodbye wave, Dr.Walcher continued on morning rounds.

I enthusiastically anticipated my immediate future for the first time since Polio was diagnosed. With Mrs. Hunky Dory's persistent encouragement for intervals of unassisted breathing time, scheduled sessions outside the tank became more frequent. My initial ten seconds steadily increased to that dreamed of minute. Strengthening tolerance for living in the outside world was not easy; fearfulness of being unable to breathe without a respirator inhibited all willpower.

Once Dr.Walcher announced my impending transfer, time remaining in isolation became an eternity. Because special equipment or recreational items weren't permitted in this unit for fear of contamination, isolation meant more than separation from germs. Staff members had situated a radio outside my door, but after a month's seclusion with minimal distractions I was really looking forward to this change. I thought, "Imagine, watching TV and who knows, maybe soon my visitors can return." Undoubtedly, leaving the severity of isolation would help me see things differently, my recovery might be moving along faster now.

Friday morning finally arrived. Dr.Walcher conducted rounds and said, "This is the big day. I've requested most of your treatments be completed this morning so you will be prepared to move by afternoon and I'm confident my request will be honored. Everyone at Riley wants you to progress, so don't let the cheering upset you when leaving isolation. I will explain various aspects of our plan when I return to facilitate your move to Ward C."

A hospital volunteer surprised me with a birthday gift. Supported by financial assistance from the Ruth Lyon's Club, Riley Hospital customarily provided patients with mementos for special occasions. The Cheer Fund lady brought a camera outfit to me explaining, "I know your birthday is on Sunday, but we don't work weekends. Since patients aren't allowed to keep personal items in isolation I'll deliver the present to Ward C, your new home."

"Thanks a lot." I said. "Maybe you could…take some pictures…of the staff…for me."

Dr.Walcher returned to coordinate preparations for my transfer. "Danny, these are the steps we will follow moving you from this unit to Ward C." he said. "The move will take about fifteen minutes. I'm sure you cannot hold your breath for the duration. Therefore, the maintenance department has generously provided a long extension cord. Your iron lung will be moved as far as possible, then we can connect you to a wall outlet until the extension cord is advanced. These actions will ensure continued operation of your respirator, negating any breathing difficulty."

"What a relief!" I thought. "When contemplating my ten second attempt at freedom I became quite concerned about the length of time required for my move." Doctors, nurses, and maintenance personnel gathered around me as Dr.Walcher gave the order, "Forward Ho!"

I rather enjoyed my excursion into a new world, getting my first clear view of the isolation unit since admission to Riley Hospital for Children. Especially enjoyable were the huffing and puffing sounds of people pushing my heavy iron lung through hospital corridors. As Dr.Walcher promised, we entered the doors of Ward C less than fifteen minutes later. People straining from moving the awkward tank looked forward to my destination site with relief. Located inside Ward C's doors were four private rooms, two on each side of the hall, and a long corridor leading to the twelve bed open ward. My location would be next to the nurse's station in a private room. I recognized some of the nurse's voices taking care of me; they had relieved Mrs. Hunky Dory, Mrs. Farrell, and Miss Bergenstout on their days off duty. Although sounding familiar, they were more attractive in crisp white uniforms than drab isolation scrub dresses. Glancing around my new room I spied a large window letting in rays of warming sun. Ward C obviously provided more opportunity for recovery, and I would never miss the tiny dark cubicle I'd just escaped. The month of October seemed to be a training session, or to coin a phrase, "boot camp" for my war of survival.

As Dr. Walcher was leaving, a group of people pushed a stretcher through the doors of Ward C. They all wore green surgical scrubs, pushing IV poles, and oxygen tanks beside the stretcher. The patient cried out and when I looked at him I could hardly believe my eyes. "Dr. Walcher!" I gasped. "Look! That is Ken. My friend from…New Castle. We go to school…together and live…in the same…town."

"What a strange coincidence." Dr. Walcher said, smiling. "Mutual friendship and support will be excellent for both of your recoveries. Now Danny, I must attend to other patients and probably will not see you until Monday. Do you have any other problems before I leave?"

"Well Dr. Walcher,…there is one thing." I said. "Do you suppose I…could have some visitors…on Sunday, my birthday? Maybe my family,…perhaps a close…friend?"

"Danny, since this is a special occasion, I will agree to expand your list of visitors. Monday we will discuss new arrangements. Incidentally," he said leaving the room, "the nurses might turn the iron lung around on your birthday then you could see out that big window."

"I don't want Ken to be ill," I thought, "but this puts me on the horns of a dilemma. I need a friend, and unknown to him, Ken just volunteered."

6
GRACE

Friday evening Dad and Mom entered my private room with smiles of happiness spreading across their faces. "We just received quite a shock." said Dad. "Your mom and I went to your room in Isolation, and they said you were moved to Ward C. Maybe some family and friends can visit Sunday, to celebrate your birthday."

"Get ready!" Mom teased. "You might even be surprised like we were today."

"I hope so, it's...been ages since...I've seen any of...my friends." I replied. "Dad, you'll never...guess who is a...patient with me on...Ward C. Remember Ken my ...good friend? You work with...Duke his father...at the factory."

"I know." Dad smiled. "It's really odd how things work out sometimes. Who can tell, maybe you guys will talk each other into getting well. If nothing else your companionship will be good for each other."

Ken's parents walked onto the ward as we were speaking. Dad and Duke exchanged greetings and expressed their delight with the new arrangements. "What coincidence! Sick friends becoming patients in this hospital at the same time." Said Duke. "Wonders never cease!"

"I'm getting suspicious." I mused. "Did you guys and ...the doctors pull...something sneaky?"

Sunday morning, November 10th, was my fifteenth birthday. Brilliant sunlight warmed the room as it reflected through my window – the beginning of a new day, indeed, a new year. My morning started with birthday wishes from all the nurses. Dr.Shoptaugh coordinated weekend rounds with staff members, bringing me good news, and bad.

"Danny we all wish you a happy birthday." he said. "It is good to see you smile again. This room is much brighter than Isolation, that alone should encourage your spirits. I understand Dr.Walcher wants you to consider letting some of your private nurses leave. Not all at once, incrementally as you improve. Allow me to introduce Dr.Schaffer, he will replace me on pediatric service with Dr.Walcher. My special training has been completed, now I must return home with my family to Colorado."

"Dr.Schaffer...I'm happy to...meet you, but am...sorry to hear...this man's...leaving." I sighed. "We've been...through rough times...together. It's sad to...say goodbye. Dr.Shoptaugh...where are you...going?"

"My family and I will be heading to Colorado Springs." Dr.Shoptaugh replied. "Danny, I can't begin to tell you how happy we all feel that you are here for this birthday. Many times we were uncertain you would leave Isolation alive. If those Air Force kids don't keep me too busy I'll drop you a note, but Dr. Walcher and Dr. Schaffer will hold the fort."

I was quite happy to learn my private duty nurses would gradually be replaced with regular staff. The ladies taking care of me the past few weeks were wonderful, but their exit meant I was getting better. Not only that, I observed young and attractive staff, many of whom were student nurses only three years older than me. "What a stroke of good luck!" I thought. "This is definitely much needed improvement."

Morning routine passed quickly as I completed all those required little duties. Mrs. Hunky Dory said, "Danny, let's try to be finished with our tasks soon because this will be a full day. Now that our breakfast is over, it is time for our bath."

"That sounds good...to me." I replied. "First I must use...the urinal."

"Sure Danny." said Mrs. Hunky Dory. "It's so wonderful we can do this without being catheterized any more."

Walking from the room, Mrs. Hunky Dory held the half-full urinal at eye level remarking, "My, we certainly did a good job, didn't we?"

Grimacing, I thought, "How could I possibly think about letting her go? The lady has helped me so much. Why should I be happy just because there are beautiful student nurses on Ward C? Oh well, someone has to do it."

"Happy Birthday, Danny!" chorused a group of people as they entered my room carrying a cake with chocolate frosting and one large candle in the center. Student nurses, regular nursing staff, and even two doctors sang "Happy Birthday".

"What a neat thing to do." I thought to myself. After receiving a birthday present from the hospital, cake was an unexpected treat. These expressions of care proved that beneath masks of solemnity, proverbially "tough as nails" people are really softies at heart.

Festivities over, Mrs. Hunky Dory said, "Dr. Walcher has given permission for more lenient visitation today involving your family and friends. Not only that, we have another big surprise later."

From depression to optimism - already changes in my life and visions of a future invigorated the air on Ward C. Shortly my visitors began arriving, bringing with them gifts and cards from my family and friends. Two of my older sisters, Vivian and Anita, entered the room smiling broadly. Vivian exclaimed, "Danny, your progress the past few weeks is unbelievable! Happy Birthday big brother."

"Not only that," chimed in Anita, "look at the smile on his face. I think this is one of Danny's happiest days in a long time. Wait 'till he sees our other gifts."

We talked for a while, I told them about the move from Isolation, and about Ken being on Ward C. "Just wait until he…is well enough…to visit." I boasted. "This place will…never be the…same."

"Listen hon," said Vivian, "we'll go downstairs now so Judy can visit for a while."

"Okay, who's coming…up with her?" I asked.

"We don't know." said Anita. "I'm sure she won't be by herself."

Expecting Judy, another sister, I was shocked when in walked Judy and Judi! "Surprise!" they said. "You didn't expect two for one, did you? Ha! Norman said to tell you 'hi', he'll be up later with one of the guys."

Judi said, "I have a big box of birthday cards and personal messages for you from kids at school. Most are cards with notes on the back. For some reason, I don't understand why, they want you to stop lying around and get back to school."

Mrs. Hunky Dory entered my room announcing, "I think it is time." With these words she and two other nurses turned my tank around facing the window. Adjusting my mirror so I could see three stories below outside the window, she asked, "Do you recognize anyone?"

"Yes! There they are! Some of my friends. I see Mike …Nancy…Valerie…Bill. Why didn't…anyone tell me…they were…coming? This is great! Not only can I …see outside for the…first time in five…weeks. My family and friends…are here for my…birthday."

On numerous occasions Mrs. Hunky Dory encouraged moving my tank back to its prior location, but I graciously refused. Spending the remaining visiting hours before the window, I hoped this wonderful day wouldn't end. The view from this vantage point wasn't commonplace to me, it was a beautiful sight. Faint rays of afternoon sun shone dimly through bare branches of towering trees as they majestically supervised activities below. In the distance I could see new buildings under construction, and cars traveling to and from IUMC. A late fall wind briskly whipped coats and jackets of people entering Riley Hospital. Crisp breezes foretelling winter's approach placed fallen leaves in neat piles along hedgerows. Watching the birth of a gorgeous sunset, I looked upward to an evening sky vowing, "Whether it takes one year or a life time, someday I will be on the outside looking in."

My first week on Ward C continued with Dad commenting, "Danny after you get familiar with your surroundings, would you object to some visitors from New Castle? The elders at the Pentecostal Church wish to anoint you and have hands-on prayer for your healing. If you agree I'll call Dr. Walcher and get special permission."

"Sure Dad. Whether I walk…or not at least…my mind…will be healed. Are these some of…the men you work…with at…Perfect Circle?"

Keep Smiling and Never Give Up!

"Yes son, they work at the factory and constantly ask about your health. The church members and many other people have held special prayer services for your healing, and that God's will be done in your life."

Polio had challenged my life to a battle that wouldn't end with one victory. I remembered Ruth's words the day she saved my life, "You can't change the fact you're physically handicapped, but you can give life meaning." Nor could I ever forget Cindy's pleas for help prior to them moving her from our room. Just before her death the words, "Help me, please help me!" burned in my mind. Sunlight faded and I watched as twilight replaced rays of hope. Tearfully, these memories became more poignant and I determined from this day forward to memorize events and people touching my life. I dreamed someday perhaps I could express my thoughts, helping others cope with the intense impact of personal challenges. Undoubtedly, pain, terror, tears, loneliness, and especially prayers were training me for a new life. Silently I vowed, "Ruth, I will continue to give my life meaning. Yes Cindy, (as you are watching) I will, God willing, try to help." As tears flowed onto the pillow I thought, "This disability won't become an excuse for dying. Never will my search for a reason to live be ended by seemingly impossible obstacles or people who've given up."

"Good morning Danny." said Dr. Walcher entering my room with his medical students. "I hear you were quite surprised yesterday. According to the chart you slept well last night following the excitement. I hope you weren't overtired."

"Oh no." I said. "It was a long…day, but I didn't …push myself. Just being allowed…to see new people …and especially…looking out the…window was good. By the way,…I'm sorry Dr. Shoptaugh…is leaving…he is a …great and…devoted doctor."

Dr. Walcher replied, "I'm also saddened to see him leave Riley, but I'm sure you will like Dr. Schaffer. Your father called with a special visitation request. I understand he's spoken to you concerning permission for your anointing. I will grant permission provided you are aware, prayers are answered at God's will. On more mundane matters, Danny, do you feel secure enough for the Ward C staff to assume some of your care? I think perhaps the evening and night nurses could be released now, but let's keep Mrs. Hunky Dory on day shift for a while. Any thoughts?"

"That schedule sounds…good to me." I said. "Only one thing…concerns me. Turning at night. Will Ward C's …nurses have time…enough for me…after caring for …so many other…people on…this floor?"

"Don't worry," interjected Mrs. Hunky Dory, "everything will be just fine. If we continue to improve, we'll soon be saying bye-bye also. Today I begin orienting staff RN's and student nurses to help provide your daily care."

"Wow!" I thought. "What more could a guy ask for? I will be surrounded by good-looking student nurses supervised by young RN's. Thank you God."

Mrs. Hunky Dory conducted an in-service program for the staff, acquainting them with my iron lung and daily hygiene. Some RN's had previously provided special duty relief for my private nurses in Isolation, but students and nurse's aides were unfamiliar with the situation. Referring to my daily attempts for increasing unassisted breathing time she told them, "Don't be frightened when he gasps or gulps, it's his unconventional way of breathing without an iron lung, but be careful he doesn't become cyanotic during this retraining of diaphragm, abdominal, and intercostal muscles. Dr. Walcher believes it vital Danny relearn normal breathing patterns. We also think it necessary he gain confidence in his ability to provide sufficient air for himself; therefore, we tend to overlook his unorthodox method of breathing."

Explaining reasons for the equipment door and relation of different portholes to my body was essential, because the staff was unaccustomed to an iron lung. My illusions about care at the hands of student nurses were soon to be exposed. Mrs. Hunky Dory proceeded to explain the process of giving a bath in an iron lung. Using my semi-draped body she reached through portholes on one side of the iron lung and patiently coaxed an embarrassed student nurse to participate in under cover exercises through portholes on the opposite side.

It was difficult to believe I was beginning my second week on Ward C. Each day revealed new progress through activities that encouraged time to move more swiftly. I could now see sunlight along with darkness. When I was admitted to HCMH on October 7th it had been one month since my last haircut. The date was now November 18th, approximately ten weeks since I'd last visited a barber. Flowing locks of my hair were draped seductively over the back of my pillow and I requested a clip job. Waiting for Miss Nash one day I was greeted by the words, "Oh excuse me, I was looking for a guy who needed a haircut. What is your name sweetie?"

In the deepest voice I could muster between giggles I responded, "Danielle! Any questions?"

Mrs. Hunky Dory brought a single rose into my room one afternoon. "Danny," she said quietly, "this is my last day as your nurse. Having survived a critical stage of illness, you must now begin the real test of your life. Keep working on your unassisted breathing; after all, you've progressed to three minutes without the respirator. These people will provide you with excellent care and the companionship of younger people. One thing before I

Keep Smiling and Never Give Up!

leave, be very careful trying to increase unassisted breathing time with these student nurses around, we shouldn't become too breathless now. Should we?"

***

"Hello, may we come in to your room now?" they asked. Three men entered my room, closed the door, and turned off the television.

"Hi." I said hesitantly.

"Good evening Daniel. We are here to fulfill the will and commandment of God." the ministering spirits proclaimed. "Our Father instructed us to pray for your deliverance, and anoint you with oil. In Romans 8:28, the Lord assures us 'All things work together for good to them that love God, to them who are called according to His purpose'. You may walk from this room tonight, or you may continue fulfilling His will from this respirator, combating the effects of your illness, but if you believe in Christ, these prayers will be granted. We have been promised our old bodies will be changed to new and our spirits will live eternally. We pray with authority given us in His name. James 5:14 in God's word directs we elders to 'pray over the sick, anointing him with oil in the name of the Lord'. James 5:16, 'The effectual fervent prayer of a righteous man availeth much'. In Philippians 4:11 we are told by Paul, 'I have learned, in whatsoever state I am, therewith to be content'."

Each man pressed his hand on my head, anointing me in the name of the Father, Son, and Holy Ghost. Amen.

***

As previously mentioned, one of the first people I saw upon entering Ward C was a neighborhood and school friend. Ken was recovering from major surgery, that would require an extended convalescence. His parents told him of my presence on Ward C and it wasn't long before he visited. Appearing gaunt and waxen, Ken rolled his wheelchair into my room. We'd been friends a long time so teenage conversation began immediately for both of us.

"Ken it sure is…good to see you." I greeted. Don't take this…personally, but I thought…you survived the operation…on your kidney. Man,…I wanna tell ya…somebody in your condition…oughta go to a hospital!"

"You should talk!" he laughed. "At least they didn't put me in a steel container to keep me out of trouble. Hey pal, how is everything in Tin Can Alley?"

I guess this was the first time since hospitalization that either of us had laughed with gusto. Yes, the road to both our recoveries had just become a lot smoother.

Every day my unassisted breathing time improved until I mastered the art of breathing for short periods outside the iron lung. My first ten seconds brought back the nightmarish terror of the initial illness, but with each additional second of freedom confidence grew and it became easier for me to remain out of the iron lung. Dr. Walcher's words, "A little more each day" encouraged my persistent efforts.

The tempo of my routine quickened, beginning with daily visits of an occupational therapist (OT). Anne's treatment for me immediately focused on psychological boosting. She brought with her different types of recreation: dominoes, playing cards, checkers with numbered labels, board games, a few books and reading material that could be fastened to the mirror on my tank. Enjoyment from participation in various mentally challenging games was essential to my well being. Too much unstructured time in my life led to boredom, which in turn gave me the impetus for self-pity. The one greatest obstacle to recovery for anyone immobilized from physically limiting problems is one's own mind. Self is the enemy.

Dr. Walcher, understanding fully any career for me as a professional athlete was dubious, decided to challenge his captive student. Sunlight not only returned to my room of gloom, intellectual rays of hope permeated my conscience. I listened intently as Dr. Walcher declared, "Polio paralyzed your body, not your brain, so Miss Stern, our hospital tutor, will visit you later today to determine at what level your schooling should resume. Danny, now that you can read books again educational studies are essential to your recovery and future. Incidentally, what are your favorite subjects? Let me guess - girls, sports, cars, and adventure. Correct?"

"I suppose...thank you is in order. For some reason ...thoughts of studying...school material...instead of playing...checkers or games...is really not...what I had in mind...for OT." I lamented. "In answer to...your question...I like history...and geography."

"Those are interesting subjects." he said. "We haven't seen many cases of Polio requiring the iron lung in several years. Just think about your location and the history you are making now."

Miss Stern rolled her wheelchair into my room uttering the words, "Good afternoon Daniel, I'm your new teacher. As you can see I too confront physical problems, so any hope of unearned sympathy from me just because you are in this iron lung is absolutely frivolous. First tell me something about yourself; things you like; what you have done; and, if you wish, how you became hospitalized."

Keep Smiling and Never Give Up!

I proceeded to tell Miss Stern about the past six weeks since becoming ill. When I got to the part about having a cold I mentioned it developed into the "flu".

"NO! NO! NO! Daniel. One never says 'the flu'." my new teacher warned. "It's influenza. We certainly have lavish opportunity for educational advancement."

"Oh boy!" I thought. "Wait til Ken meets Miss Stern." Dr. Walcher had just provided me another incentive to leave the hospital. First no visitors, now school.

Ken was able to visit longer each day as he convalesced from his surgery. My room became a meeting place for people who wished to laugh and have fun. Once, while Ken was sitting in my room watching TV, a fellow patient slipped behind him and relocated the tube leading to a drainage jar beside his chair. Stealthily, he placed it inside the back of Ken's pajama bottoms.

"Oh No!" yelled Ken. "I'm leaking!"

Everyone in the room, except Ken, enjoyed the moment of his discomfort. My friend failed to appreciate any humor in this situation, but profited from the learning experience. Ken leaned over, looked into my iron lung's mirror saying, "Your turn's coming…" At all future gatherings in my room Ken paid rapt attention to the location of his kidney drainage tube, insuring it led to and remained inside a little glass jug on the floor. I watched everyone shuffle from the room and thought, "A month ago I wouldn't have believed it possible to smile again. I remember the day of my ambulance trip to Riley and thinking I'm not like other Polios, I'll get better. Well, thanks to friends like Ken and the student nurses the sun in my life is once again piercing darkness with rays of hope."

7

COFFEE BREAK

Medical discussions, nursing orientation classes with equipment demonstrations, and guided tours - all because of my respirator. The main topic of conversation on Ward C was my iron lung. Seldom did a day pass without groups of interns or nurses reviewing my unfamiliar equipment. Prior efforts of instruction only produced inane questions:

"Is it hot in there?"

"Can you move around very much?"

"Do you spend much time in that contraption?"

I always responded to these innovative remarks with an equally clever reply, such as "yes" or "no".

Ken and I became good friends with many staff members on Ward C. Primarily resulting from age similarity, the student nurses and we developed an especially close rapport. I was appreciative of these young ladies for their help, not to mention they were fun and attractive. The Ward C staff's support at Riley encouraged my will to breathe without the iron lung's assistance. Competition with the clock became a subject for debate and wagering between personnel. A pool was organized to guess the number of minutes I would advance each week. Attempting to keep pace with these speculations encouraged lengthened minutes outside the tank, leaving me breathless. During breathing exercises portholes on my iron lung were opened, eliminating the tank's vacuum. To remain alive I gasped and gulped, forcing air down my throat, while filling my oxygen-starved lungs with life-sustaining air. A goal for Dr. Walcher was retraining both my diaphragmatic and abdominal muscles by encouraging me to breathe naturally. Well-intentioned people suggested numerous alternatives for breathing, but living without air is difficult and they were not suffocating. My goal was staying alive. I therefore, decided to rely on necessity as the mother of all invention. Facial expressions of the staff surrounding my tank ofttimes were hilarious as they watched my struggle to breathe. Some became wide-eyed and open mouthed, staring in astonishment while I gulped for air; others became flushed holding their breath while waiting for me to inhale normally.

One day amidst this exercise, Ruth from Isolation, came by to see me after her shift ended. "Oh no! Not Again!" I heard her shout as she fastened the portholes.

Snickering I explained, gulp, gulp, gulp, "Ruth, I can" gulp, gulp, gulp, "breathe on my" gulp, gulp, "own."

Keep Smiling and Never Give Up!

"Well," she said, "I wouldn't exactly describe what you were doing as breathing, but whatever works. Actually we've been getting good reports about your progress, but I wanted to see for myself. At least you aren't turning ugly blue!"

"Ruth," gulp, gulp, "you wouldn't," gulp, gulp, gulp, "believe the pressure," gulp, gulp, gulp, "I'm under with," gulp, gulp, gulp, "this breathing deal." Gulp, gulp, "These people depend," gulp, gulp, gulp, "on me for," gulp, gulp, gulp, "their movie tickets!" I quipped. I updated her about the friendly wagers and my efforts to accommodate. "They're helping me," gulp, gulp, gulp, "and it's really fun."

"Sounds good to me." she laughed. "Where do I sign up for this pool?"

Morning rays of sun streamed into my room and I was thinking about times of happiness past when Miss Nash walked through my door happily announcing, "Danny, today we begin a new era in your life. Dr. Walcher informs me you can briefly breathe sufficiently on your own, so with caution, I'll begin stretching your legs and arms while the iron lung is open. Anytime you experience undo strain with your breathing I'll put you back inside the tank to rest."

"Sounds fine to me." I replied. "So far PT...hasn't been very...tiring at all."

"Wonderful!" said Miss Nash, smiling as she opened the iron lung. "Shall we begin?"

"Ooowww!!!" gulp, gulp, gulp, "You're killing me!" gulp, gulp, gulp. "Stop! I can't breathe." gulp, gulp, gulp. "I thought you," gulp, gulp, gulp, "said stretching was," gulp, gulp, gulp, "just like," gulp, gulp, gulp, "football. Why," gulp, gulp, gulp, "didn't you tell me," gulp, gulp, gulp, "I was the ball?"

"Quiet! Stop talking and you'll have more air." Miss Nash instructed. "Your muscles and joints have become stiff while confined to the iron lung. Let's at least stretch one leg before I return you to the tank."

After closing my iron lung, I calmly breathed once more without threat of bodily injury. Wiping perspiration from my brow Miss Nash said, "Think Danny, your muscles, nerves, and joints have just survived a highly infectious attack by a vicious, unyielding disease. Dr. Walcher's harsh warning concerning the severity of this treatment following weeks of immobility was indeed sincere. Are you rested yet?"

"One thing before...you begin." I stalled. "You're pretty, and...a kind person. Why did you...choose this ...profession?"

"Flattery will get you no where Mr. Williams. Now, are you quite ready?"

"Oh I...suppose so. Get it over." I grumbled. "Only please...close the door. I don't want my...friends to hear...my screams."

Daniel R. Williams

Ken spent more time in my room than on the ward. I was grateful for his presence, encouragement, and support. Our friendship became closer because we both were attempting to cope with circumstances beyond control. Healing physically became dependent upon mutual emotional stability. Following PT, complete with moans, groans, and loud noises echoing from my room, he always came by with a joke and wiped away tears. As patients in a children's hospital, we were unable to get strong drink on the menu. Our parents provided us a supply of this instant vice, and if time permitted after visitation Ken and I would read and watch TV together while he prepared our forbidden delicacy. Evenings, after a long grueling day we anticipated quiet time and a relaxing, hot cup of coffee.

'American Bandstand' appeared weekdays at four o'clock in the afternoon. Between Ken, other patients, nurses, who were mostly students, and visitors from other floors, there were an average of ten people camped in my room with single purpose in mind - listening to their favorite song. Jimmy, who delivered the food each day, became a regular attraction as he displayed his knowledge of current music. I chose to believe it was my magnetic personality, but Ken insisted TV was really his reason for daily appearances. The motive was unimportant; we looked forward to the visits that brightened our lives. Jimmy was a walking encyclopedia with names of recording artists and their albums. Avidly listening to pop music, watching pretty girls, and learning the latest dance steps from Jimmy definitely assured me, my fifteen year old priorities had returned.

Time passed quickly on Ward C. At last my thoughts and life were occupied with subjects other than self. I became focused on gain through pain. Striving for additional time of unassisted breathing, meeting new friends, or the simple privilege of waking to light of a new day became essential. It was difficult for my family, especially Dad and Mom, to understand the contentment I'd found. The preceding seventy days had been torturous for them and many times they left my room with tear-filled eyes. Emotional suffering magnified thoughts of lost dreams for their son and knowing there was nothing they could do burdened them with stunned grief. The heartache and painful realities incurred each time they saw me were intensified, and anguish permeated their lives. No medication, pain shot or pill could ease the agony of Dad and Mom's shattered hearts. Relying on faith in God, my parents supported each other one day at a time.

With Christmas only two weeks away, Ken incessantly and hopefully talked about going home for the holidays. I chose to ignore his conversation, refusing to allow thoughts like this to enter my mind. Knowing there was little chance for me to escape, I didn't want to think about staying in Riley Hospital without my friend. Despite that mental block the inevitable discharge occurred!

Keep Smiling and Never Give Up!

Ken walked into my room with a huge smile on his face beaming with joy, "Well buddy, I'm leaving in two days."

"This is great...news for you," I pouted, "but don't expect me...to jump up and down...with enthusiasm. Ken I know...you're anxious...to leave, but...think about ...the burden...being placed on me! Entertaining these ...student nurses...all by myself...will not be easy. Who will brew...coffee each evening?"

Laughing, he joked, "Don't worry, I'll tell them to be gentle and have pity for a while until you can handle this by yourself. Don't worry, Miss Beck always takes her coffee break in this room. Hey buddy, stop lying around and get moving, Riley Hospital is only for sick people."

The nurses gave Ken a going home party that became his happiest day since admission to the hospital. I was unable to attend festivities on the ward so they brought his party to my room. Soon after the flurry of activity ended, Ken's parents arrived to take him home. Farewells were exchanged with Ken submitting to a few hugs from his favorite nurses. Then he walked out the door to a much healthier life. A big lump formed in my throat and despite persistent efforts to swallow, I choked.

There were still people in my room listening to music, watching TV, and valiantly trying to bring cheer, all to no avail. Once again I was alone. Saying goodbye to a friend was only part of the problem, I developed an intense case of hospitalitis. I decided to question Dr.Walcher, Dad, and Mom about going home for Christmas. I reasoned, "Simply because I'm in an iron lung and can barely breathe by myself, should this present any great problem?"

That evening while Dad and Mom were sitting in my room I popped the question, "What do you think...about me going home...for the holidays?" Not waiting for an expected "No", protests, or arguments, I rapidly continued, "Sure it sounds...impossible now,...but what if...Dr. Walcher ...can make the...arrangements?"

With a stunned look on their faces the simple response was a shocked, "NO! Are you serious? It's impossible! You can't do that Danny."

Never giving up easily I pleaded, "Just think Dad,...120 mile round trips...each day would...be over. Mom, you wouldn't...have to find a...baby sitter for...Andy and Millie." Talking faster than an auctioneer, and begging more than a kid in a candy store, I overcame their immediate objections. Buttressing my argument I said, "Pleeezzz!"

Conceding momentary defeat, Dad said, "I'll phone Dr. Walcher tomorrow and tell him about your idea. Perhaps he won't laugh before checking your temperature."

Pleased with myself, I watched my parents leave with a new expression on their faces. I guess Dr. Walcher won't be the only person shaking his head.

Fleeing the hospital had been on my mind since Ken made his dramatic announcement. After consideration, even I was beginning to view this wish as an impossibility. Numerous intricate arrangements were required, including the presence of an iron lung at home. I anxiously awaited morning rounds, feeling certain my request to go home for the holidays would bring an emphatic "NO" from everyone.

"Dr. Walcher, am I...ever glad to...see you today. Have you talked...to Dad yet?...Oh that's right...he's at work. Maybe he called you...though." I rattled on.

"Whoa!" said Dr. Walcher. "Slow down. No Danny, I have not spoken to your father. Is there a problem?"

"Dad said he would...call you today." I said quickly. "He just got to work...maybe he hasn't had...time yet."

Everyone on rounds was listening to our conversation. Dr. Walcher requested, "Suppose you start from the beginning and tell me slowly why your father is phoning."

Impatiently waiting for my respirator to cycle I took a deep breath and squeaked, "May I go home for Christmas?"

Staring at me in disbelief Dr. Walcher said, "Danny take it easy with these suggestions, you'll precipitate a heart attack. Have you considered the problems to be surmounted and the risks involved with this request?"

"I've thought of...nothing else lately. The problems are great," I said, "but surely you...will find solutions. After what I've been...through the risks do...not deter me in the least. If possible I...want to go home!"

Dr. Walcher smiled slyly, I couldn't be sure whether in consolation or consent. Other staff members imperceptibly shook their heads in condescension. Wondering why they were so skeptical I thought, "Just wait. Just you wait."

"Danny let me think about this for a little while." Dr. Walcher replied. "The nurses told me you were discussing a trip home, but I didn't expect this request quite so soon. Desire to rejoin your family and friends is encouraging. I promise we will study the situation. Let me talk with your parents and see what arrangements are possible. I'll try to give you an answer soon. Now staff, I think we should all repair to the lounge, it is time for his therapy. Let's go before he tries to walk."

Suggestions of this idea for a Christmas reunion with my family brought stunned responses from most people, for me it was an incredible dream that might not come true. If I went home it would undoubtedly be a very Merry Christmas; if not, well...I just wouldn't consider that possibility. Many

Keep Smiling and Never Give Up!

people dedicated to my health and happiness assured me the prospects of leaving Riley were excellent.

Developments that took place in the next few days were amazing! Shadowed by his staff, Dr.Walcher strode into my room only one week after my request, and announced, "Well Danny, I am bearing good news. According to the schedule established, you will be leaving Riley Hospital December 23rd. Beginning today you may start packing your bag."

"What?...You're kidding!...I don't believe it!" I exclaimed. "Thanks Dr.Walcher...Now it's my turn...for a heart attack."

"Danny you're younger than me." Dr.Walcher said with a smile. "You must understand the arrangements made for your approaching departure. Gulping and gasping the entire trip is obviously an impossible feat. You certainly cannot hold your breath for ninety plus minutes, so oxygen or respiratory equipment must be available. Of course an iron lung is necessary for your stay at home; consequently, we have combined both these maneuvers. Rather than move you separately it will be quite feasible to keep you inside the iron lung and load you and the tank into a moving van. A portable gasoline-powered generator on loan from the Indiana National Guard will supply electricity. Our maintenance director Mr.Sawyer will be supervising operation of the generator and everyone involved will be instructed on manual operation of the iron lung. In case of power failure you will stop at the nearest house and plug into an outlet via a two hundred-foot extension cord. Dr.Jordan, my intern, and Mrs. Wolfe, a nurse, will travel with you. Once home, Dr.Heilman will resume caring for you along with Riley Hospital and me for emergencies."

I was completely baffled by the idea of having a moving van for an ambulance. Everything seemed okay except I was concerned about talk of a power failure. A two hundred-foot extension cord to the nearest house...I wondered, pray tell, "What happens if the people aren't home?" Some parts of the plan devised by Dr.Walcher and The March Of Dimes were not very appealing, but the least I could do was be appreciative. Thoughts of a hospital stay over Christmas were depressing. Thank God, plans developed rapidly for my adventure.

A myriad of activities at home followed announcement of my impending arrival for Christmas. Family and friends made plans for my first day home. Nearly three months had passed since seeing my little brother, sister, nieces, and nephews, so I looked forward to their noise and confusion. The whole concept of my illness and the iron lung in which I lived had completely befuddled them, and attempting explanation merely increased their confusion. How does one explain to a three year old, "Your big brother now lives in a yellow tin can on wheels, with a big motor on back that huffs and puffs?"

Daniel R. Williams

Most of my friends were denied entrance to the hospital because of their age, except Judi, who was now sixteen. I could hardly wait to catch up with everybody's life. "Would they," I wondered, "be interested in mine?"

Preparing our house to accommodate the presence of my iron lung began immediately, thanks to The March of Dimes. Direct wiring providing improved electrical circuitry for a respirator was installed to ensure more efficient service. The additional weight of 800 pounds required floor jacks to support the tank. Our two-story house had no bedrooms on the first floor; therefore, Mom's dining room was converted into my living quarters. Contracting the work necessary to complete required modifications proceeded with unparalleled precision. Stories about my anticipated trip home and needed alterations to our house appeared in local media. With publicity from New Castle's radio station WCTW, and newspapers, *The Courier-Times* and *The News Republican*, Christmas spirit captured everyone's heart. Danny was coming home!

Dr. Walcher arranged for instruction of family members in the techniques of my nursing duties and administering PT. Mom and Vivian were selected for the limited education, working directly with my nurses and therapists attempting to learn a profession in two and one-half days! Watching them struggle to master these tasks was humorous, but PT caused the most difficulty for all. Mom and Vivian were hesitant to hurt me; not understanding painful physical therapy now, would prevent needless life threatening complications later. Practicing my developing willpower, I tried desperately to conceal the pain as they held my arms and legs incorrectly. Fortunately, our fears subsided more each day as we became a team striving for the goal of getting me home. Amazingly, a simple task became the most difficult to learn. To feed me each bite had to be timed with the cycle of my respirator, so my sister and mother learned to breathe quite well. After coaching and many helpful suggestions from everyone, my speedily educated nurse's aides became acquainted with daily routines. Modesty about various bodily functions made one decision simple; during Dad's working hours my fluid intake would demand discipline. I prayed never to have diarrhea.

I thought my departure date of December 23rd would never arrive! Doctors, nurses, therapists, dietary staff, and patients crowded into my room on December 22nd to convene a going home party – a celebration totally unexpected by me. Many people, doctors included, were unwilling to believe rumors of my discharge until directly informed by Dr. Walcher. Their skepticism further increased when details of the trip were explained. They came more to hear about my moving van ambulance, than to enjoy cake, ice cream, and balloons. Included in the festivities planned by Becky and other student nurses was presentation of gifts: a watch for timing my excursions outside the iron lung, and a fuzzy, toy mechanical bear playing drums. Presenting one of the gifts Becky said, "Yogi, a warm, fuzzy bear is from all of us. It exemplifies our knowledge that throughout your life you'll be following the beat of a different drummer." Along with these words, she pressed her tear-stained cheek against my face softly whispering, "Merry Christmas Danny." With tears on their cheeks my nurses smiled and doctors turned away, embarrassed by the obvious emotion.

My possessions and equipment were piled neatly around the room. As the afternoon progressed it became obvious to all, discharge was eminent. I said goodbye many times, not realizing the number of new acquaintances I'd made since entering the hospital in October. Polio closed many unknown doors of opportunity, but in turn opened others including a different perspective on the value of friendship. Whether meeting new doctors, nurses, therapists, orderlies, aides, dietary help, housekeeping, maintenance, or volunteers, each person must be valued for his or her special talents. Hospitals simply couldn't function without the services of these dedicated people. Oh yes, we must not forget the importance of every patient. Memories of certain people will forever live in my mind - whether the sun shines or clouds pass over leaving a teardrop from heaven, I will remember.

Attempting to sleep, many life-fashioning experiences encountered at Riley Hospital for Children raced through my mind. I thought about leaving tomorrow, saying goodbye to a thousand friends, and losing secure surroundings. "What is life going to be like at home?" I wondered. "Everyone here at the hospital accepts me for who I am. They talk to Danny a person, not Danny 'the cripple'. Conversations are honest with no attempt at selecting words to avoid misplaced guilt or embarrassment. That approach is comforting, because I don't want to be segregated into a 'special group'. Like everyone, I need to belong! Will family and friends welcome home son, brother, uncle, nephew, and friend; or will they welcome the disease called Polio?" With final thoughts of my trip home, the night grew late. At last I slept.

8
HOME FOR CHRISTMAS

Trying to cope with a high level of anxiety, I asked to be moved in front of the window. Recalling past experience, I knew affinity with God's creations would calm my nerves. Golden rays of sunlight gleamed brightly through glistening branches of snow-covered trees. Gazing across front lawns and over to the parking lot, I watched sunbeams bounce off windshields and dance around car tops. Brilliant glare from a blanket of snow, which had fallen overnight, forced me to close my eyes. Leaving the hospital is a happy moment in anyone's life, for me it was even more momentous, I wasn't expected to make this trip alive. What a beautiful morning! Today, I'm going home!

Routines are entirely different on Ward C this morning. Schedules are ignored, with only necessary treatments being performed in preparation for my journey. Weather reports on TV describe the temperature as a "windy thirty degrees". No telling what the temperature will be in my ambulance. Today I'm dressed in something other than clean sheets; they've been replaced by new pajamas, bathrobe, and slippers. A twinge of excitement permeated the air as doctors, nurses, and technicians relayed vital information about my trip. At noon, Dr.Walcher, the physician most responsible for my life and survival at Riley Hospital, visited me for a private and instructive conversation. His kind voice, stern words, and deep faith in God had also helped me begin recovery emotionally as well as physically. We were both being blessed with a most unexpected and very Merry Christmas present.

"Danny, I'm here to say goodbye and offer final words of advice." said Dr.Walcher. "Once this operation begins I will have little time for conversation. Although your trip is a much-awaited event, I know you are experiencing a great many doubts and some fear regarding the excursion home. We have taken precautions for your safety and comfort. Your home in New Castle has been structurally modified; accommodations for the heavy iron lung and its electrical requirements have been completed. Family and friends await your arrival. It is wise to remember these people are also burdened with fear, so you my friend will be largely responsible for acceptance or rejection of the situation. Should emergencies develop, you discovered early in your illness, panic is unproductive. Your calm demeanor is essential for controlling any problem and guiding other people's reactions. Many people have not seen you in an iron lung or heard you speak; in fact most of the citizenry have never personally viewed this respirator. There

Keep Smiling and Never Give Up!

will be sentiments of fear, sorrow, bewilderment, and some cowardly people will even shake their heads, muttering under their breath, 'Thank God it's him and not me'. You've been given a special opportunity to display a winning grace these people have never known; your choice of response will determine life's contentment. Try not to be offended by any snide, unfortunate remarks. As you know, humor is excellent for easing tension. Regardless the circumstance, there will be unhappy and devastating moments in your life. Remember, you will be looking upward to the source of your strength."

Dr. Walcher continued, "As presently planned you will remain home approximately three months. This of course depends on you and your family's health. Going home does not forfeit responsibility to pursue breathing exercises or continue the physical therapy. You now tolerate thirty minutes outside the iron lung, when you return I expect that to be tripled. Important also, don't return with your arms and legs drawn into muscular contractions from lack of therapy. I am just a phone call away. Beginning later today Dr. Heilman, your parents, but most of all you, are in charge. One request, don't disappoint any of us."

"Dr. Walcher, thank you." I continued excitedly, "There will be progress...at home, just wait...until you see me ...when I return."

"Danny this day is all the thanks necessary." he said smiling. "Do you have any questions?"

"Well Dr. Walcher," I said hesitantly, "I do have a...very important question. What happens if...there is power ...failure at home? Pump the bellows...by hand?"

"The emergency support system in New Castle is aware of the situation, and they know you can only breathe a limited time without assistance. In communications with them I have been assured of their immediate response. I have spoken to your family physician and updated him with a medical status report. Understand, this visit home is only temporary and we are here anytime you or your family require support; albeit, we are confident most problems can be handled locally."

Entering my room Miss Dennis, Ward C charge nurse said, "Dr. Walcher I have just been informed Red Ball's Moving Van is in position. Danny's ambulance is ready."

The time arrived for my caravan to freedom. Suddenly a hollow feeling formed in my stomach. "Why be nervous? After all," I thought, "this trip was my idea. Anyway I've often wondered what riding in the back of a semi-truck was like."

I was moved from my present iron lung to be transported downstairs by stretcher. As doctors and nurses placed me on the cart Dr. Walcher challenged, "Did he get a chest X-ray?"

"Oh no!" said Miss Dennis. "I was repeatedly assured they would be here in time. I'll call them again."

"Never mind." said Dr. Walcher. "I'll speak to them!"

Five minutes later the X-ray technicians appeared with a portable unit. After posing for revealing pictures I was on my way. The elevator descended and I gulp, gulp, gulped a sigh of relief.

The moving elevator jerked to a stop and then reversed direction. "What now?" exclaimed Dr. Walcher. The door slid open to a startled visitor's face on the second floor. As her mouth gaped Dr. Walcher said, "Hello. Goodbye."

Dr. Jordan and Mrs. Wolfe, RN quickly pushed my stretcher through corridors to a room where my new iron lung awaited. The hall and room were crowded with people I'd met at Riley Hospital wanting to bid me bon voyage, patting my shoulder, and wishing me good luck. Simultaneously gulping, talking, and swallowing the lump in my throat, hampered any prospects for acclimating to a different bed. Security personnel, men from the maintenance department, and doctors began moving my iron lung through doors, outside to a moving van ambulance.

"Wait a minute!" someone yelled. Ruth ran up the hall. With tears in her eyes she leaned over, kissed my forehead, then turned and walked away.

Cold air bit into my tear-stained face as I entered the outside world for the first time in eleven amazing weeks. I was momentarily blinded from the glaring brightness of sun shining on newly fallen snow. The delightful fragrance of fresh air more than compensated for winter's chill. My eyes were unaccustomed to the outside light, so squinting I tried to place faces with all the voices giving directions. I was awed by the crowd of people. Along with hospital personnel there were several newspaper and television reporters, some photographers snapping pictures, police officers, and most of all, my friends.

Dr. Walcher directed, "Quickly load Danny's iron lung in the moving van. Mr. Sawyer, please take control."

"Okay fellas let's do this smoothly, we're on TV." Said Mr. Sawyer. "I want four guys on each side. We must shove this tank inside before the gasoline-powered generator can be placed on the tailgate and started. Everybody ready? On three, heave-ho! One...Two...Three! Come on pushhhh!" Unfortunately this truck wasn't equipped with a hydraulic platform lift; thus, muscle power from numerous strong men straining with each inch of progress moved the heavy tank up a ramp to the truck. The steep incline made me stand up for the first time in three months. Swells of frosty air rushed from mouths of laboring workers as they pushed the iron lung safely inside my eighteen-wheel "ambulance".

Keep Smiling and Never Give Up!

Within seconds I was in the truck, and maintenance men secured my iron lung to the floor. Mrs. Wolfe stood beside me while preparations were completed. A news reporter and photographer stepped inside, asking for one more picture or comment. We agreed to the picture and a reporter inquired, "How do you feel, Danny?"

Gulp, gulp, gulp, "Great!" I declared.

Momentarily the National Guard's portable generator was started, and I breathed deeply once again. "Danny, are you comfortable and breathing adequately?" asked Dr.Jordan after the iron lung began cycling. "If so we're ready to travel."

"The iron lung is…working and my…breathing is fine. Let's move." I replied excitedly.

Dr.Walcher jumped inside the ambulance to say goodbye. "Danny, enjoy the holiday season and your time home. Just remember," he admonished, "NEVER GIVE UP!"

The truck roared to life and everyone took an assigned position. Dad rode up front with the driver, directing him to our home. Dr.Jordan and Mrs. Wolfe accompanied me inside the trailer providing assistance. Mr. Sawyer supervised all generator functions as it and he sat on the tailgate. City police officers assigned to escort me through Indianapolis mounted motorcycles, and their sirens wailed. Together the throng of people yelled, "MERRY CHRISTMAS, DANNY!"

We immediately discovered our semi-trailer didn't have very many shock-absorbing springs. I warned, "Dr.Jordan, this will be…a bumpy ride."

"I've come to the same conclusion, Danny." he said as he tried to remain steady on his feet. "Are you warm enough? I hope so; we can't stop for a hot drink. By the way, how far is New Castle?"

"Danny if you get cold," said Mrs.Wolfe, "I'll put more blankets on you. No kidding, how far is New Castle?"

"Believe me," I laughed, "I'm not cold…Between the pajamas, robe,…sheet, and three blankets…it's hot in here. Riley Hospital to…New Castle is…about sixty miles. You both keep falling…all over the truck. Bolting my tank…to the floor…was a good idea. Bet you guys…wish your shoes…were fastened."

Many turns and a number of potholes later we departed the Indianapolis city limits. Everyone decided the highway would be much smoother, but alas, no road is smooth under a semi-trailer. Each mile brought me closer home so the bumps and jolts were becoming less uncomfortable – or, I was just becoming numb in certain places.

Following the seemingly continuous succession of bumps, twists, turns, and jolts, Mr. Sawyer announced with sighs of relief, "We have just entered New Castle."

Dr. Jordan relayed Mr. Sawyer's periodic announcements, while grasping the side of my tank for support. Mrs. Wolfe, pale from excitement and blue from cold, braced herself in a corner of the trailer. In only minutes the Red Ball Express stopped in front of my house and backed up to the porch. I heard loud cheers of "Welcome Home Danny!" and "Merry Christmas!" resounding in my ears. The previous scene at Riley Hospital was repeated with one exception. Mr. Sawyer, frozen stiff from his tailgate journey, moved slowly while supervising the generator's removal. Unloading the iron lung and me was easier this time, since the truck was level with our porch. My heavy tank was pushed from truck to ramp by New Castle's Police and Emergency First Aid Unit officers.

Stunned silence gripped the crowd as most people spied my iron lung for the first time. Working quickly, the men completed their tasks while my friends quietly stared. At last I looked in their direction and smiled, immediately the cheers resumed. This time noise and words of welcome were less audible as everyone swallowed a lump in their throat, trying to hold back tears of happiness and fear. Looking to one side I saw Nancy my dear friend, with lips quivering and tears streaming down her face. The respirator was pushed to my new room, and any remaining semblance of confident willpower quickly evaporated.

Family welcomed me home. Aunt Ogreta, nieces, nephews, cousins, and my sisters, but no little brother. "Hi Uncle Danny! Hi cousin! Hi big brother! Glad to be home?" they chorused in unison.

Swallowing hard to control emotions I clenched my teeth answering, "Yeah, you bet!"

"Look Danny!" my ten year old niece Debbie, exclaimed proudly. "See what Millie and I made for you today? She's only eight so I helped her put numbers on the checkers. Now you can play at home like you did in the hospital."

"Thanks kids." I smiled "You did a great job. We'll play a game after these people leave."

Dr. Jordan gave me a final examination and asked, "Are you all right? Is there anything I can do before leaving?"

I shook my head "no".

"Well then," he said, "Dr. Heilman is now in charge of your medical needs. We have reviewed your chart and I told him about your necessary treatments. Remember Dr. Walcher's instructions, and good luck."

Mrs. Wolfe informed my parents concerning supplies and equipment she brought from Riley. Placing her hands on each side of my head in a hug, she said, "See you later."

"Danny," said Dr.Heilman, "if everything's satisfactory I must leave for the hospital. Call me any time you have a problem." Placing his hand on my forehead before leaving he whispered, "I'm so sorry."

Medical personnel left and the house returned to a dull roar. Judi, who'd been talking to my sisters said, "Danny we're all splitting now. Get some rest, and welcome home!"

"Hey Mom." I asked. "Where's Andy?"

"Kids, where is Andy? I haven't seen him since the van pulled up to the door." Mom puzzled.

"Grandma, he's upstairs hiding. He's scared of the big truck. The police sirens, doctors, and nurse made him cry." yelled the kids.

"Here he is." said Anita, carrying my squirming three year old brother down the steps.

The remainder of this special day was filled with much laughing, crying, and general confusion. Everyone planned a different activity my first night home and organized chaos reigned. What fun! The evening grew late and I thought, "I am the happiest person in New Castle tonight. With family and friends nearby, thank God I'm alive and well. Most of all, with heaven smiling, I'm 'Home for Christmas'."

Daniel R. Williams

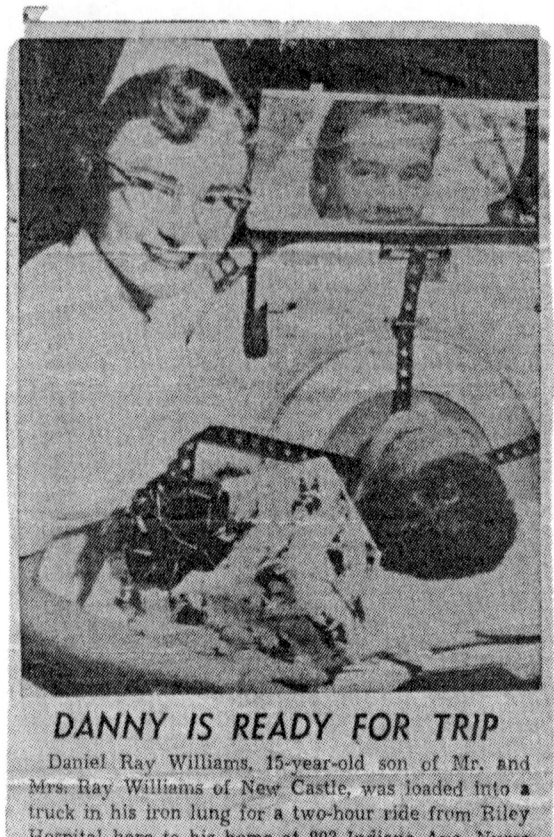

DANNY IS READY FOR TRIP

Daniel Ray Williams, 15-year-old son of Mr. and Mrs. Ray Williams of New Castle, was loaded into a truck in his iron lung for a two-hour ride from Riley Hospital here to his home at 803 Indiana Ave. Nurse Jean Wolfe is shown holding one of the gifts he received at the hospital. The truck carried a special generator to power the lung, and a doctor rode with Daniel. The polio foundation made the arrangements. This AP Wirephoto was made by Bob Lavell of the Indianapolis News.

News Releases and photos courtesy: *The Indianapolis Star* Library.

Keep Smiling and Never Give Up!

Going Home

The Christmas wish of 15-year-old polio victim Danny Williams was granted today when he was taken to his home in New Castle for the holidays. Danny, the son of Mr. and Mrs. Ray Williams, was stricken with polio Oct. 4 and admitted to Riley Hospital here three days later. Police and hospital attendants this morning loaded Danny and his iron lung into a moving van for the trip to New Castle. Accompanying him on the journey was Dr. James Jordan, Riley Hospital intern. A gasoline-powered generator provided power for the iron lung.—Times Photo by Raymond D. Bright.

9
OVERWHELMED

Christmas day was traditionally a Williams gathering to bathe in the glow of our Lord's love. As usual, everyone contributed delicious food to accompany our family holiday celebration. The children were ecstatic about their presents, and adults fellowshipped with loved ones. This Christmas was especially memorable for me; I received the gift of home-life a second time.

Some family members captured festivities with cameras. One hasn't lived until bright lights from a 1950's home movie outfit reflect off a mirror and one is temporarily blinded! The camera lights were reminiscent of another filming event only three months earlier. "Careful," I thought, "today is a time for happiness, not sorrowful memories." Wrapping paper and bows were tossed everywhere while toddlers found joy playing with empty cartons. I was particularly touched by the gift of a pocketknife from my little sister Millie, influencing gentle teasing from me, but total silence from others. Her love and thought motivating my keepsake was overshadowed by stark reality - most sheets don't have pockets.

"Thanks for the knife,…Sis. I'll just carry…it in my teeth…like Tarzan." I joked. For the first time I received the embarrassed "hush" predicted by Dr. Walcher.

My friends played Santa Claus bringing specially chosen mementos to lessen difficult and limited activities: Nancy gave me a registration diary; Valerie brought Pat Boone's book, *Twixt Twelve And Twenty*; Bill's mother sent him with homemade cookies; and Mike cheerfully presented "us" a box of cherry cordials; Judi unwrapped a portrait of herself; and I gave them "me". Today was the first time my close friends had confronted the situation in person and they tried desperately to exude an aura of coolness, but inhibited body language and stiff conversation revealed fearful apprehension. Searching for actions and words, their eyes were averted and I listened as they verbally walked on eggshells. Family also exhibited unusual restraint as they struggled to cope with reality - our lives forever changed. I felt so sorry for all of us, recovery had yet to begin.

"Hey everybody!" I proudly announced…look at this…Christmas present! Several people sent…money in cards…and letters. The cash bought…a record player…and these popular…records."

"All Right!" said Mike. "Now we can listen to music and ignore radio commercials."

Keep Smiling and Never Give Up!

"Sure." said Valerie and Nancy. "We'll even bring over some of our records. Things are looking up."

"That's fine you two," said Judi, "but I get the first dance. Uh, uh, oops!"

"Not unless Bill...holds my sheet on." I laughed.

The following days were hectic for everyone. It seemed every relative and friend stopped by to welcome me home – a drastic reversal in my life after heartbreaking loneliness. In the beginning I enjoyed every minute of their company and anticipated each knock at the door, but eventually unlimited visitation became quite tiring. Medical bulletins alerting everyone of my susceptibility to germs unfortunately became equated with "Danny is very fragile, so be careful ". Whenever a first-time visitor entered my room I heard the words: "I'll just die if I sneeze and give you cold", or "If I make you too nervous now, just say so". Repetitious, patronizing comments soon irritated the soul of my being.

Instituting a suitable routine between my family members and me proved to be impossible. Dad worked days, Mom cared for our home and two younger siblings, my older sisters were either employed or had families requiring attention, and my friends attended school. Chaos erupted in my room weekday afternoons at four o'clock. Dad came home from work, friends appeared after school, dinner was nearly ready to serve, the phone rang, then another knock at the door. Somewhere amidst all this confusion it was imperative we find time for my hygiene, therapy, and breathing exercises. What's rest? Dr.Heilman and my parents agreed on specified visiting hours to remain in effect until personal care, rest, PT, and most important to me, breathing on my own, were given priority.

Rev.Kerschner, preferring 11:00 A.M., became one of my favorite visitors two or three times a week. Each day he read aloud newspaper and magazine stories. Additionally, he read a portion of the New Testament during each visit. He asked one day, "Danny, they told me at the hospital you play checkers. Think you could beat the old man?"

"I really wouldn't want...to take advantage of you." I grinned. "After all you might...be offended and...not come back."

"Don't tell me you're chicken!" he laughed. "Where are the checkers?"

Three losing games later, he said, "That's it, I've had enough. Do you know how to play chess?"

"No." I said. "Could I master...all those moves...in reverse? Remember, I'm looking...through a mirror."

"You'll never know until you try." Rev.Kerschner goaded me with pleasure. "You'll have me for a teacher, and anyway I think your checkers are loaded. I'll bring my chess set. After you lose I want no excuses, so clean your mirror."

Daniel R. Williams

Most evening visitors were family, allowing for a more relaxed atmosphere. Grandpa and Grandma Cole had died many years ago, but Grandpa and Grandma Williams visited often. I still recall shadows of sorrow masking their faces every time they left my side. Once Grandpa asked, "Danny, do you remember when you were a little boy and we'd go fishing? I helped you hold a heavy, long cane pole telling you to watch for the bobber to go underwater. What times we had! Guess I'll never forget the look on your face."

"Yes Grandpa I remember." I whispered, voice cracking. "If only we…could do that again."

"Yes Bud," he sighed looking away, "if only we could."

Tonight my grandparents, aunt and uncle had visited me together and the air was thick with emotion. Preparing to leave Aunt Zella peered into my iron lung mirror exhorting, "Danny whatever you do, always keep smiling."

Waving bye Uncle Doc admonished, "The Lord says we are not to worry, this too will pass. Maybe not in our lifetime but always rest assured, things will get better."

At eleven o'clock next day I heard a familiar knock and Rev.Kerschner walked into my room. Without delay he stated, "It's about time you learned this game! Chess is played on a board similar to checkers. Listen closely, you have eight pawns which move forward in rank, one or two spaces optional on first move, they capture other men diagonally; two rooks who move rank and file; two knights who jump in an 'L'; and two bishops who move diagonally. Your queen is a powerful lady who travels anywhere she wants if not opposed. A king moves one square until captured. That's called checkmate. I must confess, we have a problem. How do I teach you to move these chessmen in reverse?"

"You don't." I answered. "It's like transposing…music. Looking in this mirror…while coordinating …directions. It's done automatically…by me. Now let's see, …rooks move…rank and file,…bishops diagonally, …pawns forward by one,…two optional…first move. King moves any…direction one square. Queen can do…whatever she wants…unless stopped. Is that all?"

"You remember well," noted Rev.Kerschner, "except don't forget your knight. These horses jump over other pieces in an L-shaped pattern. Don't worry, I'll show you the ropes."

I watched my smiling friend set up the chess pieces and the game began. Two minutes later I cried, "What do you mean…'Checkmate'? We just started! Is the game over?"

"I said I'll show you the ropes, not let you win!" Rev. Kerschner challenged. "You'll find a game of chess is like the life you've entered. Absolutely nothing will be given to you, everything will require work and

Keep Smiling and Never Give Up!

patience. When one loses part of his power he must adjust to the battle. Your life will resemble chess competition. If victory is to be achieved you must adapt. Want to try another game? Or are you ready to give up?"

Mom transferred to Dad the training she and Vivian were given at Riley Hospital. Most of my daily activities became Dad's responsibility, while Mom provided care for others in the family and completed household chores.

"That hurts," gulp, gulp "too much!" I yelled. "Please remember," gulp, gulp, "don't hold my muscles." gulp, gulp. "Put your hands," gulp, gulp, "under the joints."

"Danny, we can't get a hospital therapist, and I try to remember what your Mom learned in her brief training. This is the best we can do right now." said Dad. "I'm sorry the physical therapy hurts. Maybe you should go back to Riley."

Sadly, everyone's patience was wearing thin. My dear parent's valiant though feeble attempt at executing home PT was a hardship on all concerned, and it became easy to voice my irritation. At first I tried cooperating with unskilled family therapists, but PT was too painful. I failed to heed Dr.Walcher's warnings and life became unbearable for all. I cried, "Leave me alone!" each time I suffered needless pain during physical therapy, and exercise sessions became shorter and shorter. A vicious cycle of: non-professional PT, pain, immobility, discussion, argument, anger, and my refusal to participate, only intensified frequent muscle spasms. With time my arms, legs, fingers, hands, and toes contracted and I became an exasperated and dejected teenager. Willpower to overlook their lack of expertise and my weakness evaporated when I allowed circumstances to control my mind, creating a fertile breeding ground for self-pity.

"Danny?" asked Judy one day, "Didn't the therapists or nurses fasten reading material to your iron lung mirror?"

"Yeah, it worked OK," I said, "but you have…to turn the pages. Sure would be nice…if I could hold…some sort of devise…in my mouth, like…another arm."

"Well while I'm here," she said, "why don't you read a magazine or something? What happened to your school books?"

"OK, maybe I'll look…at some magazines. Concerning school,…" I said, "the books just sat…on my stand. After a month when…no one mentioned school,…I asked Mike to…return them. Anyway, I'll be leaving…soon. Hey, will you and…Norman be here…this evening? I'm looking…forward to a…game of Rook."

Weddings, funerals, and illness. It's amazing the vast number of long lost relatives and friends one meets at these times. Family and acquaintances I hadn't seen for several years dropped by, (many I'd never met before) bringing with them love and best wishes. Occasionally friends visited who only a few months ago were basketball and football teammates at church. Once, in early February two of my old buddies came by to chat. Larry, my brother by proxy, and Ralph, an older friend stuttered, "We were just on our way to the game and decided we would stop in to cheer you up."

"Good seeing you." I said. "Keep my spot open...on the team." The look on their faces indicated they were only embarrassed at my attempt to alleviate tension with humor.

"Sure." they said, self-conscious and visibly shaken at the sight of my iron lung. "I guess we better be going, the game starts soon."

"Thanks for coming. Tell all the...guys I said...hi, and good luck." They left and I wondered, "Will my good friends ever come back? Oh well, maybe they can't take the anguish of seeing me in trouble. Or else, they're scared too."

"Danny I came up with a good idea yesterday." said Rev. Kerschner excitedly. "If I pay the cost and your dad agrees to the installation, would you like a speaker phone?"

"Wow that sounds...like fun." I replied. "Are you serious? Hold it,...what's the catch?"

"I sure am." he said. "Just one thing. Now don't look at me that way, it's not so bad. After you get a phone will you call certain people inviting them to worship and Sunday School? I'll provide the list, you provide time."

"I don't know...Rev.Kerschner, this...doesn't sound easy. Do you suppose...it's possible?" I asked.

"Of course it's possible." he said. "Nothing in life worth the effort is easy. Well, you think about what I said and I'll talk to your dad."

Intrigued by the telephone offer I thought even though confined to an iron lung this could be my escape from four walls. Millie's excited voice announcing Norman and Judy's arrival interrupted my thoughts "Good," I told her, "Norman will turn...my tank around...facing the kitchen table. Then maybe we...can play cards."

"Let me get my cap gun." Andy yelled. "I'll hide and sneak up on 'em at the door."

"Danny, we've already played three games." said Norman. "I work tomorrow you know. Didn't Judy tell me somebody was teaching you how to play chess?"

"Yeah, Rev.Kerschner...is teaching me. I'm becoming ...pretty good. I nearly won...last time we played." I bragged. "Mike and Bill...also play chess...and they're good. He doesn't know...I get help...from them."

"That's great!" said Norman. "Soon you'll be a champ."

"Ha!" laughed Millie. "He's lost seventy-two games in a row! I don't know why he keeps trying."

Conversation covering the same old subjects wearied me and playing some sort of game replaced inane dialogue. I'd gotten so disgusted answering everyone's repeated questions concerning my health the pat answers became, "I'm all right, just fine, no problems." By necessity, watching television and listening to music on radio became my favorite pastimes. I was now an expert on TV game shows, and my recollection of the one hundred most popular songs on radio rivaled Jimmy's. Tapping paralyzed feet in time with music is impossible, so I clicked my teeth. Boredom makes one do strange things.

Coping with inevitable dependence on others and lack of scheduled bowel regimen created a serious physical ailment. My immobility, no privacy, and our failure to adjust caused numerous painful episodes of nervous indigestion and severe abdominal distension. Paralyzed muscles made it impossible to burp, cough, or vomit. I wished, "If I could go to the bathroom like other people, then maybe my stomach wouldn't hurt as much." Waiting until someone scratched my itching nose, asking for the TV channel to be changed, and avoiding liquids so I wouldn't need the urinal contributed to abject disillusionment. Dr. Walcher warned me before leaving Riley, "Do not let the situation control your emotions. Patience, self-control, mind over matter, willpower. If you fail to master these principles, you will lose the game of life."

Dr. Heilman came to my rescue on many occasions, day and night. Arising from sleep he would put clothes on over his pajamas and travel through the winter snow to keep me alive. More than once he stayed all night with me until certain the crisis had passed. What a doctor!

In a closed position my iron lung extended the length of our dining room, but with my bed pulled out it stretched even longer into the living room. Fellowship at gatherings while preserving any semblance of privacy proved impossible and I soon developed tremendous bladder control. Tensions were strained at times with kids noisily playing, television blaring, and loud conversation rising above the pandemonium.

Attempting to soothe the strain at one such event, Mom brought me a cup of hot chocolate. "Careful Danny, I think it's still hot." she warned.

"Thanks Mom," I said, "but my stomach…is upset and …I don't feel good."

"Come on, take a little sip, it'll make you feel much better." said Mom. "Your sister made this for you at least you can drink some."

"Ouch! Now my tongue…is blistered. Take it away! I didn't want…anything to drink…anyway." I protested vociferously, pushing the straw from my mouth.

"Oh Danny, look what you've done!" Mom cried out. "The chocolate dripped on your pillow. Now I'll have to change the cover. I wish you would try to control yourself son. A little self-control would do wonders."

"Mom,…my head…and tongue…are the…only things…I can…control." I muttered through clenched teeth, trying to modulate my voice.

Two days later, the man I needed to speak with visited. "Rev.Kerschner,…I'm glad you…came today. This Polio…isn't all it's…cracked up to…be." I spat. "My parents are…pulling their hair,…the house is in…turmoil and friends…need rationing cards. I can't eat or …sleep, and I…dread the long days…and nights. Memories of…isolation seem very…familiar. I wonder, are my…prayers getting past…the ceiling?"

"Danny, of one thing I'm sure," he said, "God does hear your prayers. When and how He answers prayer is His choice. You might not like the answer now, but remember Hebrews 12:6 'For whom the Lord loveth he chasteneth...' Let's pray."

Following prayer Rev.Kerschner sat down facing my tank and asked, "Is your mirror adjusted properly? Can you see the chessboard and all the pieces? I don't want any excuse after you lose again." he laughed.

"I hope you aren't…in a hurry." I said. "This game will last…longer than five minutes. Mike and Bill have…been teaching me…some new moves. So watch out!"

Forty-five minutes later Rev.Kerschner stared astounded at the board when I excitedly proclaimed, "CHECKMATE!!"

"I don't believe it!" cried Rev.Kerschner. "There must be a mistake someplace."

"As you've told…me so often,…an occasional…dose of humility…is good for everyone." I snickered. "I know God…just answered…one of my prayers."

"My goodness look at the time. I've got prayer meeting tonight." said Rev.Kerschner. "I really wanted a re-match."

"Sure, sure." I quipped. "What better excuse…than a prayer meeting."

"No, I really must go." he protested. "Since you began using that speaker phone inviting people to church services, attendance has increased. You wouldn't want me to relay the message, 'Danny wouldn't let me out the door' would you?"

My health deteriorated from repeated refusal of PT, and absence of vocational activities such as school or reading resulted in disastrous self-pity. One thing I could do with little help from others was increase my unassisted breathing time, at least one promise I'd made Dr.Walcher was feasible. Thirty-five minutes, forty-five, then came my dream of sixty minutes. Slowly, but surely, I was reaching the goal of two hours on my own. Some people will think, "So what's the big deal?" Five months before

Keep Smiling and Never Give Up!

I had nothing, but perseverance paid off as seconds became minutes and I reached a magical one-hour breathing on my own. For me this was a monumental accomplishment and I dreamed of more to come.

This success facilitated my participation in what could have been a most satisfying time. Either bravery or boredom encouraged agreement on my part, allowing my family to move me from iron lung to living room couch. I enjoyed being out of the tank for a short time and was grateful for different perspectives on my surroundings. Being completely separated from my respirator induced anxiety and fear which prevented any pleasure. I was naked without my steel cocoon.

"Danny," said Norman, "I keep forgetting arms and legs are under your head. If you grow any taller while hiding in that iron lung we'll start calling you, 'Wilt the Stilt'. It's hard to believe you've lost so much weight."

Lying on the couch while fresh air flowed over my body I gulped, "This is great!" gulp, gulp. "Anyone remember," gulp, gulp, "the last time," gulp, gulp, "I reclined on this," gulp, gulp, "couch? At least then," gulp, gulp, "I could wiggle," gulp, gulp, "my toes. Now I can," gulp, gulp, "only wiggle my," gulp, gulp, "nose and blink," gulp, gulp, "my eyes."

Total silence greeted my remarks. "Uh oh," I thought, "my attempt at humor isn't working. They can't take it."

Submitting to only minimal exercise was really stupid. Because my muscles were so stiff and sore, it was impossible to find a comfortable position. Continuously repositioning me at night was exhausting my father, and I knew a solution was required in the near future. Most of the day I remained flat on my back with Mom occasionally bending my knees and by evening the vicious cycle began once more.

Dad and Kenny enjoyed searching pocket change for old coins, hoping to find a rare specimen. On one such occasion Kenny yelled, "Hey Danny, I found a quarter minted on your birth date. It's really in poor condition."

"I'm not surprised...I feel like two-bits." I joked. "By the way...which date...1942 or 1957?"

March came in like a lion for me. According to the old adage it should go out like a lamb, perhaps a good omen for better times ahead. Dr. Heilman continued weathering perils of slick snow-covered streets day and night, comforting and helping me through numerous life-threatening episodes.

Physical and mental exhaustion overwhelmed everyone and emotionally, even common occurrences became a threat to my well-being. While awaiting arrival of my friends one day, I shuddered as cartoon characters screamed, television blared, and noise vibrated the room. My head and ears throbbed and I longed for solace. Unable to relocate the heavy iron lung by herself, Mom left me sitting by the living room doorway in front of the TV. Patience depleted I squawked, "Andy!.. for crying out loud...turn that TV off! Do you have to. . watch 'Popeye'...again today? I've been watching...your kid programs...everyday for three...months. Now turn it ...off!"

"Aw Danny, can't I watch him just this one more time?" Andy begged. "Please?"

Sensing defeat I growled, "Why not,...but turn the. . thing down! You forget this...is my bedroom. I shouldn't be...forced to watch...dumb little-kid...shows."

"Mommee, he yelled at me!" cried Andy, running from the room with tears streaming down his face.

"Dear God," I thought, "what am I doing? It's time to get out of here before everyone hates me." Residing close to family and friends had been enjoyable, but I was totally disillusioned as reality raised its ugly head. Trauma from being around people who months before were fellow ambulatory companions left me emotionally drained. Undoubtedly, family also suffered. A series of repugnant episodes involving my therapy and our uncompromising situation at home didn't lend itself to spectacular progress. Monotony and confinement to the iron lung slowly developed into needless discomfort for parents, my siblings, and me. My spastic and cramping muscles cried out for exercise and I succumbed to a disgusting habit of frequently demanding repositioning. Guilt overshadowed me every time I observed Dad interrupting needed sleep to willingly placate his paralyzed son's pleas for comfort. A cruel hardship affected everyone when my addiction to hourly movement increased. Yielding to circumstance and anger, I became embittered. Willpower in my life was a myth. I was learning, self-control could only be attained through years of tenacious persistence. Struggling to combat anger and my continued frustration resulting from total dependence upon others, ensured my descent into the depths of despair.

While at home I had watched others play quiz games on TV, listened to radio, and occasionally looked at and read magazines, which afforded little mental stimulation. Weeks of immobility produced serious problems of debilitation and an absence of any scheduled bowel regimen ensured Dr.Heilman would become a member of our family. I had been chosen for this life, but arbitrary limitations and everyone's refusal (including mine) to adjust had predestined failure. An old adage states, "mind over matter", but I did mind, and it did matter! Recalling Ruth's words the day my tank's porthole fell open, 'Danny you must try hard to adjust. Do it now, or you lose. Life won't change, only you.' Pained thoughts seared my mind and I decided, "Tomorrow I must contact Riley Hospital and Dr.Walcher."

The accelerated timetable for my trip home wasn't wise, so making the decision to return to Riley was easy. Waiting for the moving van to arrive I phoned one more time. "Hello Rev.Kerschner...I wanted to call...before I left...for Riley. The truck's here. Time for more...polishing."

"Thanks for calling Danny." he said. "You certainly do have a snowy trip ahead. Are you feeling better today?"

"I'm fine. My stomach is...full of butterflies... Just fear of...the unknown." I confided. "Discouragement these...past two months,...plus the terrible...strain I've been...to my family...is destroying us. Dr.Walcher will...be awful disappointed...in me. I'm not looking...forward to our...meeting. Sometimes I wonder... if my life is...worth living."

"Danny," admonished Rev.Kerschner, "Romans 8:28 tells us all things work together for good to those who love God. Don't forget an important part of polishing, as Philippians 4:11 says, 'I have learned, in whatsoever state I am, to be content. My friend, the game is never over until the good Lord thunders, 'Checkmate'."

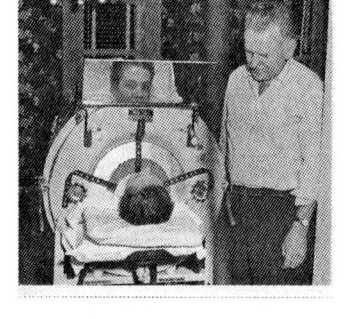

My Dad and me.
Personal Photo
collection, 1957

10

SELLERS EAST

Crisp March winds accompanied me to the emergency room entrance at Riley Hospital. Angry comments from the medical staff welcomed me upon return after three poorly conceived months at home. Other than medicine, their orders had been disregarded; physical therapy essentially eliminated; and a feeble attempt to regain control of my life was surrendered to the ravages of Polio. Miss Dennis frowned as she and the student nurses quietly moved me from stretcher to iron lung. Once back on Ward C, I nervously awaited the appearance of a man whose words of advice I'd sorely neglected.

"Please forgive me for not meeting you on your arrival from home earlier today." said Dr. Walcher. "The staff tells me you have developed some problems. Mind if I look?"

"Guess not." I mumbled. "Sooner or later…you'll find out…the truth about …my condition. Before you open the…tank I want you…to know, my…unassisted breathing…time increased."

"Hmmm! What do we have here?" asked Dr. Walcher. "Your arms and legs are a bit stiff, perhaps I will let Miss Nash evaluate this problem. Danny, I shall return later when we will have a chat. Incidentally before I leave, how long can you breathe on your own now?"

"I was afraid you…wouldn't ask after…seeing me. My unassisted breathing…time is two hours." I boasted.

"That's fantastic!" chorused the staff accompanying Dr. Walcher. "How did you manage that accomplishment while you disregarded the rest of your body?"

"Hey that was…no problem. They flipped an…on/off switch. I started gulping and…using my willpower."

"What good news!" exclaimed Dr. Walcher, sternly. "Now you can stay outside the iron lung an extended time, taking advantage of that 'willpower' while undergoing rigorous PT."

Miss Nash finished her painful examination with a frown on her face. "Danny, Danny, why did you let this happen? I try to understand the distress one endures after paralysis, but why make things more difficult in your life? Ever heard about the guy who threw himself out of a car during a heated argument with his wife? The foolish man leaped from an open door screaming, 'I'll teach you a lesson!' When you want to talk, I would like to know why you allowed this disaster."

Keep Smiling and Never Give Up!

Miss Dennis, Miss Beck, and Dr.Walcher entered my room carrying a timing clock. "Your day of reckoning has surely arrived." they said solemnly.

Dr.Walcher explained, "I have set this clock at fifteen minute intervals, to be increased periodically. The timer, along with that willpower you mentioned, will allow Ward C's nurses to take care of other patients. Our goal for you is to reach a two-hour repositioning schedule."

"Two hours! Oh man, I'm dead." I thought to myself. Boot camp was over - I was now promoted to advanced training.

Two weeks following my re-admission to Riley Hospital a blonde-haired young man of average height wearing dark rimmed glasses greeted me. "Hello, I'm Dr.Johnson from Sellers East, the Polio Respiratory Center in Columbus, Ohio. I believe Dr.Walcher informed you of my visit, I specialize in PM&R."

Eyeing him suspiciously I asked, "What is PM&R?...tell me about...this respirator...center."

Dr.Johnson replied, "My specialty is Physical Medicine and Rehabilitation at Ohio State University (OSU). A Polio Respiratory Center or Respo Center is funded by The March of Dimes and designed primarily to furnish support for people with Polio and respiratory problems. I hope you're ready to discover a new life. Are you interested?"

"Excuse me for not...standing." I sarcastically said. "Please don't be...offended if I don't... shake hands."

"No problem." laughed Dr.Johnson. "I think you should meet Dr.Oliver, our Respo Center Director. Come to Sellers East and I'll have you standing in a few months. Of course, it will be on a tilt table."

"You've got to be...kidding! I need a truck...for an ambulance. How could you...stand this tank up...on a table?" I quizzed. "I can only breathe...two hours on my ...own. That's not very...long. Do you turn the...iron lung off?"

"Danny there is a whole new world waiting for you. Why don't you drop the act? Let's discuss essentials." he said. "At the Respo Center we use portable respirators for people who cannot breathe very long on their own. I promise only a few days after arrival you'll be removed from the iron lung and transported to our therapy pool. Soon you graduate to a rocking bed, and depending on your determination, will be sitting in a wheelchair by early summer. We are developing convenient respirators called pneumobelts for vertical use, and hope to replace the iron lung with a 'pulmowrap'. Danny you may be one of the first to use these new respirators."

"Hold it you're...going too fast!" I protested. "I'm stuck in...an iron lung,...my body is a...real mess...and Dr.Walcher...tells me Columbus

Daniel R. Williams

is...two hundred miles...away. That's a long trip...bouncing along... in the back of...a moving van."

"I read about the trip home for Christmas." he laughed. "Dr.Walcher really put together some program. Please don't worry though; we use portable iron lungs along with regular ambulances. Portable only means standard tank without legs. In efforts to maximize limited space inside an ambulance, we separate motor and bellows from the iron lung. A small unit powered by the car's alternator provides pressure. A nurse from the Respo Center will be in attendance to prevent your escape."

"Listen Dr.Johnson...I tried the...rocking bed.. A few days ago. . these people...promised me...I could use ...that contraption. It won't work! I slid back and forth,...got sick to...my stomach and... it didn't help...my breathing. I spent most...of the time...gulping for air."

"Did you say gulping for air? Can you frog breathe?" asked Dr.Johnson.

"Frog breathe! What do you mean,...frog breathe?" I asked curiously. "I don't know what . .it's called, I . .just gulp air...trying to stay... alive. Staff wants me...to breathe normally...but they aren't. . the one . suffocating."

"Do you mind if I open the iron lung and watch you gulp air?" inquired Dr.Johnson. "At the same time I'll examine your arms and legs."

"Why not?" I said. "My unassisted time...has reached two hours...and fifteen minutes. I'm sore, be careful."

"Danny did someone teach you how to frog breathe? Our first priority at the Respo Center is teaching this exercise which enables you to be secure without a respirator. Often people require lessons and extended time to produce a skill or proficiency in this art, obviously you were fortunate. I think you have reacted quite well to the problem. The medical term is 'glossopharyngeal breathing'" said Dr.Johnson, "but since that's a two-gulper, we say frog breathing. Well what's the word, are you interested in coming to Columbus? Think about it, I'll return tomorrow for your answer. Just remember, it won't all be enjoyable."

I was all smiles when Rev.Kerschner entered Ward C with a chess game under his arm. "Glad you're here."

"Well this is certainly a nice surprise!" he exclaimed. "You haven't smiled this big for quite some time, and I've not lost the game yet. Do you have good news?"

"I've been talking...to a doctor from...Columbus, Ohio. He says I can...get out of this...tank."

After listening to my summary of Dr.Johnson's comments he assured, "God lives in Columbus too. I promise to visit. As always the congregation of Wesleyan Methodist Church will remember you in prayer."

Later that evening I once again surprised my parents, "Dad, Mom,...I'm going to a...rehabilitation center...in Columbus, Ohio. They have wheelchairs,...therapy pools and...portable respirators. I'll get out of...the tank and...by summer be...sitting in a wheelchair." I gushed.

Amazed Dad exclaimed, "Columbus, Ohio! Do you realize how far away that is? Danny it's hard enough for us to see you at Riley."

"Are you sure the doctor said you could get out of the iron lung?" asked my mother. "Sounds too good to be true. How would you get there? What does Dr.Walcher think about moving to another hospital?"

"Well see,...it isn't really another...hospital." I said. "It's a...rehabilitation center...known as a... Polio Respirator Center,...or Respo Center...funded by the...March of Dimes. Dr.Walcher says...if I want... to get better...I need this...special help. Guess what Dr.Johnson...told me. Oh, he's from...Columbus. I can ...frog breathe."

"Danny, what do you mean 'frog breathe'?" asked Mom.

"When I gulp air...to stay alive while...my tank is open." I explained. "He said most people...needed lessons ...but I was already...an expert."

"Danny, how do you gulp air?" asked Dad. "We thought you were just gasping."

"The medical term is...glossopharyngeal. It's much easier...to say frog breathing. I press my...tongue up against...the roof of my...mouth forcing air...down my windpipe...into my lungs. All this time...I thought it was...self-defense. Dr.Johnson...said they required ...respos to learn...this breathing...technique." With unusual excitement I continued describing Sellers East.

Drs.Walcher and Johnson entered my room the following day inquiring, "Well have you decided? I spoke to your dad and he said it is your decision. We aren't pressuring you, but your future depends on this treatment and Dr.Johnson is leaving Indianapolis to visit other Polios."

I made the decision, and during discharge from Riley I said, "Dr.Walcher,...someday I'll be able...to say thank you. When I left last time...the promise I made was... broken. You, my family,...friends, and everyone...had a right...to be disappointed...with me. After losing... respect for myself,...I won't promise...this time. I'll only say...the outcome will... be much different. I can assure you...following months of...gloom I've found... a ray of hope...for the future."

My venture to the Respo Center was sure to be different from my trip home in a moving van. A regular ambulance with portable iron lung and a nurse arrived at Riley's emergency entrance and prepared me for my journey to Columbus. Riding in a Cadillac was certainly more comfortable than transport by truck. Mrs. Rudolph (Rudy), my nurse, told me about the wonderful opportunities awaiting me in Columbus. She said, "Think of this trip as a new beginning, the first leg of an odyssey taking you to freedom."

Daniel R. Williams

Our journey ended four and one-half hours later at the emergency entrance to Children's Hospital, Columbus, Ohio. Winter darkness blanketed the area as they removed me from the ambulance and quickly escorted my portable iron lung via elevator, up to Sellers East Respo Center. Moving silently through the hall, I stared in wide-eyed amazement at so many iron lungs whooshing away oblivious to my presence. Stunned at the sight, I was brought back to earth by comments of the nurse as I entered her domain, "Welcome to Tin Can Alley."

"Things are looking up all ready." I thought. "Ken had used that phrase the last time I heard it, and life became a lot better. Who knows? Maybe this is a good idea."

"Danny, my name is Mrs. Hanover," said the nurse, "but you will learn right away I'm known by other names. Let me introduce your new roommates. Meet Jon, and this is Elmer. This handsome guy on the rocking bed is Don, heartthrob of all the young nurses. Watch out for him, he's a dirty old man. These other two guys are just ordinary troublemakers. John, our orderly, will get you settled. I must administer a butter bullet. I'll be back shortly. Some motherly words of advice, don't believe half what these guys tell you."

My father and mother peered hesitantly around the door before entering my new room. "Danny, we're sorry it took us longer to get here, but we couldn't keep pace with a speedy ambulance. We did OK on the highway, but they cheated going through those little towns. People have no respect for cars without red lights and sirens." laughed Dad. "Well it looks like you'll have enough company. We certainly can't visit here every evening like Indianapolis."

Nervously acknowledging the other iron lungs, Mom said, "Danny we can't stay long, it's so far from home. I think we should leave, don't you Ray?" Leaning over she kissed me on the forehead whispering, "See Danny, you're not the only person in an iron lung."

"Son, I've signed all the papers." said Dad. "You're a full fledged member of the respirator center. Unless it's life threatening, you and the doctors are in control. Danny I trust you've made the right decision in coming here. Like your mom said, it's a long trip from New Castle. I see many wheelchairs, maybe the doctor was right; you'll be sitting in one of your own like that guy in the corner. Just a few months ago we didn't think you'd ever be able to breathe by yourself. Son, we hate to leave you, but it's getting late and the drive home will take another three hours."

Mom waved goodbye assuring, "We'll be back soon."

As Dad and Mom left the room, tears welled in my eyes. I remembered those desolate days in isolation when I was all alone. Recalling

Keep Smiling and Never Give Up!

Rev.Kerschner's words of encouragement, I was comforted by a Bible verse, "Lo, I am with you always".

Regaining equilibrium, the guys in my room proceeded to brief me on many facets of life at Sellers East. Jon said, "You won't believe the nurses we have here. The hospital I came from held lotteries to find help when anyone needed the urinal." gulp, gulp. "Most of us go to therapy in the pool each day, and we all have our own wheelchairs. I only sleep in an iron lung," gulp, gulp, "during the day I frog breathe to conserve electrical energy. Can you frog breathe, Danny? I hear you're from Indiana, guess what, I am too. Portland. Hey Don," gulp, gulp, "tell the rookie your war stories."

"Danny? Your name is Danny?" drawled Don. "Watch out for these kids, they'll get you in trouble. Don't believe Hanover either, I'm really a sweet guy."

John the orderly, and Mrs. Dishman a nurse, walked into the room and said to Don, "OK Romeo, it's time to hit the sack."

"Aw Dish, is it that time already? You know how hard it is to watch TV from a rockin' bed." protested Don.

"Hush Colonel, you'll give our new resident wrong ideas about us." laughed Mrs. Dishman. "By the way Danny, in case they haven't told you, we're a family at the Respo Center. Use either first name or nickname, unless you speak to Miss Rickard. Call the doctors and therapists whatever you want, different names at different times. You're a resident now, no patients allowed in our home."

A young, squeaky voice from across the room requested, "Can I…have a…drink of…water?"

"Elmer spoke! He's not dead after all." shouted Jon.

"Here sweetness, take a drink." said Dish soothingly. "Don't you pay any attention to these mean ol'men."

"Don, do you really…like that rocking bed? I tried one once…and almost slid off. Not to mention I…just about barfed." I confessed.

"Well, I'll tell ya' boy." said Don slowly. "It's all right for breathing, but it's a heck of a sight when trying to use a bedpan after one of Hanover's butter bullets."

"You mean,…they don't,…Oh, you can't! How do you?" I stammered. "Surely they…turn it off."

"Well, if I'm nice," he said, "and slip 'em a couple a bucks on the side."

"I warned you about the Colonel and his war stories." laughed Dish, shaking her head as she left the room.

My naïveté' began wearing off immediately, I could tell this would be survival of the fittest. "Hey you guys,… two questions. Will someone explain…butter bullets and …what's therapy…like around here?" I asked.

"Son, you don't wanna know." said the Colonel, calmly sipping his drink.

"Don't scare him." Jon warned. "He'll have nightmares and keep us awake. Don't worry about the therapists Danny," gulp, gulp, "they're great. Real tears help sometimes, but forget about yelling and screaming," gulp, gulp, "they won't listen. I think it must be some sort of code."

"Why Jon!" snickered the Colonel. "I thought you knew they were deaf."

"Oh brother!" I thought. "Will this be fun!" Jon was correct; I had a sleepless night. We talked about the Respo Center and people into wee hours, and they promised Saturday morning I would find out about butter bullets. Conversation continued until sleep was strongly encouraged by nurses who, weary from listening to the noise, insisted we go to sleep. 'Tommy,' Mrs. Thomas, our nurse politely suggested, "Can the chatter!" Thoughts turned to family in Indiana and I tried to erase memories of the despair covering Dad and Mom's face when they departed. Hollow feelings of loneliness surged in my heart and I questioned the wisdom of coming to Ohio. Did I make the wrong choice? Already I'm marching to the beat of a different drummer."

The restless night passed and I awakened to a new day filled with dreaded anticipation. Realizing my roommate's warnings came complete with tongue in cheek didn't relieve the anxiety accompanying thoughts of today's examinations. I silently watched as Bill, our orderly, and Emma, an aide, prepared everyone for breakfast. Food was served, but not to me. First order of my day, "Weigh Danny before he eats." said 'Hixey', Mrs. Hixenbaum, our Head Nurse. "According to your records upon admission to Riley Hospital in October you weighed 179.4 pounds. Let's see what you weigh today."

"Good morning, I'm Dr.Oliver." said the handsome young gentleman with black hair, wearing a white lab coat. "Don't bother standing up fellows, I'll just take your good manners for granted. Colonel if you have no problems go to therapy. Jon it's time you went swimming, Danny and I must discuss a future for him without this iron lung."

"Shucks Doc, it sounds like you don't want us aroun'." the Colonel lamented.

"He's right Dr.Oliver." Jon piped up. "We just filled our stomachs with breakfast. We can't go swimming yet."

"Don't worry about it guys," said Dr.Oliver, "just frog and float." Dr.Oliver helped lift the Colonel to his chair and Jon to a lowboy stretcher. "Now at the risk of being rude, Mrs. Hixenbaum, please escort the gentlemen out. The iron lung will muffle our conversation Danny, so Elmer won't intrude on your privacy. Let's review your history. I see from the weight record you have been on a diet. This shows you now weigh 79 pounds. In other words, you've lost 100.4 pounds in five months. We will reverse this situation. You can be sure between exhausting activities and peer pressure, you will eat. At this Respo Center therapy takes precedence over everything! That includes visitors, games, television, stalling, you name it, **except** church services. For our own benefit we count on God to remove some orneriness from you, and to give us strength. Mrs. Leonadakis 'Leo', our social worker and counselor, utilizes every available resource. We plan to wean you from tank to rocking bed and then portable respirators. Accept pain from PT, learn from OT, and you'll enjoy the gain when you first sit in your wheelchair. PT is going to stretch muscles, ligaments, and tendons, while they generally make you want to cry. OT will provide much needed tools enabling you to perfect skills imperative for life in the outside world. Dr.Johnson will be here shortly. Do you have any questions?"

"Yes." I answered. "If you have time...Dr.Oliver, I have...many questions."

"That's why I'm here." he said. "Shoot."

"My stomach problems...are why I can't...eat. Many times I...feel so full,...it bothers my...breathing." I told him.

"You will have a regular bowel regimen here." Dr.Oliver said. "You won't be full of it any more. We'll keep you so busy, most thoughts will be directed toward getting better. Fellow Polios, doctors, nurses, therapists, many volunteers, and new friends will provide an uninterrupted flow of family life. Debilitating problems resulting from inactivity and days languishing in self-pity, yearning for the recent past, are over. You survived Polio, today recovery begins."

"Hello again, sorry I'm late. Tim, have you given him our standard greetings?" asked Dr.Johnson.

"I briefly explained the basics of our intended program to Danny." said Dr.Oliver. "Trading the tank for a rocking bed and portable respirators, along with resolving a problem in his digestive system. Dr.Johnson introduce your people."

"Today you will receive evaluations from physical and occupational therapy." said Dr.Johnson. "In addition we'll introduce you to many advances in rehabilitative techniques. Danny, meet my assistant, Dr.Olsen; Bob, PT; and Mickey, OT. Mickey will stimulate thought and teach you exciting skills. Bob will stretch your muscles and make you feel better. Dr. Olsen will repair any damages. Pain control is his forte."

"Hi Danny, I'm Mickey. I'll return this afternoon and schedule the best time for our sessions. You can tell me if you want to read, paint, or type. Have you ever used a mouthstick for turning pages?"

"First he's mine!" laughed Bob in a deep booming voice. "After the nurses complete your morning routine, I'll return for our get acquainted session. Dr.Johnson informs me we do have a bit of work to accomplish."

"Do you really think…I could ever…sit in a… wheelchair? What you are saying…sounds great, but… it sure will be…a lot of work." I joked.

Dr.Oliver frowned, exchanging glances with Dr.Johnson. Staring at me he said, "Failure is not an option in my Respo Center. To live you must give. If you choose quitting, as opposed to trying, perhaps you should consider leaving now. As of today, you either put out or get out."

I got the impression my joke was not taken with all the levity in which it was intended. "If I were a quitter… we wouldn't be…talking right now." I said, returning his intense stare.

Dr.Oliver's face creased with a grin as he announced, "Later today I will measure your vital capacity, record your tidal volume, and test your frog breathing efficiency. I've been advised you learned this life-saving ability naturally, and Dr.Johnson was quite impressed."

Dr.Johnson chimed in, "If your unassisted breathing is inadequate we will teach you to use oral positive pressure. Then Bob can schedule therapy sessions in the pool. Unless the tests reveal a problem, next week you go swimming."

"What is oral…positive pressure?" I asked.

Dr.Oliver explained, "Clenching a mouth piece between your teeth, room air is conveyed through a hose connected to a respirator, then forced into your lungs. It fulfills the same function as frog breathing."

"Suppose it blows me…up too much?" I asked.

Ignoring the question, Dr.Johnson explained how water would make a paralyzed body buoyant, allowing me to move my arms and legs. "Sometimes it even assists breathing."

"What happens if I sink?" I inquired.

Shaking his head and smiling Bob said, "Boy, why do you always have so many negative comments?"

"There will be experienced physical therapists with you in the pool, and flotation rings will be secured around your body." assured Dr.Johnson and his assembled PM&R team.

"Sounds great," I said, "but suppose that…fails?"

Bob, turning to the other people and seeing them trying to stifle a laugh, winked and said, "You have four minutes in which to say your prayers."

With morning rounds in my room completed, the entourage of doctors, nurses, and therapists left, and I distinctly heard chuckles coming from the group. Staring quietly in my iron lung's mirror I rehashed the conversations having just taken place thinking, "Maybe I received the conventional pep talk everyone gets on admission, but thoughts of enduring a daily bout of

Keep Smiling and Never Give Up!

painful physical therapy made me shudder – and I dreaded images of my paralyzed body being lowered into the swimming pool. But, Mickey said I could learn to type with an electric typewriter and paint. Her words still resounded in my ears, maybe soon I could turn pages with what did she say, a 'mouthstick'? I recalled Dr. Johnson's words the day he interviewed me at Riley, 'Dan, I promise to offer you a new life. It won't all be fun and games, actually at times you'll probably hate us, but courage, perseverance and work will guarantee improvement. You will get better.'"

11

ROCKING 'N ROLLING

A few days after admission to the Respo Center, the staff transferred Jon and I to an adjacent room in exchange for an older gentleman, Clifford, and an empty bed. Only two iron lungs whooshed away in this room, the other occupants being wheelchair jockeys who'd graduated to portable respirators.

Due to scoliosis, Jon was unable to sit in a wheelchair so his method of conveyance became a lowboy stretcher. The knee-high miniature bed on small wheels allowed him to be a participant in recreational activities and OT. Leroy used a wheelchair for rapid transit and executing long distances, but he was able to use leg braces and crutches when he tired of sitting. Slightly older and wiser, Bob had an electric wheelchair. I watched in amazement as he somehow rocked his chair backward performing a "wheelie" demonstrating four-wheel prowess. He, like everyone else, received daily PT, but the majority of Bob's exercise came from operating a joystick on his chair. In our room one either practiced verbosity or quickly lost his identity. We attempted to best each other's wisecracks, and this motivated nurses to post a caution sign beside our door reading: Beware of Mouth. I'm told they considered finding ways to deliver our medicine from the end of a long handle. I don't know why, we certainly couldn't pinch any body.

"Hello Dan'l, let's talk." said Bob, my PT, in his deep rumbling voice. "Sorry to delay the start of your day. You obviously were anxiously awaiting my arrival."

"Bob, are you...ever big. Did you play football?" I inquired.

"Sure did," he said proudly, "left end for Penn State. I'm 6'4" tall and weigh 210 pounds. I play baseball, weight lift, and I'm not deaf. Now, if you are through stalling, I must begin therapy."

Bob opened the tank, and proceeded to perform mayhem on my body. My arms wouldn't straighten, legs wouldn't bend, hands wouldn't close, and I learned a new definition of the word split. I quickly learned why Bob talked so loudly, our screams consumed much of the available decibel level.

"Well Pal," laughed Bob, "it'll be a vigorous challenge but I can take it. Can you?"

"Hi again Danny." said Mickey quietly. "Feel like some conversation? There are many things to explain. Unlike PT, OT only stretches minds."

"Does Bob always...crack jokes just...before we get ...cracked?" I asked. "He's a great...guy and I...do not want...to act like a...baby in front of...him, but that...really hurt."

"I promise not to hurt you." Mickey grinned. "Tell me what activities interest you, especially using your mind. I have books, magazines, and movie slides. I have in my hands a mouthstick, with it you'll learn to turn pages, type, and once you're in a wheelchair, paint. After you regain some strength in your neck, it's possible to write holding a pen in your mouth. The opportunities are endless."

"You're kidding." I said skeptically. "Me? Write or type? Sign my name? Really, turn pages? How about chess?"

"Tomorrow I'll bring an electric automatic page turner for books and magazines." said Mickey. "Painting is for the future, but for now slide movies are available. We have a switch that sets beside your head, allowing you to project different slides onto the ceiling with only a slight twitch. Every Thursday evening some OT and PT staff along with volunteers from OSU escort everyone to the gymnasium for movies."

Bewildered, I asked, "You mean everyone…goes to the movies? Suppose we need…something?"

"Everybody." she said. "Of course, it's your choice at first. The young people who volunteer are great. Four big guys push these iron lungs like they're having fun. Just wait, you'll see. Tomorrow at two o'clock be ready to read. Incidentally, during the movies staff will be standing by with urinals and bedpans."

While contemplating my situation, and deciding whether to be fearful of tomorrow's PT or looking forward to OT, in walked an attractive young lady with hazel eyes and flowing, long brown hair. "My name is Mrs. Wise, I'm here on orders from Dr.Oliver to continue your education. My little boy is named Danny; may I address you in that manner rather than as Mr. Williams? I see from the chart, you're from Indiana."

"Please, do call…me Danny. Yes I'm a Hoosier… I wasn't told…rehab included…schooling." I grumbled.

"Oh yes, we Buckeyes also read and write." she laughed. "Tomorrow I shall bring books and materials allowing you to keep pace with your studies, I'll contact the Indiana state authorities so you will receive proper credits. School will begin tomorrow at one o'clock."

"Now I know why Mickey encourages reading." I thought. "At least this teacher is more my age, and with a son named Danny she can't be all bad. I wonder how long it takes to comb or brush her waist-length hair."

A convoy of wheelchairs and stretchers clattered up the hall as my roommates returned from their morning swim. "Boy it's good to…see you guys again,…they haven't given …me a chance to…catch my breath this…morning." I quipped. "Why are you guys…so cold?"

Leroy and Bob in their chairs, and Jon on a stretcher entered the room wrapped in bath towels and sheets. "While in the warm water, it's great," gulp, gulp, gulp, "but once out here, you freeze!" Jon shivered.

Bob said, "Now I know why my baby daughters shook after a bath." gulp, gulp. "Leroy is a smart aleck," gulp, gulp, "he grabbed a blanket."

I grinned, "Well at least…I won't be going…to the pool if…I'm still in…this tank."

Bob winked, "Hey Jon, let's tell him." gulp, gulp.

"Let Oliver or Johnson tell him." Jon said. "We can't be the bearers," gulp, gulp, "of all bad news."

"What do you mean?" I quizzed.

Harry, one of our rehab orderlies gave a hearty laugh, "Don't let these guys shake you up, you'll enjoy the pool. Fellows, I'll be back at one o'clock for your trip to OT. Jon, remember this time before we leave, please tinkle."

"Good afternoon Dan." said Dr.Oliver, walking briskly into our room. "If you have a moment to spare, perhaps some more information is in order. I would like to see you frog breathe. Mind if I watch?" Without waiting for an answer he opened the iron lung and said, "Breathe."

Gulp, Gulp, Gulp, "How's this?" I gulped.

"Very good," said Dr.Oliver, "now try it with your big mouth shut. Like this, pull the air in through your nose. That's why God gave it to you."

Gulping silently for the first time, I said, "Hey, this works. I even get," gulp, "more air."

"Absolutely. Also you don't resemble a starving bird." he said. "Practice this whenever possible, deep breathing will keep you alive and help prevent pneumonia. Continue to frog breathe while I show you photos of various respirators and discuss their functions. As Dr.Johnson described, this small machine will supply oral positive pressure. Attached to the hose is a mouthpiece to be clenched in your teeth. Talking is out, but breathing is fine. Once you master this type respirator, pool therapy can begin. Soon we'll discuss rocking beds, chest shells, and we are experimenting with a replacement for the iron lung known as a 'pulmowrap'. Imagine a strong plastic bag encasing your body instead of this 'tin can'. One day maybe you can try a pneumobelt; it's similar to artificial respiration. An inflatable bladder is fitted within a girdle around one's waist. Room air directed from a respirator inflates the bladder pushing your diaphragm up, forcing air from the lungs. The machine cycles, releasing bladder pressure, diaphragm descends, lungs fill with air. Want to try oral positive pressure now, or would you prefer frog breathing? It's imperative you learn this quickly."

Breathless, I gulp, gulp, gulped, "Let me try it."

Keep Smiling and Never Give Up!

"OK," said Dr.Oliver, "just grip the mouthpiece in your teeth, and with your mouth closed, pretend you are frogging. I'll increase the pressure slowly; blink your eyes when you can breathe properly. In the near future we must have blood tests to evaluate the quality of your oxygen content."

"Dr.Oliver," whoosh, "it really works." I said. "Oops, I dropped it," gulp, gulp, "would you give," gulp, gulp, "it back?" Gulp, gulp, "I'm tired."

"Here Dan." said Dr.Oliver, returning the oral positive mouthpiece. "Once you're out of the tank OT will make you a collar to hold the hose and mouthpiece. Practice using oral positive and frog breathing for a few days and soon you will begin therapy in the pool."

Whoosh, whoosh, "These respirators," gulp, gulp, gulp, "sound expensive." I said. "How do people," whoosh, gulp, "afford this equipment?"

"Dan, as I have informed other residents of the Respo Center," he said, "if you had to be paralyzed, and require a respirator, be thankful it resulted from Polio. Many years ago President Franklin Delano Roosevelt was influential in chartering an organization dedicated to the health and well being of all Polios. The March of Dimes will always provide respiratory equipment necessary for your welfare."

Whir..click..click.., came sounds from the hall. "May we return to our room?" asked Bob, leading a group processional through the doorway. "OT is over, and my wheelchair battery needs recharging before this evening."

"We just finished talking." said Dr.Oliver. "Come in. Colonel why are you in this room? Won't Elmer talk to you?"

"Aw Doc you know Elmer, and those other guys sleep all the time." droned the Colonel. "Jimmy, the new nine year old from isolation, is scared to talk."

Laughing, Dr.Oliver walked out advising, "Don't pollute their minds with too many of your war stories."

Miss Rickard, wearing a crisp white uniform marched into the room saluting the Colonel. "Major Rickard reporting for duty, Sir." barked a gray haired nurse with ramrod posture. "Everything A-OK on your watch Colonel?"

"Yes Ma'am." he replied. "I quickly indoctrinated this new recruit, and for some reason he changed rooms. I guess he enjoys the company of enlisted men, like the sarge over there." he said, motioning to Bob.

"Well, if the troops are in order, I'll go review the other rooms." she said. "They are just civilians, but being asked to report off makes them feel better."

After the Colonel left our room I asked Bob, "Was that guy really a Colonel, and she really a Major?"

Daniel R. Williams

"No, Don was just a sergeant in Korea like me," replied Bob, "but since he has a southern drawl we nicknamed him the Colonel. Miss Rickard truly is a retired Army Major. After her fiancé, was killed in WWI she never married, but gave her life to the Army Nurse Corp. Since retiring she has worked here part-time, helping us learn discipline."

As Mickey promised, volunteers from OSU descended on us to participate in numerous activities. Strong male students pushed iron lungs and rocking beds to the gym while competing with captivating, petite beauties escorting those in wheelchairs. Laughter and giggles followed our speedy trips through halls and around doors, then we relaxed to watch feature movies provided by libraries and civic organizations. Fortunately for some of us Mickey was correct, bedpans and urinals were on standby. After the excitement and movie we returned to our rooms and visited with new friends, the OSU volunteers. Eugene, a muscular, bespectacled young man asked, "Do any of you guys play chess?"

"Yes." I responded delightedly, "Over here! In front of my...mirror. You move...I'll direct."

"OK," said Eugene, "take it slow until I get onto these reverse moves."

"Don't worry," I laughed, "the mirror is...on my side ...of the board."

Saturday morning I was introduced to a "butter bullet". An activity known at the Respo Center as suppository-fest is the launching ground for those destroyers of obstruction. I was de-stinkly overcome by a fragrant aroma lazily drifting under our noses and more than one of us began singing bedpan blues. My iron lung was repeatedly opened over the weekend, and I either frogged or gained experience with oral positive pressure. The nurses conspicuously dropped hints, preparing me for Monday's adventure in the pool.

Church services were conducted on Sunday morning in our rooms. Paraphrasing the Bible, with God on our side who can be against us?

Jon and I enviously watched Bob and Leroy entertaining company. Bob, from Carmel, IN, visited with his pregnant wife, obviously due to have their baby very soon. Leroy, from Zanesville, OH, saw his family often. Jon's family was from Portland, IN, his father soon to be senior minister of Walhalla, SC.'s Wesleyan church. As for me, I just got here so I made friends with my roommate's families.

The weekend zoomed by and before I knew what happened I found myself being lowered into the pool. "Dan'l just relax and let me and the water take care of everything." Cautioned Bob, waiting for my entrance into his domain.

Warm water closed around my body, and I prayed for the strength of flotation devices around my neck and chest. I'm glad Bob was supporting me; his tall athletic frame and arms were certainly comforting. My new friends had been correct, there was just no way to describe this experience. Friction from weight touching solid surfaces inhibits, if not prevents, paralyzed bodies from moving, but buoyancy of water totally reverses this immobilization. I could move my arms and legs with only the slightest quiver, and frog breathing required less effort. My main concern suddenly became the loose G-string I was wearing for bathing trunks. One more thing they left unsaid, be prepared for skinny-dipping. "Oh well, at least I'm floating in water." I consoled myself in thought.

Preparing to exit the pool, Bob moved my body over to a hydraulic lift and removed all flotation devices. "Dan'l I hope you enjoyed yourself." he declared.

Gulp, gulp, gulp, "Yes." I gasped. "It's great!"

"Take a deep breath and hold it." ordered Bob.

"Why?" I naively asked, as Bob submerged my body. His strong arms continuing to hold me, he brought me back to the surface. Choking and sputtering, I shook my head demanding, "Why," gulp, gulp, gulp, "did you do," gulp, gulp, "that?"

"Are you breathing again, or did I let you drown? Do you trust me?" asked Bob.

Squinting my eyes I ventured, "Sure I trust you," gulp, gulp, "you kept me from," gulp, gulp, gulp, "drowning."

"Good! Besides, a drowning man goes down three times." he said with a booming laugh.

I discovered my roommates were once again correct. Air blew across my wet body and froze a now defunct, straggling G-string. Coming out of the pool proved arguably to be the worst experience of pool therapy initiation. PT attendants Harry, Libby, and Wally, wrapped my shivering body preparing me for the trip back upstairs. No longer benefiting from weightlessness afforded me by water buoyancy, arms and legs became lifeless. Any diaphragmatic breathing or slight movement of intercostal muscles surrounding my chest became impossible. Bundled in sheets and blankets like a baby, I was wheeled, exhausted and shivering, along cold corridors to my room, looking forward to the security of my iron lung.

"Dan, do you have a few minutes?" asked Dr. Oliver. "I want to explain a research program, and offer you a special opportunity to contribute." Without waiting for any answer he continued, "Polios and most paralyzed people suffer gross indignity and pain of renal calculi, or kidney stones. I'm working on dietary aspects of a program that necessitates adherence to strict nutritional limits, and frequent testing of blood chemistry. Most stones are calcium; therefore, the calcium intake will be severely restricted. You possess an excellent opportunity for this research program because you only recently became paralyzed. I strongly encourage your immediate

Daniel R. Williams

participation. Results from this study could very well benefit many people. Think about it. Now changing the subject, one's use of different respirators requires periodic blood gas studies or arterial sticks. I'll perform those. Should you decide to participate in this research project, my laboratory technician, George, will be responsible for a weekly finger stick. In many instances both blood tests can be combined. We'll talk tomorrow."

Twenty days passed without company. PT, OT, volunteers from college, all filled vacancies in my daily routine, the new nursing regimen was improving my digestive problems, and lack of boredom eliminated thoughts of self, but nightly dreams were rampant with visions of loneliness and memories of my family in New Castle. I longed for home.

Thursday morning's routine changed. Our schedules were accelerated, Jon, Leroy, and Bob were hurried from the room leaving me alone. "Strange." I thought. "Why is everybody glancing in my direction and whispering?"

"Hi Danny." said Norman. "Bet you're surprised to see me. Your sister is outside the door, she'll come in soon."

"Hi brother." said Judy, wiping her eyes while walking through the doorway. "Daddy will be in to see you after he speaks to Dr.Oliver."

"It's great...to see you guys!" I exclaimed. "Did I hear you...say Dad? Where's Mom? Is anyone else here?"

"Hi son." said Dad walking into the room. "I'm glad to see you're smiling again."

"Hello Dad,...where's Mom?" I asked. "You don't look well...you're so pale."

Exchanging uncomfortable looks, Norman and Judy excused themselves. "Danny, Dr.Oliver said we should be honest with you, and there just isn't any way to say this without being blunt. Your Grandpa died last night." Dad whispered with teary eyes. He then explained, a car had struck Grandpa as he walked to their church revival meeting on Tuesday. Grandpa died early Wednesday morning at the hospital from a severe head injury, loss of blood from a ruptured kidney and multiple fractures.

Norman and Judy returned to my room. Together we cried and prayed for Grandpa and Grandma. Conversation concerning mundane matters was inappropriate, so I quickly briefed them on my activities, painful therapy, new respirators, and most assuredly, the pool. "Oh yeah, tell Mom...to send me some ...swimming trunks. These G-strings...are embarrassing. They say my...frog breathing...is very good...I should be out...of this tank in...the near future."

"Wait 'til we get home!" Judy exclaimed. "Everybody is going to be so excited."

Keep Smiling and Never Give Up!

"Danny we can't stay long." Dad said sadly. "Grandpa's funeral is tomorrow, and Grandma needs our support."

I forlornly watched my unexpected visitors leave while disconsolate thoughts flooded my mind. With my eyes closed I could see Grandpa pushing Grandma, his wife of fifty-eight years, from the path of a speeding car. Only two months ago they celebrated their wedding anniversary. Screams echoed in my ears and I heard crunching of flesh and bone as a car propelled him along the street. Thank goodness my routines had been canceled for the day. People left me alone as much as possible, and I remembered good times with my Grandpa.

Mrs. Leonadakis accompanied by a hospital chaplain came into the room. They solemnly expressed condolences, offered all possible assistance, and bowed their heads in prayer.

"Thank you…for your kindness." I said. "Everyone in our family…is upset. Especially Dad,…first, his oldest son…is stricken with…Polio. Now his father has…been killed. I'm not the only…Williams who's …suffering loss."

"Danny if you need to talk ask for me." said Leo. "I'm a good listener."

Time passed quickly at the Respo Center, with each day presenting a new challenge. It became routine to be removed from the iron lung and taken to pool therapy. Mickey, my OT, instructed me in the use of a mouthstick for turning pages, and writing while holding a pen in my mouth. She and Steve, her husband, taught us to play Bridge, and to my delight, he played chess. Once each week our recreational aides, Anita and Helen, brought a cart to our rooms laden with packages and gifts provided by a familiar group, the Ruth Lyons Fund. I managed to acquire many presents for my brother and sister and collected model car kits for later use at home.

"Good morning, gentlemen." said Dr.Oliver, when he and Dr.Johnson entered our room. "Dan, it's time for your exit from the safety of this iron lung. Your rocking bed venture begins today."

"Oh no! When I tried…using that bed…at Riley Hospital…contents of my stomach…came up faster… than the bed."

"Don't worry Dan." said Dr.Oliver. "We'll take things slowly. With your frog breathing and using oral positive we know you will rise to the occasion."

"By the way," interjected Dr.Johnson, "this week we'll begin treatment with a tilt table. You will be fastened onto a motorized platform which is incrementally inclined until you are standing upright at ninety degrees. Once you've progressed to a vertical position, we'll try sitting you in a chair."

"That's correct." said Dr.Oliver. "Shortly you will be out of this iron lung. Your body and blood chemistry must acclimate to all respirators,

Daniel R. Williams

therapy, and new positioning, because these are your tickets to a wheelchair and freedom."

"Oh boy! Here we go." I thought, as the rocking bed's motor started. Up and down, back and forth, my head emptied and stomach fell. I waited fearfully for a bile taste in my mouth, wishing I were safely back in the tank.

Dr.Oliver directed, "Pick a spot on the ceiling, stare at it closely. The queasiness will pass and if not we will give you some medicine. Tell me if your breath intake isn't deep enough and I will increase the rock. Should you need more air just frog breathe. In case you tire, we'll let you use oral positive in conjunction with the rocking bed."

"How...does...this...work?" I asked. "Should...I...be seeing...circles? My...stomach...feels...funny."

"Willpower Dan!" charged Dr.Oliver firmly. "Willpower! Think about something else, and keep staring at that spot on the ceiling. Frog. Rock for at least fifteen minutes this time. A rocking bed is effective by allowing the diaphragm to drop on the upward cycle pulling air into your lungs. A reverse downward cycle forces exhalation of air, as pressure from upward diaphragmatic motion forces you to exhale. Many people sleep on rocking beds. For instance, the Colonel."

Shortly following my second rocking bed initiation I was visited by a man in white uniform carrying a tray full of medical instruments. "Remember me? I'm back."

"Hi George." I said. "Is it my turn...to give again? What's it like...to be Dr.Oliver's...personal vampire?"

"Don't think of this as a sacrifice Danny." he laughed. "Consider it a contribution to science. Dr.Oliver asked for arterial blood gases along with your weekly donation to his diet study. He'll be here in a few minutes."

"I'm out of...places to stick." I bitterly replied. "Next thing I know...you'll be after...my ear lobes."

"Speaking of that," said George, "I could perform these weekly sticks on your ear lobes, letting your poor fingers and toes heal."

"You're not serious!" I said. "Don't you know...when a guy is...kidding?"

"Sure, but I'm not." he said. "We do it all the time."

My enthusiasm for this honored program was vanishing, I now resented weekly sticks for blood specimens. George was quite a guy, he would be humorous and tell jokes just before he jabbed a sword into my body parts. Conversely, Dr.Oliver was quiet, instructing me to, "get ready, this will sting." Slow to grasp the gravity of this situation, only two times passed before I got the point.

"Hi Colonel." I greeted. "Tried out a...rocking bed today. How do you...sleep on that...teeter-totter?"

Keep Smiling and Never Give Up!

"Yeah, I heard you were rocking earlier." he nodded. "Secret to sleepin'? Close your eyes. What do you think?"

"Well really...the bed was...rocking," I replied, "my stomach was...rolling. It was OK...but one thing ...concerns me. Can I eat...while the bed...moves?"

"No problem son, just go easy on soups." he grinned.

Within six weeks I established rapport with most of the portable respirators. My rocking bed and I reached a moving agreement of mutual tolerance. Surprisingly, all tilt table sessions began slowly. When the idea was first explained, I thought, "Simple, no sweat. I'll be through with this caper in a week." First time I elevated to five degrees, then on to great heights of ten, etc. Unlike the rocking bed that maintained constant motion, a tilt table is stationary, allowing circulation of blood to slow. Consequently, when locked in certain positions the tilt table instigated many near-fainting episodes. After a month of alarming, yet exhilarating moments, I finally adjusted to a standing position.

Following pool therapy one day when I'd ceased begging, threatening, and yelling at Bob to quit hurting me he asked, "Want to try something new today?"

"What do you," gulp, gulp, "have in mind?" I hesitated. "Are you going to," gulp, gulp, "remove me piecemeal," gulp, gulp, "from the pool?"

Laughing and without further warning he sat me up in a chair bolted to the pool frame, one arm holding my body, his other hand supporting my wobbly head. Muscular coordination had been destroyed by Polio, and atrophied neck muscles lost necessary strength to keep my head from falling backwards - I resembled a bowling ball being balanced on a pencil. Phyllis, a fellow Respo Center resident, and my pool companion today yelled, "Hurry, grab his head Bob! If he breaks his fool neck he'll be paralyzed!"

The rush of hectic activities never ended and as I lay on my rocking bed awaiting recovery from my latest encounter with Bob and pool therapy my leisurely time was interrupted by Dr.Oliver's appearance and captivating grin asking, "Are you ready for another adventure? I think it's time for a trial run with a chest respirator. Technically it's called a cuirass, but we refer to them as chest shells. You'll be properly fitted and if all goes well, you should be spending most of your time from now on in a bed or wheelchair. Dan, this will probably breathe you better than the rocking bed. As always, courage, patience, persistence, time, and above all, willpower, are keys to success."

"Now I know how a...turtle feels." I joked. "You're right, it does work...better than the rocking bed."

"You're doing great." said Dr.Oliver. "I'll return for blood gases this afternoon and simultaneously George will take your weekly donation."

Daniel R. Williams

"Danny according to the chart," said Dr. Johnson, "you reached ninety degrees twice this week. Now that you can be vertical, I think it's time to try sitting in a wheelchair."

I couldn't believe my ears. After all these months and pain my doctors just uttered the words I would never forget.

ME, IN A WHEELCHAIR!!! THANK GOD!!!

Several weeks had passed since becoming a resident at the Respo Center and during this short time I learned many important facts. The people here exhibited a rare talent of compassion. Probing for hidden strengths and weaknesses, they used persuasion, logic, pride, threats, and at times, anger to encourage or demand total effort of all residents. Courage was praised; timidity frowned upon by staff members and other residents alike. We were challenged by fellow Polios providing peer pressure to ensure determined pursuit of one's goals. Encouragement, a loving respect, and our competitive spirit instilled in us courage to endure excruciating physical and emotional pain. Confronting daily adversity gave us incentive to learn new living skills and became an educational study in survival. The dedicated staff at Sellers East Respo Center provided we residents whose lives had been altered by Polio, the best of all possible opportunities to excel in life.

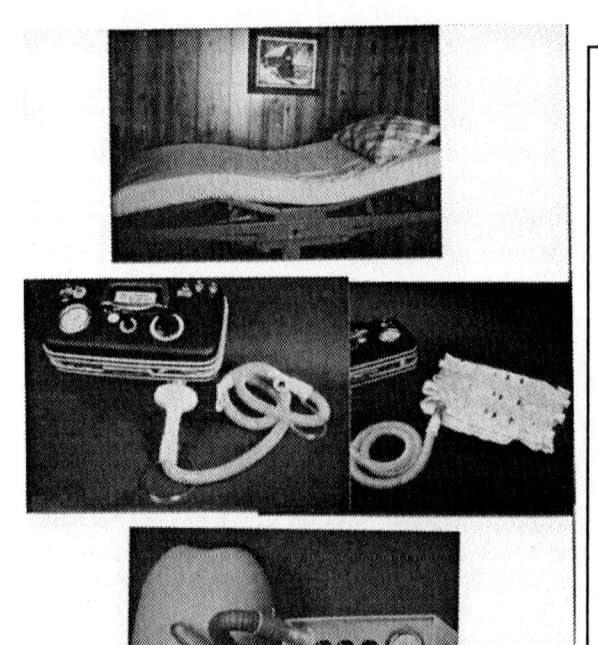

Top left: Home Rocking Bed.
Middle row: (Left) Portable oral positive pressure respirator and hose attachment, which is held between the teeth. (Right) Same Portable positive pressure respirator, with hose, and pneumobelt, which is worn around the abdomen.
Lower left: Cuirass (chest shell) and portable negative pressure respirator.
Photos Courtesy: LIFECARE®, Lafayette, CO.

12

PROMISES

The big day arrived. Doctors, nurses, and therapists gently lifted me to a chair for the first time in seven long months. "Oh Oh," I thought, "this procedure will certainly be more involved than I originally anticipated." My stomach flip-flopped more than when adapting to rocking bed or tilt table. With little hip padding remaining, my buttocks began screaming from unfamiliar pressure, and poor circulation – a complication of prolonged immobility, caused feet and legs to swell painfully.

When I first became paralyzed most people, me included, were unaware Poliomyelitis affected only motor nerves. Some times this is excellent, enabling us to experience pain and alerting us to dangerous situations. Unfortunately, we also have itches at the most inopportune times like "normal" people; and, although a blessing when attempting to prevent pressure areas, feeling pain is frustrating, when trying to attain sitting tolerance.

Proud and happy people accompanied me through corridors to the gymnasium. With a portable respirator wheeled beside my chair I entered the activities room in a sitting position for the first time. OT and PT staff members cheered loudly, applauding my accomplishment enthusiastically. A group of fellow Polios greeted my entrance with smiles, giving me a sitting ovation.

Pat, a long-time Respo resident wheeled her chair over to me saying, "Yesterday the pool, today the chair, who can tell about tomorrow!"

Phyllis, Jon, Bob, Peggy, and Leroy chorused, "Bravo!"

"Welcome." greeted Mickey. "Now we can begin seriously working on typing and painting with a mouthstick."

"Not yet," grinned Bob, "he's still mine during morning hours. Besides, I'm pushing his chair."

"Don't let me interrupt," said Dr.Johnson, "but in case you've forgotten, he's actually mine. Danny rather than put you through intense pain every day with PT on your wrists, we have decided to mold detachable splints to be worn during time outside the pool. We hope this continual stretch will more evenly distribute the pain over twenty-four hours. Now before you tire, they await you in the casting room."

"Please tell me something, Dr.Johnson." I growled. "If it was necessary," whoosh, gulp, gulp, "for me to establish a," gulp, gulp, "vertical position on the tilt table," gulp, gulp, "before sitting in a wheelchair," gulp, gulp, "why can't I stay in the chair?"

Daniel R. Williams

"My, my, aren't we touchy today." he grinned. "Bluntly, progress is slow. First, rocking bed and movement to a tilt table for short periods of time. Stationary positions are not conducive to good circulation, sitting is worse than a standing posture. Until your body has become acclimated to a wheelchair, reclining or periodic movement is necessary. Once you have reached a tolerance, it will be possible for you to sit long periods of time. Each advancement will take even longer. If within two years you've regained marginal muscle function in your limbs, perhaps you'll walk with aid from crutches. Understanding that Polios have a limited window of opportunity requires patience and persistence. Wally, take him away."

PT awaited my return from the cast room. "Come on Bob," I whined, "wasn't the idea of these splints," gulp, gulp, "to eliminate PT on my wrists and poor hands? Have a heart!"

"Recalling Dr.Johnson's words," Bob responded shaking his head sympathetically, "he said the intense pain would be more evenly distributed, not eliminated. You wouldn't want me to be fired, I must appear busy."

Squeak, creak, rattle. Mickey entered my room pushing a huge wooden frame supporting a typewriter. "Don't believe just because you're tired from PT, I forgot you. It's not wise to postpone your typing lesson until you've reached a sitting tolerance." she cautioned. "At least utilizing this devise you can learn the fundamentals of mouthstick to key coordination. Want to give it a try?"

"Sounds good to me," I said, "but how does that big... wooden frame set over...the rocking bed? This should...be interesting."

"It doesn't." she said. "We turn the bed off and fit you for an oral positive mouth piece complete with adaptor to hold a mouthstick. Dr.Johnson, Bob, and the PT's can't have all the fun."

I quickly learned a mouthstick to quadriplegics is like a good arm to baseball pitchers. With much practice, Mickey taught me how to type, turn pages, paint, and even to move checkers, cards, and chess pieces. Playing checkers was a bit difficult. Mickey taped the end of our mouthsticks in an attempt to make checkers accessible to quads without help from able-bodied (AB) participants. Moving them was simple, but we had problems when someone needed to jump. We managed to lift the checker, but couldn't let it go. Also included in my education was training to write, holding a pen in my mouth.

Later while I rested, Dr.Oliver entered asking, "Dan, how about trying to sleep on your rocking bed tonight?"

"You are kidding?" I asked timidly. "What if I get in trouble...and can't make it all night? I've never tried to ...sleep outside the iron lung."

"You won't have troubles," assured Dr.Oliver, "it will be just like rocking a baby to sleep. Surely you've taken naps during the day. If any unexpected problems arise, staff will put you back in the tank. Remember your backups, oral positive and frog breathing. Keep in mind, this is one more step toward becoming mobile."

One week later Dr.Oliver informed me, "You have done so well with the rocking bed at night, are you ready to try a chest respirator? Your blood gases are better with a shell than the rocking bed."

"I'm ready for that one...providing my ribs and skin... don't get too sore." I said. "Dr.Johnson told me...before I came to Columbus...the chest shell works...like a tank."

The anxiety of adjusting to sleep outside my cocoon of safety dissolved into restful nights. Days so completely full of activity whisked by rapidly and I personally marveled at my improvement. One day while answering wisecracks from her charges Miss Jones (Jonesy), our daytime nurse smiled, "Danny I'm glad you made it to the chair in time for the Respo's annual spring picnic. As you are aware the patio was built for Polio's, conveniently equipped with electrical outlets allowing those on respirators to relax and enjoy the event. We can relocate residents in iron lungs to the patio, but sunlight is much easier on your eyes in a wheelchair. The menu is really fantastic."

"Yeah!" exclaimed Jon. "Last year we had steak, corn, potato chips and Coke. Oh, I forgot your diet. Ha! Ha!"

Jon's snide remarks were still reverberating when dear Dr.Oliver walked into the room. "Well, your eyes are open. I trust you slept well last night, breathing and all that. The chest shell is apparently more efficient for your sleep than the rocking bed."

"I didn't have any problems...at all." I boasted. "By the way Dr.Oliver...Jonesy mentioned the patio… cookout in a few days. Don't you agree it's unjust...forcing me to... watch those people eat...all that good food...while I munch on...unsalted carrot sticks and...cardboard-tasting burgers ...without seasoning?"

"Why Dan, what happened to the dedication for my kidney research project?" quizzed Dr.Oliver. "Imagine, you, a new Polio and all the answers we could achieve. Calcium kidney stones may be a thing of the past. Anyway, you get salt."

"Yeah salt!" I grumbled. "Blood tests every week...a tray full of...lousy food and foul...tasting medicine. Ha! Dedication nothing...I'm dumb!"

Exiting the room laughing he said, "You can eat all the delicious food you want, but only for the picnic."

"Oh, I almost forgot." said Dr.Oliver returning to the room. "On August 26th some of you will be going to the Ohio State Fair. That day is three months away, so you have time to qualify for the trip."

"Hey Leroy, do you know...anything about this trip?" I asked. "What does he mean...'qualify'?"

"Sure." he said. "I think qualify means sitting up. Last year some of us in wheelchairs made the trip. We were loaded into a moving van, strangest ambulance ride I ever experienced. The bumps were terrible! The fair was fun, except for some rude people."

"Three months?" I thought. "Man, I've been trying for seven months to escape the iron lung! Guess I'll just work harder, I really want to go to the fair."

I anxiously awaited Dad and Mom's appearance at my door anticipating the surprised looks on their faces. Would they ever be shocked! The last time my family had seen me in a hospital bed was before I entered an iron lung.

"Well, will you look at this!" Dad exclaimed as he and Mom entered the room. "Why didn't you let us know the good news? You could have written."

"Danny, this is wonderful!" cried Mom. "Hold still so I can kiss you. Does this bed move all the time?"

"Slow down." I pleaded. "One question...at a time. I wanted to surprise you. No, the bed doesn't move...all the time, just when...I want to breathe. Flip the switch...I'll hold still for... a minute. Oh no! Time it so I'm level," gulp, gulp, "not standing on my head!"

"I see." said Dad. "Boy I bet it's fun feeding you on this rocking horse. Anita and Mark are downstairs with the children, they'll be up later."

"No." I said. "You guys wait outside...for a few more minutes. Oh Mom, did you bring...the clothes I requested?"

"Yes Danny. Here are your pants, shirts, and swimming trunks. Danny, are you sure it's safe for you to be in that water? What happens if you sink?"

After convincing them to wait outside, the orderly and a nurse dressed and sat me in a wheelchair. "Wait 'til they see this!" I laughed. "Better get the smelling salts!"

My parents recovered quickly from their shock of seeing me sitting up, and we all went downstairs to surprise other family members.

"Oh my word!" said Anita. "Let me sit down."

"This is great! Ready to work yet?" Mark quipped.

"Danny!" squealed Millie. "Boy, are you skinny!"

Obtaining directions from the nurses we went outside to the patio so Andy, Tina, and Millie could play on the slide and swings. As usual the Respo Center had thought of every possibility, providing a small playground for younger rehab residents and children of visitors. I remained sitting only a short time because of limited strength and my rebelling hips. The kids grew restless and Andy begged, "Bubby will you play ball with me? Pretty please?"

His innocent plea made my heart ache and I listened to Millie's comment, "Mom we don't have anything to do here, when can we go home?"

"Sorry 'bout that little sister." I sighed. "Maybe you could play tag or ball with Andy."

"We must leave." said my father. "The drive is long and the kids are tired. Don't worry, we'll see you again soon."

Midway through the next week I was contentedly relaxing following an afternoon session of OT when in walked two lab techs in white coats soliciting a blood donation from Bob. As usual, loveable Bob not only conversed with the male tech, he flirted shamelessly with the young female observer.

"Come over here,...it's safe on this side of the room." I said. "Bob is a twenty-three year old...married man. On the other hand,...I'm young, handsome, and...available."

"Hi, I'm Carol. What's your name?" asked a statuesque, 5'8" brunette with sparkling, iridescent eyes.

"Daniel, Dan, or Danny...take your pick." I said. "You look sort of young...to be hanging out with Harry, and...I'm definitely sure too innocent...for conversations with Bob."

Chuckling, she said, "I'm interning in the lab during summer break, trying to choose between this and nursing."

"Interning? Are you in college?" I asked.

"No. she said. "I'll be a senior in high school next year. Hey, this rocking bed looks like fun."

"Well you know the...old saying," I laughed, "it does have its...ups and downs."

"Oh brother!" growled Bob. "That line is a killer."

"Stop complaining Bob." snickered Jon. "At least you didn't get suckered into that diet deal."

"That's right," agreed Bob, "age is beneficial to one's experience."

"Come on guys, lay off." I protested. "I'm sacrificing good food...so you jerks won't have kidney stones. How was I to know...the lamb would taste like wool...and dear George would...visit me every week? Anyway, Dr.Oliver assured... me I could have...a steak at the cookout."

"Speaking of the devil." smirked Bob. "Hi George."

"Danny, Dr.Oliver wants a baseline blood specimen prior to the cookout, so he can track the new additives from that good food." George gleefully announced.

"Aw man, why must you...attack me in front of...Carol?" I moaned. "Oh well...get it over with."

"I have a great idea." she said. "Let me do it."

"I agree." Bob declared. "She has to learn."

"Are you kidding?" protested George. "I'm having fun."

The next day arrived and our cookout began. Not only was the Respo Center patio equipped with electrical outlets, it even had awnings for shade. Annual picnics, courtesy of The March of Dimes, Drs.Oliver and Johnson, and Respo Center staff, were planned with everyone a priority. Orderlies and volunteers heaved and maneuvered iron lungs beneath awnings for protection from sunlight. We were pleased to see Respo professionals dressed informally in tee shirts, shorts, and sandals - the cookout was our family affair. "Imagine the many different sunburns," I thought, "lobster red faces for courageous ones still hoping to escape iron lungs, striped legs beside crutches, and multi-colored arms for all of us dutifully wearing our splints."

"Everyone! Let me have your food orders." said cookout chief chef, Dr.Oliver. "I'm grilling medium, well done, and to combat anemia, rare steaks. On the blue table you'll see potato salad, corn on the cob, tomatoes, and chips. Drinks are in the coolers. Please save watermelon until last, we have no privacy curtains on the patio."

"This is unbelievable." I said to Bob. "Who ever heard of a hospital doing this for its patients?"

"Dan'l, after all these weeks you have yet to learn." he scolded. "The Respo Center is not a hospital. You and your friends are not patients. We are residents!"

The glare of outside light hurt my eyes, but fresh air mingled with the aroma of barbecue made my first cookout a wonderful memory.

"Is everybody having a good time?" asked Dr.Johnson.

In unison we answered, "Yes! A very good time!"

After the cookout I went back to my rocking bed. Bob asked, "Hey, do any of you guys know anything about moving van ambulances being arranged for the State Fair trip?"

"Sure. I went home in an iron lung at Christmas...and they transported me in a moving van." I proudly volunteered.

"Aw sure." said Jon rolling his eyes. "Stop lying!"

"Really, it's true." I said. "No big deal."

"Okay expert, suppose you tell us about your trip." Bob challenged.

Suavely I spent the next hour describing my trip home for Christmas, teaching these sociologically deprived people about sophisticated moving van ambulances!

Keep Smiling and Never Give Up!

I slept well the night of our picnic, my stomach full, and taste buds still savoring forbidden foods. The next day I greeted Dr.Oliver with, "Thanks for letting me eat some of those kidney stone growing delicacies. I was beginning to think starvation was part of rehab."

"Very funny Dan." snickered Dr.Oliver. "Don't forget, you're gaining weight. Now if you're ready, it's time you master this new respirator. Remember my exact instructions. When the pneumobelt expands exhale, relax and allow pressure to disappear before trying to breathe."

"Whenever you're rea--dy." I gasped. As the pneumobelt bladder squeezed my abdomen pushing my diaphragm upward, air was forced from my lungs. The respirator cycled, released, diaphragm fell, and I inhaled air filling the vacuum created in my lungs. I hadn't been hit this hard since football.

"What do you think Dan? Want to continue?" inquired Dr.Oliver.

"Yes, for a whi--le. At least I do--n't hold a mouth--piece. How do I eat--with this belt on?" I asked, trying to breathe with the new respirator.

Dr.Oliver advised, "Initially you should use this type respirator sparingly. Your abdomen must gradually acclimate to the pressure. I think you should return to bed now."

Following my return to the rocking bed I began firing questions at Bob, "How long have you...used a pneumobelt? I watch you feed yourself...how can you eat? Doesn't it make you sick? I'm not sure this is...going to work."

"Don't worry, you'll get used to it soon." he reassured me. "At first it's difficult to eat with continual pounding on your stomach, but it helps control gluttony. Eventually your body becomes familiar with the rhythm and it's so much easier to talk, type, or use a mouthstick. After I acquired Rancho ball bearing feeders to move my arms, being able to breathe using a pneumobelt made my life better."

"Guess I started using the...pneumobelt at the right... time." I said to Bob. "Tomorrow I get...my feeders."

Bob responded, "Independence is around the corner."

Looking at my arms suspended in slings I protested, "Is this necessary--Mickey I feel--like a pup--pet."

"Danny, just trust me." said Mickey. "They are called sling feeders. The springs facilitate movement of your arms, and hand splints allow finger and hand flexion or extension with minimal effort. Your arms will be strengthened by this adaptive equipment and compliment your mouthstick skills. I know you can type and possibly paint with a brush, perhaps some day you'll be able to move chess or checkers by hand without assistance from AB's. Slings are the forerunners of Rancho ball bearing feeders. Have patience. Are you ready for a surprise? I've finished glazing the dog picture you painted using your mouthstick. Bet your mom likes this!"

Daniel R. Williams

Observing the masterpiece I teased, "Maybe I shouldn't give this to Mom. What do you think, maybe my girlfriend?"

"Absolutely not! This is your mother's." she demanded.

Laughing I commented, "After looking at the finished product I'm convinced my future will be confined to painting pictures with words."

The day following our cookout Rev. and Mrs. Kerschner surprised me with a visit. After OT, Mickey brought them to the gym and I suggested we move to the patio. "It's great you traveled so far to see me." I said. "Have a nice trip?"

"It was a beautiful drive. We needed to see you out of the iron lung." he said. "Now that you're in a wheelchair, will I see you in church? Everyone will be amazed."

"You have my promise." I said. "After returning home I will come to church. Thanks for caring about me."

Mrs. Kerschner pressed my shoulder in response saying, "Right now we're meeting in another building, but plan a new Free Methodist Church. We don't have a sound system, but he preaches louder than this respirator."

Sunday morning after church I rested comfortably in bed waiting for my dinner tray. Leisurely rocking to and fro I thought of the past while listening to my fellow resident's visitors when I was interrupted by familiar voices.

"Want to go outside for a ride?" queried Norman.

Startled I said, "You were just here a month ago...I didn't expect you back...so soon."

"Everybody is out on the patio waiting for us, call the nurses and get in your chair." Dad directed.

Dad held the door while Norman and Mark ushered me onto the patio. "Surprise!" yelled the people waiting for me. A reunion took place for the next two hours as Nancy, Valerie, Mike, Bill, Judi, and I became re-acquainted. Anita, Judy, and Mom prepared food while Millie, Andy, and Tina my niece, entertained themselves on the playground equipment.

Looking at me for the first time outside my iron lung brought mixed reactions from friends. The last time these people saw my body and head together was before I had Polio. When entering the iron lung I weighed a muscular 180 pounds, now this skeletal frame in the wheelchair topped 82 pounds. Shocked looks were evident and conversation was once again strained, reminding me of earlier days at home.

"Hey man, did they break your arms with this therapy I heard about?" asked Mike.

"Yeah Danny," chimed in Nancy, "why are those casts on your arms?"

Smiling I said, "They aren't really casts, just splints to help stretch my wrists. Maybe someday after surgery I'll be able to feed myself."

Keep Smiling and Never Give Up!

"Maybe feed yourself?" Judi softly puzzled. "You mean you're not certain?"

"Bubby, won't you stand up again sometime?" squeaked my baby brother Andy.

The silence was deafening as I thought to myself, "Get used to this reaction and remember what you've been taught: patience, understanding, willpower."

During the days following my encounter with reality, I thought of reactions I'd received from my friends. However, heartache wasn't all that bothered me, pain radiating from my right hip prevented any progress in sitting tolerance. Attempting to alleviate the problem, Dr.Johnson ordered diathermy (deep heat treatments) and ultra sound. Bob instructed PT interns Sue and Madeline to administer daily treatments, and though I was unable to detect improvement, my sitting tolerance increased. Amazingly, this was one procedure that proved painless, sort of like a mechanized liniment.

As Leroy was released from Sellers East his departing words were, "I want to go home, but now I'll miss a trip to the fair. I wish my discharge date was later."

"That's odd," I mused, "why choose the fair over home?" After he left I stared at his vacant bed saying, "Jon didn't Leroy act sort of strange when he said goodbye?"

Jon nodded, "Yeah I noticed, like something was going to happen."

Our old friend, Elmer from next door, filled the empty spot in our room. He too had progressed from iron lung to rocking bed; still quiet and little darling of the Respo Center nursing staff. The ladies all became mothers around him and the shy baby just blushed and blushed.

Elmer's parents owned a yacht, and on his first trial visit home he became unusually brazen. Upon his return from Cincinnati, 'sweetness' was a different person gushing, "You guys wouldn't believe...what I did at home. Daddy set my chair...on the pier...then lifted me over...a railing to... the deck of our...yacht. Boy, did I ever...have fun!"

"Hey, that sounds great!" we said admiring the little guy's courage. "Weren't you afraid of drowning?"

"Shoot no!" he boasted. "I wore a life jacket. Anyway after therapy in the pool,...the Ohio River is nothing."

"Listen up fellows." announced Drs.Oliver and Johnson walking briskly into our room. "Only one month to go before the Ohio State Fair trip and despite noticeable progress, some of you should not plan on going with us. We've already talked to many of your female counterparts so you may hear uncomplimentary remarks about us and see some tears. Both Dr.Johnson and I arrived at these painful decisions in your best interest. I'm sorry Dan, Jon, Elmer; you must plan for next year. Dan, you are not physically strong enough, and your sitting tolerance is still too limited. Jon, your surgery will conflict with the trip. Elmer, you'll be leaving us before then, home is much better than a trip to the Fair. According to your parents, the trial visit went splendidly. I'm still uneasy about adventures on a speedboat. Bob, you and Jack will join Phyllis, Pat, and Peggy at the Fair."

"Dr.Oliver!" I blurted out. "It's a month away...why decide now? I've worked hard...to accomplish this goal!"

"Danny you've made excellent progress, but rehab takes time." cautioned Dr.Johnson. "Bluntly, you're not ready for a trip among strangers."

"Keep in mind," said Dr.Oliver sternly, "each person we designate to take the Fair trip has previously been home. Coping with family and friends is difficult enough without confronting inquisitive staring and rude remarks from crowds of strangers. Regardless your stoic determination to ignore cruel comments and patronizing actions, without exposure to similar circumstances in a more comfortable setting you will return to this Respo Center looking for a hiding place. Dan in your mind we are denying you an opportunity, but trust us to know best. Life outside is challenging enough without this added pressure accrued from taking a trip prematurely. You need the advantages of a home visit first to permit gradual re-introduction into society. If we allow you to attend the Fair without benefit of this valuable experience first, our decision could precipitate withdrawal from people, ensuring your seclusion. This would be tragic just as you begin the difficult adjustment to your new life. The State Fair will be over Sunday, but on Monday you still have to sit in your wheelchair. Sitting tolerance will increase as you become stronger, and experience tempers the insensitivity exhibited by ignorant people. I'm sorry you're disappointed, I know one day you'll understand."

Later, during a resident round table discussion in the gym, several people who had previously attended the OS Fair enlightened us to the love, indifference, rudeness, and many times cruelty of "normal" people. Paul recalled, "Children and elders were usually wonderful. Some people though..... A little girl offered me some cotton candy, but her mother jerked her away saying, 'No honey, these people are sick.'" Other residents added memories of frequent stares, and most all remembered being the brunt of patronizing remarks, rude words, and humiliating gestures.

Phyllis chimed in, "Danny, don't misunderstand. People can be friendly and loving wherever you go. We want you to be aware, some AB's and even occasionally one of us, resorts to condescension from embarrassment, fear, or ignorance."

Patty said, "I went last year after being home once. I believe the people are no different, just more of them. The whole thing depends on how much

Keep Smiling and Never Give Up!

your emotions can deal with at one time. Doc is right though, until you've gained some experience with familiar people, a State Fair is definitely the wrong place to reenter society."

With the State Fair trip no longer a goal, weeks slowly passed and my enthusiasm for tomorrow was thwarted. To say the least, I was still unhappy, and developed an unwarranted dislike for certain doctors. Forgetting Dr.Oliver's words about going home, I brooded about an imaginary injustice by a man who'd carefully planned my escape from the tank.

"Hi Colonel, it's good to see you again." I greeted. "How is everything at home?"

"It's OK," said Don, "but there ain't many of us good people livin' close to my grandparents. Since the death of my parents, I moved from Tennessee to West Virginia. Life was a whole lot better here at the Respo Center."

"Yeah, but things aren't great here either." I griped. "They won't let me go to the Fair."

"Somebody tol' me you were in a tizzy over this little bump in the road." he drawled. "Let me tell you somethin' I haven't tol' anybody else. Three months before I graduated from college Uncle Sam sent me a letter sayin', 'greetings'. Korea was hot and heavy so we didn't have much of a choice, be a man or be a coward. Not long after that I was in Korea gettin' shot the first time. They patched me up and then I got shot again. This time though I fooled them, I had Polio while recuperatin'. I never returned to college. What I'm sayin' son; there are a lot of things we want that we can't have and some things we don't want still happen. You ever hear the story about teachin' somebody to swim? You know, you're thrown in a lake and somebody says 'good luck'. Well, we were sorta thrown into the lake of life, but we were in luck meetin' doctors and nurses who care enough to help us learn to swim. Well, gotta go. These outpatient visits are time-consumin' and I'm very busy. Think about what I said boy, you're a teenager now, but you better grow up fast."

An outing away from the Center was scheduled and plans made for a visit by my family. Dr.Oliver directed us to an excellent location next to a river outside Columbus. I was re-introduced to the world surrounded by family who'd driven many miles for this occasion. My married sisters with their husbands and children, Dad, Mom, Millie, and Andy were all present - the serenity surpassed all expectations. Velvety green grass covered wooded, hilly riverbanks, as the silent Scioto River snaked its way through Ohio's countryside. It gave solace to throngs of people seeking escape from humid, sweltering August heat. Picnic tables and lawn chairs gave the park and its inhabitants a front row seat as we watched speedboats race along the water. Some areas were restricted to use by sailboats and their masts created

Daniel R. Williams

colorful mosaics in contrast to their blue highway. I marveled, "This day is really great! Dr.Oliver is quite a guy."

"What a quaint idea." observed the stranger. "A family picnic without forgetting the invalid in his wheelchair. Do you mind sir, if I purchase some ice cream for him and the other children?"

Dad frowned, "Thanks, but the children just finished eating watermelon and they don't need more refreshments."

"Grandpa, are you sure we don't need ice cream?" asked Eddie. "It's really hot today."

"Dad I've been up several hours. I'm getting tired and my respirator battery is getting low. Suppose we can leave soon?" I asked.

On the way back a car with three loudmouthed men pulled parallel to us. I was riding in the front seat beside Mark, while Norman supported my wobbly head. I breathed with an oral positive mouthpiece clenched between my teeth. "Aah, look at the baby sucking on his pacifier!" yelled one of the punks. "Wanna bottle?"

Reacting in anger, I quickly frogged a deep breath and gulped, "Get lost you stupid jerks!" whoosh, gulp, whoosh.

"Shut up." said Norman. "Next we'll be fighting."

Once again I was slapped with reality. No more could I forcefully defend my honor, and nobody volunteered to help. Patience and willpower gained a whole new significance that day, as I was reminded to "cool it".

A few days later Dr.Oliver informed me I would be going home for a trial visit. "I've discussed the trip with your parents and scheduled a rocking bed and other equipment be delivered this week. If everything progresses as planned and you don't get sick, prepare to leave soon. The success of your ten-day venture will largely determine when you will be discharged from the Respo Center."

"Thanks, Dr.Oliver." I meekly replied. "Please forgive me for being so childish lately."

"No problem." he said. "Sometimes projected anger can be beneficial. On to more important things. I must monitor blood gases again before you leave, evaluate your pulmonary efficiency using the rocking bed, chest shell, oral positive pressure, pneumobelt, and most especially, frog breathing."

Trying to sleep that night I couldn't help remember my step-by-step escape from the iron lung. Those first fearful times from tank to rocking bed and chest shell, then dread, thinking of sleeping outside my steel cocoon. I remembered a single night soon became a week, just as seconds advanced to minutes and hours with my unassisted breathing time. On June 7, eight months after I was diagnosed with Polio, staff wheeled my empty iron lung away. I was immediately engulfed with anxiety while bittersweet memories gave rise to respect for my lifesaving yellow "oil can" on wheels. Now I

Keep Smiling and Never Give Up!

envision sitting in a wheelchair free of pain or time limits, breathing with portable respirators. Life is a mystery, but good.

The week ended with my discharge imminent on Saturday and I'd received unending instructions from my Respo Center family. "Dan'l don't forget the sorry mess you brought to us in March." Bob reminded me accusingly. "I'm sure you can recall the pain level you were forced to tolerate because of dumb behavior. I don't want to hear a lot of screaming during PT when you return! I know it's only ten days, but muscles, tendons, and ligaments tighten rapidly unless they are exercised on schedule."

Pointing her finger Mickey directed, "Don't forget your card holder and mouthstick. Leave the sticky checkers here, we can work on that problem while you're home."

"Yes Maam!" I saluted with my eyes. "Mickey, the last time Steve and I played chess he mentioned being transferred to California. Will you be leaving soon?"

"Sometimes my husband talks too much." she grimaced. "I might be leaving soon. Don't worry though, one of the other OT's will keep you busy."

While Bill the orderly packed my belongings, Jonesy came into the room to complete last minute instructions. "Danny, allow me to introduce Mrs. Gustafson or 'Gussie' as I'm sure she will become known around here. As you know Hixey left several weeks ago and I've been temporary Head Nurse. I've been promoted to permanent Head Nurse and Mrs. Gustafson is my replacement. I want you dirty old men to treat her with respect. Now, do you have any questions before leaving?"

"Jonesy!" I exclaimed. "I can't speak for Bob, Jon, or Leroy, but I personally am crushed! When you get married, your husband better be prepared for abuse."

Jonesy laughed, "You got that right! Mrs. Gustafson, don't listen to this drivel. Danny, speaking of marriage, I will be getting married in a few months. At that time you gentlemen may call me Mrs. Maxwell. Maxey for short."

Dad and Norman came to take me home. We stopped on the way at a drive-in so I could eat burger, fries, and a shake. "Dr.Oliver will kill me if he ever finds out I ate this food while on his diet." I warned my cohorts in crime.

Dad cautioned, "Don't worry, I won't tell him. Don't tell your mother either."

Norman added, "We'll just say you forced us."

"Let's have none of that 'us' stuff, Norman." Laughed Dad. "You're feeding him, not me."

Daniel R. Williams

Returning to New Castle was a pleasure. Reclining in the front seat of our car definitely improved my view over one provided by ambulance windows, and was much more comfortable than a moving van. I observed Ohio and Indiana countryside and was reminded of my last journey in this car when the Williams family went to Florida on summer vacation one year ago. I wistfully dreamed that perhaps sometime in the future I could once again venture south. A disturbing and painful thought suddenly flashed through my mind, "Now I can't hold a deep sea fishing rod in my hands!". Temporarily shaken by reality I consoled myself, "Oh well, most sports need spectators. At least now that I'm a veteran of rocking beds, I shouldn't be subject to seasickness."

Passing several lakes Norman asked, "Remember the days and nights we spent fishing in these waters? How about it Danny, think we could come back here sometime?"

"Maybe," I smiled, "if you'll bait my hook."

"We'll be in New Castle soon." Dad interrupted. "Danny are you ready to try it again?"

Family members, close friends, and neighbors greeted my arrival home with enthusiasm. People unaware of my progress were elated, asking numerous ridiculous questions, such as: "Can't you breathe yet?"; "Do you get tired while sitting in the wheelchair?"; then the most offensive question of all, "When will you be back to 'normal' again?".

I remembered Dr.Oliver's advice, "Patience Dan, they're only human." Struggling to maintain self control I thought about many heart-wrenching events over the past ten months: denial, embarrassment, pain, acceptance of total paralysis and life in an iron lung, agonizing physical therapy, mental adjustment to sitting in a wheelchair with my only arm and hand a stick in my mouth, and now I must learn to tolerate people who ask, "Why aren't you normal?".

After a long trip home I was extremely tired and needed bed rest. The March of Dimes had previously delivered a new rocking bed, and while it wasn't familiar territory, I was home with my family. Few people had seen the rocking bed so their reaction to its teeter-totter movement was absolutely hilarious. It's amusing for users of a rocking bed to watch motions of AB's while speaking to those standing beside our beds. They're soon swaying back and forth hypnotically in time with the rocking action, attempting to maintain their breathing in sync with ours, simultaneously trying to avoid becoming sea sick. Feeding me was a new adventure for all. I knew how and when to swallow, but it was fascinating and sometimes dangerous to participate in dive-bombing antics of people holding forks. And, as the Colonel had warned one time, "It's best to go easy on the soups."

The acid test of adapting to new challenges had begun - would I live or just exist? I was informed by experts this endeavor required tremendous determination. My first trip home for Christmas in an iron lung was an answer to prayer. Returning home in a wheelchair with new portable respirators was the fulfillment of a vision, making my dream come true. Once again I naively believed after the painful struggles of preceding months, life would now be much easier. Oh what a fallacy this was proving to be! Resounding in my head were Rev.Kerschner's words when I was learning to play chess through a mirror, "Nothing of lasting value is achieved without great perseverance and valiant effort."

13
CHOICES

A trial home visit passed quickly, everyone determined to make each day a success. My personal hygiene routine and PT were performed with minute attention to every detail, I would not return in physical disarray this time. My room, adjacent to the kitchen, was permeated with enticing aromas and my salivary glands suffered great distress. Upon return to the Respo Center my alimentary canal would receive a AAA rating and blood tests would reveal Mom's strict adherence to the diet Dr.Oliver ordered. Despite my pleadings, she substituted salted carrot sticks for delicious french fries.

Taking advantage of newfound freedom I asked Judi for a date, our first since my onset of Polio. My sisters and brothers-in-law arranged a trip to the drive-in movie utilizing two separate cars. I would recline in the front seat of one car, the other for inquisitive onlookers – they decided we needed chaperones. The excitement and happiness dissolved in reality and what could have been a memorable time became an evening to forget. Instead of teenage chatter, the main topics of discussion were concerns about my respirator, decreasing battery power, sitting uncomfortably, and my inability to eat or drink. Judi was quite uneasy with the situation, and the "date" ended with her insightful comment, "I'm glad you're home again and I must say, uh, uh, tonight has been a lot of fun. Let's do it again sometime."

As she stepped from the car I thought, "Doubtful."

During an earlier visit to the Respo Center my friends' comments revealed veiled discouragement with what they saw as limited convalescent progress. The Danny they once knew would never be again. Regardless, when I returned home they expressed a desire to reclaim our past friendships by giving me a "welcome back to New Castle party". Eager to rejoin my ol' gang I readily agreed to their excellent idea.

The evening of our much anticipated celebration arrived and I was confronted with a now familiar problem. Moving me from car to wheelchair was embarrassing since it required I be lifted at each stage of the maneuver. Happily, Bill C. lived only a short distance from our house, allowing me to travel through the streets from one location to the other without being transferred out of my chair. Arriving at his home, I confronted the number one nemesis of a wheelchair jockey - steps! Mike evaluated the barrier then proposed, "We can either lift you up these steps or hike over the lawn to a side patio entrance. It's uphill and bumpy, what do you think?"

Ken, John, Bill C., Gary, Bill B., and Mike wanted to blaze a trail through the grass. "Don't look at me guys," gulp, gulp, "I'm just along for the ride."

Everyone was happy to see me, but there was a distinct hint of uncertainty in the air and tension at this party was so thick it could have been cut with an axe. Close friends I'd known for years were hesitant to mention various topics for fear I would be offended or hurt. I thought, "Why can't they understand? I wish people could be aware the unspoken glance is more uncomfortable than their admirable, but sadly misguided restraint in conversation. Vacation sabbaticals at Respo Centers should be required for all AB's. Certainly my dear friends desperately need rehab." Humor broke some of the tension and eventually close friendships were renewed. Lazy sounds of slow music drifted onto the patio and inside, couples dreamed of "April Love" while they danced to mellow strands of "Smoke Gets In Your Eyes".

At a break in the music I asked, "Where's Judi?"

The question remained unanswered as Bill C's Mom served refreshments. "Danny it's wonderful you're out of the iron lung." she said. "Would you like a Coke?"

"Let me help," said Nancy, "how about some potato chips and dip? I'm new at this feeding bit. Please be patient."

"Thanks Nancy," I replied, "but I'm supposed to remain on a diet. I'll just drink water."

"We're celebrating!" she frowned. "You can diet some other time. Eat, drink, and be merry!"

"OK, OK. Hey, nobody answered my question. Where is Judi?" I repeated.

Nervously glancing at each other, the patio cleared and people left for dancing in another room, leaving dear Nancy holding a potato chip, Coke, and the bag.

"Danny we invited her." protested Nancy. "I guess she just got tied up."

"Sure, sure." I mumbled. "I'd like more potato chips and another sip of Coke. Hey doll, let's dance."

A few hours passed when indications from my posterior and bladder helped make the decision to leave. Looking down the steep hill we held a quick conference and decided that to avoid spilling the important cargo, ME, it would be best to roll my chair backwards across the grass. The street, which had been relatively smooth earlier, was now torturous. Small bumps and tiny cracks in the pavement seemed like potholes and canyons as a result of my fatigue. Being together with friends brought happiness, diminishing the dose of reality that had slapped me in the face this evening.

Adjustment would be required of everyone if our relationships were to flourish in future encounters. Maybe next time.

I was inundated with visitors wishing to verify my exit from the iron lung and see a rocking bed in action. Amidst one quiet afternoon Mike and Bill viewed the numerous boxes of model cars, planes, and lone boat I'd accumulated while a resident at Sellers East. "How 'bout it guys, think there will be enough work here for an assembly line?" I asked.

Mike said, "This is great! We'll buy an organizer box for all the parts and shelves to hold bottles of paint and brushes. Oh yeah, we'll need sandpaper and lacquer. It's obvious what we'll be doing after school!"

Bill looked at the list of equipment needed to assemble the models and remarked, "We thought you were just kidding. I can't believe you collected all these gifts at the rehab center. It must be nice to have a fun vacation."

Ten glorious days whizzed by and on Sunday, last day of my adventure in New Castle, the Williams family held a mini-reunion at Memorial Park. Sitting atop a hill opposite the lake I languished in luxury as summer breezes wafted across water and mingled with invigorating aromas from our festive array of picnic foods. Burning wood fueled cooking grills and the smoke teased our noses as taste buds savored eagerly anticipated hamburgers, hot dogs, and marshmallows. Hearing the children's joyous cries and hefty laughter from adults assured me this home visit allowing my reentry into society was much wiser than a trip to the Fair.

Brilliant Monday morning sunlight streamed through the eastern sky dancing off our car as Norman and Dad drove me back to my other family. I was unloaded at the back door of Sellers East Respo Center, Children's Hospital to begin the final leg of my first acquaintance with rehab. Dad pushed my wheelchair onto the unit and I happily heard Jon laugh, "Oh no, look who's back! We should'a known they wouldn't keep you. Your bed is still empty."

"Yeah," Bob moaned, "we tried to rent it...but Doc said you might object. Hey, guess what happened to me while... you were gone! I became a dad for the third time...a girl!"

I exclaimed, "That's great! Another girl, what about sons?"

Bob squinted, "Yes, I want a son...I'll never give up ...but my wife has other ideas. I guess the family name... has reached an end. Anyway, it takes a real...lover to have three daughters."

"Speaking of lovers," Jon smirked, "Dan, what happened while you were home?"

"Later guys." advised Miss Rickard. "Now it's time for my questions. Did you follow doctor's orders at home?"

The following morning Dr.Oliver proudly announced, "Dan your blood tests are excellent. I'm surprised you followed my diet orders. I trust the new rocking bed worked without problems. Are you progressing with the pneumobelt? Did you incur any difficulties meeting your public?"

"The rocking bed worked swell...but you should've seen ...people feeding me with a fork." I laughed. "Despite some attempted stabbings...and food up my nose...I didn't have a problem. Getting used to the...pneumobelt will take longer, ...it's difficult eating with...that respirator pounding... my gut. I prefer oral positive...except I can't hold a... mouthstick at the...same time. I had a great...time with my family...and friends. Now that I'm back...can we talk about...the rehab surgery...you suggested before...I went home? I'd rather not think...about this during the...winter. Do you and Dr.Johnson...think it could be done...now?"

"Dan, so far as your breathing is concerned I'd agree," said Dr.Oliver, "but I don't think you're ready physically. Perhaps Dr.Johnson could better explain."

"The reports I received from therapy indicate you tried to follow our orders." observed Dr.Johnson. "You should be very proud of your accomplishments over the past few months. As we discussed before you left, rehab surgery on your right wrist and hand is an excellent possibility. Of course the amount of therapy you receive at home after discharge will determine this step. Perhaps surgery can be scheduled upon your return in the spring. It will depend on you."

"Dr.Johnson," I quizzed, "please explain once more... chances of regaining some...function in my hand following... surgery. What happens if I...don't have the operation?"

"From our previous experience," he replied, "corrective rehab surgery will assure marked improvement in both natural capabilities and use of adaptive equipment. Your ability to utilize Rancho ball bearing feeders for eating, typing, and any activities for which you now use a mouthstick should be enhanced by this procedure. Referring to returned function, essentially any gains accomplished after a two-year recovery will be considered unusual. Without remedial surgery your opportunities will be extremely diminished."

I sighed, "Sure would be nice...to turn pages and type ...without a mouthstick...holder that breaks."

Continuing, Dr.Oliver instructed, "An integral part of anyone's dismissal from the Respo Center is team conferences between you, doctors, nurses, therapists, and social worker. If you have any additional questions about the future, this meeting will be an opportunity for answers. I think OT and PT are probably ready to impart some words of wisdom."

Karen, my substitute OT, said, "Mickey left me written instructions to 'give you a rough time'. Mostly I think we should put finishing touches on projects then re-evaluate your expertise with a mouthstick."

Frowning I said, "So Mickey did leave."

Karen replied, "Yes, they moved to California."

"Dan'l, it's a good thing you didn't allow yourself to become dilapidated, and ready for recall." laughed Bob. "By the time you return for rehab surgery, I'll be in charge of the PT department. While you were home Dick resigned, and I'm in line for a promotion. Of course, that means you will probably have one of the pretty female therapists instead of my handsome face."

For two non-stop weeks I was trundled from PT to OT to X-ray to dental and eye exams. The Respo Center was intent on sending home a much healthier product than they received six months earlier, and I, departing in a wheelchair rather than iron lung, was a much happier person. My final day as a resident of Sellers East neared and I was scheduled to sit before Dr.Oliver's promised discharge conference. Opening the discussion Dr.Oliver announced, "Dan, you are acquainted with the doctors, nurses, and therapists so I'll skip formal introductions. Mrs. Leonadakis, as coordinator, will you summarize Dan's activities during the preceding six months?"

"Certainly." she replied. "Danny came to us in an iron lung, graduating to a rocking bed and portable respirators. After PT and pool therapy by Bob and his colleagues, Danny's constricted muscles were stretched, allowing advancement for seating in a wheelchair. Severe sitting discomfort, result of ischial tuberosity inflammation, was treated by diathermy and ultrasound, which helped to increase tolerance. Mickey and Karen, Occupational Therapists, provided new opportunity for him via mouthstick and sling feeders. A ten-day trial home visit has been completed and he is ready for dismissal. One difficulty, as with all disabled people, is integration into society. Danny has experienced situations common to everyone in wheelchairs, the stress of being isolated within groups of peers, and sometimes even family. His experience, acceptance of realistic expectations, time, and most importantly, maturity will enable Danny and his family to better adjust to unfortunate, and at times, discouraging circumstances. I expect him to return for rehab surgery in six months after successfully confronting and overcoming a variety of happy, disagreeable, and uncomfortable challenges."

"Dan," Dr.Oliver said somberly, "you've heard all of us speak many times of faith, courage, patience, and willpower. These are not trite words to be discarded at the first signs of problems. We promised you unlimited opportunities within your physical potential and in return our demand was only cooperation. After six months of hard work, many tears, and a few angry words the goal has been achieved. I could speak words like 'no pain, no gain', 'or 'quitters never finish', but I won't insult your intelligence. You

Keep Smiling and Never Give Up!

already know the meaning of these phrases; otherwise you would still be in an iron lung. Just allow me to say this - Polio impaired your body, not your brain. We are all chosen, still we must all make choices."

The meeting over, I returned to my room and contemplated their words of advice. Interrupting my thoughts a special person remarked from the doorway, "Danny I hear you're going home tomorrow. Why didn't you call me?" Carol asked. "May I have your address?"

"Are you kidding?" I queried. "I was going to send for ...your address. Be sure to write...once I'm home."

Bill, one of our orderlies commented as she left, "I'd sure like to date her. Do you suppose I stand a chance?"

"Friend I don't wish...to burst your bubble," I joked, "but not in your...wildest dreams!"

Saturday my chauffeurs arrived and as Dad and Norman hurried me toward the door I gulp, gulped, "You guys take care of the place," gulp, gulp, "I'll see ya next spring."

"Don't count on it!" yelled Bob. "With a new baby who ...needs her father at home,...I'm leaving too."

"Well if Dad gets a new position," said Jon, "it's bye-bye Columbus."

Leaving the city we drove westward from Ohio, directly into brilliant early afternoon September sun, its blinding rays reflecting off the windshield. The countryside quickly passed in review with pastures full of cows and horses, and fields of corn turning from green to brown awaited harvest. Traveling through small towns and cities I watched schoolchildren throng playgrounds and teenagers flock in and out of record shops and afternoon hangouts. Life, it seems, continues even if some of us received postponement dates on our calendars. Signs indicating New Castle's city limits greeted us and I felt icy beads of sweat on my brow despite late summer heat. Sudden realization this visit home would not end in ten days created havoc in my stomach and I prayed silently for strength, trying to remember my instructions.

Third time is supposedly the charm, so I eagerly looked forward to the change of seasons at home. Experience, that great teacher, had become a valuable ally in my daily life. Inexperience and exhaustion had been the main adversaries in earlier discharges home, but unlike our first encounter with reality, we were determined not to be overwhelmed. Everyone endures moments of frustration, anger, and discouragement, so perhaps this time the difference would be our acceptance of my disability and adjustment to the problems.

Once close friends willingly cooperated with schedules necessary for our sanity and my physical well being, days at home proceeded with unprecedented regularity. Morning hours were devoted to personal hygiene;

at noon Rev.Kerschner came to read and play chess; afternoons were for family visitors. Weekdays at 4:00 PM my friends from school and partners in a model car assembly line watched "American Bandstand", as Mom prepared dinner, which was invitation only. Saturday was up for grabs unless Dad worked. Our evenings were dedicated to quiet time, leisure, and the unexpected. PT, the solution to physical debilitation, rapidly lost priority. Scheduled lifestyles brought stability, but ensured frustration.

One important lesson all we residents quickly learned - family and friends count. I saved many gifts from the Ruth Lyons Fund cheer cart, most of which went to those closest to me. Not wanting Millie and Andy to believe they grew up in a hospital, I attempted to refocus their attention giving them puzzles and games for their long journeys home. Cards and magazines went to my friends, but I kept model cars and airplanes for myself. With Mike and Bill C's assistance we coordinated a model assembly line in my room while listening to popular music. Our enthusiasm in constructing models was preempted at times by sounds of favorite musical groups or songs from "American Bandstand", and attention was diverted whenever Connie, Annette, Pat, or Frankie appeared to plug their latest recording. Girls from school, while not crazy about model cars, displayed commendable patience with our new hobby. My duty in this endeavor was that of supervisor. As the guys diligently worked, I upheld the code of "cool", conversing with Nancy, Valerie, Mary, and sometimes Judi.

One day I heard an unexpected knock on the door and Mom's voice welcoming a visitor. "Guess who's here." she smiled.

"Hi Danny," greeted Rev.Kerschner, "I'm on my way home from a luncheon and decided to stop by in case you had time for a quick game of chess. I trust your busy schedule will give me the opportunity to defeat you."

"I thought you'd learned... those days of five-minute wins are past." I teased. "No more humiliation. Remember, I don't play this game...in reverse anymore and...the chess board is...in front of me now. Do you need a handicap?"

"Ho! Ho!" he laughed. "Boy, are you feeling good today. Keep in mind one thing, when you played chess while looking in a mirror there were valid reasons for losing. Now what excuse will you manufacture?"

Andy observed our chess games with great interest, even though we often competed with his cartoons. Saturday, Mike, Bill C, and I competed in chess and they taught me various new and advanced moves that enabled me to offer stiffer competition. Disconcerting mirror reflections were replaced by distracting motions of the rocking bed. My mirrored viewing had been exchanged for intermittent up and down glances.

Keep Smiling and Never Give Up!

One week prior to Christmas, *The Courier-Times* requested an interview to discuss my feelings and thoughts, comparing 1958 to 1957 following my trip home in a moving van. During the interview I was asked, "Doesn't the rocking bed inhibit reading? I'm told you like to type, but I don't see a typewriter."

I smiled, "The rocking bed is...turned off while I... read using a chest respirator...to breathe. I designed and family built...a reading rack to hold...the book over my... bed. Yes, I enjoy typing...with a mouthstick. You don't see a...typewriter because...I don't have one...at home. At the Respo Center...in Columbus therapists...taught me to... type. I hope someday...to repay them by...writing about the fantastic...support they give to...us. There's no comparing ...'57 and '58. Those days I was...living in a fantasy... totally unprepared...for the reality awaiting...me when I came home. Experience and maturity...have prepared me to...live one day at a time. Thank God I'm here...with my family, but ...I'm aware other people...aren't so fortunate. They are confined to...iron lungs and connected...to life sustaining systems...unable to participate...in family celebrations. These people only dream...of seeing their loved ones...on important holidays. Next year I hope for...rehab surgery after I...return to my family...away from home."

"Family? Away from home? What do you mean?" inquired reporter O'Giboney from *The Courier-Times*.

I answered, "A Respo Center is home away from home... the residents and staff...are family."

Three uneventful days passed when my father entered the room announcing, "*The Courier-Times* just called and a local sorority wants to present you a new electric typewriter. Do you agree to another interview, with photos this time, for the presentation?"

Astounded, I exclaimed, "Of course I agree! When?"

Serenely observing the presentation, Mrs. O'Giboney and my benefactors requested the rocking bed be stopped while a picture was taken. "Smile at the camera Danny!" prompted the photographer, "It isn't often Christmas arrives early."

"This is great!" I exclaimed. Seizing the opportunity, I stated before witnesses, "In OT at the Respo Center where ...I learned to type using a mouthstick...the typewriter sat on an adjustable...table. The keys could be raised...to the height of my...mouthstick while I...was sitting in a chair. Somebody could build that for me...huh Dad?"

Christmas was different this year. My rocking bed had created a welcome distraction for everyone, especially young children. Our annual Christmas movies were more tolerable since I was no longer forced to squint to protect my eyes from a bright light reflecting off the tank's mirror.

Celebrating Christmas had truly become a blessing. Children's voices bubbling with excitement and eyes sparkling with joy blended with words of satisfaction from adults. Carol sent me two bayberry candles and my thoughts were drawn to those special people in Columbus. I couldn't help thinking about my Respo Center family.

The Sweetheart Dance for Valentine's Day dominated most conversation as a group of friends entered my room one day. I smiled when Judi commented, "Danny, it's good to see you again." My dear friend then promptly removed herself from the gang, preferring instead to remain seated with her eyes glued steadily on the TV. A blanket of uneasiness covered a usually festive gathering and my other friends awaited the inevitable. Attending school and listening to hall chatter they'd known for some time what I only suspected. Reality again asserted itself; Judi was dating someone else.

Attempting to regain control of the situation, I tried to inject some humor. "Which one of you lucky girls...will be my date for...the big dance Saturday...evening?" You've heard of "lead balloons"!

With unaccustomed eagerness the group decided to leave early. Mike expressed each of their thoughts clearly as he stated, "It's warm in here, anybody else need some air?" My friends exited in single file taking great pains to not look toward me.

Judi, the last to leave my room, hesitated then laying aside the friendship ring I'd given her before Polio touched my arm whispering, "I'm sorry."

"We both have new...friends." I said. "You know we had ...some good times together. I hope you'll come back...to see me some day. I'm glad you've been...honest. Not many girls would've...stuck around this long. Thanks Judi."

The daily routine had its ups and downs, but my rocking source of breathing stripped a gear. Emitting a low squeak at first, the noises soon became frantic screams for help, the bed's sound becoming unbearable. For me to obtain an adequate breath the rocking bed needed to elevate forty degrees, then reverse to a ten-degree inversion. As it struggled to reach a level position earsplitting squeals, scrapes, grinds, and one final "ker-chunk" made everyone question its imminent demise. Irritation turned to danger as a holding gear began slipping markedly when the foot lowered. Many times as my head rose I had images of swan diving to the floor, so Dad called The March of Dimes respirator equipment rep. and he sagely advised adding oil to the gearbox. Needless to say, oiling didn't relieve the machine's cry for help, so without mechanical repair the bed was no longer safe.

Keep Smiling and Never Give Up!

Listening to a one-sided conversation I overheard Dad ask, "Are you certain his bed can be repaired in two hours? .....Yes, Danny can lie on the couch that long....I hope you are correct with the time estimate."

Dad walked back to my room and I grumbled, "What's up? This rocking bed won't last... much longer."

"The equipment representative just informed me he'll be here early in the morning." said Dad. "He says it's not a rare problem with rocking bed gearboxes, and he can repair it quickly. I warned him about your breathing, but he said it wouldn't take long to fix the bed."

My father remained home from work so he and Mom could transfer me from bed to couch. Mr. Quickfix arrived early with his tools in a paper sack, ready for a quick fix.

"Don't you worry Danny," he said assuredly, "it's only 7:00 A.M., we'll be through here in two hours. Do you rock on this bed often, or do you stay on the couch?"

Gulp, gulp, "Only when I lie down to breathe." I joked sarcastically.

At ten minutes 'til eleven, Mr. Quickfix explained our difficulty was a shaved and destroyed cog in the gearbox. I commiserated with his problem and he intoned the following, "I guess you lie down and breathe a lot Danny. Some of the gear has been eaten away. I don't have a gear-puller in my tools, but I'll get it and a new gear on my lunch hour. I'm sure where I work they'll lend me the tool. Once I locate the part it won't take any time to repair the problem. If you don't care, I'll grab lunch while I look for a gear. A strenuous workout always makes me shaky because I have low blood sugar and after this morning I'm really tired. I hope you're all right for a while, if not I'll return immediately with the parts and tool."

"Danny won't you eat lunch?" pleaded Mom. "Why are you trying to set a record on an empty stomach?"

"You'd better eat," encouraged Dad, "I wouldn't count on Mr. Quickfix finishing soon. Do you need oral positive, or do you still want to frog breathe?"

Gulp, gulp, gulp, "Unless this guy works nights too," I smirked, "I'm going to frog until he leaves."

Afternoon shadows shaded Mr. Quickfix's sweating face as he steadily labored on the gears of my rocking bed. "Ray it's dinner time," called Mom, "come and eat."

"It won't be too long now Danny." Mr. Quickfix meekly stated. "I almost have the damaged gear off, so don't worry I'll be through in just a little while. I promise."

"Danny, it's eight o'clock," said Dad, "don't you think thirteen hours is long enough without your respirator?"

"I wish you wouldn't push this," Mom worried, "you'll get exhausted."

At twenty minutes after eight I began to realize why Dr. Oliver insisted we learn frog breathing. Oh was I tired.

"I got it!" shouted Mr. Quickfix gleefully. "The gear is on and working, once I oil it the job's done. It took a little longer than I expected, but I've never worked on the gearbox of a rocking bed. Until today."

Gulp..gulp..gulp, "You really fooled me!" I responded. gulp..gulp..gulp.."No problem, I just passed," gulp..gulp.. fourteen hours." Gulp..gulp..gulp."I've been breathing," gulp..gulp.."on my own today." Gulp..gulp.."Thanks a lot Mr. Quickfix." gulp..gulp..gulp.."Boy! If those guys at," gulp..gulp.."Riley could see me now!"

Monday the mail arrived and Mom announced, "Danny, you got a letter from Dr. Oliver."

"Oh no, did my draft notice arrive?" I snickered.

Ignoring me Mom continued, "I wonder why he's writing?"

"Open the envelope Mom," I urged, "maybe we'll discover...the answer."

Mom read, "Leo and I will be visiting in your area soon and would like to schedule a date sometime in the next two weeks. Please answer within ten days."

"Oh, Oh," I sighed, "Suppose I could be sitting in my wheelchair that day?"

My question went unanswered as Mom studied the letter. "We met Dr. Oliver, but who is Leo?" she asked.

"You met her too," I laughed, "Leo is our nickname for...Mrs. Leonadakis the...Respo Center social worker."

Two weeks later they arrived to assess my debilitating physical status and evaluate any progress. "No offense," I said, "but Dr. Oliver...why are you here? It's mid-March and ...when I left the Respo Center...you told me to expect...a visit in late spring."

"Dan, I'm hurt. We're visiting in Muncie and Carmel, and decided killing two birds with one stone would be quite feasible. So to speak." he grinned. "Let's have a look at those wrists and elbows. Have you been following the rigid therapy program Dr. Johnson designed?"

Before I could answer, Dr. Oliver picked up my stiffened wrist and tried straightening it frowning, "Hmmm, I really don't think so. What about your elbows and knees? Never mind, I can see without touching them."

"Wait a minute...I've got some good news." I shouted to avoid the pain from his examination. "My breathing is... much improved. I frog breathed for...fourteen hours!"

"Yeah, and then slept for two days." Dad reported.

Dr. Oliver stared, "Remember me? I've been your doctor for over a year. Don't try those diversionary tactics Bob and Dr. Walcher warned me about.

Keep Smiling and Never Give Up!

I'm pleased your unassisted breathing time improved, but then breathing isn't optional. I trust you appreciate your irresponsibility regarding PT."

"Dr.Oliver, I think Danny should be commended for those frog breathing efforts." Mrs. Leonadakis commented. "I'm sure he'll profit from additional time off the respirator, this strength will obviously assist him while enduring the needless and painful physical therapy he'll now require."

"Mr. Williams," Dr. Oliver addressed Dad, "could I speak to you in another room?"

Leo said, "Danny why don't I keep you company while Dr. Oliver is discussing matters with your father? Tell me what you've been doing. Reading, painting, typing, or any of the skills OT taught you at Columbus?"

"I read a lot." I said glumly. "Mostly I watch TV... and listen to music...on the radio with...friends. The guys and I...organized a model car...assembly line. My minister, some friends...and I play many...games of chess."

"What do you read?" she asked. "Science fiction?"

"Forgive me for interrupting." said Dr.Oliver returning to my room. "Dan, I think you should come back to the Respo Center in the very near future. The planned rehab surgery to improve your hand function can't be performed now without painfully aggressive therapy to realign your wrists, fingers, and arms. This and the surgery will take several weeks and as you've previously been informed, the cast must remain on your arm at least three months. Your parents agree with my decision, but they say it's your choice. Well Dan, do you think you're strong enough? Shall we try again?"

"The sooner the better." I sighed. "This is terribly embarrassing. What can I say to all my friends...when I get ...to the Respo Center? I promised this wouldn't happen."

Dr.Oliver patted my shoulder and said, "Dan, sometimes it's easier to teach, than to do. Families and friends also require rest and rehabilitation at times. I'll arrange for your re-admission in two weeks. When you enter Sellers East Respo Center's corridor, read and memorize our motto."

Daniel R. Williams

Personal Photos:
Left-Residents, family, and staff enjoy Patio cookout, Respo Center, Columbus, OH, 1958.
Right – "Chef" Dr. Oliver, Director Respo Center, Columbus, OH, 1958.

14

HERE WE GO AGAIN

"Well look who's back." groaned Maxey. "The wheels of progress are rolling, bad pennies always return."

"Hi everybody." I greeted. "Don't act so happy to see me. Have you taken care," gulp, gulp, "of the place," gulp, gulp, "while I've been gone?"

"Dum de dum dum." hummed a person in white uniform as he sauntered up the hall. "I'm sure glad to see you Danny! I'm running low on bloooodd." George quipped.

"Oh no! Can't I even," gulp, gulp, "get settled in my room," gulp, gulp, "before you start attacking," gulp, gulp, "me with your weapons?"

"Just cool it!" retorted George. "Dr.Oliver said get a finger stick, it won't take a second."

"Remember," I shot back, "the diet's over." gulp, gulp. "Be quick!" gulp, gulp. "I can't sit," gulp, gulp, "around this hallway," gulp, gulp, "all day."

George smiled, "Here Pal, let me turn your hand over."

"Wait a minute that hurts!" I protested. "Don't bend," gulp, gulp, "my wrist or fingers!"

"Oh man, here we go again!" muttered George.

"This room looks familiar." gulp, gulp, I said, being ushered into my new abode. "Great! Three rocking beds at once. Now that I'm back in bed...the AB's will really be...swingin' and swayin'. Hey Maxey, have you...heard from any of the guys?"

"Meet your new roommate Jerry." she responded, "Now about the guys: Jon will be here next month for spinal surgery. Bob is due for an outpatient visit. Elmer just left after a checkup, he's fine. The Colonel visits us occasionally, ornery as ever. Phyllis is getting married, and if all goes well Pat begins college in September."

"Sounds good." I said. "What about Leroy?"

"I was afraid you'd ask." Maxey answered hesitantly. "Leroy died of pneumonia this winter."

"Who was Leroy?" Jerry inquired. "I heard some people talking...about him. Was he a friend?"

"Yes, Leroy was a good friend,...he was a roommate once ...we and two other guys...went through both horrible...and happy moments at the...Respo Center. Jerry, we all support...each other." I studied my new roommate rocking lazily in his bed and quizzed, "How old are you? Where did you get that red hair...from your dad or mom? Then again, maybe...you just blush a lot."

"Aw come on,...I'm not blushing," Jerry replied, turning fire-engine red, "and I'm eleven years old. Pop said I got this hair from my beautiful mother,...Mom says it's so I... won't get lost in the dark. What's your name mister?"

"My name is Danny, Dan, or Daniel...your choice. Don't call me mister,...that's my dad. How long have you been...a resident? I see the posters...are you a baseball fan?"

"Sure am!" he answered excitedly. "Some day I'll...be a sports writer. I've been here two months,...but Mom says it's...only a matter of time...until I walk. Did you know I...had Polio? Did you have Polio too?"

"No, I'm just lazy. Hey Maxey...other than getting... married, anything new...with you or the staff?" I inquired. "Heard from Hixey lately?"

Maxey answered, "Mrs. Hixenbaum hasn't visited for some time, we haven't heard anything new. Oh, Mrs. Gustafson is leaving soon, her husband has been transferred to another Air Force base. So far we don't have a replacement for her. Well enough gossip, there are other residents at the Respo Center who need my attention. Be careful what you tell this young child, Elmer spoke to him before he left and the girls have schooled him quite well."

"What girls?" I asked. "Just what have all...you good people been...telling this boy?"

"I mentioned Phyllis getting married." replied Maxey. "Pat is here for a thousand mile check-up and possibly for rehab surgery, after recovery she's college bound. Now, you two get acquainted, I'll be back later."

"Hello Dan'l, good to see you." said Bob in his booming voice. "What trouble did you bring back this time?"

"Hi Bob." I said hesitantly. "Get the whips ready,...I blew it. My wrists are deviated,...fingers contracted, arms stiff,...and my knees bend only enough for sitting. Sorry."

"Not half as sorry as you will be friend." Bob frowned. "What about your legs?"

"They're tight, and...I still can't dance." I smiled.

"Watch it, pal." laughed Bob. "Remember the pool? Don't get upset, but I can no longer be your PT. The demands of my new position won't allow me to spend time with people like you. Meet your new physical therapist."

"Hi Danny, I'm pleased to meet you. My name is Rolene. Some of my fellow graduates interned here last summer, they told me about you. Remember Sue, Madeline, and Betsy? My good friend Sheila also works here at the Respo Center."

Keep Smiling and Never Give Up!

"I can see you two will get along fabulously." Teased Bob. "Now give the guy a chance to answer before we leave."

"Sure, I remember them." I replied. "We had a lot of fun. The stretching was a pain...but therapy in the...pool was great. Does this mean Bob...won't be holding me in... the water any longer?"

"Yes, I will. Don't worry. My five foot three inches may look tiny next to Bob, but I'm strong. See my muscles?" demonstrated Rolene. "They'll never let you drown."

Bob laughed, "You guys work out the details, I'm late for a meeting."

Rolene and I talked for a few minutes reviewing my past history then she said, "I'll be back in the morning with a schedule, right now a paraffin bath and an anxious resident await my attention. See you later."

Watching her walk away I thought, "How lucky can I be?" Bob was 6'4", muscular, and hairy. Rolene had a soft voice, blue-violet eyes, and hourglass figure. She left my room and I observed raven black hair nestling comfortably around her uniform collar. My teenage heart throbbed. I dreamed.

"Good morning Dan." said Dr.Oliver. "Have a nice trip to Columbus? You know Dr.Johnson. I'm pleased to introduce Dr.Larrick. If you qualify, he'll be the orthopedic surgeon performing rehabilitative surgery on your hands."

"Hi Danny," greeted Dr.Johnson, "Tim informed me about your fourteen hour frog breathing marathon. I'm impressed! He also forewarned me about your irresponsibility regarding physical therapy. May I examine the crime scene?"

A few minutes later, coping with a racing heart, sweaty brow, and muffled cries I thought, "Oh Williams! How could you have been so stupid? It would have been much easier to tolerate amateur therapists, than to go through this again."

"Danny," Dr.Larrick said, "may I examine your wrists, or do you need some recovery time?"

"Be my guest Doc." I moaned. "Take your best shot."

After a few minutes of excruciating pain, I regretted my bravado. Shaking his head Dr.Larrick stated, "Son, these wrists and fingers are a mess. Dr.Johnson informed me you were nearly ready for surgery seven months ago. Don't you realize how important this could be? What happened?"

"It's a long story." I replied dejectedly. "A problem of priorities...and the path of least resistance. I hope my chances aren't lost. Can you still help me?"

Dr.Larrick said softly, "I'm not sure. After this cursory examination, your right wrist and hand present strong possibilities, but I'm hesitant

Daniel R. Williams

regarding surgery on your left hand. I warn you, any hope for this procedure's success depends on successfully stretching your muscles, tendons, and ligaments, through painful intensive PT, pool therapy, and paraffin baths. Wrist splints must remain in place at all times of inactivity. In six to eight weeks I will examine, re-evaluate, and provide my prognosis. How much pain can you tolerate?"

Trying to appear nonchalant in front of Drs.Oliver and Johnson, not to mention Rolene, I said with boastfulness, "I can take anything for a while."

"It will take longer than just a while to resolve your problems." said Dr.Larrick seriously.

"Give me six weeks with him," assured my new dream girl friend, "we'll be ready for surgery."

"Your optimism is encouraging." said Dr.Larrick.

Dr.Johnson added, "To facilitate the process and help with stretching I'll immediately arrange to have new wrist splints for Danny."

"Hi Danny, my name is Harriet. I'm you're new OT. Dot left and Karen is now in charge of the department. That move leaves me in charge of you. The old records show Mickey and Karen assisted you with typing, painting, and turning pages with a mouthstick. Do you want to continue this program, or try something different until your rehab surgery?"

"Please forget the painting." I pleaded. "Just help me type, write, and read."

Harriet responded, "When you come to the gym later I'll set up your schedule. As Dr.Johnson says, we'll prepare you for rehab surgery, so expect a lot of exercises using Rancho ball bearing feeders. Ever squeezed a rubber ball?"

Dr.Johnson nodded, "Ranchos differ from sling feeders. Dr.Bennett invented arm support systems for Polios while he was Director of PM&R at Warm Springs. Later, Dr.Bisgrove added ball bearings to the device and labeled it a reacher feeder. Progress from Rancho Los Amigos Rehab Center in California led to further modifications. You will no longer be attached to spring supported slings. The bracket fastened to your wheelchair will hold mobile arm supports moving upon highly sensitive ball bearings - hence the name, ball bearing feeders. Soon after reconstructive surgery, more freedom awaits you."

"You mean I might be able to move my arms and hands? I didn't realize the surgery could be that important to gaining independence." I replied.

"Yes Danny, that's why physical therapy while you were home was so important. Not to worry though, we still have time." Dr.Johnson encouraged.

Later while sitting in my wheelchair I tried to control the urge to scream when they extended my arms out and away from my body as Drs.Oliver and

Larrick injected a numbing solution into both brachial nerves. The resulting lack of sensation was a temporary blessing during their manipulation and realignment of my wrists while casting new splints.

Recovering next morning, Rolene and Harriet entered the room waving a paper. "We have a schedule." they chorused.

"Oh,oh," gulp, gulp, achooo, "sorry." I sneezed. "This hay fever is murder. You were saying?"

"Rolene gets you in the morning and late afternoon. We will have OT after lunch." advised Harriet.

"Sounds good to me." I gulp, gulp, achooo, sniffed.

Rolene proceeded to utilize Bob's methods as she bent, stretched, and disarmed my growing infatuation. Without question, her hands were much softer than Bob's and her eyes much sexier, but pain is no respecter of persons. At first I welcomed relief from the excruciating pain associated with my new splints, but I soon realized what Rolene had meant when telling Dr.Larrick, "We'll be ready for surgery in six weeks". I wondered, "Can I survive?"

"Gee, wish I was...that brave." said Jerry. "Your new therapist...is mean. When she stretches my legs...I cry."

Sensing a need to be a strong male role model to Jerry I bragged, "Kid, some day you'll...understand the necessity ...of being cool." My bravado tenuous, inside I trembled at the thought of future pain.

"Excuse me." Maxey interrupted. "Danny you're moving next door. Orders from the boss."

"Why are you moving me...to another room?" I wheezed. "Are you concerned my sneezing...and runny nose could be... contagious? Or maybe I'm allergic...to this place."

"You just need a change of scenery." answered Maxey. "When you return from the pool this morning all your stuff will be relocated."

"Ouch, Rolene." gulp, gulp. "Take it easy." I begged. "Are they paying you," gulp, gulp, "by the tear? And just think," gulp, gulp, "I was falling in love. After you've made," gulp, gulp, "a pretzel out of my body," gulp, gulp, "please let me," gulp, gulp, "float for a few minutes. It feels great," gulp, "to move my arms and legs," gulp, gulp, "in this warm water. I'm so weightless in the pool," gulp, "it's amazing how heavy I become when lifted," gulp, "to the stretcher."

Using flotation devices attached around my waist she back-pedaled, pulling me through the water, which allowed my lifeless arms and legs to float freely. "Rolene it's impossible for you," gulp, gulp, "AB's to understand," gulp, "how wonderful this feels. Let's stay in the water," gulp, gulp, "a little longer. You know I dread," gulp, gulp, "that miserably cold trip," gulp, "through the arctic corridor," gulp, gulp, "to my room." Gulp,

Daniel R. Williams

aah aah achooo, "Oh man! This hay fever," gulp, gulp, "is killing me." I wheezed between sneezes.

"Time's up! Harry and Libby are ready for lunch and they're waiting for us to leave the pool. Tomorrow is another day." Rolene summarized. "Anyway why are you so anxious for more therapy?"

"Ah..ah..ah..chooooo." gulp, gulp. "Oh, I need help, please." I sneezed on the way back to my room. "Maxey, get me to a hospital," gulp, gulp, "I'm failing fast."

"Don't bring that sick person in here with me!" yelled a familiar voice as I entered my new room. "Wait 'til I see Doc, he should have warned me about this situation."

"Let me introduce your new roommates Danny." Announced Maxey. "Jon's back, and since you two can't stand to be in the same room with each other, Dr.Oliver arranged a reunion. Tom has the other bed. Now don't be shy, get acquainted."

"Am I glad to see you,...now maybe things will get back ...to normal around here." I laughed. "When did you arrive? I hear you're in...for more back surgery. What's up?"

"We got here while you were in the pool." replied Jon. "My parents are on their way to South Carolina. Once I have surgery, my back will be strong enough to support me," gulp, "sitting up. Of course it's back to the tank for a while. Your nose is all red. Why are you sneezing? Are you really sick?"

"Sick?" I wheezed. "No, I just," gulp, "can't," gulp, gulp, achoo, "breathe. It's hot and staff...opened windows and...spring air lets in...all that pollen." Ah, ah, achoo gulp...gulp. "Rotten hay fever!" Achoo, gulp, achoo.

"Are you taking medication?" asked Jon. "What do you think Tom, are we safe to be in the same room with this guy?"

"Wish the only thing wrong with me was hay fever." Tom whined. "I'm paralyzed."

Suppressing a laugh, then sneezing I wheezed, "Hey Jon, did you hear him? Now we really gotta worry."

"Don't be rough on Tommy." said Maxey walking into the room. "He had Guillian-Barre`, three months ago, and doesn't feel well right now."

"What is Guillian-Barre`, Maxey?" quizzed Jon. "How'd he get in the Respo Center with us Polios?"

"Guillain-Barre`, is a virus producing the same physical effects as Polio. The good thing for Tom, his paralysis is only temporary. With luck he'll walk out of here," Maxey explained, "especially since he's healthy and twenty-two."

Making a surprise appearance at the door Carol charged accusingly, "I heard you were back. Why haven't you called? If it weren't for my friends in the lab I wouldn't know you are here. Thanks."

126

Keep Smiling and Never Give Up!

Achoo, achoo, "Things have been hectic...since I got... back, and now," achoo, achoo, "I'm sneezing...my head off."

"Well don't let it happen again." she ordered. "When you arrive, ask a nurse or somebody to call. Are you all right? Why are you sneezing? Those casts must be new, they don't have any signatures. Did you have an accident?"

"Slow down! I have hay fever. My arms aren't broken, ...the doctors are just trying to...straighten both wrists ...for rehab surgery. Actually they are just...reminders of my abject stupidity." I quietly lamented.

My lunch tray arrived and while Carol fed me I told her of my winter at home. Upon finishing lunch our visit was interrupted as orderlies Nate and Harry readied me for OT. I was shoved down the hall with sneezes and gulps trailing my exit and announcing arrival for afternoon recreation.

"Morning sneezy!" quipped Dr.Oliver. "Feeling better? Hope you guys aren't too unhappy being roommates again, but I didn't think it was proper to subject little Jerry to your obnoxious behaviors. On the other hand Tom needs strong and mature encouragement. He's old enough to handle your abuse."

Achoo, achoo, "Doc, can't one of you intelligent men... do something about this," achoo, achoo, "hay fever?"

"According to the chart, your therapy is progressing as we anticipated." interjected Dr.Johnson. "We brought Dr.Olsen along hoping to interest you in a radical, non-medicinal idea for solving your hay fever problem."

Dr.Olsen nodded commenting, "Since orthodox medicine hasn't been effective against your hay fever I'm offering an alternative remedy. Are you interested? Have you ever been hypnotized?"

Achoo, achoo, "You're kidding!" I wheezed. "Who, may I ask,...will frog for me while...I'm out?"

"Hey Doc, haven't you heard? Geniuses and dumb people can't be hypnotized." joked Jon. "And he's no genius."

"Don't pay any attention to him." I nasally protested. "He's just jealous...of my red nose...and bloodshot eyes." achoo, achoo..."I'll try anything to help."

"Follow my instructions Danny." Dr.Olsen directed. "Pick a spot on the ceiling and stare while you listen to my voice."

"Wait a minute!" I gasped. "Give me my chest shell." Achoo, achoo.

Once my chest shell was adjusted Dr. Olsen continued, "Slowly, sloowly, slooowly, you're getting very sleeepy. Think of cool waters, colder waters, cooolder waters."

Opening my eyes I looked at Dr.Olsen exasperated, "See, I told you...it wouldn't work! Now what Doc?" I demanded while glimpsing at Jon. "Jon, why are you laughing?"

"I don't know how, but he had you under." Jon reported. "Ask Tom, you haven't sneezed in an hour."

"Be serious." I said. "Man, it's cold in here,...someone close the windows."

"Surprise!" chirped Rolene, as she pushed an Everest & Jennings wheelchair into my room. "Your new wheels are here, Harry from Adaptive Equipment will build a platform to carry your respirator beneath the seat, and a Hoyer hydraulic patient lifter is waiting in the gym to go home with you. Now Daniel you'll be just like the other big boys, sitting up in your own wheelchair. Ready for PT?"

Forty minutes later, my body was in total agony, and I cried, "Oooh, oooh," gulp, gulp, "you're breaking my wrist. Please have mercy."

"That's enough for today." announced Rolene. "See you in the pool tomorrow."

"Now I understand why you enjoy the pool." wisecracked my good friend Jon. "With a doll like that for a therapist the suffering would be worth it."

"Jon, what are you saying?" I protested aghast. "She's an older woman."

"Suurre." he smirked. "I seem to remember you told me she was only twenty-one."

Sunday, my day of respite arrived and I envisioned quiet solitude. Interrupting my fearful thoughts of tomorrow I heard, "Hello stranger." My father, Norman, and Mark came into the room asking, "Did you get our letter about today's visit? Hope so, everyone's waiting in the lobby. Where's the new chair you wrote about? Come on, get up! Your mom wants to visit that beautiful site by the Scioto River."

"Hi little brother." chimed my sisters as I entered the lobby. "You're looking good. What a shiny new wheelchair!"

Hugging me Mom appraised, "Danny I think you're gaining weight, have you been on the scales lately? Why do you have those casts on again? Don't they hurt?"

"The casts have become part of my body," gulp, "except in the pool and for therapy." I explained. "Remember both my wrists were drawn to the outside," gulp, gulp, "they must be realigned before surgery next week." gulp, gulp, "I wish I'd worn my splints," gulp, gulp, "while home last winter."

"I know PT and those splints hurt." said Mom. "Are you sure all this is worth the effort?"

"Who knows Mom." I said. "If everything works I should be," gulp, "able to feed myself. Even now, I'm using a new type ball bearing feeder," gulp, gulp, "and I'm learning to type using my hand and arm. You got my letter, I typed it using the feeders."

Keep Smiling and Never Give Up!

"Danny, what's a feeder?" asked Millie.

"Sis a ball bearing feeder," gulp, "is something that will help me feed myself, and type." I explained. "It's a metal tray," gulp, "holding my arm to help me move. A steel rod is fastened to a base," gulp, "and balanced on tiny ball bearings. The slightest pressure," gulp, "makes my arm and wrist move at my command."

"Oh, it's part of your bed." she nodded affirmatively.

"No, I have to be sitting in my wheelchair." I replied. "The feeder is bolted on its frame. Once balanced, my arm," gulp, "will move like yours."

Listening quietly to my explanation Mom proclaimed, "We can feed you Danny and your sisters will write your letters. Don't you think it's best if we take care of everything?"

I sighed, "Mom of course you could do all these things for me," gulp, gulp, "but I **need** to help myself."

Impatiently and thankfully Millie begged, "Can't we go now? I want to see that river again."

Driving northwest through Columbus we admired the OSU campus, then continued on to Scioto River. When returning we drove south to see Lockbourne AFB then north back to the Respo Center. En route I thought aloud, "Sure wish there'd be some way I could try on and buy a pair of shoes."

At the first convenient time Norman stopped the car for discussions with Dad, who was riding in a second auto. After receiving directions from a local service station attendant, we proceeded to the nearest shoe store. Finding a parking place in front of the business Norman said, "I'll go in and speak to the clerk, maybe he'll bring some samples out to the car. Your dad said you probably wouldn't need boots."

More than willing to accommodate Norman's request, the salesman knelt beside our car's open door and front seat as I tried various styles of shoes. Twenty minutes later I was proud owner of a new pair of black penny loafers. "Thanks everybody." I stated. "Lacing and tying those old shoes was very time consuming. Wonder how much wear these soles will give me?"

After returning to the Respo Center my family prepared for their trip home. Dad advised, "Danny, if you're certain rehab surgery on your wrist and hand is good, it's okay with us. Remember, it's your choice."

Despite Rolene's best efforts and my sweat and tears, the rehab surgery was delayed once again. Two weeks later in a final conference before surgery Dr.Larrick informed me, "Danny, PT on your right wrist has finally progressed enough, so plan for surgery Thursday. In ten days recovery should be sufficient for corrective surgery on your knuckles. It's imperative your fingers flex enough to fit the retainer and cast. A word of warning, prepare yourself for intensive therapy following the first procedure."

Dr.Johnson added, "The therapist will devote whatever time is needed to accomplish our goals."

As promised, a short interim between operations ensured painful therapy to achieve goals necessary for successful rehab surgery – the most agonizing PT of my life. Not only was my wrist sore from the recent operation; six-day-a-week PT sessions made my fingers and knuckles swell, and brought tears to my eyes on many occasions. I'd previously worn removable splints, but following the wrist fusion I was encased in a permanent cast, which denied me paraffin baths or soothing pool therapy. Trying to follow doctor's orders, Rolene forced herself to administer aggressive PT while closing her ears to my groans and cries. Glistening eyes avoided my tears and I was comforted knowing her heart shared my agony. Following a physically devastating weekend of therapy, my fingers and hand became so swollen scheduled surgery was postponed indefinitely.

The swelling diminished after a week of bedrest with my hand elevated, receiving only range of motion. Examining me Dr.Larrick confirmed, "I want you to undergo two days of PT, then expect surgery Friday. This time we'll go easier with the stretching, it won't be as bad."

Dr.Johnson asked, "Do you have any objections to being a subject for teaching purposes?"

"Not unless I have to watch." I quipped.

Entering my room Rolene announced excitedly, "I've been given permission to watch your surgery! After what we've gone through the past nine weeks, I'm entitled to keep tabs on you. Of course Sheila will watch with me in case I faint or get woozy at the sight of your blood. Do you mind?"

I shook my head, "Man! After waiting all this time now when you fall for me, I'll be out cold!"

After my operation I was transferred to a special room with Jon, who had recently undergone spinal surgery. Moans and groans were over for him, but mine were just beginning. The final stretch of my knuckles had been accomplished under anesthesia, and now swelling inside the cast was torturous. During surgery tendons had been relocated and knuckles were encapsulated with stainless steel, preventing extension of the fingers on my right hand.

"Well, how are my two favorite pains this morning?" Dr. Oliver greeted. "Jon I know you are better. How about the pain, Dan? Is your chest shell working properly?"

"Doc the surgery wasn't bad, but this cast is too tight for comfort." I moaned. "Could I have some medicine?"

Keep Smiling and Never Give Up!

"Danny, we thought you might be hurting intensely this morning," said Dr.Johnson, "so I brought Dr.Olsen with me on rounds. Hypnosis worked for hay fever and he thinks perhaps you might be interested in utilizing it for pain control."

"Hi Danny." said Dr.Olsen. "Want to try something for your pain? Remember what I said. Mind over matter."

"No offense Doc, but this involves a little more than hay fever." I argued. "I remember what you said, but as I told another doctor once, I do mind and it does matter."

"Hypnosis worked before, Dan," said Dr.Oliver, "give it another try before I order medication. First let Dr.Johnson examine the cast, and determine if it can be loosened."

"Once more now." intoned Dr.Olsen. "Focus on a spot, stare at the ceiling, and listen to my voice. Slowly, verry sloowly, slooooowly, relaaax. You are getting sleepy now. Sleeepy, sleeeepy. Your right hand is cold, coold, coolder. Think of it snowing outside. It is so quiiiet…Wake up! Danny, do you feel any better?"

"I'm not sure…would you look at my cast?" I asked. "The circulation must be cut off - my hand feels so cold."

A week in bed did wonders for strength, but once back in the wheelchair, progress slowed. Harriet pushed my OT as diligently as Rolene pursued my surgery preparation. I used Rancho ball bearing feeders day after day, intently hoping to strengthen muscles needed for feeding and typing. During this time Rolene persistently worked on my left fingers and hand, optimistic I'd soon be ready for further rehab surgery to facilitate use of my left arm. Refreshing swims in the pool with Rolene were a distant memory because a permanent cast on my right hand and wrist terminated my happiness. PT and OT had become dreaded work, rewards of which were yet to be determined.

On rounds one morning Dr.Oliver recommended, "Dan, we think it would be wise if you spent the next two weeks at home. Perhaps some rest is in order."

Dr.Johnson agreed saying, "Obviously you can't receive extensive physical therapy at home in preparation for more corrective surgery, but Dr.Larrick has informed us success on your left hand is questionable. I suggest you use the time to strengthen your right arm and become proficient with the Rancho feeder."

Rolene interjected, "Good! Danny's left hand is too swollen for me to continue aggressive therapy."

Harriet said, "Look Dr.Johnson, isn't he moving his arm well? I've provided customized utensils for feeding himself and please notice, he's typing everyday."

"Danny, this is more than we expected." he said. "Are you satisfied with the progress achieved?"

"Yes, more than satisfied." I said. "Especially when I move...my arm and hand even wearing...a heavy cast. Imagine how much easier...it'll be for me to feed myself...type, and turn pages...once the cast is off."

"Excellent!" Dr.Johnson exclaimed. "What are you typing? If it's a letter I won't be nosey, but it appears to be a story."

"Oh it's nothing important," I said, "some thoughts I'm putting together. As I told Mickey earlier...since I'm not an artist...I paint my pictures with words."

"Mind if I read?" he asked. "Hmmm, why don't you think about being a writer some day?"

"Who knows?" I responded. "Maybe I will some day."

15

MOTIVATE OR VEGETATE

Whoosh, sssss, boom, crack, sparkle, "Wowee! Fireworks are pretty huh Danny?" shouted my little brother. July 4th, members of the Williams family took possession of a Memorial Park hilltop to see New Castle's Independence Day celebration. I arrived at the gathering flat on my back because Dad and Mom had recently purchased a station wagon preparing for a summer vacation in Florida. Kenny and Mark lifted me to the ground on my chaise lounge with snide remarks referring to me as "Your Highness". More than a dozen nieces and nephews along with parents, siblings, and brothers-in-law enjoyed a picnic and festivities among throngs of strangers. Trying to appear as just one of the crowd, I nonchalantly reclined in comfort as darkness interrupted by occasional bursts of manmade galactic lights concealed my autographed casts and debilitated body. A mutual blending of spirits ensued while each of us marveled aloud as flashes and exploding splendor graced the horizon.

While recuperating from last night's excitement of loud cherry bombs and dazzling Roman candles I listened curiously to knocks at our front door. I heard Mom say, "Yes, please come in. Danny's room is this way."

"Harriet! What brings you to New Castle?" I inquired. "Checking up on me, huh?"

"I'm driving to California for vacation." she quickly explained. "The route paralleled New Castle, so I decided to stop by and observe your progress. It's nearly noon, why are you still in bed? A feeder is useless unless you sit in the wheelchair and strengthen your arm. Don't you ever feed yourself? I see a typewriter sitting atop that box, but unless you have a table, it's too low. Your mouthstick doesn't extend far enough and I dare say there's no way to maneuver the feeder at that angle."

"It's good to see you Harriet." I said, ignoring sharp questions. "So you're driving to California. I trust you have enough...vacation time for this delay. Are you driving on...US 40?"

"No, the map said US 36 was the Ernie Pyle Highway, and I enjoy historical sites." she said. My road map directs me to US 40 as I approach Illinois."

After visiting for about an hour she departed with one final question, "Shall I inform Dr.Oliver of your strenuous inactivity and lack of progress?"

"Harriet, in all seriousness," I intoned, "considering your route,...and distance for a round trip...to California, I'll see Dr.Oliver...long before you."

Harriet's words rang in my ears as I watched Mom scurry around the kitchen preparing lunch. "Maybe I should get up this evening." I shouted, raising my voice above the din. I refocused attention on the TV game of "Concentration" as my request met predictable silence. The two-week vacation with my family in New Castle concluded and I returned to Columbus where I was royally chastened.

"What do you mean, a few times?" demanded Dr.Johnson following my response to his question about sitting in the wheelchair a few times?"

"Well, Dad works days and Mom can't lift me from my bed to the wheelchair by herself," I explained, "so I only used the feeders evenings and weekends. Mostly, I just read and watched TV. Oh yeah, I played chess."

The words barely slipped from my mouth when I realized how idiotic I sounded. I guiltily looked around at doctors and nurses who'd given so much of their time to help me, and then my gaze settled on Rolene. First with eyes widened in disbelief as she shook her head side to side, then placed both hands to her brow, lowering her head incredulously. Never before had I felt such shame. The anguish and pain we both had endured for me to achieve successful rehab surgery was dangerously close to becoming an exercise in futility.

"Did you get any of your physical therapy this time?" asked Dr.Johnson. "Or did you once more take the easy way out? When Harriet returns she will continue assisting with strengthening of your arm in the feeder. Rolene, you will continue with intense stretching on his left wrist and hand. Understand Danny, you have only a limited time in which to regain strength in these Polio-damaged muscles. Our efforts continue, but we need cooperation from you and your family."

"Dan, we don't wish to belabor this point," Dr. Oliver stated, his eyes locked on mine, "but the hydraulic patient lifter was provided so one person could transfer you from bed to wheelchair."

As usual, private conversations sometimes have a way of becoming gossip and by afternoon I began receiving silent indignation from my fellow residents and their therapists. Rolene barely acknowledged my presence and PT that day was definitely not enjoyable. Midway through our quiet session I implored, "OK, I'm sorry! Yell at me, say something."

A smile barely forming on her lips she said, "Suffer!"

And suffer I did. Painful stretching of my left hand, practicing with the feeder, and repeated, exhaustive strengthening gave me all the opportunity I needed for repentance. Residents, although visibly displeased by my failure to successfully confront adversity, were aware from first hand experience, the difference between home and our Respo Center.

Days passed, eventually all was forgiven, and I began anew, struggling to regain respect of peers and staff. One afternoon Bob came into our room

Keep Smiling and Never Give Up!

instructing, "OK you guys, listen up! I'm proposing a trip to the hospital's softball game against players from University Hospital. I'm captain and you know many of the other players: therapists, kitchen staff, orderlies, even some doctors. The Medics, that's us, are in need of avid support and we've volunteered you. Therapist or nurse will accompany each person who chooses to go. Initially we planned to use our personal cars, but discovered many of them are inaccessible. Have no fear, a flurry of phone calls and negotiations produced an answer to our problem - a local taxi company offered their services in exchange for publicity. Think about my offer, I'll get your answer in a few days."

Immediately I had visions of riding in the back seat of a Chevy with Rolene. With a little coaxing I was matched with my favorite PT. Six of us were shepherded to waiting autos as Bob and the other AB men present transferred us from chair to taxi. Rolene and I patiently waited while Bob lifted the others, noticing that each required the presence of an AB to provide neck support once seated. "What luck!" I thought. "This will be more fun than the pool."

My thoughts of happiness became despair as I heard Bob frantically yelling, "Hey over here! We need help. Rolene quick! Someone needs to hold Betty's head and I think it'll be better if you stay with her while I lift Dan'l in the car and hold his head during the trip."

Disconsolate exasperation ripped my heart apart as Bob lifted me from my wheelchair. "This is disgusting and humiliating!" I thought to myself as the taxi bounced over rough streets to the ball field. "Imagine, I was supposed to have Rolene's soft arm around me, and here I sit with a football player's hairy, muscular arm bruising my neck."

After several days my damaged ego healed when Dr.Oliver requested assistance, "Dan, I need a favor. Will you please demonstrate frog breathing skills during one of my student seminars? The requirements are simple, just breathe, and I will do the rest."

"Sure, Dr.Oliver,...I'd be happy to help. Will I get any credits?"

"Lady and gentlemen, this is Dan." Dr.Oliver introduced me for show and tell. "He is convalescing from effects of Polio and kindly consented to demonstrate seldom used life-saving breathing techniques this morning. Dan will you take a breath and count until you expend the air?"

Gulp, gulp, gulp, gulp, "one, two, three, four, five... twenty-seven, twenty-eight, twenty-nine."

Leaning over me, Dr.Oliver whispered, "They're supposed to think you're sick! Take a normal breath to display your limited tidal volume, count until the air is expended. Then frog breathe and count again."

Amid snickers and stifled laughs from the audience, Dr. Oliver explained the slight misunderstanding to his medical students, and encouraged another try. I then proceeded to count, this time reaching only fifteen before exhausting my unassisted volume of air.

Back in the room while telling the story Jon laughed, "You're kidding! Last year I did the same thing. I think Dr.Oliver has a hard time catching on."

"I did exactly what the man...told me." I teased. "At least they know I can count...beyond three. Will Eugene and the volunteers...be here this weekend? Think they'll continue...the chess tournament...even though some people... are going to the fair?"

"Maybe, who knows?" muttered Jon. "Sure wish I wasn't ...trapped in this...tank. I wish I could...go. Have you decided...about the fair...this year?"

"Not really," I hesitated, "a lot of people are going."

"Yeah, most everyone." replied Jon. "I think all... the therapists are. Sure wish I could go."

"Danny, sure you're not coming with us?" Rolene asked.

"Yes." I insisted. "Jon and I must practice our chess in preparation for the tournament. Think how much stronger my arm and hand will be after moving chessmen all day. I'd probably get paired with Bob again anyway!"

Later accosting me in the gym Dr.Oliver demanded, "What did I just hear? You aren't going to the fair tomorrow? I caught all that grief last year for nothing? What's up?"

"Nothing important," I hedged, "birds of a feather, you understand."

Occupational therapy afforded me opportunities to use a mouthstick with an electric typewriter. Subsequent pressure from certain doctors resulted in my becoming editor for the Respo Center newsletter. Drs.Oliver and Johnson personally required that respo residents learn to frog breathe – hence our newsletter, *Croakers' Chronicle*. I must admit, editing facilitated my therapy and simultaneously enabled Anita, our lovely redheaded recreational therapy secretary to become a more productive assistant. When I was first asked to assume the position my quick response was, "Hey, this is a really big deal. I'm now a writer." Experience soon taught me my mouthstick would produce the majority of all articles while enhancing stories from various staff contributors. If all else failed, - hurray for fillers from *Reader's Digest*.

Writing was enjoyable and basically fun, but recruiting and organizing submissions of articles to *Croakers' Chronicle* by many other people became nothing less than drudgery. Willing friends on PT, OT, and nursing staffs, assuring that Danny did not croak over the chronicle, rescued me! We reported sports, recreation, current events, opinions, gossip, deaths, and in many instances, births. Therapists, doctors, nurses, and we Polios can be quite creative. Rumors concerning the length of time a dear aide and orderly stayed in the tub room, or who won the last wheelchair race, were all topics of serious discussion. I expended lonely hours combating effects from near-nervous breakdowns as deadlines hovered over incomplete copy. More than once I became point man for migraines.

After checking on Jon and me one day, Miss Rickard threw her hands up complaining, "Danny, if you keep any more items from the gift cart we'll have to move you to a private room. What are you doing, opening a business?"

"Could be." I teased. "Cards, puzzles, cosmetics, and games are always in demand. Need something? The toys are for my little brother and sister, I save the models for me. Everything else is negotiable. Interested?"

Miss Rickard shook her head and walked out.

"Hi guys, having a good day?" asked Carol, entering our room. "Just completed registering for fall classes at OSU. How about it? Think I'll make a good nurse?"

"I don't know...about good," quipped Jon, "but doll, you're a breath...of fresh air."

"Speaking of fresh air," I remarked, "Carol, why don't you take me down to the patio, and let's escape the hot air around here?"

"I don't understand one thing." she said as we walked and rolled to the elevator. "When you were on a rocking bed your speech was hesitant. Jon's speech in the iron lung is fragmented. It's obvious when you 'frog', but you talk like the rest of us when you are sitting in the wheelchair. Can you please explain this to a budding student nurse?"

"Okay." I said. "Remember, this is your first clinical nursing instruction. No one can overpower the cycling of an iron lung - when it breathes, you breathe. A rocking bed is smoother, although we're still required to adjust speaking rhythms to coincide with the moving bed. As you mentioned, frog breathing for most people is obvious gulps. While I'm sitting in my chair, I breathe with a pneumobelt. Breathing cycles of the respirator are more natural and once we adjust to the abdominal pressure, speech is unaffected. That, my dear, concludes today's lesson on heavy breathing. Carol, now that we're alone, tell me about this nursing career."

"I decided the advantages of providing care for people far outweigh taking blood and using needles all day." Carol said. "Not only that, OSU's school colors are attractive."

"If ever I heard a reason for such an important career choice, this is definitely it." I teased. "I agree though, I'd much rather see a cute nurse than a nasty ol' lab tech determined to stab me with needles and hurt my body."

"Seriously, my parents and I think a nursing career has a more promising future. Who knows, someday I may be your private nurse." Carol smiled coyly.

"It's good you stopped by for a visit today." I winked, changing the subject. "According to schedule, my tour here is ending. I'm leaving soon, returning in September for a cast change as an out-patient."

"Glad I'm here in time to say good-bye. Promise you'll call when you get back." directed Carol. "I'll write."

Jon's convalescence allowed him moments of freedom out of his tank, so I sat and he lounged by the nurse's station. Once while relaxing at our usual spot in the hall Jon cried, "Well I'll be, will you look at that? I don't believe it! Here comes Tom walking toward us on crutches."

"Uh oh, hope he doesn't hold a grudge." I mumbled.

"Man! Do you believe that?" charged Jon. "I think we should've held out for Guillain-Barre`!"

"Hi guys. I'm back for a pound of your flesh." warned Tom, motioning with his raised crutch. "Remember the hazing you gave me when I first came to the Respo Center? Well, I just wanted to say one thing. Thanks."

Jon's inability to remain outside the tank for extended periods of time left me sitting by myself in the corridor. Ol' bloody George approached and invited me to accompany him to the lab for brother-to-brother fellowship. Although I'd grown to dread his appearance during working hours, we spent many evenings talking, joking, and laughing while he studied microscopic results of Dr.Oliver's most recent blood tests taken from an unsuspecting dietary convert. As George took me back to my room one evening he confided, "Danny boy, I hate to admit this, but I'll miss needling you."

"Oh man!" I moaned. "Is that the best you can do? I gotta be honest," gulp, "you've been a pretty good brother. One thing George," gulp, gulp, "you better be more," gulp, "careful. I think you're," gulp, "stuck on yourself."

Departure day arrived and I left my family in Columbus and headed home for two months, though it hardly seemed worth the effort. With my friends concentrating on school I faced a steep decline in socialization. Rev.Kerschner, answering a summons from God, built Park Place Free Methodist Church and I envisioned a perfect time to fulfill my promise. Speaking to Dad I explained, "I made many vows last year and none are more important than going to church now that I've been given a second chance at freedom."

"Danny, are you sure another trip so soon won't be too exhausting?" asked Dad. "You haven't been home very long."

"Rev. Kerschner will be pleasantly surprised and I suspect God will be smiling." I conjectured. "Unless the trip from Columbus made you tired, let's go."

Upon arriving at the church I was transferred from our car to my wheelchair. Dad and Norman pushed my chair across the gravel parking lot

Keep Smiling and Never Give Up!

bumping over rocks to a smooth walk. I longed for a wheelchair with shock absorbers as my kidneys and posterior screamed. Finally my chair rolled onto cement sidewalks leading to the door and I was abruptly forbidden entrance by one of many barriers confronting all who travel on wheels - Steps! I remember thinking, "God, you're not making this promise easy to keep." Momentarily two muscular young lads appeared at the door. I declared, "I'm so happy you just volunteered," gulp, gulp, "to lift my chair."

"Oh, sure." they stammered. "Just tell us what to do."

Assisting Norman and Dad, they lifted me up the steps and I entered church.

"Danny, you didn't tell me you were coming!" exclaimed Rev. Kerschner. "I didn't expect you here so soon."

"Remember the Bible says, 'I can do all things through Christ who strengtheneth me'." Gulp, gulp, gulp, I smiled. "Besides, it's my duty," gulp, gulp, "to personally hear the sermons you preach." gulp, gulp, gulp. "Sorry to be rude," gulp, gulp, "where is your nearest outlet," gulp, gulp, "or do you have a heavy duty," gulp, gulp, "extension cord?"

He laughed, "You can either sit in front with me, or in back with the other young people."

"No offense," I gulped, "but maybe I should stay in the back," gulp, "I don't want to disrupt your sermon." Finally connected to an outlet I gasped, "Thanks Rev.Kerschner."

Confident one of my promises had been kept, I focused attention on the immediate future and began extended usage of the chest shell, eliminating need for continuous rocking bed respiration. My reasons were valid since fastening any written material on the bed's frame was quite difficult, and reading was my doorway to life's experiences. Words became my avenue for escape from daily, monotonous boredom. Dad's job at Perfect Circle then yard work on Saturdays occupied his spare time - rest for him became a rare commodity. Mom provided care for Andy and Millie, placing severe limitation on my extracurricular activities. Opportunities to sit in the wheelchair on a regular basis didn't exist, preventing any development of proficiency with my new feeders. My faithful mouthstick substituted for turning pages and I read while lying in bed, an utterly demeaning futility resulting from failed attempts to profit from aggressively painful PT. I watched dreams of anticipated physical improvement following corrective rehab surgery, fade into clouds of neglect.

Three weeks later, Dad, Norman, and I traveled to Ohio keeping an outpatient appointment for removal of my cast. I watched as Dr.Larrick's resident sawed the plaster apart and cut remaining layers of gauze inside, revealing crusty dead skin. He then snipped the dried, blood-soaked stitches and directed, "Clean him up and scratch his itches."

After soaking my hand at home to repair the detrimental effects from months of immobility, disparaging remarks were made by family members, "I didn't know it would look so bad, it really is ugly." Obviously people had expected immediate success. Results from the first attempt to feed myself minus weight of a cast and minimal experience brought more discouraging comments. My parents insisted, "We could do this so much easier and faster ourselves. Danny, you went through all that pain and surgery for nothing."

Six weeks of disappointing efforts to capitalize on the opportunity to strengthen my newly won freedom of movement left me despondent. I welcomed return to the Respo Center.

"Boy, am I glad…to see you!" exclaimed Jon when I once again entered our room. "Eugene has been…busy with college and…my chess game…is suffering. I dreamed about…Carol's companionship,…but realized you…might object."

"Why should I object?" I joked. "Carol wouldn't have anything to do with you anyway. You really shouldn't play chess with me; playing Eugene is your only opportunity to win. Remember who won the championship?"

"Maxey," yelled Jon, "get me another…room, quick."

"Well Dan'l, what sort of disaster did you bring to us this time?" Bob quizzed. "I guess you know our PT staff is being depleted by your workload."

"What do you mean?" I asked. "I simply try to provide employment for you people. Besides, after comments from my family I'm convinced you sent home damaged merchandise."

Bob laughed, "You're so lucky we aren't stretching your whole body this time around! Seriously though, you'll have a new PT this session. Rolene resigned."

"What!" I exclaimed. "She didn't say anything to me about quitting. Why did she leave?"

"I'm not sure," Bob replied, "many of us are leaving. I'm heading for Cleveland this spring to continue doctorate studies at Case Western. Maybe Rolene foresaw the absence of certain people."

"Sheila," I quietly commented, "it's fine if you're my new physical therapist and I like Betsy too, but I'll really miss Rolene. Why did she leave?"

"Who knows." said Sheila, avoiding the question. "She resigned in September after your outpatient cast change."

"This is my…sixth Thanksgiving…in a hospital." lamented Jon. "How many for you,…Danny?"

"Only my second." I related. "If I'd been chosen for Polio at eight years of age like you, it would probably be many more. Wonder what's for dinner?"

A few evenings following Jon's and my Thanksgiving meal I dutifully played chess with a good friend from OSU. "Aha, Checkmate!" Gil declared. "Come on Dan, this is three games in succession. You aren't trying. What's wrong?"

"Sorry Gil." I apologized. "A dear friend left me and my future here at the Respo Center looks bleak. Maybe I'm just getting weary of hospital life."

Gil counseled, "In my studies for a PhD in psychology I've gleaned an important lesson you must learn and always remember. Attitude adopted for any situation can determine successful outcome or contribute to utter failure." Returning later in the evening he presented me a book entitled, *As A Man Thinketh* by James Allen confiding, "Dan, the words and thoughts in this book have buttressed me throughout multiple disadvantageous episodes in my life. I know if you read and absorb its contents you too will profit from its wisdom."

Although I appreciated Gil's concern, time seemingly continued to move at a snail's pace and I lost interest in what had once been eagerly anticipated goals. Entering my room Dr.Oliver surmised, "Dan, you've been here only a few weeks, but serious consideration should be given to spending Christmas at home with your family. I know it's a long trip for only two weeks; but Christmas is a very important day for togetherness."

I passively accepted Dr.Oliver's suggestion because a lull in my progress made any disagreement irrelevant. I'd anticipated fellowship with my family, but this year holidays at home were only a short respite from drudgery. Watching Andy and Millie play with new toys; hearing ooohhs, aaahhs, satisfied giggles, and gleeful sounds of joy emanating from nieces and nephews gathered around the glittering Christmas tree, I silently gave thanks for their innocent childhood. I glimpsed the contented countenances of adults and realized how much God had blessed our family. Glancing over to the hand-knitted red Christmas stocking Carol had sent hanging beside my bed, I thought of friends far away. Guiltily, I envisioned Jon celebrating another lonely Christmas confined to his iron lung, surrounded by our Respo Center family.

Two weeks of questionable relaxation flew by before I knew it. Dad, Norman, and I left for Columbus with tires rhythmically intoning, "Don't go back, don't go back". Gazing at passing scenery I determined this would be my last journey to the Respo Center at Children's. I'd wasted many months undergoing the pain of PT, three surgeries, and who knows how many hours in OT, struggling to regain a semblance of fulfillment only to have my hopes and dreams dashed. My endeavors to regain a limited measure of independence seemed pointless, one step forward and two backward. Despite the valiant efforts of so many people to give me hope, I still confronted demons of irrelevancy in my life. Our car sped forward as a dark pall of gloom weighed heavily on my heart.

My greetings to the Respo staff were hidden behind a facade of holiday cheer as Norman escorted me through the door. "Hi." Jon mumbled as I entered our room for the last time. "Have a…Merry Christmas?"

"Sure." I replied. "Did you?"

"Guess what!" announced Jon. "You'll soon…hear. Dr.Oliver is…leaving and they…are closing our… Respo Center. I hear he…is going overseas."

"Sorry to hear the bad news." I remarked. "It doesn't matter though, I've already decided this is my last trip to Columbus. Everybody's leaving. Most all our friends, Bob and now Dr.Oliver. Rolene didn't even say goodbye. Who's left? Besides, this rehab isn't all it's cracked up to be."

"Whaddaya mean,…who's left?" demanded Jon. "I'm left! Stuck in this…tank with two…more operations …to follow. Things really look…bad right now."

Saturday after my return Carol kept Jon and I company as we watched OSU play basketball. I must say, she'd never espoused any prejudice before, but we were repeatedly told IU didn't stand a chance against Lucas and Havlicek. "Just wait," I challenged, "soon Pavey and Rayl will join Bellamy, then the pendulum swings." Following Carol's discourse on OSU's future I winked at Jon and asked her, "Would you like to play some chess? I'll be happy to teach you."

"Oh goodness, it's time to go!" she exclaimed.

A few days later Mrs. Leonadakis intercepted my return from OT announcing, "Danny we must discuss your discharge. It's important you are prepared to confront future problems after leaving the Respo Center."

"Why not?" I gulped. "My schedule is clear."

Later in her office, Leo said, "Begin by summarizing a daily routine at home, then we'll progress to your ambitions and goals for the future. Several factors are converging: you're approaching eighteen, and you've reached that crucial two year mark for maximum return of muscle function following acute Polio. Time for procrastination is over. Now tell me, why do you consistently allow physical regression during home visits?"

"It's not a simple matter of **allowing** these things." I protested. "They happen. At the Respo Center I'm totally surrounded by residents and staff who've become family. A person experiencing similar problems is a great companion. Staff respect us for what we are, always encouraging us to try harder, but happy with any progress."

"Your comments sound familiar." she reassured. "I think everybody who passes through this Center experiences many of the same difficulties. Paralysis of a family member doesn't devastate only the individual, but also loved ones. Therapy at the Respo Center has been designed to maximize corrective rehab surgery, but your records indicate repeated patterns of inactivity at home. I cannot reiterate strongly enough, persistent practice using ball bearing feeders for typing and feeding yourself must be continued at home. Sitting in your wheelchair is a prerequisite to independence. I will contact the Indiana educational authorities upon dismissal regarding transfer of your credits. This and similar vocational matters require quick attention, we can't allow your rehab to be a failure."

I declared, "Believe me, I don't ever want to undergo the agony of rehab therapy again, and it won't be my choice to waste my surgery or efforts put forth by this dedicated staff. What can I say? The people can't go home with me. We all do our best at home even though there aren't shifts of nurses and orderlies on duty. One problem, New Castle doesn't have professional home therapists for PT or OT."

Nodding she confided, "Not being paralyzed, I honestly can't say I understand. However Danny, from experience and discussion with other residents I know the vast problems you and your family confront. When Dr.Oliver and I visited your home he instructed you to memorize the motto of this Respo Center. I'm sure you've seen it mounted over the main entry, 'Motivate or Vegetate'. Motivation has become part of your life while enduring months of painful treatments, including surgery and rehab. The path of least resistance can lead to despair, please don't go home and vegetate."

On morning rounds next day Dr.Oliver summarized, "Dan this will be the last time we conduct staff rounds with you present. Your dismissal over the weekend denotes completion of a long and painful rehabilitation. Jointly, we hope you have benefited from our efforts enabling you to construct a meaningful and resourceful life."

Dr.Johnson stated, "You've progressed from confinement in the iron lung to using portable respirators traveling by automobile through the country side. Never allow negative attitudes, yours included, to diminish your accomplishments. Someday I expect to read about them."

"Dan, if by chance you haven't heard," said Dr.Oliver, "opportunity for a position in Sweden has arisen. I'll soon be leaving the Respo Center. Dr.Johnson will continue to be Director of Physical Medicine and Rehabilitation until this Center closes. Good luck, my friend."

The evening preceding my discharge from Sellers East I was surprised by a visit from my dear friend, therapist, and pool companion, Rolene. "I'm very glad you came by before I left for the last time. How did you know I was leaving?"

"Sheila told me you were here and being dismissed." Rolene responded. "I wanted to say goodbye. Seems everyone is leaving the Center, I guess it's for the best."

The ride home from Columbus evoked mixed emotions. I'd soon be with parents, siblings, and old friends, but saying goodbye to residents and staff who'd become family brought a tear to my eye. Thoughts of no longer seeing these special people created an ache in my heart.

The excitement of coming home quickly and predictably evolved into the status quo of my past. The presence of an unused typewriter sitting atop a box on a table in my room left me disconsolate. Dad and Mom were weary at day's end and weekends were my only opportunity to sit in the chair. Strengthening my arm and gaining experience with feeders was rare and I inwardly groaned at my loss. Home only one month and already I relied on a mouthstick for turning pages and TV became an important source of intellectual challenge. As when Harriet visited six months earlier, the typewriter sat much too low for accommodation to my wheelchair and its usage was minimal. Shortly after returning home physical therapy lapsed into boring and indifferent nonchalance. Excuse and rationalization are always prevalent in failures, and while environmental pressures greatly influenced my actions, I am totally responsibility for unwise, detrimental choices.

A fabled January thaw had yet to begin and heavy snow continued to blanket Indiana. While looking out my bedroom window at the cottony white pureness clinging to branches of our evergreen shrubbery I happily observed Mark walking to the door. "Hi brother." he greeted. "Danny, the basketball season will be over soon, would you enjoy going to a game? Anita says Jackie, one of her friends, will go to the game with us so we won't have an odd number. Understand? What do you say?"

"I may need snow tires on my wheelchair." I laughed. "If you want to try, I'm willing."

"Jackie, this is my brother." introduced Anita. "If he gets fresh or pinches, let me know."

The New Castle Chrysler High School field house was very crowded as Mark pushed my chair along the concourse. People gathered in small groups creating mini obstacle courses on the pathway to our seats. "It's good I brought a chair with me." I teased. "The place has standing room only."

"Yeah, there sure are a lot of people here." Mark said. "Notice the way they move over when they see you coming?"

I joked, "It's a combination of love and fear."

During halftime I re-established old friendships while continually answering the question, "How are you?" Watching the ball game being played by my former classmates elicited both pride and envy.

Keep Smiling and Never Give Up!

Contemplating the irony of me enduring two and one-half years of anguish competing with death for my life, while they attended school, had girlfriends, drove cars, and bounced balls, provoked unfounded bitterness. I said hello to Ray and Sue, struggling to maintain control of my emotions as Mrs. Hendricks my first grade teacher, hugged me whispering, "Amen". Mark bought popcorn and Coke, Jackie dutifully smiled, Anita contentedly watched as friends waved 'hello', and I faded into thoughts of yesteryear.

On the way home Anita asked, "Did you have a good time tonight? I guess from the reception you received, people do remember the past few years."

"It was fun." I responded. "Many of those people were just surprised. Mostly they remember the pictures and story of my trip home for Christmas in a tank. My wheelchair left them speechless."

Several evenings later while memories of my trip to the game remained vivid Mark came to visit. "Care if I watch TV with you tonight?" he asked. "Anita had to work late again and I'm busy baby sitting Tina."

"Of course I don't care." I smiled. "You and Sis don't spend much time together anymore. Problems? Mom will fix us a snack. Would you like something to drink?"

"Never mind." shrugged Mark. "I'm not hungry. Maybe Tina would like some hot chocolate."

A couple days later my sister visited by herself. "Hi, is Mark coming later?" I inquired. "Want to go out again?"

"No, big brother. I think we should talk. So much has happened, I don't know where to begin. Danny, I don't know what to say." Anita uttered dejectedly. "Mark and I tried desperately to conceal our problems, but marriage between us isn't possible any longer. You may be paralyzed and sit in a wheelchair, but you don't have a monopoly on trouble."

The winter of 1960 became a blur of disconcerting and painful realities. As months dragged by I lost family, use of my feeder, Rev.Kerschner transferred to another church, and friends who'd been my connection to life stopped coming by to visit. Mike, my brotherly friend, remained loyal, but school and work even prevented our usual camaraderie. With eager anticipation I awaited spring's rebirth, hoping for a new beginning. The one bright spot in my life was that I no longer had to bid farewell to parents or siblings as they left me behind in the Respo Center.

Easter Sunday once again became a day of miracles. Ten family members went for a drive after dinner. Gusty, warm breezes wafted odors of succulent springtime flowers through open windows of the station wagon. While adults happily sat in front serenely observing the countryside, children played in back, innocently entertaining themselves. Naively, they all assumed security.

Daniel R. Williams

"Ray, look out!" yelled Kenny. "That semi tanker isn't stopping. Hold onto something!"

Wham! Bang! Crash! Screams of my mother and sisters blended with cries for help from the children. Crunching of metal was momentarily interrupted by a sickening thud when Andy's head slammed against the tailgate window. Piercing sirens wailed, red lights flashed, and emergency personnel pulled injured and broken bodies from the car wreckage. Dad lifted my little brother from the mangled automobile, looked down at the unconscious and bloody child in his arms and sobbed, "Dear Jesus, help my baby son. Not him too."

A rush of activity transpired at Henry County Memorial Hospital emergency room following the accident. Thoughts of bumps, bruises, cuts from flying glass, and broken bones now gripped the minds of everyone being treated. Thank God, no deaths occurred. The Lord's presence was evident.

"Mr. Williams," said the doctor, "Your wife and Millie sustained back injuries, Andy head and leg lacerations. The X-rays indicate Mrs. Brummett and Kennetha are also being admitted with minor back injuries. Other members of your family fortunately received only cuts, bruises, and shock."

"The truck driver said he was blinded by sunlight." Said Kenny. "I think he was drunk!"

Dad explained to the police, "I watched him through my rearview mirror and straightened the car's wheels as he gained speed, but it was too late. Oncoming traffic prevented my turn and I thought he would stop before hitting us. I'm thankful our injuries aren't any more serious."

Meanwhile at home after receiving word of the accident by phone, Judy frantically rushed to the hospital. Norman stayed with me a short time until Mike arrived to "Dan sit". Dad brought Andy home Monday and my heart broke as I watched him struggling to move from chair to chair, his leg severely bruised and unable to bend at the knee. Bandages covered the stitches and mending lacerations to his head. Mom and Millie were discharged from the hospital Wednesday and other injured family members went home after a few days recovery. Life eventually returned to regulated chaos.

Summer would be here soon and I was anticipating life outdoors for a change. With front and rear steps, sidewalk accessibility for my wheelchair was impossible unless strong arms lifted my chair over the barriers. A transfer from bed to chair was difficult at best, the hydraulic patient lifter provided for our convenience was stored in the attic. I often watched sports on TV, read books, studied the encyclopedia and dictionary, eating meals while a loving family fed me, avoiding time-consuming use of ball bearing feeders. Days became weeks, and weeks became monotonous months. My close friends were now planning their college careers or searching for jobs. Some were planning marriage and family life. The days of after school visits, playing chess, enjoying music, or watching "American Bandstand" were joys of the past. The transfer of Rev.Kerschner to another church near Evansville eliminated Bible stories, devotions, and treasured spiritual fellowship. Life was changing for everyone, including me.

Days of loneliness were interrupted by mail delivery. Friends from Columbus continued to write, asking each time of my progress. Carol was particularly faithful with much encouragement, letters, cards, and occasional gifts. A lone fellow Polio survivor from New Castle visited me many times, offering words of wisdom gleaned from years of experience. JJ was chosen for Polio at age six, but through intestinal fortitude, assistance from his family, and faith, he not only completed high school from his wheelchair while breathing with a respirator, but also attended Earlham College. Empathetic of a stagnant situation from first-hand knowledge, he told me to contact University of Michigan, Ann Arbor, one of the few remaining Respo Centers. JJ said Dr.Dickinson, "Dr.D", was similar in his approach to my description of Dr.Oliver.

Taking JJ's advice I typed a letter to Dr.D. "Sir," I wrote, "for well over a year I have endured kidney problems, numerous infections, and recently passed kidney stone number five. For reasons I prefer not to explain at the moment, I do not often utilize my wheelchair or a ball bearing feeder. My lift is in the attic, and the feeder, for which I endured rehabilitative surgery, is stored in a box. If possible may I come to the Respo Center at Ann Arbor?"

16

THE PENTHOUSE

The elevator door opened and I entered another world. A sign above the Penthouse Respo Center's entrance welcomed, "Halitosis is better than no breath at all". I chuckled to Dad and Norman pushing my chair, "JJ didn't tell me anything about Michigan's sense of humor. Ann Arbor will be fun!"

"Danny? Hi, I'm Jean." greeted the nurse. "We've been expecting you. Dr.Dickinson will meet you later, now let me show you to your bed."

Preparing to leave Dad remarked, "The distance from Ann Arbor to New Castle is 230 miles and it's getting late, so Norman and I must start home. We probably won't be able to visit often, but next month when we return from Florida I think a July picnic is in order. Oh, the nurse said they would bring you an afternoon snack. Call if you need anything, we'll see you later."

Click, click, whirrr, "Hi, I'm Corky." a sandy-haired, rosy cheeked young lady announced as she approached in her electric wheelchair. "Welcome to the Penthouse. Ever been to a Respo Center?"

"Sure," I said, trying to be cool, "I spent a long time at Columbus. What's this place like?"

"Let me give you a tour by words only, I don't want to waste my battery." laughed Corky. "Dr.D. is our director, he looks like Gary Moore. You'll like him; he's a nice man and smokes a pipe with delicious smelling tobacco. His assistant Dr.Sullivan is just great, of course what can you expect from her, she had Polio like us. We call our Respo Center the Penthouse because it's built atop University of Michigan's twelve-story main hospital building. Actually we're the thirteenth story, they don't number the main floor. Our ward has sixteen beds plus an examination or isolation room. You can see there are windows on two sides affording a beautiful panorama awaiting us each morning. Where you from? Ever been to Michigan?"

"I'm from Indiana." I answered. "New Castle, it's a small town. Know what a Hoosier is?"

"A Hoosier! Poor baby!" she teased. "You apparently have been deprived of beautiful scenery, so I'm sure seeing our Michigan countryside is a sight you'll never forget. I want you to meet the other residents. There's Bill, Linda, Ron, Pat, and Bob, our resident artist. Have patience with Pat, she only had Guillain-Barre`. Oh yes, last but not least, little Billy, everyone's pet."

Keep Smiling and Never Give Up!

"I like this setting." I remarked. "Those large windows really provide a great view. After so many months of seeing four walls, this is like a breath of fresh air."

"That's what most new residents say." Corky responded. "When I first had Polio, mobility was non-existent, but now that I've been 'rehabbed' my little chair and I go most every place AB's travel. Except up steps!"

"OK Corky, relax." directed the 5'8" nurse's aide in a canary yellow uniform, her pony tail of deep auburn hair and green eyes accentuating a deep tan. "Danny, would you like some cheese and crackers? Maybe something to drink? My name is Judy and your every wish is my command. Almost! Beware of Miss Corky; she's after a husband. Oh Corky, don't blush so much, he understands. The shift is changing; get ready for another round of introductions. Oh oh Corky, here comes Dr. D and company. Let's take a walk."

"You take a walk, AB." Corky joked. "I'm smart enough to ride."

"Good afternoon Mr. Williams." said the short, handsome man with a crew cut, smoking a pipe. I'm Dr.Dickinson, or Dr.D, as I'm known around here. How do you feel? Have you rested enough from that long ride to discuss your problems?"

"Pleased to meet you." I replied. "I was informed you resemble Gary Moore, how true. My father is Mr. Williams. Call me Dan or Danny. Where should I begin? Kidney stones and urinary tract infections; lack of activity. How much time do you have?"

Arranging chairs, Dr.D and his entourage sat down to listen. "Dan, let me introduce my colleagues." Dr.D began. "Meet Theresa, our social worker, Marge your OT. You've met Dr.Riflin, our resident, and Dr.Sullivan my assistant has accompanied Barb, your PT, to a seminar. Introductions are complete, now the floor is yours. We're listening."

I summarized, "At Columbus I was admitted dependent on an iron lung, advanced to a rocking bed, and I now breathe with portable respirators. I endured fourteen months of PT, three seemingly futile corrective rehab surgeries, and was discharged home in 1960. Since then I've spent most of my time in bed passing kidney stones, struggling with UTI's, and watching all the gains I made in Columbus, vanish. Dr. Oliver gave me an opportunity to participate in experimental dietary research for prevention of renal calculi - a regimen involving strict adherence to a low calcium diet along with numerous blood and urine tests. The diet helped eliminate calcium stones, but I've since been inundated with magnesium and oxalate kidney stones, passing my fifth jewel a few days ago. Other calculi passed at home were similar in appearance, multicolored with sharp edges, and painful!"

"We read about Dr.Oliver's research program." Commented Dr.D. "Perhaps lack of sweets and ice cream contributed to your minimal weight gain. You mentioned rehab surgery?"

Theresa joined the conversation, "Yes Danny, about your operations. I'd like to know the purpose."

I explained the therapy and surgery on my right wrist, hand, and knuckles. "At the Respo Center I sat in my wheelchair daily, progressing to feeding myself and typing using a Rancho ball bearing feeder. The situation reverted to pre-rehab days after I went home."

"This is a familiar lament of many handicapped people." said Dr.D. "For the most part nobody is responsible. It's a result of limited time, ignorance, and an unfortunate lack of ambition from everyone. Regarding Dr.Oliver's diet, your failure to utilize a wheelchair for sitting, and absence of activity, contributed to your kidney problems. Would you be interested in renewing your proficiencies with ball bearing feeders? I can't promise anything until evaluation."

Theresa expounded, "I think it would be advantageous if you capitalized on new and modified ball bearing feeders. I know it shouldn't require very much PT or OT."

Marge interjected, "Listen to Theresa. Technology has achieved remarkable advances in recent years. Sophisticated and intricately balanced devices are replacing the original ball bearing feeder. We will design a custom unit to assist you with your particular requirements. Danny, you might require some additional PT, but..."

"Hold it!" I declared. "PT is out. OT's fine. Forget surgery, and no more research diets!"

Smiling, Dr.D said, "I promise, no more stretching. We have a great OT staff though, and PT range of motion is, more or less, painless. Until we eliminate your kidney problems, you will be living each day in your wheelchair, so you might as well take advantage of the time by using your feeder. We have received your previous medical records from Columbus; they charted your weight at 106 pounds on dismissal. Prior to breakfast tomorrow, an admission weight will be obtained. I will order OT, and PT will schedule an exercise program."

Following our discussion about my future I spent the afternoon getting acquainted with residents, nurses, aides, and orderlies. I gazed enthralled out pictorial windows at a Wolverine sunset as night blanketed my new horizon. Earl, one of our orderlies, awakened me as morning sunbeams danced across my breakfast tray complete with Michigan blueberries swimming in rich thick cream. I was eating enthusiastically when Marge greeted, "Good morning Danny. Dr.D. directed OT to schedule a program with Rancho ball bearing feeders."

My mouth full of blueberries, I nodded agreement then she continued, "Tell me about your experience with feeders and the equipment you've been using."

I mumbled, "Obviously my experience utilizing different appliances is only part of the problem. My feeder is stored in the box by my bedside stand and I seldom have a chance to use a wheelchair."

"I'm curious, did you have a hydraulic patient lifter at home?" Marge questioned.

"Yes." I replied. "My parents thought it was too time consuming, dangerous, and casters were the wrong size to fit under my bed. My lift is stored in the attic."

"Such a waste, such a waste." she lamented, retrieving my feeder. "Ah yes, an old type. I assume you've used a mouthstick to turn pages while reading or typing. What do you think about painting? Bob, one of our residents, is a mouthstick artist. Have you ever played chess or checkers?"

"For sure." I answered. "Without a mouthstick I'd be lost. I spend most of my time reading. When I can sit up I type, but the mouthsticks are continually breaking. Forget painting, my only talent rests with the written word. Chess has been limited recently, my friends are busy with numerous other activities or have moved away. My brother who's seven and my eleven-year-old sister are learning chess, but don't yet give me much competition. Actually they've learned to manipulate me, playing only after I agree to help with their schoolwork. Don't tell them I said that."

Laughing, Marge promised, "Tomorrow I'll arrange for a visit to our Adaptive Equipment Department. The engineers have developed unbreakable aluminum mouthsticks with plastic mouthpieces molded from dental impressions. Afterwards I'll take you to the OT Department in Kresge Memorial building."

The remainder of my first full day was occupied by many tests, X-rays, and breathing evaluations. Dinner trays were collected and I was watching another Michigan sunset when I heard Judy's now-familiar voice ask, "Danny, wanna take a ride to the cafeteria with me? It's my supper break and I hate eating alone. On the way back I'll give you a short trip around University Hospital."

Moving through long, crowded corridors I remarked, "This place is huge! I can't believe the size of that cafeteria. Incidentally, why did so many people move aside after noticing your name tag?"

Judy smiled, "I'm glad you enjoyed the tour. What I've shown you is only a small part of University of Michigan's Medical Center. The reaction to my nametag is common from most people when they see the word, 'Penthouse'. Residents are best, staff is tops, and we have good food and movies. They think we're just spoiled rotten."

Daniel R. Williams

"Don't worry about it." I responded. "From what I know about March of Dimes and Respo Centers, only the best work on these units. They're just jealous. Thanks for the tour. By the way, I forgot to tell you my sister's name is Judy."

One week after my arrival I was moved across the ward next to a bed occupied by a young man my age breathing with an endotracheal respirator. Introducing myself I said, "Hi, I'm Dan or Danny, I hear you're our resident artist."

"Hi, I'm Bob." he grinned. "I heard you...tell Corky about...coming from Indiana. Sorry you waited...so long to...see Michigan. My brother's named...Danny. He'll be here...this weekend. Don't worry...we won't get... you two mixed...up. He's much younger. Ask Judy."

"Yeah." laughed Judy. "First of all he's not in a new wheelchair, and second, he's cute."

"Zinng!" giggled Doris the RN. "She got you!"

"Not really," I dryly remarked, "I'd rather be called handsome than cute." Turning to Bob I inquired, "I know you're on positive pressure, what type unit do you use?"

Bob answered, "It's a new...respirator. See the... valve on my...pillow? A hose connects...my trach to. . the unit...under my bed. The valve permits...me to talk ...slowly between...each breath."

"Hey Doris, what about those roast beef sandwiches you promised?" I teased.

Doris answered, "Danny, this is movie night. The food will arrive later. We also have popcorn tonight."

Unlike Columbus, movies were brought to our bedside. Construction of the Penthouse had included a built-in movie screen, eliminating transporting residents to a different location. The only thing required for Thursday's movie was a good film and refreshments. Three much younger residents were enticed with early bedtimes; two older people slept from boredom, the rest of us enjoyed a weekly movie. Glass surrounding the Penthouse gave invitation to starlight shining through windows, and dreams of a world beyond.

Friday morning Marge escorted me to Adaptive Equipment, where I became acquainted with Larry and Dick, two geniuses who formed the intricate pieces of equipment for all of us from sheets of steel, plastic, aluminum, wood, etc. Unique machinery helped them design aids to assist us in developing a convenient and more independent life.

"This is Danny." said Marge, introducing me to the two engineers. "He needs some new mouthsticks. The unbreakable lightweight ones you've invented. Since he'll be using it for many activities it must be custom fitted for his mouth."

"No problem with light weight and unbreakable," joked Dick, "but custom fitting that mouth will require patience."

Marge smiled, "It sounds like you guys will get along fine. Danny if you're all right, I'll return later."

I watched, fascinated as they manufactured strong, thin aluminum mouthsticks with molded plastic mouthpieces, their machines turning, twisting, and rolling the metal. Dipping the custom mold repeatedly in a vat of hot liquid plastic, Dick formed a pliable and comfortable means of clenching the all-important instrument between my teeth. Returning later to the Penthouse with my new toys I became known as, 'have mouthstick, will travel'. "At least nobody can deny me use of this convenience." I thought. "With my new mouthstick I can turn pages to read and maybe sometime, type while lying in bed. Now reading and typing might be enjoyable."

Next morning Dr.D announced, "Dan, I think you should receive new respirators for your chest shell, oral positive, and pneumobelt. The small Bantam will sit underneath your wheelchair seat allowing you to be more mobile and can be powered by battery. These portables will facilitate travel and I encourage ventures into society at every opportunity."

The Penthouse resembled Columbus's Respo Center in many ways. Each year Dr.D and staff organized an outing for the residents, sporting all the amenities associated with patio cookouts. The party menu was similar to the food we ate at Columbus and festivities resembled a family reunion with one measurable difference, we were thirteen stories above ground level. A portion of the Penthouse was outside, yielding us a balcony overlooking Ann Arbor and UM's campus.

As the days passed I spent many hours strengthening my arm and hand in the Rancho feeder. Once situated within the feeder support, Marge placed a steel weight in my hand and I moved my arm repeatedly by using my shoulder for leverage. Gripping small rubber balls I exercised the flexing power of my fingers, then held custom designed eating utensils while relearning skills required for daily living.

Faith, a nurse's aide, participated in lady's softball leagues and made arrangements for some of us to attend one of her games. Judy's husband, Don, volunteered his car and services for our trip to suburban Detroit. Refusing to stay home by herself while we boys had a night out, Judy insisted on accompanying us as chaperone. After the four-and -a-half hour trek from my hometown to Ann Arbor, 35 miles to Garden City seemed inconsequential. The journey did prove a little embarrassing since Don's car wasn't equipped with headrests, and my weakened neck muscles still required support. As her husband drove, eyeing me suspiciously, Judy sat with her arm protectively draped around my neck. What could I say? It was Don who volunteered his services for this trip.

During the game numerous fans warily glanced toward our direction, but after four years of disability my adjustment to people's unintentional cruelty had matured with humor and wisdom. Following the game, Don, Judy, and I headed back to Ann Arbor. Using my pneumobelt with a battery-powered respirator during travel and the game, several hours had elapsed and my pressure began to slowly decrease. While monitoring the gauges Judy reflected, "Your battery is losing power, can you frog until we reach Ann Arbor?"

"I think so." I gasped. "If not there's only one smart solution. I hope Don understands."

Judy grinned, "If not, I'd be forced to give you mouth to mouth until we arrive at the Respo Center."

Don, looking at me through narrowed eyes, drove faster.

Dr.D's advice to "socialize at every opportunity" gave me a completely new perspective on life. No longer confined to a bed surrounded by four walls, I once again encountered freedom only previously experienced at Respo Centers. As we earlier planned, Dad, Mom, Millie, Andy, Judy, and Norman came to Ann Arbor for a Sunday afternoon visit. My parents, recently home from vacation in Florida, anxiously awaited a chance to review my progress. The long distance between New Castle and Ann Arbor made frequent visitation impossible so taking advantage of brief moments together, we relaxed and enjoyed ourselves at a park near University Hospital. Mom observed, "Danny, you're looking healthy. I guess Michigan air must agree with you."

My sister Judy remarked, "It looks like you've gained some weight. Maybe it's just the new color in your cheeks."

"You're right! Ten pounds, and feel great." I assured. "I've regained the four pounds I lost at home and now weigh 112 pounds. Guess what? OT's are training me with new type feeders. I'm in a more advanced rehab program."

Dad frowned, "Are you serious? Rehab again?"

"Not PT," I stated, "too much pain, little gain. I'm working with a new type ball bearing feeder, so far feeding myself at least one meal a day. I also have a new aluminum mouthstick, lightweight and unbreakable. They insist I type a lot which is great! I like writing. This battery-powered respirator makes travel so much easier, you wouldn't believe where I went last week." I described my journey to the softball game near Detroit.

"Danny, you went to Detroit with strangers?" questioned Mom. "Not only that, what about your kidneys? Didn't the ride hurt you?"

"First of all Mom they weren't strangers, these people are my family away from home." I declared. "My kidneys are fine. Sitting in a wheelchair everyday and doing something other than lying in bed makes a remarkable difference. All the diets in this world won't stop stones or infections. Dr.Oliver told me this before leaving Columbus and Dr.D. also concurs with his judgment. Mobility is the answer to good health. It's a shame we didn't heed the advice before, because I feel so much better sitting up, traveling, having a life outside my room at home. Dad, when I return suppose you could unpack my lift from the attic and we might begin using it at last?"

"I'll think about that Danny." Dad answered. "I guess it'll fit under your rocking bed once we install the correct size wheels. Time wise it's just so much easier and quicker for me to lift you from your bed to the wheelchair."

"I know Dad, but Mom could transfer me when you're at work." I hinted. "Also, lifting me wouldn't be so hard on you when you're tired."

"Why Danny, I couldn't transfer you to a wheelchair all by myself." protested Mom. "What if I dropped you?"

Andy interrupted pleading, "Danny can I play with your chess set while you're here at the hospital? Mom said no, unless Millie played a game with me."

"Before you tell him yes," directed Dad, "ask him what happened to the black horsey."

Norman said, "Boy this sure is a pretty park. I'd like to fish in that river. Maybe after you come home we'll all spend some time at the lake."

"By the time I get home it'll be ice fishing." I joked.

Norman laughed, "I'm not sure about that. With all your equipment the weight would send us to the bottom."

"Danny, are you really going to stay here for a while?" asked Judy. "Do you honestly believe there's a chance they can help you with rehabilitation?"

I responded, "I'll soon be nineteen. Hopefully, I'll get better using a ball bearing feeder and add to my skills with a mouthstick. You know I can already turn pages with my mouthstick and regardless the school system's refusal to accept my credits from hospital studies; I've gained more knowledge from reading and self-instruction than I ever did studying with private tutors. Some day I want to pursue an advanced program, by correspondence if necessary. My grasp of knowledge has been tested here at the Respo Center and I scored well above average. Experience with this type ball bearing feeder and utilization of my new mouthstick to turn pages when reading, guarantee independence from continuous supervision. Once I'm able to feed myself regularly, write via the typewriter, and read leisurely, I'll have achieved my goal. Then the excruciating pain from intensive PT and multiple rehab surgeries performed at Columbus will be worth the effort. Amazingly, I'm already feeding myself one meal a day even without long term strengthening or practice. The more consistent my training, learning,

Daniel R. Williams

experience, and daily discipline, the more independent I become. These are tools necessary for me to have an independent life."

"Danny, this all sounds grand," they said, "but do you really think it's possible for you to attend school?"

"JJ did it!" I challenged. "He not only graduated from high school, he went to college. After classes each day his attendant provided personal hygiene and put him in an iron lung for a restful night's sleep. Fraternity brothers took notes and escorted him from class to class. I can do it too with support." As daylight faded my family departed for the long trip to Indiana and I went home to the Respo Center.

Upon my return to the Penthouse Bob was talking to some guys who he introduced as buddies from Saginaw. After weeks at the Respo Center I'd gained enough confidence to engage in conversation with other resident's friends. Listening to their conversation about old times my curiosity overwhelmed me and I pleaded, "Bob, will you or your company please tell me what happened? How did you get a broken neck?"

Bob said smiling, "You wouldn't…believe it. I dove into…a gravel pit…where we'd…gone swimming…the day before. The bottom had…shifted overnight…and next thing…I knew these…guy's feet kicked…me while searching…for my body. I guess the…water wasn't deep…enough. My neck broke…at C2-3. Marines lost…a good candidate."

"I can't believe my luck!" I said. "Not only are you a semi-chosen person with paralysis, you like the Marines."

"What do you…mean, semi-chosen?" demanded Bob.

"Well, with all due respect." I quipped. "Instead of having Polio, you fractured your neck. You gained the status of living at a Respo Center by accident. Oops, better move before your buddies let the air out of my tires."

Laughing, Bob retorted, "Hey guys…don't you think…Polio paralyzed…more than his…body?"

Hearing giggles and approaching footsteps I looked over to see Doris and Judy walking to our side. They chorused, "Wanna buy a pizza this evening? We'll pay half."

"Sure." Bob agreed. "I can hardly…wait to see…Danny feed himself…pizza!"

Keep Smiling and Never Give Up!

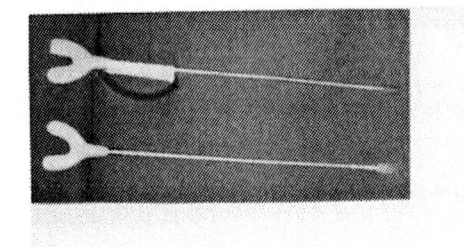

Personal photo: Aluminum Mouthsticks with custom-molded plastic mouth pieces.

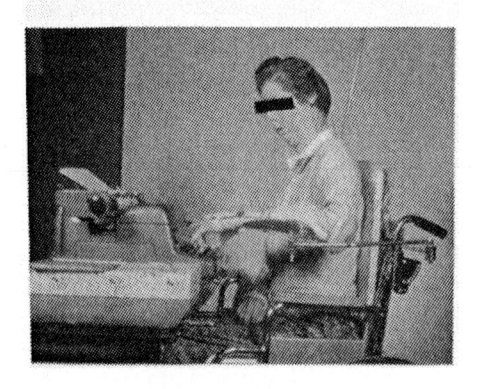

Photo Courtesy: University of Michigan Medical Center, Occupational Therapy Division, Ann Arbor, MI.
These mobile arm supports (Rancho Ball Bearing Feeders) support and enable one to move and guide one's arms and hands to type, paint, or feed oneself.

17

NEW HORIZONS

"Hey Danny!" shouted Corky from across the room. "Have someone push your chair over here, I want you to meet a good friend from the nursing home."

"Hi Corky. What's up?" I asked as Earl, the orderly relocated my wheels. "Watch it man, don't get me under that rocking bed."

"Danny, meet Noah." introduced Corky. "Noah also likes to play chess, and he's champion frog breather of the Respo Center. I told him about your exploits at Columbus and, oh never mind, I'll let him tell you."

"Nice meeting you Noah." I said. "What outlandish lies has Corky been telling you?"

Blushing, a shy redheaded young man nodded recognition.

"Lies! Boy are you something!" exclaimed Corky. "Go on Noah, tell him about your frog breathing and chess."

"Well, I was...champion of both...last year. Actually, I was...one of only three...who could frog. Chess is easy. The rocking bed...makes AB's nervous. They try breathing,...in time with the...respirator. It's a distraction...for them. Sort of a...handicap." Noah laughed.

I nodded grinning, "I used a rocking bed after escaping the iron lung, but it's impossible to enjoy reading with all its movement. While rocking I'd frog breathe to control my speaking cadence so AB's wouldn't feel abnormal. The poor souls were really confused. Oral positive, chest shell, and pneumobelt help me to talk much easier. Noah, I'm happy to learn you play chess, sometime soon we'll have a match. You know Corky will help us move the pieces - right Corky?"

Through clenched teeth Corky replied, "I'd be honored."

Rehab II progressed as planned. Shortened PT sessions and greatly increased OT expanded my visions of independence and hope for the years ahead. During my brief residence at the Penthouse a nighttime RN and I became close friends as we discussed both our futures into wee hours of the morning. Jan, a petite strawberry blonde, became my regular afternoon companion, especially on weekends. On a particularly sunny Sunday we were touring the hospital grounds when she asked, "Dan, remember that little grove of trees near the parking lot? The one surrounded by a flower garden?"

"Sure. You mean the one with a sitting area for AB's? What about it?" I asked, intrigued. "It's at the bottom of a steep hill."

"Why don't we go down there and sit in the shade?" she coaxed. "It's still early. Going downhill I'll turn your chair backwards so you won't fall out."

"Why not?" I hesitantly answered, picturing the loonngg downward journey.

As my chair rolled slowly backward down the hill I saw a thirteen-story hospital grow taller and a mountain formed before my eyes. While maneuvering my wheelchair, respirator, and battery under the swaying branches of leaf covered shady trees, Jan sighed and scolded, "See, I told you we wouldn't have any problems."

Shadows crossed our faces as afternoon rays from a red Michigan sunset created patchwork along a sidewalk and path leading back uphill to the hospital. "Jan what time is it?" I inquired. "I'm getting hungry, and the sun is setting."

"Oh wow! It's almost five o'clock, time for dinner. I guess they'll think you've been kidnapped." she teased.

With all my equipment secured we prepared for a return trip to the hospital. A few minutes later I heard grunts of strenuous exercise emanating from behind my ear.

"Ooohhh, deeaarr, stop dragging your feet!" Jan moaned and groaned. "You're supposed to be helping me. You must be gaining too much weight."

Knowing the heavy breathing in my ears did not result from a romantic interlude, I began to worry as my wheelchair wavered in its direction toward the hospital. "Jan, are we going to make it to the top? Maybe you should lock both my brakes and rest."

"I can't reach your brakes! If I let go, it's bye-bye. How close are we? I can't see with my eyes shut!" whimpered Jan, gripping the handles on my chair.

"We're only half way!" I nervously replied. "Carefully roll my chair back down the hill, then go for help."

Jan struggled to maintain control of my chair while we timidly sought refuge at the bottom. Exhaling with relief she gasped, "OK, your brakes are locked and the respirator pressure is set. I'll be back in a few minutes with help."

"You better be quick," I declared, "my battery power is almost depleted."

"Don't worry." she promised. "I'll be right back. Now promise you won't go any place."

My mouth opened as I glanced bemusedly in her direction and we both burst out laughing. "It's the heat." I said. I watched forlornly as Jan's wilted and exhausted body trudged up Mt. Never Again. Realizing my loneliness, I became aware of saturated clothing, and began watching with trepidation a bee circling amidst trees and flowers of our summer place. The liquid flowing down my brow confirmed perspiration was the cause of my wet pants, not fear. I quickly calculated the time it would take Jan to walk uphill, traverse the long corridors of University Hospital, ascend thirteen stories in an elevator, and then casually explain why I remained outside in a valley of despair. Prayerfully I began contemplating my midnight snack.

"You've got to be kidding!" Doris exclaimed. "Danny's sitting down there by himself?"

Blushing and humble, Jan squeaked, "'fraid so."

Shaking her head Doris directed, "Carl, go get Danny!"

Straining, Carl pushed my chair back up the hill, every step accompanied by a disapproving snort. "Tell me," huffed Carl, "how much does this chair, with you and your equipment, weigh?"

"Well," I replied, "when weighed on loading dock scales 280 pounds. If little Jan can push me down the hill, surely with all your muscles, you can push me up."

Jan, exhausted and embarrassed, stoically walked beside me, retracing the path of our Sunday afternoon stroll.

Eventually giggles and hushed whispers subsided and our reputations recovered. The annual frog breathing contest was held and I barely defeated Noah for the championship. A dedicated, ethnocentric Wolverine, Corky convinced Dr.D to give Noah a rematch and coaxed both of us to try again. The big day arrived and we "frogged" to everyone's amusement.

"Come on Noah!" encouraged Corky. "You can do it. Get that frog breathing title back."

"Easy Noah." said Dr.D. "Maybe you should relax before trying to out-frog Dan. Remember he's a few years younger."

"Gulp, gulp, gulp, gulp, gulp." Noah gulped.

"Noah! Are you all right?" demanded Dr.D. "Blink your eyes if you need my help. Stop! Exhale!"

Whooosh, gasp, gulp, gulp, "Thanks," gulp, "Dr.D. How much," gulp, gulp, "air did I," gulp, "frog?" coughed Noah.

"Well, at the risk of your health, you beat him by one hundred cubic centimeters." replied Dr.D, frowning. "Sorry I had to stop you, but winning a contest is not as important as remaining alive."

"Is that why...you pushed on...my chest?" asked Noah. "After I frogged...the air in...I couldn't let...it out. At least Indiana...didn't beat...Michigan - huh Corky?"

Dr.D smiled, "I think now you should rock and rest."

Marge diligently worked, teaching me how to perfect the fine art of feeding myself. Combined with previous training at Columbus and my expertise with fake food, I was becoming proficient with the real thing.

Keep Smiling and Never Give Up!

Certain foods presented all the difficulty one needed for starvation. "Come on, come on Danny." Doris encouraged. "Don't quit now, keep trying."

"Easy for you to say. These peas won't stay on my fork and forget soup. Marge is getting me swivel-handled spoons. I don't suppose while cutting up my pork chop you could give me a bite of peas?" I cajoled. "After all nurse, surely you wouldn't let a poor guy become malnourished. Would you?"

"You won't starve," Doris insisted, "and I won't cheat. Stop stalling, eat! Marianne will be here soon with Edgar. I thought you two were supposed to play chess tonight while she works with the other residents."

"You're right." I conceded. "Just in case, order me a roast beef sandwich this evening for snacks."

"Hi Edgar, ready to face defeat?" I teased, greeting my new visitor. "Marianne, you'll probably return to a broken and severely humiliated husband."

"Gads!" Edgar harrumphed. "I must say, are you well?"

"Evon, just sit that tray of sandwiches on the table by Bob." instructed Doris. "I think somebody's trying to fudge since he can't feed himself sandwiches, but let's have pity on the poor guy. Otherwise, if he loses I'll get blamed. Please feed Danny between chess moves before he 'starves'."

"Hey this tastes good!" I exclaimed. "Bob, why are all you people staring?" Suddenly I became a fire-eating dragon as Anne, Bob's mother, his dad Bob Sr, little brother Danny, Evon the orderly, and Doris burst into loud guffaws.

Gulp, gulp, gulp, "What did you do to my sandwich?" I gasped. "My throat's on fire!!!"

"I raised some great peppers this summer." smiled Bob's Dad. "Do you like the red or green ones best?"

Doris demurely winked.

"Checkmate!" Edgar once again humbled me before people I'd previously considered friends.

"Great! You're all plotting against me." I protested. "Edgar, in view of the fact your father was an English chess champion, you shouldn't resort to such shameful tactics."

"Mr. Williams, assuredly defeating you requires no such additional assistance." sniffed Edgar in his British accent. He waved bye and said, "Better luck next time ol' chap."

Acquiescing to Dr.D's advice on socializing, I savored various amenities provided by Ann Arbor and invited Jan to dinner, hoping for an opportunity to assist her recuperation from snide remarks following our downhill fiasco. Accepting my invitation she suggested, "Invite Carl and his date then perhaps this way I can apologize."

Carl, his date, Jan, and I planned an evening of fun. Corky had recently been discharged from the Penthouse, and now lived at a nearby nursing home. Jan drove while I sat in the front seat with her, Carl and Corky in back, with our wheelchairs stored in the trunk. A cord adapted to the cigarette lighter powered my respirator.

"Carl did you call the restaurant yesterday to confirm our reservations?" Jan asked. "This is Friday evening and it looks extremely crowded."

"Oh, no!" Carl growled. "I knew there was something I forgot. We'll never find a place now."

"The way you guys are dressed we better try a much more informal setting." Jan said disgustedly.

Corky piped up, "I know a quaint little place. It's a small restaurant and bar."

"What if I get carded?" objected Carl.

"Don't worry," I said, "I'll just gasp a couple times, distracting them from the situation. You drink coffee, tea, or water, and don't stumble on the carpet."

Corky gave directions to a lounge in Ypsilanti, twenty miles away. Mountainous steps confronted us in front of the entrance presenting a barrier to our candlelight dinner.

"Corky, why didn't you tell us they had steps?" Jan quizzed. "Have you really been here before?"

"Yes, but I forgot to tell you - my brother carried me into the restaurant." she answered sheepishly.

"No problem." stated Carl. "Which one is first? I'll carry one of you, while Jan brings the chair."

"Sure you'll be all right waiting outside by yourself?" Jan asked with concern. "It's dark already."

"I'll be fine. Just don't order before Carl carries me up these steps and inside to our table." I pleaded. "Jan, I could get the impression you don't like my company. You're always leaving me alone, waiting for my dinner."

I sat nervously outside the lounge door while Carl and Jan took Corky into the restaurant. Flashing neon lights and illumination from the open door spotlighted my position as exiting patrons did double takes in amazement, observing me sitting in a wheelchair before a flight of steps. Surely they were wondering if I was attempting to use the power of positive thinking. "Swell!" I thought. "What if the cops drive by? They'll never believe this story."

"Why did you take so long?" I snapped when Carl and Jan returned. "I was propositioned twice."

"Sorry, this place is crowded." explained Jan. "We had to wait for a table. Then Carl had to re-assemble Corky's electric wheelchair."

"Yeah," Carl grumbled, "I'm holding this gal in my arms while people tried not to stare."

"Are you ready?" asked Jan. "Corky's in there all by herself. We can't leave her alone."

"Poor baby," I mocked, "at least it isn't dark inside."

Carl scooped me up, straining as he climbed the steps. Entering the lounge, we squeezed by a piano, which sat inside the door. At the same moment Carl turned sideways to slide past, the piano player raised a drink to his lips. My shoe toe bumped his glass, splashing liquid onto the piano keys, puddling on the floor. Wide-eyed, mouth agape, the poor guy nearly fainted! Everyone seated at the bar simultaneously turned, looked at us in disbelief, and in unison, firmly put their drinks on the bar. We all started laughing. Covering her mouth, Jan giggled, and Carl's strength drained from his body. "Quick!" Carl yelled. "Bring that chair he's falling!"

Sitting comfortably around our table while awaiting the waiter I snickered, "Did you see those guys at the bar pale out? I bet they never drink again. I should get an award."

"You? This was my idea." Corky said exasperated.

Recovering from the initial excitement, we enjoyed our dinner and left the same way we had entered. Safely back in the car we decided a short drive was in order, embarking on a trip to Jackson, Michigan. Jan pleaded, "You have to see the artificial water falls they've constructed."

9:00 PM was not the most intelligent time to venture on a journey taking three hours. Something we ate must have affected our ability to make wise decisions. About forty miles from our objective Jan's car ran out of gas! I know, suuurre, you're thinking. The vehicle slowed to a stop, and not realizing it was a fuel problem, Jan attempted to start the engine again. Her efforts were futile and she looked beseechingly in Carl's direction. "Oh no! You're kidding." he cried. "I can't go for gas, we're in the middle of nowhere."

"Well, don't look at me." I said. "I'm afraid of the dark. Besides Jan, we're not parting," gulp, gulp, "again! Carl, this is your fault anyway. You forget to make reservations." gulp, gulp, "Someone better do something fast. The motor's off," gulp, gulp, "and my respirator doesn't have power. Jan's a nurse," gulp, gulp, "so if I need mouth to mouth," gulp, gulp, "I want her to be," gulp, gulp, "my angel of mercy."

Carl, an able bodied red-blooded American male, meekly volunteered for the hike. Off he trudged into the black of night searching for someone to believe our woeful tale. He eventually returned with enough fuel for a short trip. Dear Jan tried to start the car only to discover the starter had broken during earlier unsuccessful restarting attempts. A look of disbelieving horror spread over Carl's face as he began another desperate forage searching for assistance. As the witching hour of midnight approached, Carl, a young premed student who should've been at home tucked in bed, used gifted intelligence to rescue his helpless companions. One hour later we watched a police car and tow truck with lights flashing approach our car. We heard Carl desperately plead, "See, I wasn't lying." He stared at Corky and Jan mumbling, "You girls are bad luck!"

After a short discussion with embarrassed occupants of Jan's car, the police left laughing and shaking their heads. With a push from the tow truck we were on our way. Sensing Carl's discontent we gingerly asked, "What happened?"

"You wouldn't believe it if I told you," Carl growled, "the police didn't. The friendly service station was closed when I got there the second time, so I tried locating a pay phone to call for help. The station is five miles away and since I was almost in town, I looked for a cafe or bar. The man inside a local tavern let me use the phone, instructing me who to contact for assistance. The place was crowded and after my phone call I decided it best to wait outside on the curb. I was standing in front of the bar when a police car drove by and officers demanded an ID and explanation for my presence. I attempted to explain why I was in that vicinity and they said, "Okay buddy, that's a good story. Have you been drinking inside this saloon?"

Carl continued, "I showed them my underage ID and again tried to explain the situation. Just as they'd invited me to take a seat in their cruiser, the tow truck I was waiting for arrived, and its driver verified my story."

Shrieks of laughter accompanied each word of Carl's sad story as we began moving once again. "Considering the hour, perhaps we should visit Jackson another time." I suggested. "Wait 'til the Penthouse staff listens to this explanation. We'll be famous."

"Don't laugh." begged Jan. "I work there!"

"I work there too." protested Carl. "At least I did."

"Don't worry people, I'll tell them Corky was driving." I joked. "Seriously, thanks Carl. I needed my respirator. The power has been off for nearly three hours."

Jan parked her car outside the nursing home where Corky lived, absent-mindedly turning off the ignition. "OH! NO!" she cried out. "Now what?"

"Maybe they have an unoccupied bed." volunteered Corky.

"Make that two." Jan sighed sadly. "I'll share yours."

Carl transferred Corky from car to chair, and began his weak explanations to the charge nurse. With a plea for some understanding, he shanghaied three of the more stout nurse's aides to push Jan's car so it would start. Finally we drove up in front of the hospital about 2:30 AM, where Jan parked atop one of many hills, purposely turning off the ignition.

Keep Smiling and Never Give Up!

"At least we have a steep downward slope should we need to restart the car for a quick get away." she explained.

"Ahhh yes, doll." I winked. "Isn't this our hill?"

Approximately 2:45 AM Jan pushed my wheelchair into the Penthouse, encountering greetings of, "Well, look who's back at last." For some reason we did not receive warm welcoming comments upon our return to the fold.

"At the risk of sounding rude," Frank, the charge nurse demanded, "where have you been? Better yet! Why'd you come back?" Not waiting for an explanation, he looked at Jan and smirked, "Remember the downhill ride? I heard rumors about you two. Never mind! I won't believe anything you tell me anyway. Surely you wouldn't try to feed me that old excuse, 'We ran out of gas'. Especially since you were driving." I angrily told Frank to cool it. Jan tried without success to explain, but the charge nurse just shook his head. "Oh come on now." he taunted. "You can do better than that."

By now the entire Penthouse was awake, listening to our conversation. Amid giggles, laughs, rolling eyes, and smart remarks, fellow residents expressed their support with winks and words of, "Way to go!"

Dr.D conducted rounds next morning, or later that day. Approaching my bed with the chart, his opening comment was, "I hear you were out rather late last night."

Lowering my gaze, I grinned, "Actually this morning."

"Dan, this is no laughing matter. What happened?"

"Yes sir." I responded, beginning my explanation.

Flabbergasted, Dr.D interrupted, "Dan consider yourself temporarily grounded. Can't you just imagine your parent's reaction if they heard their eighteen-year-old son was bar hopping into wee hours of the morning? Cavorting on lonely roads? Especially with one of my nurses!"

I exclaimed, "Bar hopping! Cavorting? Where did you hear that sick nonsense? I was only following your advice to socialize. I chose to do it in a very civilized manner, in a public diner situated beside a well-traveled Michigan expressway. Perhaps the teller of this outrageous story is a bit jealous. Better check your sources."

Taking a puff on his pipe Dr.D replied, "Maybe I jumped to conclusions. Anyway for my sake, let it rest."

The lapse in my freedom and mobility created by rumor and innuendo refocused my energies. Despite the needless overreaction to Frank's mythical renditions of my dinner date with Jan, Corky, and Carl, rehab continued with a feverish pitch. Theresa tried unsuccessfully to convince my parents they should purchase another feeder, bargaining instead with local charitable organizations to fund the cost of new equipment. Repetitious practice using ball bearing feeders and mouthstick while typing helped me regain latent proficiency with various abandoned and neglected skills. The corrective rehab surgery performed at Columbus became a treasured asset in my quest for independence. Transplanting tendons and muscles; fusing my right wrist; and encapsulating metacarpal knuckles on my right hand to assist extension were now invaluable. Feeding myself dinner and typing had become eagerly anticipated exercises on my path to a new life. One typing exercise was a letter to my close friend Carol from Columbus, telling her about once dreamed of achievements.

The Penthouse Press was a resident written newsletter, formatted similar to *Croakers' Chronicle* at the Respo Center in Columbus. Executive Editor Marianne, who wrote articles and utilized material from residents asked, "Danny would you enjoy writing stories for the newsletter?"

Whether my writing experience with Respo newspapers had preceded me, or Dr.D discovered ways to deter my socializing by regimenting unstructured time, remains a mystery. In any event, I "assisted" with *The Penthouse Press*. I preferred writing, and lack of responsibility in organizing the paper promised an interesting challenge. This was soon to change! After I willingly accepted the position, resident newspaper staffers completed their rehab, leaving the Center. I coped with their absence, once again inheriting resident editor of a Respo Center paper. Fortunately Marianne, a vivacious AB, was my co-manager, her writing expertise and long-suffering patience produced wonders for our newsletter. Unfortunately I found Michigan no more endowed with willing writers than Ohio. Once I'd bid farewell to fellow resident writers the responsibility for their contributions fell at my doorstep. Obviously any spare time I had for socializing was severely limited. "Interesting," I thought, "wonder if Dr.D is aware of this situation? Hmmm."

While a Respo Center resident at Columbus I won a chess tournament between other residents, staff, and volunteers. The Penthouse chess contest was open to anyone professing a verifiable interest in the game, resulting in a larger group of excellent players. Sadly this time around I definitely operated from a "handicap". I made it to the final round, competing against Noah and Edgar. A big difference between the tournament here and at Columbus was the rule insisting we utilize rehab training. In consideration of my new skill with a ball bearing feeder, I was required to manipulate my own chessmen! Struggling to exhibit finesse with my feeder eliminated any chance to perform stunning feats at chess. I therefore quickly became a spectator. Good excuse, eh? The Penthouse chess championship regretfully traveled overseas to jolly old England, safely within the grasp of dear Edgar.

Temporary curtailment of my outside adventures produced needed penitence for the unplanned late night excursion and Dr.D lifted my probation, giving his blessing for a trip to the movies. Amidst crude remarks

Keep Smiling and Never Give Up!

from judgmental people as to the wisdom of our friendship, Jan transferred to another unit leaving Carl, my convenient and willing companion. I was pleased when Carl suggested a night on the town. In an effort to eliminate need of automobiles and late night walks for gasoline he decided to push my wheelchair through city streets. Although a fraternity brother offered his car for the journey, Carl disregarded the warning concerning hilly terrain, preferring to "hoof it".

"Tonight will be simple." grunted Carl while struggling up the first hill. "Our trip is only two miles. Last time I walked ten miles for gasoline, and got insulted too."

One mile and numerous hills later I casually inquired, "Carl, how long have you lived in Ann Arbor? Are you aware this is one of the more hilly areas in the lower peninsula of Michigan? Perhaps we should trade places for a while."

"Shut up!" gasped Carl. "Next time you watch movies at the Penthouse with everybody else."

"Aren't we grouchy! Remember you said, 'I'll pick you up in my buddy's car about six'? It was your idea to walk."

"You're not walking! I forgot all your equipment was so heavy, and I've been in Ann Arbor two years." he snarled. "These hills are not this big in a car. I'm absolutely and summarily convinced YOU, not the girls, are my bad luck."

Reaching the movie theater Carl wiped rivulets of sweat from his furrowed brow, purchased tickets, secured my chair in the center aisle, connected my respirator to an outlet, found a cool quiet place to sit, and collapsed.

Following the second presentation of the movie I deemed myself an expert on the dialogue of "Judgment at Nuremberg". Looking at Carl contentedly sleeping his life away in a cool dark theater I suddenly remembered Dr.D's admonition. "Carl wake up man! The movie's over." I snapped. "If you sleep through this one more time I'll be late again and we both know what will happen. Remember, it's only two miles."

En route to the Penthouse Carl remarked, "I'm sure glad it's cooler now. See Danny, I told you this would be a good evening. We could invite Jan and Corky to dinner, but they would probably want to drive."

Carl and I retained a very close friendship even though he refused to go on any outings with me, Jan, or Corky for dinner or movies. Certain ruthless colleagues persisted in singing renditions of 'over hill, over dale', whenever Carl came on duty, but he ignored their snide remarks, continuing to encourage my rehabilitation and on-site socializing.

Daniel R. Williams

Returning to the Penthouse after a difficult afternoon in OT I commented, "Boy, am I hungry! I'm glad it's dinnertime. Hey Judy, where's Ron?"

Judy answered, "Frank and Dave pushed his iron lung out on the balcony. Ron wanted some fresh air before evening. He better come in soon, it looks like rain."

"Someone please help me bring Ron back inside." Frank requested. "The sky looks angry and I can't push that tank by myself. Ron's also ready for dinner."

"Here comes the food." announced Judy. "Frank, carry a tray and make yourself useful."

"Okay, but just for a minute," Frank bargained, "Ron's waiting for me to bring him back inside."

About twenty minutes later rain began pelting furiously against windows as thunderclaps reverberated throughout the Penthouse and streaks of lightning illuminated darkened skies. "Where is Ron?" demanded Doris.

"Oh #X%*!" shouted Frank. "I got busy and forgot about Ron. He's in his iron lung outside in the storm!"

I smirked, "Frank you're such a good nurse! You of all people who had the haughty audacity to challenge Jan and me after our misfortune. Physician heal thyself!"

A mass exodus of nurses and orderlies stampeded outside to Ron's rescue. Amid a mixture of curses directed at Frank and "Thank God" for everyone else, Ron in his tank was soon retrieved from a front row seat to nature's fireworks.

Nonchalantly feeding myself I stared at Frank and shook my head. "One question nurse," I chided, "ever think about finding employment elsewhere? Maybe another state?"

Following three more long months of rehab Dr.D and his staff gathered round my bed announcing, "Dan, in a few days you will be ready for discharge. The progress you've made in such a brief time is remarkable; especially the expertise developed using customized ball bearing feeders. Combined with more diversified uses of your mouthstick, I think this has been a successful rehabilitation. Your unassisted breathing time has increased as a result of persistently practicing frog breathing. I'm satisfied, does anyone else wish to offer any comments?"

"As you are aware," stated Marge, "Danny's arm and hand movements were so weak we designed and manufactured a custom ball bearing feeder. In addition to skills he's acquired with a mouthstick from long hours of practice; hard work and forceful persuasion have allowed him to enhance his typing with use of this special feeder. Our goal of Danny feeding himself at least one meal a day has been achieved. Excluding any unforeseen

Keep Smiling and Never Give Up!

complications, and assuming he'll receive continued steady encouragement after going home, I think rehab for now has been completed."

Theresa summarized, "Mental aptitude tests, discussions with Danny, and his desire to write indicate definite goals for independence. Although his formally sponsored education was limited by bureaucratic red tape, he has overcome this disadvantage by self-instruction. He personally combated a tragedy resulting from a paper jungle and registered high on our educational profile. In short, Danny has potential for success, he only needs opportunity and encouragement."

Dr.Sullivan, speaking from experience charged, "Outside encouragement is only part of the answer. Danny himself is responsible for making wise, appropriate choices."

My last weekend at the Penthouse arrived much too soon and I spent the final hours Saturday evening telling fellow residents and staff who had quickly become family goodbye. While discussing the baseball season and Detroit's chances at winning a pennant, I was greeted by Edgar and Marianne. "Well ol' chap, we hear you'll soon be departing. For your information, we too shall soon be leaving the colonies; my wife and I are proceeding home to a more civilized world. I have earned my PhD in political science and Marianne misses her mum."

Marianne interjected, "Danny, my husband is keeping the proverbial English stiff upper lip. His father is ailing."

"I'll miss both of you." I confided. "Your friendship and kindness in visiting me have brightened my life. Edgar the chess games were challenging and special, my knowledge revolving around intellectual warfare is progressing. I'm especially appreciative of the opportunity Marianne gave me to write for *The Penthouse Press*. Collaborating with you on its production has solidified a lasting friendship. Marianne, I'm sure you will continue teaching special ed, but Edgar pray tell, what possible advantage do you hope to receive from your doctorate in political science?"

"Your wit of mind is exceeded only by the intensity of your body's paralysis." Edgar quipped. "Since Marianne must tend to various odds and ends in preparation for our exodus, what say, you and I engage in one final game of chess."

Marianne directed, "Danny don't dignify his remarks by listening, his English father mistakenly informed him he was part of the British aristocracy. I'm sure you know we both have enjoyed our relationship with you, and seriously, when you return to Ann Arbor we will be gone. Don't forget to keep writing stories, maybe someday they'll be published. I will leave you two now to one last chess game."

Nearly one hour and many moves later (extended I'm sure by Edgar's desire to leave me with a favorable and indelible impression) I proudly

Daniel R. Williams

exclaimed, "Checkmate!" Hmmm, after so many untold losses, why did this win occur now?

Warm summer months of exposure to Michigan countryside became more vivid as I observed Bob paint beautiful scenery while clenching in his teeth a mouthstick attached to paint brushes. I watched him create intricate pictures depicting leaves and flower petals painted with an exquisite precision unsurpassed by many AB's. His creative artistic renditions of waterside life, boats, docks, and fauna were impressive. Imagine lying in a reclining position with a frame suspended before him specifically for painting pictures on canvass and paper. Everyone was awestruck by his mastery, marveling as he originated heavenly reproductions from his uniquely clear perspective. It's rare to meet people with real courage and I'm thankful for the privilege of Bob's friendship. While observing him paint I recalled many able-bodied people who squander God-given talents. With unabashed admiration and envy I thought if only I could write words like he paints. What a divinely wonderful gift Bob has been given.

Anxiously awaiting Dad and Norman's appearance Sunday to take me home I conversed with Bob's family and Penthouse staff. Bob Sr. offered me a sack of red peppers in memory of a special sandwich and Danny, Bob's brother, assured me he'd keep Bob in line. Anne, Bob's loving mother, hugged my neck promising to faithfully write letters. Saginaw, their hometown was nearly one hundred miles north, eliminating any quick round trips. Every weekend they lived at a motel so they could visit Bob at the Respo Center in Ann Arbor. What an incredibly close family.

Just as I thought my farewells were complete in walked Carl with his girlfriend. "Hi Danny, I wanted to introduce you to my new movie companion. She wouldn't believe you're real and questioned my honesty when I told her how you and the girls got me in trouble."

"Carl, thanks for coming to say goodbye before I left." I grinned. Looking in her direction I shook my head saying, "He's a nice guy, just be careful what you believe."

"Danny!" Carl exclaimed. "Next time, YOU go for gas."

Entering the Penthouse at noon Dad remarked, "Ready to travel? Norman and I will pack your belongings in the wagon then return for you. What's in the box?"

"It contains my new custom built ball bearing feeder." I responded. "I now feed myself and type. If all goes well after this rehab, I'll be writing."

18

SHADOWS UNEXPECTED

"Danny let us help." urged my parents. "They said you could feed yourself, but this really takes too much time and effort. Wouldn't it be easier if we did it for you?"

"No, just give me a chance." I protested. "Of course feeding myself will take longer. Don't forget, today is the first time I've used this feeder since coming home from Ann Arbor two weeks ago. Without practicing and exercising every day the muscles in my arm are certain to weaken. Unless I sit in my chair more often, independence is just a dream."

"Danny you really haven't been well enough to use your wheelchair or new feeder." Mom said. "Do your side and back still hurt as much sitting up as they did in bed? I wonder how you traveled so many places at Ann Arbor without having kidney problems."

"I know." said Dad. "He wasn't riding 230 miles on his back, bouncing on a lounge chair in the rear of our car. If the hospital just wasn't so far away."

"My side's killing me and I'm nauseated, Dad please put me back to bed." I pleaded. "Better call Doc and tell him I'm having a rock slide again."

Dr. Heilman stated to my father, "I gave him additional pain medication. I think he should go back to the hospital. First acute Polio, now kidney stones and infection. Danny's paralysis obviously contributes to his kidney problems, but immobility interrupted by lengthy, bumpy rides is definitely a reason for these recurrent illnesses."

I heard Dad speaking into the phone, "Dr. Dickinson this is Danny's father. He has a kidney infection and our family doctor says it's the result of kidney stones. Dr. Heilman's given him pain medication because his chest shell is putting pressure on the place he hurts. The rocking bed's movement increases pain, and he's having breathing problems...Yes, he just got home, but our doctor believes he should return to Ann Arbor. What do you think?...Are you sure? It's really a long trip. OK, I'll ask him."

Laying the receiver down Dad returned to my room where Dr. Heilman and I waited his instruction. "Dr. Dickinson said to use oral positive pressure as much as possible to relieve some of the pain caused by the shell, and to frog breathe. He said if you feel like making the trip there will be an iron lung awaiting your arrival."

"No! No! No!" I shouted adamantly. "It took months for me to escape that prison, I'm not getting back in the tank!"

"Danny listen." Mom pleaded. "You've got to breathe. Besides it'll only be a little while."

"You don't understand!" I exclaimed. "A minute is too long. I can't go through that ever again."

"Son," Dr.Heilman said, "I can't keep giving you pain medicine, it's affecting your breathing."

Surrendering disconsolately to overwhelming odds I said resignedly, "Why not? Let's go."

After a quick call to Norman, Dr.Heilman medicated me for the trip and shortly we headed for the Respo Center in Ann Arbor, nearly five hours away. Fortunately with power for my respirator via the car's alternator, I rested. As promised by Dr.D an iron lung stood at the ready, prepared to imprison me in a life I'd thought was history. When they closed the tank, sealed its portholes, started the motor and bellows whooshed, my pain eased. I breathed comfortably for the first time in many days. As feared, horrible memories, which had encompassed my days in isolation after first being placed in an iron lung, forced me to relive searing anguish.

Due to the late hour we arrived, darkness was settling, so after hurried consultation Dad and Norman departed for home. I watched their reflection in my tank mirror as they walked away from me toward the elevator. Alone again, this time my heart ached as I thought about all the gains I'd lost. Exhibiting bravado in view of staff and fellow residents, I tried vainly to restrain tears welling in my eyes. Just two weeks ago progress had surpassed everyone's expectations, but now I found myself once again viewing life through an iron lung mirror.

The next morning Dr. D advised me of his plan to locate the source of my problem. "Shortly, Earl will escort you to X-ray where you'll receive a special radioactive dye which will highlight the calculi within your kidneys and urinary system. Once diagnostic procedures are completed I'll meet you here to conduct the usual pulmonary examinations. Dan, you realize return to the iron lung will necessitate blood gas studies. Are you breathing better?"

"I'm breathing fine...Dr.D. Can I have...any pain medicine...before taking all...those tests?" I inquired.

"Sorry Dan." he apologized. "You need to be strong and alert during these tests so you can frog breathe adequately. I will order medication for pain control once you return to the iron lung. Before I leave, welcome back. Even though you were only home two weeks."

"Thanks a lot...Dr.D. It's really great...to see this...place." I remarked sarcastically. "I hope the... tests won't...take long. The pain is...really sharp so ...please be sure...you write that...order."

An eternity passed while I endured endless testing and multiple X-rays. The technicians were all sympathetic to my plight because they were aware of my previous improvements. They knew me from times I'd been pushed through the halls of University Hospital and I repeatedly answered, "Why are you lying on a stretcher instead of sitting in your wheelchair?" Fortunately they chose to ignore my foul mood. En route to the Penthouse following tests, I heard, "Danny! Danny! Why are you back? What's wrong?" As her familiar voice reached my side Jan grabbed the stretcher continuing, "You should've called. I'm on duty now, but I'll be up later."

My tests completed, I finally returned to the Penthouse and rest. I refused to eat, but accepted frequently offered glasses of liquid. Exhausted and dozing, I silently praised Dr.D for ordering my pain medication while saying to myself, "What a way to end summer!"

I watched in the mirror as Dr.D approached my tank, his head down, "You have an infection. I don't know how you got them, but there are three stones in your right kidney, and two in the left. All but two are passable, we think it's best to wait this one out rather than create any additional problems. You are on a potent antibiotic regimen, so please drink copious amounts of water, and staff will periodically reposition you in efforts to flush the stones. I understand waiting for results is frustrating, but it's preferable to impulsive surgical intervention."

"This is just...great." I lamented. "Dumb diets... blood tests, and...finger sticks for...nothing!"

"Don't be hasty in your judgment." cautioned Dr.D. "We don't know the content of your stones. They may not contain calcium, in which case your previous diet was appropriate."

"Be patient, Danny." encouraged Dr.Sullivan. "You must drink at every opportunity, and tinkle lots."

Little did I realize their importuning me to drink more abundantly included meals. I shuddered when my dinner tray arrived, but was amazed at the variety of liquid food. When Jan had come to visit and comfort me last night I was sedated from pain medication; this evening I looked forward to seeing her, even if it was through an iron lung mirror. While awaiting her appearance I challenged Evon to a game of chess, but had second thoughts considering he was on duty. "Evon, I sure...do appreciate...this chess game. Since Marianne...took Edgar home...while I was...on a brief ...sabbatical...I lost my...chess partner. I'm afraid you...might get in...trouble though...playing chess on ...work time."

"I may work here as an orderly," Evon replied, "but we all need intellectual exercise. And you need water."

"Don't ask me...to drink any...more." I protested. "I'm ready to...burst. My parts will...get rusty."

Walking up Judy charged, "Your parts are already rusty. Drink! Here's Jan, she'll pour some fluids down you."

Evon joked, "You better drink, it's checkmate anyway."

"Am I ever glad...to see you!" I sighed. "Judy and Evon...are picking on...me."

"I'm sorry," Jan soothed, "here, calm down and drink."

"Aw Jan,...I'm tired of...swallowing. Can we just ...talk a while?" I requested. "The atmosphere here... is changing."

My patience began to wane as I awaited stone delivery and the September days of summer slipped by, warm weather a memory. Storm clouds were replaced by streaks of gray forming across Michigan skies accentuating perspectives of a bleak autumn. Newly employed nurses orienting at the Penthouse listened to roars of approval and boos of discontent echoing from the UM football stadium as sounds of athletic warfare permeated the Penthouse windows. Thirteen stories below and one-half mile away, a hundred thousand fans filled the poignantly cold air with loud enthusiasm. Listening to joyous sounds increased my level of impatience as I waited for problems to pass. I attempted different distractions including a telephone call to Carol in Columbus. Even though realizing Dr.Oliver had left the now-closed Respo Center, I remembered better days and envisioned more rapid progress at Ohio State University. Without discussing my intentions with Carol, I called Dad to ask, "Will you come...pick me up...at Ann Arbor...then transfer me...to Columbus? I've now waited...six weeks without...improvement in...the situation. If I get... lucky maybe...bumpy roads will...shake these stones... loose so...they'll pass."

Dad hesitated, "I'm not sure this is a good idea, but I'll call Norman and see if he wants to take a joy ride."

"Dan, you are making a big mistake." Dr.D warned. "How will you breathe without an iron lung for an overnight stay at home? Remember, Columbus is no longer a Respo Center."

"It doesn't matter...my friends will...take care of me." I reasoned. "Breathing wise...I'll tough it...out with my...chest shell. There are...380 miles...from here to...New Castle...and OSU. If nothing else...the ride might...bounce a stone...loose. Dr.D...I've got to...try something. I'm wasting...time."

"Dan, listen to me." he cautioned. "You've lived in an iron lung for six weeks, your breathing must be reacclamated to portable respirators. Don't expect miracles at Columbus. Hear me. Your decision is against my medical judgment."

A disheartening scene greeted me upon arrival at Columbus. A once dynamic Respo Center had deteriorated into a shell of its former magnificence. In the short time since my last admission, the doors of Sellers East had been closed and its area relegated to storage and classes. I was placed in a semi-private room so small, my bed's head and footboard touched the wall where particles of hidden dust fell onto my pillow. I cringed, experiencing the disgust and utter humiliation of one deceived by time. With great sadness I decried my stupidity and wondered if I could bend my knees far enough when asking for Dr.D's forgiveness.

After examinations and summarizing my medical history I stared forlornly at the cracked ceiling above. Interrupting my silent discourse with memories, Mrs. "BB" Hanover entered asking, "Danny are you comfortable? Why have you come back to Columbus? We heard you were in Ann Arbor."

"Mrs. Hanover I'm glad to see you." I smiled. "Maybe I just missed your 'butter bullets'. I thought a change might speed things up. I'm trying to pass stones. Basically, I'm fine. What happened to our beautiful Respo Center?"

Shaking her head she laughed, "I guess I've never heard of anyone traveling so far to get a suppository. Once the Respo Center closed and special people stopped coming here, everything went down hill. The old staff has mostly left. Speaking of leaving, anything you need before I go?"

"Well there is one thing," I ventured, "would you phone someone for me? Remember Carol? She's now a student nurse at Children's Hospital and lives in the nurse's quarters. I can't wait to see the surprise on her face."

"No problem." BB answered. "See you later."

Late that afternoon as I planned a strategic retreat, in walked the one bright spot of this lost battle. "Carol, am I ever glad to see you! Oh, surprise!"

"Danny, what do you think you're doing? I could hardly believe my ears when Mrs. Hanover called and said you wanted to see me, here!" Carol voiced her exasperation. "When we talked a few days ago, you didn't mention a visit."

"Carol, I knew you were rotating through Children's for your clinical nursing experience and I certainly didn't want to bring added pressure to your life." I explained. "Lying in the iron lung at Ann Arbor was discouraging and I needed a more rapid solution to my problem. Now that I'm here I see impatience and good memories really clouded my judgment. Thank goodness you're here, I need support. Incidentally, would you feed me supper?"

Kissing my forehead she said, "Sure honey, drink!"

The same tests were repeated, antibiotics resumed, and liquids forced. The days were spent in a drab cubbyhole as I contemplated my next move. The urology department quickly snapped into action, scheduling surgery for

Friday. "Maybe I should take things a bit slower," I thought, remembering Dr.D's warning that impulsive surgery could be complicating.

"You're what? Are you crazy?" demanded Carol. "Danny you don't even have an iron lung! What respirator will you use after surgery? Do you realize this means a tracheotomy? Is there something I'm missing? I know you want to get well quicker, but come on, be patient, wait this out!"

"Thanks a lot." I quipped. "First I return to remains of a beautiful Respo Center only to find it a shadow of its greatness; I get ensconced in a phone booth; I'm yelled at by a dear friend; and doctors threaten me with knives. What support!"

"Ordinarily that would be funny," remarked Carol, "but this is not a laughing matter. You're facing major surgery tomorrow, without any preparation for your respirator. It's difficult to understand how you are breathing now with only a chest shell. Submitting your body to needless pain isn't wise. I'm here to support any effort to improve your health but I do wish you would seriously consider the consequences of your actions. Maybe it would help if you just swallowed your pride and returned to the Respo Center at Ann Arbor. I know they have more expertise with iron lungs than we do at Children's because we no longer have a Respo Center. Danny I'm glad you came back to OSU, but no more surprises."

"Carol, you're making great sense." I conceded. "Guess you've become quite the nurse and philosopher. Please call my parents and give them a message. You're right, I'm going home and wait this out. Thanks for being here for me."

After quick consultation with the surgeon I withdrew my consent and BB hurriedly packed my belongings. Saturday a veil of shame covered my face as Dad and Norman squeezed into the phone booth. Dad bewailed, "Danny, this is ridiculous! We delivered you to Columbus on Tuesday, and now this weekend you're coming home still loaded with stones and infection. I don't wish to be nosey, but would you like to travel any place else your highness?"

Following a bumpy and painful return ride to New Castle my stoic resolve drained into the urinal. As predicted, the journey assisted in dislodging gravel, stones, and created further problems with infection. Surrendering to discomfort I requested Dad phone Dr.Heilman. When he arrived I tried to rationalize my behavior over the past few days saying, "I don't know what happened Dr.Heilman. The long trip between Ann Arbor, New Castle, Columbus, and New Castle again surely caused the problem. Maybe the bleeding will stop soon. It hurts, but I've already passed two stones."

Keep Smiling and Never Give Up!

"Danny a large portion of blood fills your urinal every time you go to the bathroom." Dr.Heilman cautioned. "You'd better return to Ann Arbor. I'll personally speak with Dr. Dickinson at the Respirator Center."

Midway to Ann Arbor Norman grumbled, "Danny, this time you better get it right! The forecast is for snow. Before you know it, Ray and I will need a doctor for kidney stones from all the traveling we've done as your chauffeurs."

"Well look who's back." smiled Dr.D. "Couldn't breathe that Ohio air, huh? We kept your bed warm while you were on a tour around the tri-state area. Seriously, let's get some more pictures and, since you're back in the iron lung, you will require more blood gas studies. According to your dad you've lived in a chest shell for ten days. Your CO_2 must be elevated because after only a short time in the tank your color is improving and you're becoming sleepy. Perhaps we physicians are right, oxygen is important. The quart of bloody urine you brought from home is en route to the lab for analysis. I will order its disposal unless you need physical evidence of your little caper. I imagine inner contemplation of your impatience will occupy many days and nights."

"Yes sir! I'm staying...right here. Expect me... for Thanksgiving...if necessary." I humbly replied.

"Happy Birthday, Danny." chorused the Penthouse staff.

Time passed with ever decreasing speed, while boredom of my situation enhanced the monotony of each day's reality. November 10th, my nineteenth birthday, was celebrated in the Michigan Respo Center. Three stones had passed and each day I anticipated another delivery. Mary, one of our new RN's, displayed a distinctive longing for northern Michigan and homesickness shone in her eyes as she announced, "Mom says the snow is already two feet deep in the Upper Peninsula. I can't wait until my Christmas days off work. I'm gone!"

"Turkey dinner was excellent for cafeteria food." Earl reported, returning from his Thanksgiving meal provided by the hospital. "Danny, did you enjoy your food?"

"Sure." I muttered. "Feeding myself...Thanksgiving dinner...was last summer's...goal. Rather difficult to ...achieve while trapped...in this tank. Oh well,... grin and bear it."

After returning from my adventurous journey to Columbus I spent another six weeks in the iron lung. Reacclimating to portable respirators became necessary following extended periods of living within the vacuum of a tank; therefore, I tried on many occasions to breathe with chest shell and oral positive pressure. Stamina I once had evaporated, passing with kidney stones, infections, and time wasted in idleness.

Daniel R. Williams

"Dan today we're transferring you to bed once again so you can attempt breathing with a chest shell." Dr.D stated. "According to X-rays, two stones remain in your kidneys, but you've stopped passing gravel and the infection has cleared. Once you're breathing sufficiently with a chest shell maybe going home for Christmas can be achieved. I'm certain you'd rather be in New Castle during the holidays. An unnecessary absence would only precipitate depression."

Steeling myself to the discomfort created when I used the chest shell, I gained strength from Bob's example and encouragement from staff while adapting to portable respirators again. The experience of escaping an iron lung twice left me fearful I couldn't triumph a third time. While staring at snowflakes sliding down warm penthouse windowpanes I awaited Dad and Norman's appearance to take me home. Inwardly I vowed if at all possible to avoid future imprisonment in a steel cocoon.

"It's snowing heavily." announced Dad, as he and Norman packed my respirators and other belongings onto a stretcher. "Maybe we can get away from here before the roads are really impassable."

Looking out a window Norman mused, "Does Michigan ever have anything but snow during the winter?"

I grinned, "Yeah, sometimes they have lots of ice."

"Humph!" Norman grunted. "Ready to leave?"

"Yes, but I don't," gulp, "shovel snow or change tires. Dad did you install," gulp, "heavy duty springs in the car?" I laughed. "I'd prefer a smoother ride," gulp, "then maybe I could spend winter in New Castle. Let's go," gulp, gulp, "I'm not in the habit," gulp, gulp, "of frog breathing."

Enjoying the secure comfort of home, relaxing in my own bed wearing a chest shell, seasonal festivities became more inviting. "Merry Christmas family! After a Thanksgiving in Michigan it sure is good to be home for the holiday. Dr. D is correct," I nodded, "hospitals can be depressing."

"Danny isn't my Christmas puppy cute?" Millie gushed. "I always wanted a Collie and since he looks like Lassie, I'll call him Laddie."

"Get ready little sister," I advised, "your puppy will quickly grow bigger than you."

"Thanks for my new chess set Danny, now I won't have to borrow your game." Andy grinned.

Weeks passed and I longed for days of old when friend's visits were part of my life and memories burned brightly. I soon realized convalescing from a bout of kidney stones and lack of any goals led to apathy. Strength lost during iron lung incarceration left me unable to sit in a wheelchair and denied me use of my feeder. I continuously utilized a chest shell enabling extensive reading of books containing stories about real people and places. These pictures in words gave me glorious avenues for education, recreation, and escape. Encyclopedias, dictionaries, world almanacs, magazines, and newspapers, replaced formal educational opportunities abrogated by petty bureaucrats and red tape jungles. Biographical novels and non-fiction literature allowed me participation in life, joining in activities and visiting many places forbidden all people coping with paralysis.

Weekends were time for visual recreation. As I watched a football game one Sunday Anita entered my room announcing, "Danny, I want you to meet Jim, the man who will soon become my husband, and your new brother-in-law. We're planning an early springtime wedding."

"Pleased to meet you Jim." I responded. "Anita told me the very weekend I was diagnosed with Polio in 1957 you had delivered milk to our door."

Jim replied, "That was a few years ago. Now I install plumbing and soft water systems. You could say my business is fixing rusty pipes."

"In that case," I said, "how about fixing mine?"

While reading *Accent on Living* I became interested in constructing a typewriter table to fit over the bed, such as the one Mickey my OT had wheeled over me at the Respo Center in Columbus. After consideration I decided it would be much too involved for Millie or Andy to build at their age, and Dad didn't need another job. In time, maybe in time. For now I would have to find contentment in reading.

Alone in my room behind closed doorway curtains one morning, I heard Laddie barking furiously at strangers outside the house. I tried calming him with clicking noises and calling his name. Then I watched horrified as he responded to my kind signals. All eighty pounds of him burst through doorway curtains, leapt onto my bed, and landed on top of me while I sat enthroned on the bedpan. Wagging his tail, whoofing, and slathering my face with his livery wet tongue we became lifelong buddies. Prior to this intimate encounter, I had only admired Laddie from a distance because of his size. His enthusiasm for a new friendship was crushing.

April Fool's Day arrived and I began arranging a return to Ann Arbor. Several months had passed without any decline in discomfort resulting from two recalcitrant kidney stones, which had refused all efforts of delivery. These stubborn "gems" caused infections requiring antibiotics, which negatively influenced any possibility of regaining my strength. Lying in bed was excellent for reading, but eliminated any hope of progress in sitting tolerance or feeder experience. Letters to Dr.D requesting re-admission to the Penthouse for a checkup and evaluation brought an affirmative reply.

"Danny will Laddie be safe by himself while we take you back to Michigan?" asked Millie. "He gets so lonely."

"Don't worry Sis, he's big enough to take care of him-self, and you'll be home safely by bedtime." I assured her.

Daniel R. Williams

Mom, Millie, and Andy replaced Norman for this journey back to the Penthouse. The station wagon was fully packed with respirators, wheelchair, personal belongings, and me in the back. Repeated illness had accentuated my inability to breathe comfortably without oral positive assistance, and frog breathing quickly depleted my strength. Years had gone by without my fear of suffocation surfacing, but sadly I now required backup, necessitating a battery-powered respirator. Approximately 125 miles from our destination, panic struck. "Daddy the car's on fire!" screamed Millie.

"Dad, my respirator is burning." gulp, gulp. "Battery cord is smoking." gulp, gulp. "Fire is coming," gulp, gulp, "out the side vents." gulp, gulp. "Pull off the road!"

"Oh my Ray! Hurry!" cried Mom. "What if those paper sacks catch fire?"

The slow speed dictated by Fort Wayne traffic presented a dilemma, but vehicles parted and Dad slammed on the brakes bringing our car to a sudden stop on the berm. Scrambling to the tailgate Dad jerked out the battery cord and snatched my burning respirator from our station wagon. To be sure, life had just sunk to a new low. Without battery power for my respirator I was forced to rely on emergency hand bellows (ambu bag), and my trusty frog breathing for survival.

Andy whimpered, "Daddy are you sure the car won't burn up? I'm scared! Let's go home."

Millie, my twelve-year-old sister, in a precocious and professorial tone assured, "Everything will be okay little brother. I'll help Danny breathe with his emergency hand bellows. Remember? He taught us how to use them in case we had trouble with his equipment."

Exhausted from frog breathing and re-instructing Millie on how the hand bellows must be cycled with her breathing, I arrived at Ann Arbor. "Danny, it's good to see you again." welcomed Doris. "Why are you so pale? Come on, your bed is ready. Bring him over here, Earl."

"No!" gulp, "I'm wearing," gulp, gulp, "my pneumobelt. Connect my respirator," gulp, gulp, "to the outlet now." I gasped. Breathing comfortably for the first time since we left New Castle I sighed, "Thank you! Oxygen really helps alleviate suffocation. Let me rest a few minutes and I'll tell you what happened. Everything's fine now."

A few breaths later Dad left for the return trip to New Castle and Doris intoned, "I'm glad you're sitting in your chair. Danny, let's go to the porch where we can have a private discussion." After connecting my respirator to an outlet she sat down beside me revealing unhappy news. "We waited until your return before telling you. Bob's dad died."

"What? Oh no! What happened? When?" I questioned.

Keep Smiling and Never Give Up!

Doris hesitantly spoke, "In January he had a massive heart attack. Bob Sr. walked upstairs one morning to dress, and when he didn't come back for several minutes Anne went up to the bedroom, finding him sprawled on the bed, already cyanotic. Resuscitation failed and medics had to carry him past Bob's bedroom across from the steps. At their request, I went to Saginaw and stayed over a week at Bob's house to take care of him while Anne coped with the funeral. I thought you should know this prior to Bob's return. It's still a sensitive subject, so please be tactful in your conversations with Bob, Danny, and Anne."

"I can't believe so many people wrote letters to me at home and yet didn't tell me anything about his death. Why?" I asked in frustration. "I'm glad you told me."

My first week back at the Penthouse was interesting as I had penetrating discussions with equipment reps from The March of Dimes. "Tom, are you serious?" I asked horrified. "I've been using this unit ten months and you're now telling me the cooling fan doesn't operate on battery power? Thanks a lot pal! Do you realize we were almost toast?"

Jerry, another equipment rep said with relief, "Luckily no one was injured. Don't worry, the newest respirators are equipped with backup systems for auxiliary power should AC not be available. You'll be outfitted with one of these new units, obviously your old respirator is history."

Wednesday morning Bob arrived as Doris explained, "OK guys we've rearranged the beds so you two can tell each other wild stories. Danny, Bob recently had a tragedy in his family, so I'm sure he needs a friend right now. It's strange you both manage to show up at the same time."

Most of the familiar staff were still employed at the Penthouse, but there was a steady influx of new residents in for medical checkups. Carl was now in med school, Evon had left for Phoenix, and Dave was a fire fighter. Don applied for entrance to the California State Highway Patrol and if selected, Judy would obviously move with her husband. Jan was planning to climb the mountain of marital bliss. With all the changes, father time was exacting a disastrous toll upon the residents and Respo staff family at Ann Arbor.

Corky edited *The Penthouse Press* from her nursing home room several miles away. Our resident family of Polios was slowly dwindling. Thanks to Salk and Sabin, Polio attrition was reaping a harvest without replacements. Spinal injuries like Bob's swimming mishap, Bill's uneven trampoline descent upon his neck, or auto accidents filled the Penthouse. Some uninformed people declined an opportunity to experience the excitement of Polio, opting instead for Guillain-Barre` from an allergic reaction to immunizations against influenza, ensuring a covert avenue to rehabilitation. The increasing absence of new Polio was both encouraging and frightening as we began to understand that although our time in history was secure, our unique era was indeed ending.

Reconditioning my body to wheelchair and feeder was a dull, boring experience. Rehab had become a repetitious and futile exercise. Drs. D. and Sullivan, along with Theresa and Marge confronted me one morning challenging, "All right Daniel, snap out of it."

Theresa said, "I did not strive to acquire your custom feeder so it could sit idly by your bed. The sooner you've readjusted to its use, the sooner life will improve."

Dr. Sullivan charged, "Danny the infection is gone and your kidneys are better, so stop giving us Polios a bad name. I think you should look around young man, we are a vanishing breed. Only the resilient will survive."

"I think these ladies have summed up your situation." Dr.D. concurred. "Kidney problems were rare while you were active and except for the extra baggage of renal calculi, nothing has changed. I'm curious, why don't you venture out with your friends? Go to a show, or maybe dinner. Please though, do not stay out until 2:30 AM."

Shamed by their cutting observations, I decided to get back some of my self-respect. Phoning my friend I yielded, "All right, Corky, I'll write some stories for the paper, if you promise not to quit your job as Editor."

"Great!" she exclaimed. "Let's celebrate! I'll invite Carl and you ask Mary to dinner. Just like old times."

"No way!" I protested. "I won't be yelled at again."

Corky snickered, "Maybe you're right."

"Hey Earl," I beckoned one day, "let's have some fun. After lunch step outside and pocket a small pebble, when you return I'll use the urinal, then you drop the rock inside. Innocently ask Doris to empty it because you're busy helping Bob, and watch our blushing nurse go bonkers."

"Forget it man!" objected Earl. "You're passing kidney stones and they're straining your output."

"Earl," I explained, "that's what makes this plan such a beautiful idea."

"Danny if I do that, I might get fired." Earl worried.

"Don't fret ol' buddy." I calmly assured. "I received instructions from Dr.D to 'get a life'."

Earl returned from lunch with a rock the size of a big walnut. "Are you sure this is smart?" he asked, before it dropped noisily into the half-full stainless steel urinal.

"Now sit it on the table, pull Bob's curtains, and call Doris to empty the urinal while you assist Bob." I directed.

Earl hesitantly followed "our" plan sweetly requesting, "Doris please assist me over here while I suction Bob."

Keep Smiling and Never Give Up!

"Oh Earl, I've got my hands full." protested Doris. "I will be there in just a minute."

"Hey you guys, stop laughing." I warned. "Even if you are behind a curtain, she'll hear you."

"Here I am." said Doris. "What do you need?"

"Would you please empty Danny's urinal, he needs to go again and I'm right in the middle of suctioning Bob."

Doris responded, "Sure I'll empty it, but I won't give Danny the urinal. That sir, is your responsibility."

Clang! Plunk! Doris screamed, "Oh my word! Earl, you rat! Wait 'til I get my hands on you."

"Don't blame me." he grumbled. "Blame Danny."

I listened to Doris's totally unnecessary verbal abuse, then winked saying, "Remember the pepper sandwich? Gotcha!"

Listening to conversation and laughter permeating our Respo Center when Earl's practical joke became known, I was certain my life had rebounded, especially when word leaked about Doris's retrieval of a rock from the torn sieve. With this encouraging note I directed my life to a higher level.

Everyone was anxiously awaiting the heavyweight fight between Liston and Patterson, including residents and staff.. Taking advantage of an opportunity for entertainment I said, "Everybody agreed? The loser pays for our pizzas."

"Let's see now." said Mary. "We all draw numbers from a box, and if our choice gets knocked out or loses in this round, we pay for the pizza. What if it's a draw?"

"No problem. We'll just split the money and each pay our own bill." I explained. "Sarge, while you were in the Marines didn't you tell me operation directors were neutral and not required to buy their own ticket?"

"Not a chance, Dan! You fork out dough just like every one else, or don't eat." he ordered. "Okay everybody, quiet down! It's time for the match and I want to hear when Sonny knocks him out. It better not be quick, I drew round six."

"No way Vern..." Bob laughed. "Patterson will win."

The "fight" ended quickly and we enjoyed our pizza.

"Good morning Mr. Williams." Dr.D greeted on his daily rounds. "Well, haven't you been a busy little bee lately? First you scare one of my nurses to death, endanger another orderly's employment, and now you organize a numbers racket! When I said start living your life again, I didn't mean for you to go about disrupting ours in the process. Especially with some of my employees! I called your father. (Pause) Don't worry, I just told him you're ready for dismissal."

183

Four days after returning home Dr. Heilman moaned into the phone, "Oh no, not again! He just got home. It must be the ride that shakes everything loose. Strain his urine. I'll be there in a couple hours."

Three weeks later I arrived back at the Penthouse, to gleeful words of staff members. "You just left!"

While I was absent staff rearranged beds once again and I was now living in a different area of the Center. It took nearly all day for Bob's bed to be moved next to mine, so I met some new friends, Howard and Betty. David their son, a resident or should I say patient was convalescing from a hit and run auto accident. Howard was a well-known professional football player, so David was visited by his father's team and I fortunately made the acquaintance of Terry, Nick, Joe, and, of course, Hopalong.

I went to sleep each night watching purplish clouds as they drifted by Penthouse windows. Shivers of loneliness and awe accompanied my gaze as I looked at flickering lights of Ann Arbor's skyline. Eventually my eyes drooped lazily and exhaustion of another active day consumed me in restful sleep. One night I awakened to shrieks of panic and I humorously observed George, the night orderly, pleading with Mary to release him from bondage. Inexplicably she'd lured him onto a portable tilt table (platform on wheels), strapped him helplessly, and now shoved him mercilessly around the Penthouse. I watched as Mary, our quiet, shy, demure, loveable sweetheart of an RN, circled the ward with her prisoner, consoling him as he begged for mercy. Disappearing around the corner I heard George scream, "Please, let me go!" Completing another tour of the Penthouse I heard Mary's giggles and his screams fill the air. Mary was indeed having fun! Trying to control my laughter and attempting to present deep concern for George's safety I said, "Mary, remember the dear supervisor will be here some time tonight."

With a devilish grin on her face she said, "I knooww. She just left."

The final days of summer left us with humid, sweltering weather. Penthouse air circulation thirteen floors up was usually excellent, but today's suffocating atmosphere clung oppressively. The stunning unobstructed view from my corner location between two large windows forced me to watch irate skies and consider avenues of escape. The beautiful setting which afforded us a magnificent countryside panorama became menacing as we witnessed a yellowish green horizon and heard dire storm warnings broadcast on TV. I nervously stared at swirling black clouds just beyond my eagle's nest hideaway, contemplating our pathetic lack of protection. Rumbles of thunder and streaks of vicious lightning encompassed us and intrepidity surrendered to vulnerability. Torrential rains spewed through open windows, drenching everyone.

"Close the windows!" yelled Mary. "But leave them open enough for the pressure to equalize."

Keep Smiling and Never Give Up!

Staff rushed around the Penthouse battening down every hatch, attempting to shut out an invasion of sheeting rain. A terrible roaring noise deafened shouts of alarm as windows shattered, our feeble and broken defenses breached by angry expletives of Mother Nature. I looked back at Jeri only to receive a face full of glass. Flying missiles were everywhere! Our bodies and beds were blanketed by millions of minute glass shards, but thankfully the slashing fragments caused no serious injury. David escaped danger since his bed sat strategically behind a solid wall protecting him from harm. Bob received a minor cut, and my eyes sustained corneal damage. Mary pushed the emergency button and staff reacted with courage, speed, and proficiency, moving us to the hall for safety. Provisional repairs to a now windowless Penthouse were quickly completed and residents received first aid. Incredibly, none of the staff sustained injury and life soon returned to "normal". Doctors bandaged Bob's cut, flushed my eyes with saline, and restored a semblance of calm before the delayed supper trays were delivered. Quiet ruled once again as we thanked God for our safety amidst a stormy September 13th afternoon.

When Dad and Kenny brought me back to the Penthouse six weeks ago I had purposely sent my wheelchair and feeder home to New Castle. I knew the physical exhaustion accompanying more rehab would probably drain my body of needed strength, delaying recovery from another kidney stone and infection. Staff along with Dr.D had been quite upset with me saying, "You're giving up Danny and letting Polio win. The Respo Center is no place for quitters."

Their words ringing in my ears, I watched Mary, a PT, who'd become a good friend, administer exercises to Bob as tears of anger stung my eyes. Biting my tongue I thought, "You AB's just don't understand the problems." Turning my head in Mary's direction I asked, "If I cajole the orderly to get me a borrowed wheelchair, would you accompany me this evening to the cafeteria for a Coke and sandwich?"

"After what I just heard," she replied, "you need it."

Sensing their encouragement was falling on deaf ears, Dr. D eventually gave me a green light for dismissal. "Dan, I think it's time for you to travel home again."

In recent years leaving the Respo Centers had given me inexplicable moments of regret, but confronting separation now didn't seem to matter. Many of my friends were either gone or anticipating change, which promised to leave a void where love and respect had reigned. My thoughts centered on these traumatic future events as the evening shift went off duty. Before she left Judy walked to my side commenting, "I will have moved to California by the time you come back, so I'd better say goodbye now.

We've made some great memories, don't forget those days when you're feeling down."

I smiled, "Are you kidding doll? Please drop me a note sometime and don't forget us."

Judy hugged me saying, "I could never forget you, Bob, or the other special people. Danny, I know you haven't let a few setbacks defeat you, but there's no doubt in my mind the guy I'm talking to today wouldn't go to Detroit with me. You better think. Enough lectures, see you again I hope."

Aware I had received some friendly advice to shape up, I quietly began setting goals hoping to get my act together. Previously when I'd ignored similar thoughts the results were more disastrous consequences. Events connected with recent incidents in my life underscored a need for more determined action. The promise I made long ago to do my best was being neglected, I decided inane procrastination must end.

Previous years of painful rehab effort was decidedly in the process of being wasted. I spent monotonous days at the hospital in bed, drinking water, and taking medicine. This time around I'd totally ignored rehab, but I had no doubt following multiple X-rays and cystoscopies I would glow in the dark. Forlornly watching out Penthouse windows while awaiting Dad and Kenny's arrival, I struggled to combat the vicious emotional cycle of bitterness and defeat in which I was now entrapped. Although historically the ride home had always been disastrous to my health, I decided crisp autumn air foretold a Michigan winter, another reason to leave. An unusual silence cloaked the subdued conversation in our car on the way home as we all contemplated the trauma on my body resulting from other journeys to Indiana. Cold breezes of discontent and seeds of impatience encompassed my thoughts, "Didn't I do this last year?"

19

CHANGES

The trip home from Ann Arbor was uneventful. Familiar potholes and expected bumps foreshadowed a predictable rapid recurrence of kidney problems. In less than a week after my arrival home in mid-September I gave birth to kidney stones. In keeping with past experience, an infection followed with all attendant repercussions. Dr.Heilman was again summoned and I received the customary dose of antibiotics.

After repeated visits to accommodate my usual problems Dr.Heilman said, "Danny it's been nearly three weeks since I began this regimen. You need X-rays and another cystoscopy to determine if I'm treating your problem correctly. At the risk of precipitating further difficulties, do you feel well enough for a journey back to Ann Arbor?"

"With all due respect, Dr.Heilman. No!" I charged. "The trip's too long, riding dislodges more gravel, infection and pain then inflict damage. Quite simply, I'm tired. Testing only takes a few days, so what do you think about contacting Robert Long Hospital at the IU Med. Center in Indianapolis?"

Approaching the emergency entrance at Long Hospital Dad remarked, "Did you like this shorter trip better Danny? It sure is easier for us to travel 60 rather than 230 miles to Ann Arbor."

"Yeah boy I like this trip." chimed in Andy. "Remember going home we get to stop for White Castle hamburgers."

Thanks to Dr.Heilman's pre-admission arrangements with colleagues at Long, I was escorted through emergency to my room. I stared in amazement at a sign over the doorway to the unit entrance, "Ward C". What irony! Five years ago I began an odyssey through the pitfalls of Polio as a patient at Riley Hospital less than two blocks away. Now by a quirk of fate I entered Ward C again - same pew, different church.

"Welcome Mr. Williams," greeted the nurse, "your bed is ready. I trust you can educate the staff and me about your respirators. I'm sure you're familiar with hospital routine so please have patience as we learn. I've never worked with this type respirator. Is it new?"

"Hmmm." I pondered. "So I'm now a hospital patient." I answered, "No, ma'am, I've used oral positive respirators over four years. It may look like a compact suitcase, but the Bantam is really a positive pressure machine. Years ago when I graduated from the iron lung it was already in use."

"Oh, were you in an iron lung?" she inquired. "Then I bet you probably know several people who are still employed at Robert Long Hospital."

"Probably not." I said. "My original hospitalization occurred in Riley's isolation ward."

"Just by chance," she said, "do you remember Mrs. Hunky Dory? We were classmates many years ago."

"Mrs. Hunky Dory was my private duty nurse for two long months." I said. "Incidentally, I'm Dan, not Mr. Williams."

"Your dad introduced you as Danny. I like that better. My name is Mrs. White. Where were you hospitalized when you got out of the iron lung?"

"I've been a resident of two different rehab centers. The Respo Centers at Ohio State and University of Michigan." I explained.

"At the risk of displaying my ignorance, what's a Respo Center?" she questioned.

"A Respo Center is simply a contraction of respirator and Polio rehabilitation center." I began. "They are places where agony of defeat is snatched from the jaws of despair, emphasizing Churchill's words, 'blood, sweat, and tears'! They, fortunately, gave me a second chance."

Mrs. White smiled, continuing a cursory orientation of Ward C and introducing me to the nurses. Indicating a cute little student nurse, Mrs. White stated, "Danny this will be your nurse for the day. Dottie is our Dixie Darling."

Dottie blushed. "Aaww Missus White. Hi Danny."

"Daniel, my name is Dr. Waters. We will begin tomorrow morning with blood tests, IVP, and more X-rays. I have scheduled a cystoscopy in two days. Dr. Heilman is my friend and he instructed me to take good care of you."

I scanned twenty beds along the walls of Ward C. They were all occupied with sick people! "This is a bad place." I thought. Gone were happy times at the Respo Center.

"What's that noise? Can't a guy can't get some needed rest at this establishment?" shouted a patient on a circular bed. "I'm going home!"

"Shush Jim!" scolded Dottie. "Our new patient breathes with a respirator, you'll hurt his feelin's."

"More than that'll hurt if he wakes me up again." Jim threatened. "What's wrong with him anyway?"

"Danny had Polio, he's paralyzed too. Neither one of y'all could punch your way out of a paper bag." Dottie joked in her Tennessee drawl.

Jim ordered, "Flip me back. I gotta meet this guy. At last there's somebody here who might know what's up."

As the circular bed revolved on its frame like a Ferris wheel, Jim assumed a supine position. Spying my respirator he snickered, "Man, you look uncomfortable with that turtle contraption on your chest."

Keep Smiling and Never Give Up!

"Surely you jest." I sniffed. "Strapped to that silly monstrosity, how could you accuse someone in a regular bed of looking uncomfortable? I've been demonstrating Polio, what happened to you? I hope it wasn't a dumb accident."

"Well I could start by telling you I was in the Navy, but you probably wouldn't be impressed." He chortled. "My name is Jim and basically the swimming pool where I dove was too shallow and I fractured my neck. I'm visiting Long this time for skin and kidney problems. Who are you?"

"As Dottie said," I replied, "my name is Dan unless you are speaking to certain motherly types, then I'm Danny. It must be something in the water, my plumbing system is also on the fritz. I'm paralyzed from Polio, but never mind if I can't walk or move anymore, dancing never was a big deal. I met a guy at the Respo Center in Ann Arbor who fractured his neck while swimming and was totally paralyzed. From what he said, I guess the bottom moved for him also! Bob had a C2-3 break requiring respiratory assistance via a trach. When we were residents at the rehab center he was in for treatment of a decub on his tailbone. After seeing his situation I'm thankful only motor nerves were lost when I had Polio, so sensory nerves can warn me of pressure and help prevent trouble. I've never had a decubitus."

The remainder of my first day at Long was filled with blood tests and routine X-rays. Next morning I received the promised IVP and my kidneys were highlighted by radioactive dye. Dr.Waters delivered the expected news with his morning visit. "Dan, you have two large stones, one in each kidney. Also there is a large accumulation of small stones or gravel on both sides. Tomorrow, plan for a cystoscopy."

I observed a young nurse visiting Jim, assisting him at mealtime. Not wanting to intrude, I refrained from asking her name or their relationship. The second day he shouted, "Hey Danny Boy, meet Sue my girlfriend."

"It's a pleasure to meet you Sue. I truly admire your courage." I teased. "Tolerating that guy requires a lot of patience. I'd rather be called Dan, but you know how some people can be, especially those stubborn Navy types."

Later in the afternoon I was taken to a treatment room and prepped for a cystoscopy, another in a long succession since Polio. For those of you unfamiliar with this procedure, one is placed in "stirrups" as for childbirth and the urologist introduces a urethral catheter with a scope through which he views one's bladder. Experience had muted my embarrassment and discomfort associated with this exam, but today's cysto was a bit different. The room in which it was performed had windows level with a driveway into ER. Midway into the exam I glanced at the window witnessing a carload of people going by with their mouths agape, viewing what surely resembled pornographic filming. Obviously someone neglected to ensure privacy by closing window blinds, thereby exposing me to the public. I suavely commented, "Do you think I could charge admission for this show?" After initial screams, angry words from my doctor, and muffled laughter from technicians, dignity was restored.

The change from Respo Rehab Center to ordinary hospital was traumatic. Close friendships developed during lengthy admissions are quite different from momentary fellowship in acute illness. Surrounded by "patients", Jim and I quickly accommodated each other's need of encouragement, friendship, and camaraderie. Confronting this abrupt alteration was too depressing, so I chose to go home and recuperate following four days of examinations. I adhered to doctor's orders, swallowed medicine with copious amounts of fluids, and rested. Incessantly reading was now difficult due to the weakness of my eyes, so I responded by allowing my dear babysitter, TV, to hypnotize me once again. Circumstances prevented my sitting up to type, so Vivian and Judy took dictation as I practiced the art of writing. The situation in which I now found myself created much dismay, as I couldn't erase thoughts of having endured pain, work, and elective surgery enabling me to use a ball bearing feeder, only to see my goal of independence destroyed. Endless Rehab days of repetitious practice ended, and I suffered the indignity of losing my ability to type. Sitting in my wheelchair was a seldom-afforded luxury as suffocating dependence on other people continued choking my life. Days of autumn passed slowly, monotony gained speed.

I quietly celebrated my twentieth birthday at home with good memories inundating my thoughts while reading birthday greetings from many dear friends. Family, doctors, nurses, and acquaintances remembered me at this time in my life. I especially appreciated a card from Aunt Zella reminding me to "keep smiling".

The house overflowed with family members as together we celebrated Thanksgiving, two weeks after my birthday. With three married sisters all bringing specially prepared food, the menu was much improved over customary hospital cuisine. One more holiday at home and I would set a record unmatched since diagnosed with Polio. I gave thanks while eating turkey with my family.

One month later I cheered, "Merry Christmas everybody! Today indeed is a special time together. Do you realize I haven't celebrated three holidays at home in five years? We've found a great way to remember 1962."

Early spring arrived without more kidney problems, but my vision became increasingly blurred. The shattered glass that scratched my eyes during a Michigan storm last fall was interfering with my preferred avocation, reading, making it a chore. Stinging, unfocused, watery eyes indicated need of an appointment with Dr. Burnett, Ophthalmologist.

"Of course it'll work everybody." I assured. "I grew up in this neighborhood and all the driveways and curbs are familiar. I rode my bicycle, delivered papers, and played many years on these sidewalks."

"Let's see," Dad ruminated, "I lift you into your chair at noon, taking you down the steps before I leave for work. Vivian and Judy then push you over sidewalks and through the driveway cutouts to Dr.Burnett's office one mile away. You return, Jim stops by on his afternoon break and helps bring you back up the steps. Once home, you plan on remaining in your wheelchair until I get off work at 11:30 PM. A twelve-hour marathon including bumpy rides on steep hills. Danny, you can't be serious."

"Think about it this way Dad." I reasoned. "Either we follow my plan, or you miss another day's work. Of course, Mom could use my hydraulic lift and put me in bed."

"Mush, you girls!" I encouraged. "We're almost to the hilltop. Keep pushing! If you love me, don't let go."

Dr. Burnett greeted, "Welcome to my office. Be seated ladies. I'll be with you in a moment Dan."

"No problem, my chauffeurs need a rest." I joked. "Dr. Burnett, would you examine me while they stay in the lobby?"

"Certainly Dan." Dr.Burnett agreed. "What do you mean chauffeurs? I thought they pushed your chair to my office."

I answered, "They did. I don't have a hydraulic cartop lift, and they can't carry me. Dad's at work and I refuse to walk on weekdays. Besides, they need exercise."

Amidst harrumphs and chagrined stares from Vivian and Judy, Dr.Burnett chuckled, "I don't see a seat belt securing you to the wheelchair. Aren't you worried about falling out of your chair as you descend hilly Indiana Avenue?"

"Rest assured I've thought of that." I asserted. "My sisters will just roll me backwards down the hill, sloowly."

Heat from exertion motivated them to navigate a shorter route home. Midway to the bottom of the first hill I once again experienced a surge of adrenaline similar to that day in Ann Arbor when Jan and I climbed Mt.Never Again. Aware additional help was nonexistent, Vivian and Judy strained to control the speed of my descent. Many huffs and puffs later we made it home as they vowed to think twice before shoving me around again. Personally, their big brother enjoyed the new exercise program.

As previously scheduled, Jim appeared at 4:00 P.M. and pulled my wheelchair back up the steps. Although I sat in my chair for extended hours at the Respo Centers my parents having never been a part of this life remained unconvinced I could persevere until Dad returned home. Games of chess and cards with my brother and sister grew boring so watching TV helped pass the time while Mom worked upstairs. By 10:00 PM I began to feel the effects of my journey and quietly sought to maximize comfort, asking Millie to recline my wheelchair. For those unfamiliar, a semi-reclining wheelchair must remain sufficiently balanced to provide a stable foundation. When this balance is disturbed the chair assumes a precarious position, especially with a heavy portable respirator sitting beneath the seat. Attempting to relieve pressure on my posterior I asked, "Millie, would you please move my feet off the pedals and place them on the floor?" Weariness apparently clouded my judgment because I overlooked the fact my wheelchair was not braced against a wall. Millie lifted both feet at once following her big brother's irresponsible request as scenes of horrible consequences flashed before my eyes. No sooner had she raised my feet than the wheelchair tipped backwards, bouncing me head first on carpeted floor. My thirteen-year-old sister stared down at me with bulging, fright-stricken eyes, on her ghostly pale face.

"Now you've done it!" yelled Andy. "Wait 'til mom sees this. Hey Mom! Millie's killing Danny."

Peering down at my crumpled form, Millie gasped with a shaky voice, "Are you okay?"

Trying desperately to sound calm I frog breathed deeply gulping in response, "Sure, I'm just practicing Yoga."

"Oh." she said. "What's Yoga?"

Sensing this wasn't the greatest time in the world for a deep discussion I ordered, "Go get Mom."

"I called her." yelled Andy. "See Mom! I told you she dumped him."

"Millie, what are you doing to your brother?" demanded Mom. "Danny, what are we going to do now?"

I growled, "Mom, sit me up." Gulp, gulp, gulp.

"Oh Danny, you shouldn't be in your chair." Mom stated.

"Then Mother I suggest you go upstairs and get the lift and put me to bed." I reasoned.

"Danny I can't operate that lift." she reiterated.

Dad arrived home from work two hours later to confront Mom's sage words of wisdom and advice. Something sounding like, "Ray, don't ever leave him in his chair again!"

Reverberations of my trip to Dr. Burnett echoed through the house for quite some time, and I endured another setback in my quest for independence. Although I wasn't grounded, bed became my foundation for the immediate future. Reaching out for freedom presented more of a dilemma than expected. Consoling myself while reading one day Judy reported as she delivered my mail, "Here's a big envelope from Columbus, let me hold this card for you to read."

"It's an announcement for Carol's college graduation." I revealed. "Tempus fugit! I can hardly believe four years have flown by. I know she'll be a great nurse."

Judy asked, "Is she the girl who writes you letters?"

"Yes." I answered. "And she always sends birthday and Christmas gifts. She sent Paul McElroy's *Moments of Meditation*, which has been quite helpful to me. She probably saved my life with her wisdom the last time I was in Columbus. Wouldn't she be surprised if I RSVP'd in person, appearing at her graduating ceremony from OSU School of Nursing? I'll never forget her."

The following day my eyes were re-focused on a wondrous world of exciting words when Dr.Burnett personally delivered my new glasses commenting, "It's easier for me to drive than for your sisters to huff and puff up that hill. The corneal scar tissue impairs clarity, but these lenses will eliminate some of the strain. Perhaps now you can resume reading."

One day as I read, Dad fastened a letter to the rack stating, "These glasses must help your eyes, your sisters bring you a lot of books, magazines, and newspapers from the library."

"Can you believe this?" I asked my parents. "Remember Bob from Columbus? He doesn't have a seat belt on his chair and while riding outside two weeks ago, the wheelchair hit a bump and he hit the deck. I warned him about wheelies. Dad maybe a seat belt would be a good idea."

The rebirth of God's green earth emerged from beneath winter's snowy cloak as trees budded, flowers bloomed, and birds joyously sang of life soon to be hatched. Accepting an invitation from Anita and Jim for a Memorial Day picnic at their house, we bathed our bodies in soothing warm sun as springtime breezes lazily wafted scents of new mown grass in our direction. Mouth-watering aromas from encapsulated molecules of barbecue smoke from grilling hamburgers and hot dogs tickled our taste buds as they passed under our noses.

Varrrrooommm! Varrrooommm! Varrrooommm!

"What a beautiful Memorial Day." Mom said. "Anita, I'm sure happy you and Jim invited us to this picnic. Remember when we used to do yard work on this day while listening to the 500 mile race on radio?"

"The afternoon sun is really becoming uncomfortable." I complained. "Could we get in the car and take a ride?"

Jim offered, "I've got an idea. Let's put Danny, chair and all, in my van. We'll drive around New Castle and show him what's been happening to the town. How about it, Danny? Interested in an all-expense-paid tour?"

"Fine with me!" I agreed. "My face and wrists are on fire. Anything for shade."

Monday morning I awoke with bags of edema clinging to my cheeks; huge blisters on my forehead; backs of my hands swollen tight; and a bright red bulbous nose. Responding to my pitiful pleas of distress, Mom immediately began placing cold soaks on the painfully sunburned areas. By Wednesday I'd become weary listening to, "Danny you should stay inside more!" Although ignoring their unsolicited advice, I began experiencing familiar pain in my sides so Dad telephoned Dr. Heilman. "It's another kidney infection." he diagnosed. "I think it best if you would consent to admission at the Respo Center for examinations and thorough evaluation. Apparently the deep sunburn precipitated an infection which traveled to your kidneys. Danny, it's been nearly a year since you were at Ann Arbor, feel strong enough for a 230 mile trip?"

Entering the Penthouse Doris, narrowing her eyes, said, "Danny, you really timed your trip perfectly. Bob's waiting for you. He just returned from surgery to remove a kidney stone, so take it easy you two."

"Dan, it's good to see you again." greeted Dr.D. "I've been told you're having plumbing difficulties. Oh, Oh, when did you get that sunburn?"

"Hi Dr.D. Yeah, kidney troubles again, but this is the first time in almost a year." I boasted. "Until I acquired a sunburn one week ago, my health was fine. The doctor at home said they might be connected."

"Possibly." Dr.D nodded. "An infection will migrate to the vulnerable area of your body. No problem, we'll simply correct the situation. What about your chair and feeder?"

"In summary Dr.D, I sit in my chair once a month. Only for special occasions, never using my feeder. Basically, my rehab failed. I want simply to convalesce, recover from the kidney infection, receive necessary examinations, treatments and medicines, then go home. Rehab goals without diligence and supportive encouragement are futile. The suffering and hard work associated with the rehab program don't fit the reality in my life."

"Dan I sense a lot of anger and exasperation." Dr.D confided. "Channeling inner turmoil and emotion into a productive effort is the only way to avoid embitterment and defeat. At least while you are at the Penthouse, I suggest you take advantage of our assistance and sit in your chair whenever possible. How long has it been since you've been out to dinner or a movie?"

"Actually, I haven't attended a movie since leaving the Respo Center over a year ago." I replied. "Obviously from my sunburned condition I've been outside - the first venture since going home last year. I'm not what one would refer to as a social animal at home. Most of my time is spent reading, watching television, sports, news, current events, and game shows which mentally exercise my thought processes. Through reading I've traveled thousands of miles and visited dozens of countries while participating in the adventures, visions, dreams, and hopes of other people. Though reality is limiting, the horizons of my life are endless. Thanks to reading I'm very privileged to have a ubiquitous view from the words of every writer who ever painted pictures with literature. I've fancied myself the primary character in more than one thousand books and innumerable magazine articles, which brought facts, life, and information before my eyes. Any constraint placed upon my life is dictated only by the fallibility of my mind."

Dr.D nodded affirmatively, "You have a solid grasp of an unfortunate situation, but to achieve significant gains it's imperative you participate physically as well. While here, as I've said before, you should be more motivated. We will talk again tomorrow, rest and think of what I said."

"I couldn't help...overhear Dr.D's...conversation." said Bob. "Unless you make...some new friends,...don't count on...much social life. Most of our...old gang has ...left. Only Mary,...Doris, and Earl...are still at ...the Penthouse. Jan got married. You knew Judy...and Don...moved to...California. Corky's searching...for newsletter...writers. Be careful! Carl has another... girlfriend. I've only seen...him once since...returning to...Ann Arbor. Everything has changed. This place... is becoming...too much like...a regular hospital."

I shuddered inwardly while listening to Bob's summary of our beloved Penthouse's sad state of decline into just a "normal" hospital. Sighing I reminisced, "Man, remember the good ol' days? I die laughing when I recall Doris's scream as she noisily dumped a large rock from my steel urinal."

Bob chuckled, "That's nothing...remember when we... talked Evon into...putting a fake...spider under my... bandage? We had some...really good times."

"Good times! Ha!" I snorted. "Don't forget how Judy retaliated for the nursing staff that evening when she put teddy bears on our shoulders then read kid's bedtime stories to her captive audience. I really liked her before that!"

Bob smiled, "Don't lie...you still...like her."

"Well," I conceded, "I do miss her. Hey, remember the bottle of scotch we gave her as a going away present?"

Bob grinned, "What a...night! I miss her...too."

I mused, "It's too quiet, we need some excitement."

In compliance with Dr.D's admonitions and the totally abject humiliation my reputation had suffered from peers, I knew positive reclamation of my pecking order was demanded. The Penthouse balcony presented an inviting view of the city lights below, offering excellent opportunities for a variety of activities. In communicating with orderlies and friends on various units, I enlisted cooperation from my remaining cohorts.

Daniel R. Williams

With willing accomplices we organized Man's Night. "Take my word for it guys - this game will be cool. I distinctly heard Dr.D say, 'socialize and motivate'."

In the past we had used the balcony quite often to play cards, and this one game in particular will forever remain etched in my memory. Five of us were seated around a table which held a large amount of coins - possibly, two or three dollars in pennies, nickels, dimes, and quarters. Everyone was bedazzled by a fortune to be won or lost. Abruptly, our table overturned and money went flying. A blinding flash of white invaded our recreation zone, accentuated by grunts and groans of unmistakable discontent. It was Miss Oxley! The new evening charge nurse didn't look happy.

"What's going on out here? I won't have any gambling on my floor!" she bellowed. "Lee, get back in there and do some work! You other guys get to your floors, right now! I want all of my people back inside immediately! I can just see headlines in tomorrow's paper, 'PENTHOUSE RAIDED! NURSE ALLOWS GAMBLING IN HOSPITAL!'. Well misters, I'll tell you there's no way that's going to happen on my shift!"

In retrospect, I understand why the good lady in white was upset. In fact, I've even developed compassion for Dr. D's dilemma. I assume full responsibility for all unhappy conclusions associated with our effort to achieve a balance between socialization and isolation. My problem undoubtedly had been in choosing the wrong type society. Honestly, I'm proud of one fact. Miracles were enacted for many passersby that evening when, thirteen stories below, pedestrians were showered with pennies from heaven.

Earl greeted me next morning with a smile, "I heard you and the hospital mafia were involved in an unofficial bust yesterday evening. I'm curious, do you spend an entire year at home devising these little schemes?"

Dr.D entered the ward, approached me slightly smirking. "Dan, I think you're getting better. When I expressed wishes to see you matriculate into life once again, I didn't exactly have a gambling parlor in mind. I don't think it's appropriate, especially with the employees on my unit!"

One day nearing the end of my "recuperation" while Earl escorted me to the cafeteria he asked, "Would you like going out to see a movie, and maybe stop for a pizza? Ask Mary, I think she'll go with us. Just one thing, no funny business. We will be back by midnight."

The planned excursion took place without great fanfare previously associated with such adventures. We saw a movie, stopped for pizza, and returned to the Penthouse. I really love those two for their kindness and consideration, but the recreational excitement was no longer the same. My teenage years had been eclipsed, and expectations were well beyond rebellion. I wanted more than to be simply, "entertained".

Keep Smiling and Never Give Up!

Bob had recovered sufficiently from surgery and was now working with OT perfecting his painting skills, producing beautifully unique scenery on greeting cards. What had begun as a therapeutic exercise, evolved into a promising vocation. With the assistance of counselors and his mom, he began developing talent into a potential livelihood.

Sadness ensued as my Penthouse stay waned and I watched Bob serenely creating swirls of heavenly beauty from globs of blue, green, and yellow paint. I casually spoke to him contrasting life at home and the Respo Center, nonchalantly revealing, "I won't be coming back soon. Maybe never."

"Really?" asked Bob. "You aren't…coming back?"

"Think about it." I said. "Ann Arbor is 230 miles from New Castle. Indianapolis is only 60 miles. My kidneys take a beating every time I travel the distance and the Penthouse is no longer enjoyable. You said yourself it's really just a 'hospital' now. Some day residents of the Penthouse will be required to wear name bands. Can you imagine?"

Grinning, Bob said, "Wouldn't be…surprised. You're right…Saginaw's a…lot closer…than Ann Arbor. It would be…easier on Mom…and Danny to…visit. My friend Claudine…said when she. . stopped at your… house in…New Castle…on her return…vacation trip …from Texas…you were still. . in bed. What gives? Don't you…sit in your…chair at home…like here?"

Ignoring his question I suggested, "Doris, let's order a big pizza tonight. Invite what's left of our friends for a going away party."

Only a half dozen or so friends accepted our invitation to the pizza party. Where once the Respo Center would have been crowded, we now counted the people without difficulty. I shuddered inwardly as realization slashed memory, choosing next day to discuss my questionable future with Dr.D.

"Dan, certainly I think IUMC can provide you with more than adequate medical care. They probably don't offer rehab opportunities available at Ann Arbor, but decreased travel will be more agreeable for your family and kidneys." Dr.D. continued, "I'd like you to speak with our new Social Worker before leaving The Penthouse. I know Theresa had a unique flair for communicating, indeed solving many problems, but please give Mrs. Queen a chance. Perhaps there's an area in which she can assist."

"Dr.D I truly appreciate your concern; however, I'm not interested in new ideas involving rehab." I proclaimed. "Theresa's valiant efforts remain in a box; a seldom-used typewriter sits idly by; and a hydraulic patient lifter awaits my independence. The wheelchair will probably remain like new for some time. Thanks to health problems on my part, and lack of ambition from other people, rehab training was meaningless. Painful cries, curses, and

Daniel R. Williams

tears were to no avail. Intense PT, OT, surgery, excruciating pain, and exciting dreams of hopeful anticipation were all wasted. I adamantly believe my role in this life is to remain much as that ball bearing feeder. Until heaven smiles, I'm stored for later use."

20

REALITY

The Respo Centers from which I received so much support and improvement at the hands of skilled, professional staff members were fast becoming a part of history. Compassion of these wonderful people combined with the enjoyment realized from camaraderie of fellow residents made these unique, but timely healing environments, a vitally important pathway to successful living. The healthy attitudes instilled at these Centers concerning disabilities promoted essential goals of physical rehabilitation. Confronting devastating problems ensures, by necessity, an accelerated maturity and emotional stability required to compete in the world. Unquestionably, paras and quads must approach physical problems with special answers, but retain equality with AB's in their desire for respect and life. Most people respond immediately to their body's demands; conversely, we must accept physical limitations. A mental adjustment is crucial for us if we're to successfully overcome difficulties presented by illness or accident. Any movement taken for granted by AB's, but an impossibility for handicapped people, must be confronted with grace, courage, patience, and spiritual enlightenment. Rather than negating our humanity, these challenges only increase our yearning to be independent. Re-education is imperative.

The happiness of coming home was overshadowed by loss of familiar friends and fellowship in Michigan. Immediately following our long journey from Ann Arbor, a routine episode of kidney stones, infection, and pain pummeled me again. As Dr.Heilman brought the usual antibiotics, pain medications, and collected urine specimens he intoned, "Danny, it's the same old thing, you're passing another stone. Antibiotics should control the infection that will inevitably follow."

Ten days passed and my physical condition continued to deteriorate unabated. Dr.Heilman determined a stone hadn't passed and was concerned it might be trapped in my ureter. Infection worsened. I panted breathlessly, unable to relax, struggling against my chest respirator. Those of you "lucky" readers who've endured kidney stones know it's impossible to find a comfortable position. As my paralyzed friends are aware I'm not the first to endure this agglomeration, but I believe it necessary to verbalize their silent comments. Immobility, disgusting waves of nausea, and squeezing constant pressure from a chest respirator, which fit tightly over my abdominal area, intensified the pain. Minute by minute, hour by hour, each time vacuum forced the shell (respirator) against me I emitted moans and groans, decrying my mode of traveling on a chaise lounge in our automobile.

Daniel R. Williams

Incessant pains refused to ease, hematuria increased, and oral antibiotics failed.

"Danny, please try to eat something." pleaded Mom. "At least drink some juice. Are you cold? You look so weak and blue. Ray, call for help! Danny fainted!"

"Okay now?" asked medic officers Hankenhoff and Baker.

"Ray, I got here soon as possible. What happened? Why did you call the first aid unit?" questioned Dr.Heilman.

"We didn't know what to do." Dad answered. "He can't eat, each time his chest respirator cycles he becomes pale. About an hour ago he stopped breathing and turned blue. The medics revived him with oxygen, but he fades in and out. I know his bed is soaked from perspiration. Today's problem was all new to us, other times he could frog breathe while shouting directions."

Dr.Heilman warned, "Ray, I think you should take him to the hospital, but Ann Arbor is too far away. Let me make a call to Indianapolis, meanwhile phone this number and tell them I've ordered a tank of oxygen for home."

"Mr. Williams, I'm Chuck. You know Clarence, meet Don and Vaughn." said the medic officer. "We're ready to take Danny to Indianapolis."

Six years earlier an ambulance had taken me away from home following the onset of Polio, now I was again whisked away from my family en route to the IU Med Center.

I tried focusing my blurry vision on unfamiliar ceiling and walls, searching the brush marks overhead. I visually explored strange equipment surrounding my bed. Scanning the room my eyes were drawn to a lamp and chair beside a little desk where I saw one of my former private duty nurses who'd taken care of me in isolation at Riley Hospital. "Oh no!" my mind raced. "Not this again! I'm having a bad dream." Quickly averting my gaze, I tried desperately to remember.

"Danny!" exclaimed the nurse. "Thank God, you finally opened your eyes. Don't worry, you're a patient in Robert Long Hospital. Remember my name?"

"No ma'am." I replied. "Where am I? What happened?"

"After passing kidney stones an infection left you in a coma." she explained. "Forgot my name, huh? Danny, under the circumstances I'll make an allowance. Think about it a while, you'll recall my name. The registry offered me this job and when I found out it was you I expected an iron lung. When you're better you must bring me up to date. All six years. Please excuse me while I go to the nurse's station and tell the charge nurse our good news. Apparently you two are friends."

Keep Smiling and Never Give Up!

"Who?" I asked as she left the room.

"Hi Danny." greeted Sue. "Thank goodness! At last you are getting better. Jim is driving me crazy. Every day he asks questions about your health."

"Sue! What are you doing here? What am I doing here!" I demanded. "Oh, sorry, didn't mean to sound unhappy. How long have I been here?"

"Danny, I'm the charge nurse." she answered. "You've been here three days, welcome."

"Three days!" I drowsily repeated. "Oh yeah. Now it's coming back. Sue, why am I in Indianapolis instead of home in New Castle? Last I remember, I couldn't pee. Oh, sorry. Hey, you didn't have to transfer units just because I arrived."

"Oh brother!" she said. "Mr. Williams, this floor is my assigned unit. First Jim, and now you. Oh well at least you're awake, maybe someday you'll make sense. Jim said you were too ornery for anything bad to happen. Call me if you need help Mrs. Farrell."

"That's it!" I exclaimed. "Hello again Mrs. Farrell. Sorry I didn't remember your name."

After an intern's cursory examination Thursday evening, I went back to sleep naturally, until abruptly awakened at 6:00 AM the next morning. "Hello I'm Dr.Greenlee, resident of this service for another week." said a young man wearing street clothes hidden beneath his white lab coat. "Don't be concerned about IV's in your arms, after fasting for several days you were dehydrated. A serious infection required powerful antibiotics in the IV fluid. Are you alert enough to explain the respirator? Upon admission your dad helped us immensely, but I think it important you school our staff, including we doctors. We tried putting you inside an iron lung, but for some reason it was ineffective, compelling us to rely on your present apparatus."

Trying to cope with his questions I answered, "Pleased to meet you Dr.Greenlee. I'm feeling stronger all the time now that I'm breathing better, when can you remove the oxygen? The stone surely passed, my pain is nearly gone. I have to frog breathe at times and my side hurts, but I guess the crisis is over. I have flashes of memory about the iron lung fiasco. No offense, but the iron lung wasn't at fault. You guys were! Someone set the positive pressure much too high and prior to me fainting I remember yelling in my dazed condition, 'turn that down!'. Needless to say, you didn't listen."

Laughing, Dr.Greenlee responded, "I guess it's unusual for us to hear patients tell us where to go and what to do. We'll check your blood gases before discontinuing the oxygen. If those results are adequate, I will schedule X-Rays and cystoscopy. You did pass a stone. An IVP will reveal any damage your body sustained."

"Danny, I'm sorry." said Dad. "The doctors wouldn't let me adjust the iron lung pressure. Clarence and Don drove the Unit with you screaming, 'turn the sirens off, I can't stand that noise!' Vivian and Anita said lab techs stuck you thirty-two times while attempting to start IV's, before they were asked to 'leave the room'."

As usual, I accepted care from many student nurses. My respirator became a daily class instruction aid, and I followed previous medical advice by being social. The evenings were especially enjoyable because I could relax as Sue and I talked about the life she and Jim were planning. "Sue, that's great! When is the big day? Tell Jim you two have given me hope. If a wonderful person like you agrees to a marriage proposal from a man with his personality, then certainly I, a very humble and shy person, will definitely have no problem finding a wife. After he completes verbally destroying me, tell him I think he's a very fortunate man. Uh oh, Sue I'm so sick to my stomach!"

"I'll give you a shot for nausea. It should alleviate your evening sickness." she laughed.

"Do you really think the medicine will help?" I gagged. "Look at all those bottles of drugs that are mixed in my IV. Uh, uh! Jaw stuck! Can't shut mouth!"

"What were you saying about Jim?" she teased. "Speak up Danny, I can't understand you. Oh dear! You're not just joking are you? I'll call Dr.Greenlee stat!"

"Close your mouth Danny!" ordered Dr.Greenlee. "Your face looks like you sat on a hot stove. The nurse said you were having difficulties with some medicine; obviously it's a reaction. IV Benadryl will solve the problem. See, the medicine is working already, your mouth is closing and in a few minutes you'll be speaking as usual."

"Oh no!" said Sue smirking. "No more peace and quiet."

Dr.Greenlee informed me, "Tomorrow we've scheduled that IVP I mentioned, but it's impossible for me to be there with you. Today's my final twenty-four hours on isolation. In the morning a new resident will report for duty and you can honor him with your words of wisdom."

I grimaced, "Sorry to hear that. At least I'm better and can answer questions now. I feel much more comfortable with you though, we've all learned a lot this week."

"Don't worry Danny," Dr.Greenlee smiled, "Dr.Ryan is an intelligent and good man. You'll get along fine."

The next day I went to X-ray as planned, except without meeting my new doctor. Lying on a cold, hard table I began seeing yellow swirls and black dots before my eyes, and cold perspiration beaded on my forehead. I heaved, "Help, I'm sick!"

Keep Smiling and Never Give Up!

"Doctor!" yelled the X-ray technician. "Mr. Williams is having a reaction to the IVP dye."

"I'll call your service resident." he said. "I'm not familiar with your respirator and difficulty breathing. He will administer medicine to counteract these symptoms."

"No!" I demanded. "Page Dr.Greenlee, tell him I'm in trouble."

After the flurry of excitement Dr.Greenlee insisted, "I am not your doctor. Why didn't you let them call Dr.Ryan?"

I growled, "I haven't met Dr.Ryan. Anyway, he doesn't know anything about me. Thanks Doc."

One month later at home I heard from my sisters, "Happy Birthday Danny! Well brother, at times we didn't think you would make it, but at last you're legal. How long will it take Dad to fasten your typewriter shelf on the wall? What will you write first? Have you abandoned ideas of a book?"

I grinned, "Ask Dad about the shelf. As for writing, who knows?"

"Here comes JJ." Mom announced. "I hope neither he nor his attendant sit down on the icy steps or sidewalk."

"Mom, without being rude," I snickered, "JJ is already sitting on the ice. Anyway ice isn't his main concern, our steps without a ramp are his biggest barrier."

"Happy birthday, ol' buddy." greeted JJ. "Couldn't you do something about those steps? How do you go any place? I installed the seat belt on my chair so I wouldn't topple out in places that require rappelling techniques."

Following a brief, but enjoyable visit from my friend I watched as the attendant pushed his chair toward our front door and steep ice-covered steps waiting outside. Frequent comments by various people like Dr.Burnett, Bob, Corky, and JJ extolling the virtues of a seat belt gave me incentive to have one installed on my wheelchair.

"Is this what you wanted Danny?" asked Judy, displaying a long webbed strap. "Are you really sure Millie and Andy can do this? Aren't they awfully young?"

I humbly replied, "Sis, with my supervision they could build anything. Trust me!"

"Hey Danny, Mike's here!" shouted Millie. "I thought he moved away. He hasn't been here for a long time!"

"Of course he moved away Millie." I chided. "Evidently he's passing through town on his way to Louisville. Mike is earning college money by driving a fuel tanker truck out of Fort Wayne. I'll sure be glad to see him."

My old buddy and I conversed for a long time about our years of growing up together, then decided to play chess. I surprised my teacher by frustrating what used to be a simple and quick defeat. Eventually Mike proclaimed, "Checkmate! Well you're much better at this game now; do you realize we have been playing over an hour? I'm glad I came by today, we had a good visit."

"Mike, did you catch Andy observing our chess game? He wants to start playing chess."

"Go ahead." Mike encouraged. "Everybody has to learn sometime, take it easy though."

"Forget it!" I declared. "If he wins, he wins. He'll earn the victory or learn from defeat. Remember when you, Bill, and Rev.Kerschner taught me to play chess? My friend, I lost seventy-two games in a row. Take it easy? You guys didn't!"

Chuckling as he left Mike waved, "See ya later."

BULLETIN: PRESIDENT JOHN FITZGERALD KENNEDY HAS BEEN ASSASSINATED IN DALLAS, TEXAS
11/22/63

Thanksgiving season was a dichotomy for everyone in our country. While being thankful for many personal blessings, the fellowship and togetherness of family and loved ones had become especially important – a fact made much more poignant by the tragic murder of our country's leader, accentuated by his family's suffering at this moment in time.

The hiatus between holidays passed quickly and I heard a familiar voice call out as he rolled into my room one day, "Merry Christmas!" greeted JJ. "You're becoming a real bed warmer, Santa Claus will know where to find you. Hey, what have we here? Is this the birthday present you referred to in our conversation last month?"

Looking proudly at my recently built typewriter shelf I commented, "It's great. I can reach the keys without strain to my neck. Also it isn't necessary to clench a mouthstick so tightly between my teeth. I already bent the aluminum."

Christmas over, days flashed by with wearisome boredom. I read, and read, and read. For a change of pace, whenever reading books became too monotonous, I read magazines. Judy and Vivian made weekly visits to our local library, bringing home up to fifteen books each trip.

"JEOPARDY!" became my choice TV game show, truly taking the place of a noonday tutor. Listening and viewing college basketball with Dad and Norman was an enjoyable routine, and Sundays I reserved time for watching professional football warfare. Dad and Kenny were quite boisterous in support of the Chicago Bears, while attempting to denigrate predictable success of my Cleveland Browns. Unfortunately, cheering on Milwaukee's Braves would soon be impossible following their planned

move to Atlanta, but their change of address didn't alter my loyalty even if they were losing.

Weekends and some days in between I wrote many letters or developed short stories at my new typewriter shelf. One must establish disciplined habits when trying to write, but developing a routine was impossible due to limited time in my wheelchair. With my ball bearing feeder stored in a box, a mouthstick became the extremity of necessity. Utilizing a mouthstick to type required practice and I took advantage of every opportunity. Whenever health problems allowed I spent many strenuous hours attempting to compose short stories for submission to various publications.

As usual, just when I thought things were better health wise, the old devil raised his hand saying, "Guess who?"

"Why is this happening now?" I groaned to Dr.Heilman. "I haven't been outside my room since returning from the Med Center last year! You can't blame these kidney problems on a bumpy ride. This is maddening and ridiculous!"

"Sorry Danny." replied Dr.Heilman. "I really think you should go to the hospital for X-rays and tests."

Following a short two-week stay at Robert Long, I returned home convinced hospitals are too full of sick people. Once feeling better, I readily acceded to Andy's request for a chess match. My little brother quickly lost three games in succession and midway through the fourth Mom lamented, "Aw Danny, why don't you let him win? He's just a little kid. He might get discouraged and not play anymore. You aren't being very fair to Andy."

"Mom, if he wins, he earns it. If he loses, he'll try harder next time." I responded. "I'm not about to give him undeserved success. Schoolteachers won't give him A's just because he's a cute little boy. Someday, my little brother will be grateful that I demanded he strive for excellence. In the world where I've lived since having had Polio, 'fair' is glaringly absent from our vocabulary."

A sweltering August day the mail arrived and I was greeted with a blessedly small, but much appreciated monetary surprise, and a big ego booster. A popular magazine purchased one short story I'd previously submitted. Assuredly, retirement could not be built from the income I received, but it did wonders for my desire to confront a frightening, blank sheet of paper. Writing is best described as creating a literary masterpiece of art by using words of wisdom to paint pictures from thoughts hidden deep within one's heart.

As I watched TV, gentle soothing breezes caressed drapes at my window. My cousin Barbara and daughter Debbie from Hammond were visiting when someone knocked at the back door. Mom answered, "Why of course Danny will be happy to see you. Danny's dad's at work, but maybe we can help lift the chair. Bring him up the driveway to the porch."

With everyone assisting in scaling the steps, Jim and Sue honored me with a surprise visit. Sue pushed his wheelchair into my room as Jim exclaimed, "Hi ya Danny boy! It's good to see you friend."

"Hi big mouth!" laughed Sue. "Any reactions lately?"

"I wanna tell you buddy," he began, "those steps gotta go! How do you ever go out in your wheelchair? The driveway in back isn't bad, but those big steps up to the porch are killers."

"Jim, I rarely venture off the porch. Mostly I travel to the hospital and back requiring the use of a stretcher. As you can see my wheelchair has become a resting place for odds and ends. I'm not odd, and my end seldom sits there. Enough concerning me, I'm sure glad you two got married. It certainly did remove a great dilemma from my life."

"What do you mean?" asked Jim.

"I was trying desperately to stay single, but with Sue available I began to question my loyalty to a good friend."

Sue teased, "Danny! You didn't tell me."

"Jim," I asked, "is it just an ingrained Naval slowness or were you playing hard to get? Why did you delay so long before allowing her to shove you around in that wheelchair?"

"Now I know why your mouth stuck open." Jim responded. "You talk too much. Seriously, you should get a Kartop lift like us, then you could visit our home while I insult you."

I laughed, "My pleasure ol' buddy. Speaking of home, where've you two decided to live, New Castle or Tipton?"

Jim replied, "My aunts, uncles, cousins, and parents reside in so many places we decided to follow Sue's family to Fort Wayne. If I recall, didn't you tell me a tale about a trip through our fair city?"

"Fort Wayne? Sure." I laughed. "I had a flamin' good time there once, on one of my many trips to the Respo Center at Ann Arbor."

"Ah yes." said Jim. "I remember our discussions about your extracurricular activities at the rehab facility. Well Sue, we've honored Danny Boy with our presence longer than two hours. Shouldn't we depart? It's a long trip home. If you ever get down those steps in one piece, come visit."

Last minute amenities were exchanged and I bid farewell to my dear friends admonishing Sue to drive safely. As Mom and Barbara watched Sue transfer Jim from wheelchair to car via Kartop lift Mom mused, "How does she do it, I couldn't."

"It works the same as my bedside lift." I sighed. "One day perhaps I'll get married and my wife and I will travel."

Barbara commented, "Danny that would be wonderful."

I continued reading and watching TV, spending less time at my typewriter. Glow of success quickly faded following receipt of repeated rejection slips. Visits from my friends were non-existent, their lives were understandably directed toward promising futures, not dependent on past memories of agonizing dreams or visions of a disparaging present. Every day many long hours were devoted to focusing my thoughts on magazines and novels, images and words enabling me to enter a world beyond these four walls. I traveled to Turkey with Mike as his letters described Air Force life where he was stationed; played golf and fished with Norman as he recalled his activities; worked on cars with Kenny; installed plumbing with Jim; and listened as Dad described work and referred to friends such as Fred and their lively talks about baseball. I became part of a team with my professional sports heroes and in early November cast my first presidential vote, 1964, the twenty-second year of my life.

Happy Birthday, Danny! Happy Thanksgiving, Danny! Merry Christmas, Danny!

"Whew, that wind is bitter outside!" shivered JJ, as an attendant pushed his ice-cold wheelchair into my room. "My body brace freezes when I travel during the winter so I probably won't thaw for days. I briefly considered making you a snowball, but was afraid you'd throw it at me."

"Yes, Mr. Williams." said JJ's young assistant with an athletic build. "Be glad you're home in that warm bed."

Embarrassed, JJ instructed, "Uh Tommy, why don't you go to the living room and watch TV? We need to talk."

I smiled, "The 'Three Stooges' are on."

A new year sped by with ever-increasing slowness. Judy and Vivian made frequent library visits trying to satiate my voracious reading appetite. In addition to many magazines, I averaged four or five books each week. Only news, sports, variety, and TV game shows contributed to any recreational enlightenment. I'm ever so thankful for educational shows like *"JEOPARDY!"* and *"COLLEGE BOWL"*, my schools of the air.

A far away place became an increasingly common topic in the headlines as Vietnam captured our national pride. Latin America thrust itself upon us as paratroopers and Marines found themselves fighting in the Dominican Republic. Unrest grew violent and ugly in major United States cities, as civil rights became a euphemism for rioting and burning. At home I listened stoically to the sound of new music as it crowded out the ballads and rock and roll of Connie, Ricky, Elvis, and Pat. Despite many parent's objections to their dress and songs, we were invaded by John, Paul, George, and Ringo.

Inconsistent mobility in my wheelchair proved damaging to kidneys as usual and I confronted a familiar nemesis. "I can't believe it! Not again!" I groaned. "Dr.Heilman, I'm exhausted. I haven't ridden in the car for ages, are you sure it's another infection? Maybe it's just my tenth stone and I can pass it at home. Bring on the pain medicine, lots of water, and antibiotics. It'll be over soon, then I can return to my busy life. I'll be fine!"

"Danny it is an infection, and you know what happens if those stones get caught. You need a urological evaluation and X-rays." admonished Dr.Heilman. "I'll phone the Med Center, you get ready to leave for Indianapolis."

"Ward C is filled to capacity." explained Dr.Leaky, my urologist. "Since you won't be here long, I've arranged for your admission to the isolation ward. They're familiar with respirators and the nurses are fantastic."

As predicted, tests and X-rays were quickly completed and I returned home within two weeks infection free, though still carrying ballast in each kidney. Resuming my reading I was skeptical but supportive as President Johnson, bowing to pride, pressure, and politics, deployed Marines to Nam. Consequently, along with books and magazines, my days were now devoted to corresponding with many friends and relatives in a bloody, undeclared war. Imagination became blatantly ugly as reality confirmed images of human and material destruction. Television newscasts seared everyone's mind with pictures of death and stories destroying our innocence. American cities continued to burn with racial unrest, and Detroit, a special part of my life, became a statistic in the 60's revolution. I was acutely aware letters from Michigan friends had become strangely infrequent in my daily mail. Thinking about them and myself I read with concern Bob's letter of invitation. Love and friendship overcame caution and I stated, "Dad, I need a complete physical exam and re-evaluation of my health and respiratory status. If I write Dr.D and schedule a few weeks stay at the Penthouse, can you simultaneously take Mom and the kids to Florida? Your planned vacation should be a rest for everyone. Assuming everything materializes, suppose I could hitch a ride to Ann Arbor?"

"Welcome back to the Penthouse." greeted Doris. "Well, it certainly has been a long time since your last admission. We thought you had been banned from University Hospital. I know you'll be surprised, Bob got here this week. You two must have mental telepathy, your timing is incredible. Bob! Look who's here."

"Doris said you only recently arrived." I winked. "Are you having more troubles, or did you come back for a rest?"

"No trouble." he grinned. "Like you it's...been two years. I need a... checkup. Judy's back...in Michigan,...she'll visit soon. Mary works...evenings. Earl's on...another floor. Everyone else...is gone."

After talking much of Sunday evening reliving good times, we slept, anticipating a new beginning tomorrow. The morning sun streamed through

Penthouse windows as I heard a familiar voice, "Hello stranger, did your kidneys survive the long trip from New Castle?" asked Dr.D. "What can we do for you? I hope it's just a checkup, if you have additional rehabilitation with feeders in mind you've waited too long. The glorious Penthouse will soon be a museum of memories."

"It's good to see all of you." I remarked. "Is Dr.D. being good to you, Dr.Sullivan? I've been a patient at IUMC in Indianapolis. In the past two years I've had five UTI's and kidney infections, passed three more stones, and donated my appendix to medical science. Most doctors are excellent, and the nursing staff is well acquainted with my situation. Unfortunately they're lacking in rehab and facts pertaining to respirators. I not only need a physical, but would also profit from pulmonary functions evaluation. Don't be concerned about further rehabilitation as an option for me; it's no longer important. I'm curious, why did you say I'd waited too long?"

Dr.D responded, "Dan we'll do a thousand mile tune-up and before long you'll be ready to roll. I'm sure you know that with decreasing cases of new Polio and vanishing needs for Respo Centers, The March of Dimes withdrew funding for our Penthouse. Don't worry though once other establishments are required to provide necessary support, they will acquire knowledge needed for your survival."

Dr.Sullivan remarked, "Remember what I told you once, only the resilient will survive. Whatever you do with the rest of your life, make it count. Some day Polio will be a footnote in history, but we can't be forgotten."

Lighting his pipe as he walked away Dr.D said, "Never!"

Life as a Penthouse resident still had moments of humor regardless our sadness. Staff, especially veterans of Respo Center follies, had poignant memories of the past. Doctors and nurses encouraged me to drink a glass of liquid at least every hour and much time was consumed with the consequences. Knowing Doris, our evening charge RN, was a bit shy I tried to await the orderly's return so she wouldn't suffer another consequence. One evening, unable to stretch my bladder any further I gritted my teeth and pleaded, "Come on Doris! Why can't you give me the urinal? First you force me to drink, and then ignore my pleas. Stop blushing, help me do my duty!"

"I'll call Earl so you won't be embarrassed, hold it until he gets here from the fourth floor. I'm certain you won't pass another big kidney stone this time." she smiled.

I winced, "Doris, this is no time to hold a grudge. I can't cross my legs!" Just as my eyes began watering, Earl emerged from the elevator. Upon hearing my tale of woe he laughed heartily.

Daniel R. Williams

Several days later Anne, Bob, Danny, and I conjectured if Judy would have time to visit between classes in nursing school, when all three of our sweethearts, Judy, Doris, and Mary, appeared. "What a surprise! Today may be the last time we have a chance to visit." I lamented ruefully. "It's really great you timed this reunion at shift change. All of you have been subjects in my dream world, so it's difficult to leave since we probably won't ever see each other again. Judy, I think it's disgraceful that after becoming single you lived so far away; Mary for some unknown reason you got married without even consulting me; and dear Doris, I won't forget how you blushed each time we flirted - even now. Bob and I correspond occasionally relaying current information about everyone, especially you good-looking nurses, so we'll stay in touch. Remember the good times, take care of yourselves, and keep smiling."

For the next few days an atmosphere of emptiness filled both Bob's and my heart as we acclimated to a future without promise of camaraderie at the Respo Center. Laughter, joy, and happiness associated with the Penthouse were evaporating as staff and residents ventured into other avenues of life. I was therefore quite contented to hear Dr.D inform me, "Dan the tests are completed. You are free to leave after being outfitted with new respiratory equipment. It's doubtful you will return to Ann Arbor in the future for medical reasons, so allow me to offer my best wishes for your health. Don't neglect monitoring your kidneys, and needless to say, always be cognizant of respiratory functions. Should you need any assistance with pulmonary problems call me and I will try to assist in locating necessary answers."

As Sunday noon approached I bid a heartrending farewell to one more special friend. With a huge lump forming in my throat I choked, "Bob I'll always cherish our friendship and be forever grateful for the opportunity to know someone so courageous and talented. We may never meet again on earth, but sometime in eternity our spirits will mingle." Turning to Anne and Danny trying to convey thoughts of encouragement and love I stammered, "You'll always be in my thoughts. May the sun never set on our memories of each other."

Dad walked onto the Penthouse announcing, "Your mom and the kids are waiting for us downstairs, let's go home."

Watching the countryside as I traveled to Indiana, my thoughts were blurred with memories of a life never again to be encountered. Diminishing Polio cases meant disappearance of suffering and death for many people along with loss of a unique institution, the Respo Center.

From my window at home I observed autumn's rainbow as leaf colors changed from gold to brown. JJ wrote to say he was returning to Ann Arbor one more time, regardless word of the Penthouse's closure. I cautioned him

Keep Smiling and Never Give Up!

of Dr.D's remarks, but he departed for Michigan before receiving my letter. I was quite amused when JJ returned three days later.

"Danny you wouldn't believe it!" JJ exclaimed. "It's a hospital! Like you said, the Penthouse is closed. I was in a regular room, forced to wear an ID band. Can you imagine? It was distressing. These people required orientation to my tank and respiratory equipment. Our knowledgeable staff was gone! When the Penthouse lights were turned off everything changed for the worse, 'progressive nursing care' included. If assigned to one group, a resident, excuse me patient, was avoided by other staff members. I was assigned to the red team, so blue and green team members ignored my pleas for assistance. The lights may have been turned off in the Respo Center, but it's also dim elsewhere in the hospital. So long Michigan!"

Snickering I said, "JJ, at the risk of sounding crass, I told you so! Apparently, AB's are in charge."

In customary fashion JJ responded, "Yuk, Yuk, Yuk!"

Once settled at home the frantic busyness resumed and I eagerly anticipated weekend college and pro football games. In an effort to clarify radio reception from Cleveland, 300 miles away, I convinced Andy and Millie to assist me in a small feat of communications engineering. "Come on kids! All you have to do is run this tiny wire under my window and fasten it to a steel rod in the ground."

Millie challenged, "Danny, are you sure it'll work? I don't think Mom will agree with this project. If we get in trouble, it's your fault."

"Oh come on Sis." Andy mocked. "Are you chicken? Hey Danny, where's the steel rod?"

I smiled at my little brother's ambition, "It's in the garage. Remember that leftover axle from my old derby car? Find it then use Dad's sledgehammer to pound the rod down into the ground outside my window. Tightly wind this wire around that rod and push it under the windowsill. Come in here then and we'll connect it to the radio ground post. Be very careful, and please don't hurt Dad and Mom's bushes."

Our day's construction completed, I basked in perfect static-free reception when suddenly Dad bellowed, "I don't care if radio reception of your Cleveland Browns is better! That steel stake might have damaged our evergreen bushes."

Happy Birthday - Happy Thanksgiving - Merry Christmas.

Millie announced, "Danny, I've invited one of my good friends from high school to stay overnight. Together we'll welcome in 1966 at midnight. She's an attractive young lady so please be on your best behavior."

Smiling, I chuckled, "I'm sure you didn't tell her any naughty stories about me, Sis. What's her name?"

"Kaye."

21

TWILIGHT TO DAWN

An aura of roaring silence foretelling the solitude and boredom of a new year followed Christmas holidays of l965. History once again repeated itself as I incessantly read and watched television. Friends my age were in college, gone to war, or married and residing in far away places. Bobby, my new chess partner, had enlisted in the military. Fulfilling his duty, while making a career of seeing the world, Mike's training and duty station locales in the U.S.A.F. afforded me many different scenarios for imaginary travel. Loopholes for evasion of traditional responsibility had developed for those not wishing to satisfy their country's moral and legal obligations. Avenues of escape became identified as three C's: contacts, college, or cowardice. My family and friends chose none of these; some people used all three. Woodrow my cousin, visited often while home on leave from the Marines. I say proudly, he served multiple tours of duty in Vietnam. Aware living life through their perspectives was unhealthy, I continued attempting adjustment to my reality - a quest challenged by priorities in other people's lives.

Answering my request, Millie declared, "Danny I'm too busy to play chess right now. Anyway it isn't fair because you always win."

"I'll play." volunteered Andy. "I almost won last time and if I keep trying, before long, you're mine. You should play chess with me anyway, after all I did help fix weighted bottoms in the chessmen and build a storage box."

"You're right little brother, set up the board." I said smiling. "Take it easy though. How many losses is it now?"

"Well, it's seventy, but remember you lost seventy-two games before winning." he said defensively. "So watch out!"

Valentines Day had become an insignificant celebration in my life; it paralleled the cold weather outside. Most of the girls I'd known were now married, and oddly their mates objected to them sending me cards of endearment. Marriage to these wonderful young ladies had crossed my mind on many occasions and I only wished them the best. Regardless any altruistic thoughts on my part I couldn't help envying the lives they'd been given to live. Fortunately my loneliness diverted me from bitterness while I consoled an aching heart accepting salutations from TV news anchormen and reporters. Stoically I immersed myself in evening news film about men and war in Nam, empathizing when they bemoaned 'Dear John' letters. I thought, at least someone called them 'Dear'.

Periodically Dad cut my hair expressly fulfilling for me an act of vanity. Following these routine barber sessions I appropriated time in my wheelchair for writing short stories, fillers, and letters to the editor. Also on my list were letters to relatives and friends in Vietnam.

While deeply engrossed in an exciting re-run of "From Here To Eternity" there was a knock at the door. Answering, Mom escorted a guest to my room. "Forgive my intrusion," JJ apologized, "we were in the neighborhood and decided to stop by before going home."

I greeted, "Glad to see you. You're definitely not an intrusion, I was just watching television. Sort of taking a break from my busy schedule. Read any good books lately?"

"Actually I haven't." he answered. "I've been too busy writing my column and planning the radio program's guests. I'm curious, what happened to your typing? I see letters to the editor, why don't you try getting reimbursed for writing opinions? Who knows, it might lead to a column."

"Writing on a scheduled basis is impossible for me." I explained. "Anyway, I don't want overexposure."

JJ asked, "What are your plans for acquiring a medical checkup? Since our choices are restricted to conventional medical facilities, how do we select the best hospital?"

I teased, "Why JJ, aren't you traveling to Michigan? The Penthouse may be closed, but Ann Arbor is still open."

"Yuk! Yuk! Just you never mind." he admonished.

Following a pleasant conversation between two kindred spirits separated by years, but allied by circumstance, my emotions ebbed as I watched JJ and his attendant leave the room. "See ya friend, don't roll anyplace I wouldn't."

Spiritual support and growth were limited at this time. In years following Rev.Kerschner's transfer to a new church location, ministerial activity failed to materialize, and my scriptural nourishment withered. Emptiness was created when I abrogated my responsibility to follow God's commandments, ignoring freedom to choose another pastor, and obviating all personal accountability. It was easy blaming the other guy. The biblical directives I'd received from Rev.Kerschner were blurred in their importance as I drifted into a struggle for human and personal significance.

I submitted articles for publication, but received many rejection slips, which only magnified my frustration. Words of admonishment for allowing circumstance to control my life echoed from the past. Kidney stones, infections, and days required for recovery constantly plagued me, even though my travel was rare. Immobility exacerbated the difficulties I now confronted, occasionally demanding medical attention, antibiotics, and pain medicine to forestall hospitalization. Closed Respo Centers combined with my dislike of hospitals, monetary expense, and physical exhaustion encouraged display of my adamant refusal to submit to X-rays and examinations. Dr.Heilman's son and other doctors increasingly substituted in his father's practice so during one house call I asked an obvious question, "Is Dr.Heilman Sr. retiring?"

Dr.Heilman Jr. responded, "Yes, unfortunately. Dad's past retirement age, having devoted much of his life to the welfare of other people."

I silently exclaimed, "Oh no! What now..."

On a rare occasion when my parents allowed other people to provide me companionship while they went shopping, I kept Grandmother Williams out of trouble. "Hi Grandma. Glad you came over. It sure looks sunny today."

"Ray, you and Velma go buy the groceries." she ordered. "Danny and I'll get along just fine. You two be careful and take your time."

Dad nodded, "Thanks Mom. Are you sure staying here by yourself with Danny won't be any problem?"

"No! My goodness he's no trouble, so long as he stays in that bed. If he starts moving around I'll swat 'em just to show him who's boss." she chuckled, escorting them to the door. Returning to my room she pointed her finger at me and said, "Son that was for their benefit, this is for mine. Do not move!"

"Grandma," I laughed, "if I do move, one or both of us will be scared to death. Tell me some secrets about Dad."

Andy returned from school with two questions. "Are we going fishing tomorrow? Did you get food for the picnic?"

Eleven months following my last breath of fresh air and feeling warm sunshine, I inhaled the invigorating scent from flowers and grass blowing across blue waters. I dreamed of previous fishing trips while offering sage advice to young family members. I relished the children's wide-eyed joy and excitement when they yelled, "I got a bite", or "Look, Uncle Danny, I caught one!". It's amazing how much better a meal tastes when barbecued outside, and the enticing aroma as it mingles with nature's ingredients is indescribable. The day passed quickly and I thought, "If only my time in bed while imprisoned within four walls could speed by as quickly." As I bounced along in the back of Dad's station wagon I felt an uncomfortable pressure on my back from straps on the chaise lounge. Silently I ventured, "One day I'll travel sitting, then my view will encompass more than oncoming headlights."

Resuming my vigorous daily schedule, life continued with books, magazines, and TV competing for attention. A special exception highlighted this routine as weekend baseball games regularly appeared on summer TV, alleviating some boredom. The rocking bed seldom saw action for respiratory assistance, with most support provided by a chest respirator

Keep Smiling and Never Give Up!

along with my pneumobelt. This was indeed fortunate, since Dad could provide most maintenance required for these units, I was no longer honored with the presence of Mr. Quickfix. Scanning magazine pages and reading stories about distant places once more became my ticket for adventure. I inundated myself in articles about Nam, knowing full well were it not for Polio; I would be alongside my relatives and friends. I sent many cartons of items rarely found in their locations, along with my letters of encouragement to Mike, Eddie, Woodrow, Bill, Bob, and other friends. I thought this a small contribution to their well-being, and somehow might supplant my absence in obligation to God and country.

While studying some informative literature in my quest for enlightenment, I was stricken with the familiar pangs of physical discomfort. Kidney stones were on the move and I understood the adage, "familiarity breeds contempt". After all my usual remedies, Dr.Heilman was soon contacted and a house call requested. "Danny you need blood tests and new X-rays." Dr.Heilman proclaimed. "I want to leave you in the best health possible when I retire."

"Dr.Heilman I'm sorry you're retiring, but I absolutely refuse admission to the hospital unless it's life or death." I declared. "Tell me, now that your car knows the direction to my house and can bring you here in your sleep, will you occasionally allow it to drive by for emotional stability?"

Grinning, he responded, "You're right, it will probably be necessary to remove the tires from my car, otherwise it will be trying to leave the garage at two in the morning." Squeezing my arm, he bid me farewell and best wishes.

The Williams family enjoyed a summer picnic reunion and in deference to those who wished to fish we assembled once more beside cool, blue water. Lazily watching the excited children playing and adults distracted by conversation, my eyes darted to a nephew satiating his kindergarten curiosity dangerously close to the water's edge. I shouted, "Anita or Jim, you better grab Kent! Hey Sis, after you save him will you please bring me more potato chips?"

The flaming sun set behind forested overgrowth, shadows cast over placid waters created fleeting images, and streaks of red cut across the sky as dusk approached, instilling in me dread of returning to my four walls of existence. Picnic baskets, coolers, and fishing tackle were reloaded into our car and my chaise lounge with me aboard was then secured in the station wagon. Everyone's thoughts lingered behind as a good day ended and we began our bumpy journey home.

Within a week following our excursion I was once again afflicted by the usual maladies of fever, pain, and nausea. Dad observed, "Apparently fishing and picnic adventures are too much for you. I phoned Dr.Heilman Jr. and he agreed to come here after his last appointment."

Following examination by my new doctor I was informed, "Danny, I will continue assisting where Dad left off at his retirement, but I think you should return to the hospital for X-rays and blood tests."

Shaking my head I said, "As I told your father, no! If you'll help me at home, hospitalization won't be necessary."

Dr.Heilman smiled, "If you insist."

Utilizing a rare opportunity to stay in bed I willingly played chess with Andy. Shortly I proclaimed, "Checkmate! Andy, little brother, you're getting better. Keep trying, someday you'll succeed in winning."

"Shoot!" replied Andy in disgust. "I almost beat you. Let's see, seventy-three losses."

I nodded, "That's right bud, you've now set the record for most chess losses in this house. At least you're still making an effort to win, Millie won't play anymore."

Although socializing privately with friends was nearly impossible, Dad and Mom agreed to participate in activities where I could be transported while lying on the lounge. As autumn approached we convinced Judy to pack a lunch and join us on one last outing before winter. Scheduling difficulty had prevented her attendance on previous trips so she agreed to be part of our memory scrapbook. School days for Millie and Andy would begin soon, so this picnic was bon voyage to sunny days and beautiful sunsets - adventures ripe in sweet nostalgia. I deplored the end of an opportunity to see blue skies and my soul withered when thinking of life within four walls, but I simultaneously felt guilty enjoying my life of comfort, knowing many men were dying in a war gone awry.

The rolling thunder of monotony resumed when autumn and winter merged into one bleak atmosphere. Memories of summer fishing and picnic trips sufficed for excitement as I buried myself within other people's lives through books, magazines, and TV news. Halloween and trick-or-treaters camouflaged by costume and revelry provided release for tension. Entering our home in disguises designed to exact horror and surprise, they were intimidated after espying me and my respirator in the adjacent room. Mouths agape they hurriedly exited while ignoring tricks, but quickly storing treats in paper sacks.

"Happy Birthday Danny." chorused my family. "How does it feel to be an even two dozen years old?"

Looking at Kenny who had the same birthday I said, "Ask him. He surpassed that maannyy years ago. Now if I can but convince somebody to build me a typewriter table on a frame, which will roll over my bed, I'll be happy. Andy? Dad?"

Keep Smiling and Never Give Up!

Happy Thanksgiving.

"Andy how 'bout it, will you help me build a typewriter table to fit over my bed? I'll supply brainpower if you'll provide the muscle." I reasoned. "The lumber yard promises to deliver all supplies."

"All right." said Andy. "If Millie helps too."

"Well Merry Christmas at last!" I sighed. "Building my dreamed-of table begins after supplies arrive. Provided of course, enough room remains for construction."

Impatiently awaiting Andy's agreement to begin work on my rolling over-the-bed typewriter table, I counted the days until an idea etched in my mind for quite some time became reality. One day while reading, Millie and a guest entered our front door and I overheard my sister direct her friend, "Wait for me in the living room, I have to run upstairs."

I beckoned, "Will somebody catch this newspaper? It's falling!"

Turning my head toward the unfamiliar voice asking, "Can I help?" I unsuspectingly gazed into lovely, warm, brown eyes, peeking around my newspaper, a vision of innocent seductiveness. Suddenly those dreams, which had been suppressed as I forlornly watched friends and family leave to fulfill duty, seek marriage, happiness, and fortune were alive again. The soft loving voice emanating from a vivacious personality immediately captured my heart and now encompassed God's answer to prayer. We only briefly met when she, thirteen months ago, visited Millie on New Year's Eve. Her angelic face and sparkling eyes immediately inflamed my heart with undying love. "Kaye you look great!" I exclaimed. "You must come by more often. If you'll please forgive me, what's your last name?"

"Dan, it's Williams, same as yours. Millie and I are in the same homeroom at school."

"Oh yes." I stammered. Though trying unsuccessfully to divert attention from the charming magnetism in Kaye's eyes, my imagined debonair demeanor quickly dissolved and searing hot flashes covered my face. Little capillaries opened and I became angry for allowing this teenage doll to turn a once cool, sophisticated young man into a tongue-tied little boy. Without thinking I impulsively chortled, "Williams huh? If you'll marry me, you won't have to change the name on your driver's license." Oh well, I've had better days.

Blushing Kaye laughed, "We barely know each other."

Entering the room Millie asked, "Okay you two, what's up? I heard laughter, let me in on the funny."

"Millie, I think Dan just proposed." Kaye teased.

Narrowing her eyes Millie grinned, "A new sister eh?"

As they left I winked at Kaye, "Don't forget now."

Daniel R. Williams

The difference between Valentine's Day this year and last was phenomenal; my broken spirit had just begun healing. As Cupid's holiday approached I developed an innocently covert scheme to send Kaye a Valentine without her knowledge of its origin. In discussions with Millie I learned she had plans to attend the sweetheart dance with a "boyfriend". I felt compelled to subvert Kaye's attention from her unsuspecting companion, and enlisted the help of my questioning sister.

While thanking Millie for the lovely card she chose I nonchalantly instructed, "Now Lefty, if you'll just write these words of endearment with your right hand and neglect to sign my name, I'll let Kaye think it's from 'Junior'."

"Danny this isn't very nice you know." Millie objected. "What if she thanks her date for the kind thought, and he's too embarrassed to tell the truth?"

"Who cares." I replied. "All's fair in love and war."

Two days later Millie entered my room laughing, "Danny! You won't believe what happened. On their way to the dance Kaye thanked 'Junior' for the Valentine. Flustered because he forgot to send her one, he mumbled, 'Oh, you're more than welcome, I guess'. Kaye knows he didn't send her the card with that romantic poem. Now she's on the warpath quizzing everyone if they know who sent the mysterious Valentine. I gotta tell you brother, when she questioned me I almost let the cat out of the bag. My gut's still sore from trying not to burst out laughing while looking innocent."

Happiness at Andy and Millie's agreement to begin work on a long awaited typewriter table had been short lived when it became obvious my brother wouldn't be available until the wrestling season ended. Patience was rewarded even though Valentine's Day passed and the Ides of March were upon us. Late winter winds accompanied delivery of supplies from New Castle Lumber Yard and I imagined myself using the finished product. Judy inventoried, "Twelve 2x4's, a 40x24" sheet of 1" plywood, 2-60x48" sheets of 1/4" plywood, nails, bolts, and chains, threaded rods, electrical box, light fixtures, stain and sandpaper, four casters, steel piping, one 8'- 4x4, several feet of conduit wiring, and miscellaneous hardware. Danny, it's all here. Pay the man."

As Judy handed the delivery man my money Mom walked in exclaiming, "Oh my goodness! Your room is full. Now Danny, you know Andy can't put all this together."

I protested, "Of course the room is full Mom, what did you expect at our building site? The brainwork is mine and I need Andy's muscle. He'll do just fine."

I received information from The March of Dimes telling about their annual telethon. It merely confirmed statements by Dr.Oliver following my

Keep Smiling and Never Give Up!

first admission to a Respo Center. While the thrust of this wonderful organization would now be directed toward birth defects, we respo Polios were assured necessary respiratory equipment support for the remainder of our lives. Thank you President Roosevelt.

Some time later Judy encouraged, "Danny, why don't you listen to WCTW in the morning? The radio station is having a contest and the prize has reached one hundred dollars. I think you'd be interested in the subject: military history. Let's see if you remember anything from all the books we've been bringing you from the library."

"Aw come on Sis, it's on too early." I groaned. "How could I call anyway, I can't reach the telephone."

"Tch, tch, tch, you're just chicken." she goaded. "Dad can phone the answer to me and I'll contact the station. I guess we could split the prize."

"Why should I split the prize? One doesn't usually pay his hired hand fifty percent of the profit." I joked.

"Beetle Smith? No way!" said Dad. "He's in the comic strips. What's the real answer?"

Impatiently I stated, "Tell Judy the answer is General Walter Bedell Smith. Eisenhower's Chief of Staff on D-Day."

"You're crazy! Oh, not you Daddy." Judy exclaimed. "I think Danny's nuts. I'm not going to sound like an idiot by phoning in that answer. Is he mad at me?"

"This was your idea." said Dad. "Call the station!"

The day following Judy's phone call to WCTW she entered my room sheepishly asking, "Danny where do I put your half of the one hundred dollar prize?"

Inwardly smiling I answered, "Well actually Judy, use some of my prize money when you go shopping to buy a lovely birthday card. Something with roses or hearts."

"Why? It isn't my birthday." she quipped.

Imperceptively shrugging I stated, "Tell you later."

Judy returned from the store asking, "OK, what's next?"

"Since you obviously owe me a favor," I explained, "the card will need your hand for my signature."

"Oh, oh!" Judy cringed. "You're not going to enlist me in your forgery ring like Millie!"

"Remember Bedell Smith? Now please write." I pleaded, "Happy Birthday Dearest Kaye. Guess who?"

Bang! Bang! Scrape, Whirrr! The sounds of construction echoed through the house as Andy, and occasionally Millie, worked diligently to complete building my typewriter table.

"Danny, I'm not sure these kids are responsible enough to control these power tools." commented Dad. "Maybe Andy shouldn't use the circular saw."

"You're right Dad." I agreed. "It would be much better if you cut all the wood. Thanks for volunteering."

Several days a week it became necessary to engage in an incentive program. I sighed, "Okay Andy, it's time for our game of chess. Remember, only three then we work."

One afternoon Millie came home from school carrying two yearbooks and I joked, "You sure have a big ego."

"Oh this isn't mine." she replied. "We exchanged books so different people would have the opportunity to write some words of wisdom. This is Kaye's yearbook."

"Hhmmm!" I mused. "Wonder if a kind person would help me sign my name? Perhaps even a poem of endearment."

"No!" said Millie. "I won't be your accomplice again."

"Hey Andy." I yelled. "Want to play some more chess?"

"Are you sure this is all right?" asked Andy. "What if that girl finds out it's my handwriting?"

"Don't worry." I assured him. "Millie won't tell."

"Who says I won't? My guilty conscience burns." Millie frowned. "Anyway, Kaye will know when I return the book."

"No offense Sis," I remarked, "but you must learn to be more creative. Ask Carolyn to return three different books at once to other girls. Include Kaye's in the mix."

Work on the typewriter table was temporarily suspended while Andy participated in springtime sporting events. As I was reading a book, giggles filtered into my room.

"Hey Danny." teased Millie, peering around the doorway. "Are you dressed for a fashion show?"

Kaye, Millie, and their friend Janice entered my room gracefully twisting and twirling as satiny, flowing formals radiated an electrifying display of beauty and finesse. In unison my spirits, circulation, and pulse zoomed as I soared into an era of euphoric speculation. Millie and Janice were well dressed; however, the third model captivated me. Clouds of gloom parted and, mesmerized, I whispered, "Hello Kaye." Quickly regrouping I said, "Millie, I know you're attending Senior Prom. I just met you Janice. What about your plans Kaye, I suppose you'll be dating 'Junior' again?"

"No, I'm attending a church party." she answered. "How did you know about 'Junior'? He and I don't talk much anymore. I embarrassed him Valentine's Day so now he's dating another girl."

Solemnly I remarked, "I can't imagine why anyone would do such a thing, but if he's that weak of character you're much better off going to church. If the party ends early, perhaps we could play a game of checkers."

Graduation day completed, Millie began summer work. A void took presence in my life as Kaye departed for Tennessee to spend the summer with her grandmother Ollie. Oh well, at least 'Junior' is here in Indiana with me.

Sitting in bed before my new rolling typewriter table I lauded, "Andy you did a fantastic job! It's perfect! Maybe now I can type with my mouthstick while in bed. Brother, if you'll remember the skills you learned while building this stand, somebody will give you a great job someday."

Beaming with pride Andy blushed, "Thanks a lot!"

Laying mail on my bed one day Mom commented, "Aaahh how sweet. Look! A postcard from Kaye in Tennessee. She's so considerate. Millie's got a wonderful friend."

After visiting each local military recruiter my sister Millie enlisted in the service of her country. Without any encouragement from me. Really! She resisted peer pressure coercing her into college, and determined to be an entirely independent person, preferring freedom of choice – signing away four years of her life to the U.S. Marine Corps!

In the autumn of 1967 a vacuum filled my life as Kaye left for Marion College, Millie marched off to boot camp in San Diego, Andy played football, and I read and dreamed. My correspondence continued at an accelerated pace now that I could type letters easily from bed. Writing short stories encouraged me to begin planning a newspaper column. I chose not to interfere with Kaye's studies by sending her letters because I really didn't know how to explain 'Junior'.

"Happy Birthday Danny." said my dwindling family. "Any special requests this year? Now that Andy's finished your typewriter table, let's put him to work on a new house."

Mom lamented, "Twenty-five! It doesn't seem possible. Only yesterday my fourteen year old baby had Polio."

"Yeah Mom." Andy chuckled. "Quarter of a century!"

Celebrating my birthday was complete as an old friend, Mike, appeared at the door with a beautiful young woman on his arm. "Happy Birthday old buddy!"

"Hi Mike," I greeted, "welcome back to the world."

Grinning, Mike happily announced, "Meet Mary Lou, soon to be my wife. If all proceeds on schedule, January 27th is going to be our lucky day."

Mary Lou smiled, "Happy to meet you Danny, Mike's told me a lot about you and both your exploits when you were growing up."

Laughing I said, "Hope he told you he instigated most of our activities. Seriously, pleased to meet you. Tell me how you ever convinced this guy to get married."

"Well Danny, it took a little while," she said, "but he finally got smart. I agreed to overlook his bad habits."

Thanksgiving day became a cherished moment in my life. After family festivities, while mutually bemoaning gluttony, there was a knock at our door. Escorting her into my room Vivian said, "Danny, look who's here. One of Millie's girl friends from school, Kaye."

"Well hello." I welcomed. "Glad you could come. Mom said you might be here when Millie called from California. While we're waiting tell me about college."

Following a flurry of long-distance phone conversation Dad groaned, "Good land, that phone bill will be enormous! Everybody in the family, Danny by proxy, Kaye, and there's no getting Velma to say goodbye."

I coaxed, "Vivian, I don't have any flashbulbs so would you usher Kaye outside for a photograph? I'm sure Millie would like a picture. I'll send it in her Christmas card."

Vivian coughed, "Millie's coming home for Christmas. The film won't be developed in time. Sure it's for her?"

"Well you never can tell," I explained, "Just take the picture! If it isn't developed in time, it's mine. Agreed, Kaye?"

Confronting December's holidays required patience and a Solomon-like discernment of the future. Millie's homecoming was eagerly anticipated, but my newly recognized affection for Kaye presented me with a dilemma. I knew I must either be honest with her concerning my feelings or be willing to silently suffer in anguish each time we met. Reckoning day would soon be upon me, Christmas break at college neared.

"Welcome home Millie." cheered the family in unison. "We're glad you're here for the holidays."

Millie gushed, "Believe me it's wonderful. Living so far away from home at Christmas is really lonely."

Ten days passed rapidly and plans for the new year were foremost in everyone's thoughts. Another kidney infection mitigated any decision I presently made and I surrendered to the tribulations engulfing my life. My sister made plans for evening church services and I remarked, "Look at it snow!"

"Danny stop stalling!" Millie demanded. "Kaye wants to see you, what do I tell her? She's only home from college until early January, are you suddenly shy? I know you don't feel well, but is there some other reason? I'm beginning to wonder if you're hiding something. Should we talk?"

"What can I say Sis?" I replied. "Honesty from me will either begin a closer relationship between us, or inhibit any future friendship. What if I write her a letter? If I dictate a letter will you take it to her at church tonight?"

Dictation complete, Millie exclaimed, "Whooooaaa! I thought I saw sparks flying the last time you were together, but I didn't realize the situation was this advanced. Are you serious?"

"Listen Marine, don't get smart!" I ordered. "Besides, you weren't even here the last time we were together. Just please deliver my letter to Kaye when you go to church."

Millie hesitated, "Sure, if that's what you want, but I can't tonight. You know this is New Year's Eve and Kaye's singing. A solo, no less."

"Fantastic!" I grinned. "Give her my letter before she stands up in front of the congregation to sing. I couldn't ask for a better time to test her willpower."

Returning home from her New Year's Eve date and church service, Millie could hardly contain her exuberance. "Well, I gave Kaye your letter prior to her solo. When reading it she paled out. You'll never believe what she chose to sing tonight. 'OPEN MY EYES, THAT I MAY SEE'."

"How appropriate." I said. "A match made in heaven."

Enthusiasm for life's rewards rapidly accelerated as my typing now included letters to Kaye. Written discussions to get acquainted proved difficult, and our letters became long distance dates enabling us to understand each other's hopes, aspirations, and perspectives. Kaye's goal was to become a Registered Nurse or Medical Doctor and I dreamed of creating successful literary contributions. Fading visions awakened and together we prayed for happiness and love. Valentine's Day approached and I was content knowing this year 'Junior' and various other "friends" were history.

Mom answered the phone then entered my room announcing, "Kaye is calling. She's home on semester break and wants to visit you. Shall I tell her it's okay?"

During our visit and conversation I confessed to a most dastardly act associated with last Valentine's Day. I shyly explained, "It would probably be more romantic for me to now sign your cards with my name rather than just, 'Guess Who'."

"So you're the one!" Kaye said accusingly. "A birthday card too? Poor 'Junior'. I could offer my belated thanks, but wouldn't you rather have a kiss?"

After Kaye's brief visit Mom fired insistent questions regarding our conversation. "Danny what did she want? Your sister isn't here anymore, so why did she come?"

"Mom, Kaye's a nice person and I'm thankful she thinks about me." I replied. "Our conversation was private."

I continued writing letters to my friends and family in Vietnam. With the addition of Kaye to my life, writing had indeed become a labor of love. Studies and classroom time usurped much of her day, but in an effort to assist with the financial responsibilities of an education she began working as a part-time nurse's aide at Marion General Hospital. The frequency of Kaye's letters prompted dissension between Dad, Mom, and I because they adamantly disagreed with any thought of their son having a meaningful relationship with a woman. Ironically, regardless my paralysis, Kaye's parents were more willing to trust their daughter's future to her choice. We both prayerfully sought God's will for our lives.

Unbelievably March was here again, but this time rather than contemplating uses of a new typewriter table I dreamed of future happiness. As Kaye's birthday approached I asked, "Judy, will you do me a favor? On your way home please stop and order flowers for Kaye."

"Danny," Judy answered, "I don't mind shopping for you, but shouldn't we ask Mother and Daddy first?"

"Judith! I'm twenty-five years old. Don't ever ask me that again! Is your answer yes or no?"

"Yes," she said hesitantly, "but don't ever tell them I helped. Now what do you want?"

"Tell the florist I want eighteen red roses delivered March 9th, to Marion College. Explicitly sign the card with these words: 'Happy Birthday! My Dearest Kaye, Love, Dan'."

The next day Dad prompted, "Danny, why don't you end this ridiculous relationship before someone gets hurt? Surely you realize, as a young college student Kaye will be dating other men. I think you should just try to forget her. She doesn't have a well paying job, it's best if we keep taking care of you."

"Listen to your dad." said Mom. "She shouldn't write to you anymore. We know what's best, you're paralyzed!"

"Dad, Mom, relax!" I pleaded. We aren't eloping. Kaye must finish nursing school and I'm hoping to earn a living writing short stories, a newspaper column, or even a book."

"Oh Danny," they scoffed, "that won't happen. Once she graduates from college her attention will stop. As for you earning a living...remember Polio! We'll take care of you."

Following this predecessor of many arguments I decided immediate action was necessary. The next day when my sister visited I requested, "Judy will you do another favor for me? Please take my money and rent a P.O. Box."

"Danny why do you need a post office box?" she asked.

"I'll continue writing and receiving letters from Kaye, just at an alternate address." I declared. "This is Dad and Mom's home, I'll respect their wishes so long as I reside in their house. Consequently, for Kaye's letters I'll need a P.O. Box. I trust you, or someone, will bring me my mail."

"Danny I don't understand their position." she replied. "Yes, I'll reserve a P.O. Box and bring Kaye's letters."

"Dan, why?" responded Kaye in her next letter. "It doesn't sound rational to me and I don't agree, but if you say mail letters to a P.O. Box or your sister's house, I will."

I was comfortably engrossed in a study of World War II when I heard mortar shells landing beside the hallway phone. "What? Millie, you don't mean it!" exclaimed Mom during her telephone conversation with my sister. "Well you can't stay in the Marines now that you're married. ...Are you sure?... OK, I'll ask him...If you're wrong he's going to be mad."

"Danny that was Millie calling, she and a Marine named Malcolm were married. She said marriage was permissible for women Marines. Is that right?" asked Mom, expecting denial.

"Yes Mom." I answered. "Until she gets pregnant it's permissible for her to remain an active duty Marine."

"Well I never dreamed..." said Mom. "You don't act at all surprised. Did you know?"

"Me?" I innocently replied.

Following a family furor over the ills of sending one's daughter to an "unsupervised" military base, the humdrum of life continued. I thought it disgusting my little sister was now a married Marine, while at twenty-five I surreptitiously got my mail smuggled from a P.O. Box. Time provided opportunity for most people to accept Millie's elopement and I was quite pleased when Judy reported, "Norman and I are going west for our vacation. While in California we hope to visit Millie and meet her new husband. Vivian will bring Kaye's letters from the post office during my absence."

While Judy and Norman traveled west I contented myself with visions of once seemingly unattainable goals. Reading and typing were interrupted when I played a thrilling game of chess with Andy. "Eighty-nine games! I can't stand it!" my little brother grimaced after our exercise in futility. "Someday I'll beat you at this game!"

"Hey Mom!" I yelled. "Andy needs another consolation sandwich to ease the pain of loss."

Andy growled, "Just wait! Ready for another match?"

I wrote to Kaye explaining that Millie and her husband would be home on leave in late June and implored, "If at all possible you and I must spend some time together."

Daniel R. Williams

My little sister and her new husband arrived and Millie kissed me announcing, "Danny meet Marine L/Cpl Malcolm. You both enjoy similar subjects, I know you'll like each other."

We all exchanged amenities and over the next few days became acquainted with our newest family member. It proved easy discussing favored subjects with him, especially Nam. One unfortunate aspect of his demeanor was partiality toward Purdue University - even Marines aren't faultless. Malcolm challenged me to a chess match and, hesitant to display anti-social behavior, I cautiously accepted. Hours later Millie appeared at his side asking in frustration, "When will you two be finished? I want to visit my friends."

"Patience little sister." I urged. "All young men need to learn humility."

"Yeah." said Andy, watching our game. "I shouldn't be the only humble person in this house."

Moments later following my words of wisdom I looked in horror as Malcolm shouted, "Checkmate! I don't believe it!"

Running into my room Millie cried, "What happened?"

Malcolm proudly replied, "Your Big Brother just got a dose of humility."

While I looked stunned at the board of defeat, Andy put his hand on my shoulder comforting, "I know the feeling."

Anita and Jim planned a family dinner honoring Malcolm and Millie. I willingly accepted the invitation, but asked, "Are you sure I can invite Kaye? I know it's your house, but Dad and Mom won't come under those circumstances."

Anita replied, "I'm preparing enough food for everyone. Of course we want you to invite Kaye. As for our parents, they're welcome, I hope they come to the celebration."

"Listen Danny." said Millie. "Malcolm can transfer you from wheelchair to car, we'll stop by Kaye's house and bring her with us. When we return home he'll lift you back in bed and I'll help secure your chest shell for sleep."

On June 29, 1968, Kaye and I began the second phase of our courtship. I watched her as she nervously walked toward the car. "Dan, meet my mother, Myra. Dad's at work. Mom, this is Dan." Although we met three years ago Kaye hadn't seen me sit up like a big boy. After nervous introductions we proceeded to an enjoyable dinner with family. Together at last in a setting away from home Kaye became acquainted with me for the first time in a wheelchair. Looking at the chair she asked, "What's this piece bolted to the frame?"

"That's a long story." I sighed. "The bracket attached to my chair held a device known as a 'ball bearing feeder'. I once used it for typing and feeding myself."

"Oh, why didn't you tell me?" Kaye asked excitedly. "I wouldn't have fed you if I'd known. Does it still work?"

"No." I mumbled. "Not any more."

Sensing unwillingness to discuss the subject further, Kaye relegated this topic to another day. With cooperation from my sisters and brothers-in-law, we took our first step on a journey toward happiness and fulfillment.

The next day warming rays of sunlight flickered through towering oak trees as siblings and their mates savored food, fellowship, and happiness at a family picnic in Baker Park. Everyone enjoyed togetherness at a hurriedly planned going away party for Malcolm and Millie. We all anxiously watched for our parents to appear, aware of their negative reaction to Kaye's presence at dinner the preceding evening which they refused to attend. A heavy pall of indecision settled over everyone as we dreaded future repercussion. We prayerfully anticipated Dad and Mom's attendance at today's gathering, fervently hoping the summer breezes would bring a succulent change to misunderstanding.

Kaye's eyes nervously darted over the roads leading to our location and she repeatedly asked, "Are you sure it's OK for me to be here with you? I don't like being responsible for family arguments."

"Yes." I declared. "Someday, God willing, you will be their daughter-in-law. They must accept that now. It's so obvious your presence is important to me; I'm sitting in my wheelchair for the second time in two days. Outside!"

Vivian and Anita snapped pictures while staring at the park entrance as I contemplated my life at home after today. My parent's reluctance to allocate love and devotion while accepting my adult emotions and mature choices influenced their decision to not participate in our festivities. Sadly they and we missed the opportunity to love and give thanks.

I agonized over continuing conflicts surfacing between Dad, Mom, and me. Added to this dilemma was the knowledge of their sincere love and demonstrated devotion to me during the eleven years since my affliction with Polio. Perhaps my care, and stress associated with providing innumerable trips from home to hospital, prevented any possibility for them to accept another person in their son's life. My distress soon became obvious in Kaye's letters, "Dan it's miserable to be perceived as a wedge in anyone's parental relationship."

I didn't know how to explain something to my fiancé, that I couldn't understand myself, but responding to her questions I wrote, "the disagreement between my parents and me doesn't involve you personally.

Since Polio I've never received any enthusiastic support for a new endeavor, and especially this time, which involves eventual independence. Needless to say, obstinacy is definitely more pronounced now that a woman is in the picture. Without a miraculous change in their mind, I'll forever be a fourteen-year-old baby/boy/son paralyzed from Polio. The Lord is directing our situation."

Dad endured a physical ailment precipitated by lifting me without using my hydraulic patient lifter. This problem, his job, and stress associated with our continued arguments, increased my feelings of guilt. One day during conversation concerning summer vacation I meekly suggested, "Why not pay for two or three weeks at a nursing home for me, and all of you go to Florida for some needed rest? Maybe Eddie or Jeff could accompany Andy so he'll have a buddy. Mom you've been dreaming of living in the Sunshine State, look around for a perfect retirement home site."

Dad willingly and quickly agreed with my suggestion and while they were gone I was a resident of Park Riley Nursing Home. My perceived sense of a gloomy future had encouraged me to research various nearby facilities, choosing Park Riley as a preferable respite. Admission procedures were a unique experience. As the young nurse's aide took inventory of my possessions she nonchalantly reached into my mouth and authoritatively asked, "Do you have any identifying marks on your false teeth? We must register all dentures in case you lose or misplace them."

"Let go!" I warned through clenched teeth, "Doll if you don't get your hand out of my mouth I'll bite your fingers! I'm only twenty-five and I take my dentures to bed."

"Oh! I'm so sorry!" she gasped. "It's just a habit."

Once staff familiarized themselves with my respirators and hygiene requirements, life became a breath of fresh air. Susie and her giggles; Chatty's devotion to detail; Barb's medical adroitness, and Mary's motherly love exemplified the care at my temporary home. My first adventure into another world was indeed successful. I sat in my wheelchair every day participating in varied activities at Park Riley, and its close proximity to Anita and Jim's house made visiting with them quite convenient. They transported me; sitting in my wheelchair, in back of Jim's pickup while I watched with awe the sights, sounds, and people of Greenfield. Jim conducted his soft water business from home and Anita was office manager so I conversed with customers and was treated to home-cooked meals. I must say, the bologna sandwiches were excellent and I dreaded thoughts of returning to four walls. My ball bearing feeder remained stored in a box, but I was in heaven.

Two weeks into this vacation, Anita invited Kaye for a cookout. Scheduling was difficult because she worked at the hospital during summer hiatus. My recall of the barbecued food is nonexistent, but suffice to say, the grill didn't produce the only glowing embers that memorable day.

Dad, Mom, Andy, and Eddie returned refreshed from their Florida vacation as tanned and sunburned bodies testified to the enjoyment of a pleasant break in routine. Eddie's USAF enlistment signaled his prompt departure from New Castle, and Andy prepared himself for football season, but Dad and Mom were evermore rigid in their opposition to my dreams of self-sufficiency. I decided to embark on a plan to relocate regardless Kaye's doubts about its advisability. No longer could I submit to a life without goals or sustainable hope of achieving even minimal success. If only my parents could understand. I not only resisted their rules at home, but I risked my relationship with Kaye by discounting her counsel for long-suffering. I continued to investigate a number of options for accomplishing my life's dream.

As summer ended and time for Kaye's return to college neared I reached an irreversible decision in my life. With resolute goals in mind I asked Judy for another favor, "When Mom goes to the doctor will you consent to calling Kaye and extending my invitation for her to come here at 2:00 PM? I know she just returned from visiting her grandmother Ollie in Tennessee, and we must talk before she leaves for Marion. Don't worry, it'll only take thirty minutes."

Judy pleaded, "Danny, don't ask me to get in trouble."

"Listen Sis, they only said no more mail." I advised. "Visitors weren't mentioned."

"That reasoning sounds suspicious to me." she argued. "I'll probably regret this, but okay. Thirty minutes."

A knot of unquestionable fear formed in my stomach and I summoned all the reserve suaveness I possessed as I waited for Kaye to arrive. After what seemed an eternity, Judy let her in the front door and excused herself while I silently prayed for words of wisdom and strength. Looking into Kaye's loving eyes and feeling her lips touch mine I whispered, "Do you have any idea how much I've missed you? Honey, it's so wonderful to see you again, even if only for a short time. I've tried on a number of occasions to test your willpower, patience, and fortitude, but truth and difficulty only seem to strengthen your resolve. Now without any doubts, I'm asking for all your love, patience, and trust. Will you..?"

"Stop!" exclaimed Kaye. "Don't forget I promised Dad I would graduate from college."

I acknowledged, "I have no intention of asking you to break a promise you made to your parents. Listen carefully, whether it takes three, six, or ten years my question is the same. Please let me finish speaking this time. I

Daniel R. Williams

know it's Friday, September 13, I love you regardless the date. Will you marry me?"

"YES!"

22

BURNING BRIDGES

I welcomed the days ahead with new optimism, encouraged by Kaye's acceptance of my marriage proposal. The interim between dream and fact was irrelevant as hope propelled our lives toward a distant vision. My fiancé began her second year in college as I continued feeble attempts to initiate a writing career. Research, short stories, book outline, and personal correspondence occupied my time, however with JJ's support I submitted an idea for a daily newspaper column. I sought this opportunity to develop writing skills planning and anticipating future quests. Unfortunately, the managing editor of *The Courier-Times* decided I would receive a negative response to my chosen subject - a history of New Castle. His reaction was understandable, since each day brought further bad news about a war taking place thousands of miles away. Parents buried sons, wives buried husbands, children buried fathers, and some people protested, but the majority searched for answers through quiet contemplation. Headlines trumpeted war and brutality. With these grisly facts in mind, why would anyone be interested in the past?

My parents defied any discussion of a relationship with Kaye. Regardless my age of twenty-five, expressing personal feelings for her promised verbal conflict. Disappointment and anger became routine, suffocating influences in my life, but intermittent correspondence with Kaye provided temporary respite. Although writing often, I attempted to conceal the increasing discouragement overtaking me, while assuring her of my eternal love. Promises of enduring support sublimated for actions, as letters became our lifeline for long-distance courtship.

Painfully, I realized the only way we could achieve our goals in life was for me to leave the protective confines of my parent's home. I wrote Kaye of my thoughts and quickly received a curt reply. Answering her letter I pleaded, "Try to understand. It's not a question of wanting to change my residence, rather one of requirement. Certainly Dad and Mom love me, the devotion they've shown to my well-being is more than evident. Sadly, they adamantly refuse to acknowledge I am no longer a baby boy or a fourteen-year-old son. Unwillingly to change their limited view of the present prohibits any opportunity for future happiness. Despite their choice not to accept my maturity, I must be allowed to live as an adult free from parental control. I respect your opinion, but this time I must do what I think best for all. Shortly I'll arrange my exodus from their house."

Daniel R. Williams

Responding to my announcement Kaye wrote, encouraging me to, "Be patient. If I could stand on weak knees before a church congregation on New Year's Eve while singing solo with a shaky voice, you my dear can also cope. Stories you've recounted from rehab days prove you and adversity aren't strangers. As for us, if God wills we be together nothing anyone can do or say will prevent that from happening. So what if the column idea isn't viable at this time? Talk to JJ again, I'm sure he faced rejection at first."

Coincidence or the hand of God, who can say, but eerily I once again felt the pangs of kidney problems. Dr.Heilman was summoned and appropriate medicine prescribed along with his observation, "Danny, do you realize how long it's been since you've had blood tests and X-rays? I'm convinced you should be hospitalized for a more thorough evaluation."

"Sorry Doc, not yet." I replied. "I don't have time to waste on something so insignificant as tests. I'll soon be requesting your referral orders to Robert Long, but with luck this can wait until mid-November."

Dr.Heilman stated, "I understand from your letter all attempts to write a newspaper column failed, any change? Danny, there is a possibility the Clinic could help you educationally through a course for transcribing medical orders. You realize any such employment wouldn't offer an adequate income. Don't you think it's advisable to remain at home letting your parents support and take care of your needs?"

"Dr.Heilman I appreciate your concern for me, but this involves much more than my needs. I'm no longer a child and I've made a decision to leave!" I asserted. "There haven't been any changes concerning the column and while I realize you are trying to offer help, it's inadequate. Platitudes, though well meaning, and discussion of future arrangements can't solve a problem so complex."

"I understand." he nodded. "Be advised, we don't have nursing home facilities in New Castle equipped to accommodate your respiratory needs and our new convalescent center won't be open for approximately eighteen months. I'm quite certain your admission to this facility would require funds exceeding any income from the employment I suggested. Perhaps consideration for submitting your column to another newspaper is an option."

"Thank you for your words of wisdom." I intoned. "I've already done that."

After administering pain medication and ordering the usual antibiotics Dr.Heilman prepared to leave. Cognizant of my determination he advised, "Call when you need me."

Events moved rapidly during the next few days while I closed doors that could never be opened again. Fortunately my brother and sister assisted me,

Keep Smiling and Never Give Up!

unwittingly of course, in preparing for the move. Andy asked, "Danny why am I packing your books in these boxes? Aren't you ever going to read them again?"

Judy asked, "Why are you storing all your things in the attic? What are you doing? Does Kaye know?"

"Please just trust me." I requested. "In time you'll all know the answer. Including Kaye."

The emotional self-protection, which I'd hidden behind for more than a decade since Polio, demanded reticence as I continued efforts to relocate my residency. Questions asked by family and close acquaintances became contests between my right to privacy and their quest for truth. Unhappily, this mode also included Kaye, my wife-to-be. I purposefully gave brief, superficial explanations of my plans to her; certain she'd not only worry, but also object. Choosing confidentiality I acknowledged, "Hospital first, convalescent center second, our home third; knowing faith, love, patience, and hope will always sustain us through future tribulations. Aunt Zella encouraged me many times to, 'Keep smiling!' Soon after I had Polio a nurse's aide who saved my life, and Dr. Walcher, admonished me, 'Never give up!' I'm certain our future will be fraught with challenges; those watchwords mustn't be ignored as we confront yearly, weekly, indeed daily trials.

Later I commented, "Andy, now that football season is over suppose you have time for a game of chess?"

Excitedly Andy agreed, "All Right! What's up? I know you're not feeling very well."

"No special reason little brother." I responded. "Just thought you might want to try winning. Unless I'm mistaken, your record for chess losses in this house is secure at 94. Don't let my frail condition fool you. I offer no quarter!"

I watched my brother's eyes sparkle as he anticipated victory with each move. "Oh wow!" Andy exclaimed wringing his hands nervously. "Two moves and you're mine!"

"Don't get excited prematurely." I cautioned. "As Yogi once said, 'it ain't over 'til it's over'."

"CHECKMATE!" Andy bellowed. "I can't believe it! Hey Mom, I won! Hey Dad, I beat Danny at chess! Finally! Now after 94 losses I can hold my head up high. Danny you must have a fever. I gotta write Millie!"

"Happy Birthday Danny." said the remaining members of my family at home. Inwardly, anguish over consequences of recent decisions created trepidation and I fervently hoped my choices were correct. Nevertheless this year, 1968, was my final birthday celebration in Dad and Mom's house. Next day I could no longer postpone reality and requested the doctor be called.

"Dr.Heilman thank you for coming once more." I stated. "My health is deteriorating, the kidney stone and UTI demand more than a house call. I can't eat and the pain is too severe, I'm ready to submit. Would you please arrange my admission to Robert Long Hospital?"

The following day despite nausea and pain, I sat up in bed and typed a letter to Carlton Bishop, equipment rep, at The March of Dimes respirator pool in Augusta, Georgia with a request for pickup of my rocking bed in late November. As I completed the letter I became physically unable to write more so I awaited my sister's appearance next day. "Judy, I was unable to type Kaye a note last night. Will you phone when she returns home from college for Thanksgiving break to give her my IUMC address? Also, please mail this envelope."

"Sure Danny." agreed Judy. "I'll call her."

I responded, "Thanks for everything Judy."

The evening before leaving I reasoned with my parents, "Dad, perhaps this break will help you rest and regain some of the strength you've expended the last eleven years. We both know lifting me isn't good for you. Just think Mom, while Andy's in school your only responsibility will be to avoid loneliness. Not to worry though, I'm certain Judy and Vivian will visit occasionally."

"Danny we don't know what you have in mind," said Dad, "but you won't be in the hospital many days. The doctor is only asking for tests and X-rays."

The following morning I embarked on a new adventure as we left for Robert Long Hospital in Indianapolis. Riding in the back of Dad's station wagon I arrived at the emergency entrance and was eventually assigned a bed on Ward D. "This is interesting." I thought. "Admission to the hospital on day 13, assigned to bed number 13, in a semi-private ward of 13 patients. I can't wait to tell Kaye."

After perfunctory conferences with appropriate people Dad assured me before he and Mom left, "Your sisters will be visiting soon, if you're here that long. The doctor said it would be a brief stay so we'll probably be back shortly to take you home. After all, it's just for X-rays and tests."

"Dad, the 'doctor' was only a med student." I remarked. "He's never seen me before, and I have several problems that weren't discussed. Please take my word; I won't be home in the near future. I'm planning on more than a 'short stay'. Before you leave, remember what we discussed earlier, I've initiated irreversible changes and directed The March of Dimes to pick up my rocking bed. You'll be contacted in a few days to schedule a mutually agreeable date toward the end of November."

Mom chided, "Oh Danny, what makes you think they'll do as you say? Anyway, when did you talk to them?"

Keep Smiling and Never Give Up!

I sighed, "Mom, it's my respirator, of course they'll answer my request. Look at it this way, now you'll have a dining room again. Why not order new furniture?"

As Dad and Mom walked away I was conscious a vacuum of needless misunderstanding created heavy hearts for everyone. Between nauseous gags and vision blurred by a fever, I awaited word from the doctor in charge of my case. Shortly a dark-headed, young, muscular man with horn rimmed glasses stood beside my bed announcing, "Danny we have completed the blood tests and your chemistry is in need of adjustment. We'll immediately begin intravenous feeding. Now the next question, which arm do you prefer?"

"Either arm Doc, but prepare for difficulty." I warned. "My veins are sadly depleted."

Seven unsuccessful attempts later Dr.Bender sighed, "It will be necessary to perform a surgical procedure exposing a vein, allowing insertion of an intravenous catheter. I will do this with local anesthetic, so you won't feel any pain. The cutdown will take about thirty minutes."

After completing the procedure I nodded, "Thanks Doc. Your little operation hurt less than repeated needle sticks while you probed for a vein."

John the orderly, Donna RN, and Phyllis a nurse's aide, transferred me to the stretcher in preparation for travel to X-ray. "Watch the IV tubin'." instructed Rosie, Head Nurse, her Irish brogue filling the air. "There ya' be Danny Boy. See ya' in a wee bit."

Returning to Ward D from X-ray, I was both disgusted and angry. Rosie phoned Dr.Bender to explain and received comments directed by proxy to Radiology. "Well doctor, he was in X-ray and 'peers they were a wee bit rambunctious."

Within minutes Dr.Bender stormed onto the ward charging, "They did what? Who pulled this cutdown out? The man only has two arms."

Rolling her green eyes Rosie meekly said, "Yes doctor."

Dr.Bender apologized, "Danny, I'll return shortly and put an IV in your other arm, but first I'll discuss this situation with certain staff in Radiology."

Days later I was feeling better, though still weak and nauseous. Lack of adequate nutritional intake and stringent antibiotics to combat a virulent infection continued taxing my body. Liquids and some solid foods were encouraged, but my digestive system rebelled. Even thoughts of Thanksgiving food failed to entice my taste buds.

On rounds Dr.Bender stressed the importance of continuing a regimen of forced liquids. "Danny, the stone will not pass unless you drink copious amounts of fluids."

Looking at him I shook my head and said, "Yes Doc, I'm well aware of the routine. I've received those instructions eleven times before when passing stones."

"We're giving you strong antibiotics so I think the situation will soon show marked improvement." He stated, and then added, "Oh, X-rays revealed two stones."

Since I hadn't been in close proximity with seriously ill patients for a long time, I was hypersensitive to other people's problems. One afternoon my heart wept for a fellow voyager on the ship of woes, as I listened while he begged the medical staff for help. The curtains were drawn around his bed as doctors and nurses worked frantically to save his life. I'll never forget his screams imploring the doctor, "Don't let me die! I can't die! My wife! My wife!" With a final gasp, silence permeated the ward and I watched them walk away, shaking their heads as they left his eternally quiet bedside. My eyes welled with tears. "What will happen," I wondered, "when my time on earth is over?" I anxiously awaited visitors, hoping the anguish would end.

Anita and Jim visited only hours after this unsettling event. I reviewed recent happenings with them and my eyes brimmed with tears exhibiting an unusual emotional response to life and death struggles. It was quite strange relating the past few hours, considering my history of life in a hospital. The abruptness of his death, my own poor health, and weariness, resulted in realization of my mortal vulnerability.

Dabbing my tears Anita said, "Here's some information that will distract your attention. Mother and Daddy got a phone call today asking for a date to pick up your rocking bed. They'll be here this evening and they're not happy."

"I'm lying here with both arms wounded, two IV's, and a catheter. I can't eat or drink, X-ray staff is determined to inflict bodily injury, my roommate croaked, and I should worry about this? Wake up!" I demanded.

Thanksgiving day arrived with my appetite nonexistent. In an effort to encourage gluttony, a dinner tray containing traditional holiday goodies was delivered to my bedside. Large servings of turkey and dressing, candied yams, and cranberry sauce covered the plate. I observed the feast and gagged! For an unknown reason, stomach and throat were at war with my body.

Kaye, accompanied by her sister Faye, surprised me with an unplanned holiday weekend appearance. "It's good to see you." greeted Kaye leaning over to hug me. "Why didn't you tell me you were sick? You can't keep secrets from me now that we're engaged. Tell me what's wrong. Why IV's?"

"Sorry I couldn't reveal the extent of my problems, but you would've worried instead of studying. I'm fine. Don't worry about these IV's. It's like a radiator that requires flushing, IV's pour liquid in the top and a catheter drains it out the bottom. Except for eating solid food I'm getting better each day."

The visit was limited by Kaye's scheduled return to the college campus. Leaving me with a goodbye kiss Kaye said, "It's been three weeks since I received a letter from you, try keeping me informed. I'll be home next month during our Christmas break. What other surprises do you have in mind?"

With furrowed brow I explained, "I've been in contact with social agencies seeking accommodation at a convalescent center. I'm assured these efforts will be successful, most probably before Christmas. In the meantime, remember my words from the beginning of our relationship. Faith, love, patience, and hope. Above all, Keep Smiling, and never give up!"

Regardless my stomach's rebellion at Thanksgiving food, Kaye's surprise visit comforted me and I dreamed of a life-to-be. The following morning awaking from an unusual rest, Dr.Bender stopped by while reading my chart and shaking his head, "Danny the infection is under control, and you've been sufficiently hydrated to correct the chemical imbalance in your blood. Since you're still not eating well I've ordered barium X-rays of your GI system hoping they will define the problem."

"Oh fantastic Doc!" I growled. "I can't eat or drink without gagging and you want me to swallow barium? Thanks!"

The next evening following my experience of choking on a quart of white chalky liquid to determine the cause of nausea, Dr.Bender introduced his colleague, "Danny, meet our expert in Gastroenterology and General Surgeon, Dr.Openhouser. He has reviewed your X-rays and wishes to explain the situation."

"Pleased to meet you Mr. Williams." he said, extending his hand. Embarrassed at my inability to acquiesce in usual amenities, he glanced at Dr.Bender who explained my limiting circumstance. "Forgive me, I forgot." he mumbled. "X-rays indicate two problems: a condition known commonly as hiatal hernia, controllable by diet so surgery is not advisable. The other more pressing problem involves a constricted valve between your stomach and small intestine. We can eliminate this situation surgically."

Looking askance at Dr.Openhouser I questioned, "Is the problem life-threatening? Is surgery required immediately?"

"It isn't life-threatening." he responded. "You could wait, but it will continue to worsen as you grow older if it isn't corrected. As for the hiatal hernia, discomfort from eating particular foods will dictate whether you religiously ascribe to the necessary diet. Shall I schedule additional examinations and prepare for surgery before Christmas?"

"NO!" I adamantly declared. "There will be no surgery. I don't have time. When it becomes impossible to eat, then surgery will be an option. Until then, diet is the answer."

Dr.Bender said, "Then Danny you must force yourself to eat soft food. Ignore the taste, just swallow."

"Doc," I sighed, "those words are familiar. Seems I've swallowed a lot of stuff in my life without liking it."

The weeks of December passed uneventfully as I healed from a kidney infection and regained my strength. The renal calculi didn't pass willingly and apprehension over surgery ensured avid adherence to my diet. My strength gradually increased as I forced myself to swallow food like medicine. Initial discussions with a social worker proved fruitful and I prepared my exodus from Long Hospital - six weeks after an admission for a "few tests and X-rays". On Christmas Eve as Donna was completing my morning back care she exclaimed, "My goodness! Why haven't you said your hip was sore? Doesn't it hurt? I'm paging Dr.Bender now!"

"Danny what's this I'm told about a decubitus on your left hip?" charged Dr.Bender as he examined the inflamed and sensitive area. "Why didn't you tell me your hip was sore? I'll order an immediate orthopedic consult."

Notwithstanding the holiday, within hours after a shocked Dr.Bender examined my rear end I was greeted by one more specialist intent on invading my body parts. "Hello, I'm Dr.Shaver, Orthopedic Surgeon. May I look at your hip?"

Sensing I was outnumbered and without a leg to stand on I agreed to his request. Following another examination he diagnosed, "This bone spur must be surgically corrected now to prevent irreparable damage from a more serious decubitus. Danny I know this is quite a surprise, do you have any questions?"

"Only one." I said disgustedly. "Do you mean ballroom dancing at the New Year's Eve party is out?"

Dr.Shaver and his med students left chuckling, "Don't worry," he said, "in a few days all will be well."

Christmas Day was a contrast in emotions. I welcomed Kaye to my temporary abode, trying to maintain a proverbial "stiff upper lip". Strained facial expressions and conversation couldn't hide unspoken tension. My sister accompanied Kaye for our holiday visit; because I requested Anita purchase a special gift. Amidst our joyous Christmas atmosphere I presented Kaye a compact engraved, "Merry First Christmas, Love Dan".

Keep Smiling and Never Give Up!

Kaye's first Christmas presents to me represented more of my dreams than she could possibly fathom. Unwrapping the gift, she revealed a personal portrait for my bedside. Then excusing herself for a few minutes, she returned carrying a small fishbowl containing a live goldfish."

"What a wonderful gift." remarked Donna passing my bed. "Have you named your new pet?"

"Kaye." I innocently snickered. "Oh, you're referring to my Christmas present. No. We haven't gotten acquainted yet. Why don't you nurses pick a name?"

Unwilling to dampen the spirits of all present, I tried waiting until shortly before they left to inform Kaye and my family about the impending surgery. Smiling while I watched them leave I repeated, "Merry Christmas, Happy New Year."

December 26th signaled the beginning of a challenging environment on Ward D. Hong Kong Flu had been prevalent for weeks throughout central Indiana, but only recently had begun to affect hospital procedures. Visitors were screened and required to take appropriate preventive measures such as gown, mask, gloves, and washing hands in a special solution upon entering and exiting the nursing units. Most elective surgical procedures were postponed; unfortunately, mine was no longer elective. As I informed Dr.Shaver, "No problem, let's get it over. Anyway, I'm still recovering from a bout of Hong Kong Flu eleven years ago. A mistaken diagnosis was my introduction to Polio. I'm probably immune."

Dr. Shaver reluctantly agreed to do the operation as scheduled because of my hip's deteriorating condition. As the nurses and orderly positioned me on a stretcher bound for surgery, Rosie asked, "Danny Boy, can I be doin' ya' a turn 'fore ya leave us this mornin'?"

"Yeah Rosie," I drowsily replied, "don't forget to feed Big Red. Don't let him out of his bowl. See you later."

"Okay dearie," she said, "I'll be feedin' our fish for ya'. After surgery yul' sure be be'in a pain in the rear."

Following surgery for removal of a hip bone spur I was recovering quite rapidly when disaster struck. I developed a wound abscess requiring another incision and de'bridement. I was feeling much better, even to the point of enjoying food once again when calamity disrupted my staid life. Awakening in early morning hours following one of my healthier days, I was stricken with a terrible headache, nausea, aching body, and the return of an elevated temp. "Well Danny," Dr.Bender said, "You have Hong Kong flu."

Between moans of despair and groans of pain I observed my pregnant sister Millie through bleary eyes. "I'm glad to see you Sis, but you shouldn't be here. What happens if you catch this bug? Malcolm get her out of here, please."

"Hey listen, I tried to stop her, but right now she's bigger than me." he joked. "Millie's your sister and we all know stubbornness is a family trait."

"Danny don't be upset. Malcolm will be leaving for Nam soon, and this is our Christmas." explained Millie. "We'll only be here a minute. How are you really feeling? Is Kaye all right?"

I assured my baby sister, "I'm not upset, just sickly. Kaye's fine, meet Big Red, her Christmas gift to me. The nurses named him for Indiana University; he's an unofficial mascot for Ward D. I'm not sure, but I think he coughed too a while ago."

Malcolm laughed, "He is green around the gills."

An urge to smile was overpowered by a choking cough as I grimaced, "Remember last time I had Hong Kong flu in '57? It weakened my body so much I developed a case of Polio. I wonder, what next??" Attempting to hasten their exit I bid them farewell, surreptitiously hoping they would leave me to my misery. I coughed, "Thanks for coming you two or should I say three? I'd rather accompany you to Lejeune or Nam Malcolm, but hey, we all have to be someplace. Merry Christmas!"

The next twenty-four hours my hacking cough worsened. As a result of a paralyzed diaphragm I was unable to muster enough strength for productive expectoration. My temperature elevated and breathing became increasingly difficult. I tried frog breathing to inhale deeply, facilitating coughing to relieve chest congestion, but my weakness ensured failure. Crying out in my soul for strength from God, I thought, "Flu didn't get me the last time, but without divine intervention I'm perilously close to crashing soon."

Dad and Mom entered Ward D wrapped up like two mummies. "What's going on?" questioned Dad, his voice muffled behind the mask. "Millie didn't say you were back in isolation. I guess she didn't want us to know you're so sick."

"I'm not in isolation, Dad. You are!" I coughed. "The hospital is undergoing a flu epidemic." Cough "This reverse isolation technique will" cough, cough, "prevent its spread. For now," cough, "tell everyone to stay away. I'm fine."

Soon after my parents left, Kaye and her mother arrived for a visit. I again received obvious questions. "What's happening? We knew about the flu epidemic from TV news, but not these measures. The sign reads, 'FAMILY ONLY'. Are you sure it's permissible for us to be in this ward?"

"Actually, it isn't" I coughed, "we must get married today! You saw the sign," cough, "Family only. I'm just teasing," cough, cough, "they know who you are."

Evening approached and my respiratory condition worsened. A dedicated respiratory therapist (RRT) administered inhalation treatments

Keep Smiling and Never Give Up!

called intermittent positive pressure breathing (IPPB), every fifteen minutes. I was also given nasal oxygen. Even though posted signs stated minimal visiting hours, Kaye was allowed to remain at my bedside most of the time. Barb the evening RN, called Dr.Bender reporting increased congestion and more breathing difficulty. Shortly, an X-ray technician arrived with a portable machine. Rick, RRT, held an oxygen mask over my mouth and nose allowing me to breathe while the chest X-rays were taken. Diane and Joanna, two other RRT's assisting Rick encouraged him to, "Take a break. We'll stay with Danny until you return."

"No, not until Dan is better." he replied grimly.

I encountered a sinking feeling as I slipped beneath a suffocating fog. Reality struck with Barb's question, "Do you want us to call your family?"

"No! Don't call." I wheezed. "Nothing they can do. I want you to go home Kaye. It's late, you and your mom must be tired." Cough! cough! cough! "It's sixty miles to New Castle." Cough! cough! cough! "Please be careful."

Kaye protested, "Dan I can't leave with you this sick. What do I tell your family?"

"Tell them nothing!" I pleaded. "They'll just worry. I'll be fine." Cough! Cough! "Remember honey, faith, love," Cough! Cough! "patience, hope, and always keep smiling."

Kaye hesitantly walked from the ward, glancing backward toward her future. I coughed, choked, gagged, and spat as Rick, Diane, Joanna, and Barb worked furiously in an effort to keep me alive. I hadn't been aspirated since acute Polio days in isolation at Riley Hospital. I can honestly report, time does not enhance this procedure's attractiveness. I repeatedly asked Barb for results of my X-rays, but unwilling to frighten me, she changed the subject every time - her silence shouting an answer. Momentarily Dr.Bender arrived at my bedside and I asked him, "Is" Cough! Cough! "pneumonia spreading to both lungs?" Cough! Cough! Cough!

"Yes, there's no point denying the obvious." Dr.Bender acknowledged. "We now have a race on our hands."

My eyes weakly sought confirmation of time from a wall clock and I thought, "Kaye should be home soon, it's almost ten o'clock. This is now your fight, Jesus."

"Saying goodbye to Dan that evening was one of the most difficult things I've ever done in my life. The silence was deafening as Mom and I left the waiting room. Visitors were aware of a serious situation; each person understanding his or her loved one was also vulnerable. I don't remember much about leaving, except my knees were weak and I had a knot in my throat and stomach. Mom said I was pale as we silently walked to the car. Upon return to New Castle I disregarded Dan's demand and called his family with a medical update. I then went to my room, knelt down, and prayed."

"Danny, Danny, can you hear me?" demanded Dr.Bender as he smacked my face. "Can you breathe easier?"
The room revolved in slow motion while people standing beside my bed seemed to weave back and forth. I desperately tried to focus on the person slapping me, eventually his head stopped spinning. There was momentary silence as I opened my eyes to expectant gazes of the medical team. A hush covered the group. I smiled weakly, "Why are you just standing around?"
A sigh of relief filled the air and one by one each of these wonderful people said, "He's better, I'm going home."
Watching night personnel remove the bedside emergency equipment, my eyes searched for the wall clock, "2:30 A.M."
The next day Joanna greeted me saying, "You certainly look better today than you did last night."
"I must have been really sick! I remember looking down from the ceiling watching you and Barb holding my oxygen mask and turning me while Rick and Diane played drums, beating on my back. What a strange, detached sensation." I reported.
Jo frowned, scratching her head as she walked away.
Awaiting arrival of lunch trays I watched and listened as Donna and an excessively quiet gentleman patient observed sleet and rain outside our window. Donna innocently stated, "Sure is coming down hard."
Without a moment's hesitation, this man who previously hadn't spoken a word during my stay on Ward D replied, "Better down than up."
Still chuckling to myself about the conversation I'd just heard, Dr.Bender entered Ward D. As he examined me and ordered X-rays to confirm my obvious improvement I confided, "Thanks doc for helping clear my lungs last night. You, the nurses and RRT's will always be appreciated for your efforts to save my life."
"Just doing our jobs." he modestly responded. "I can't help thinking God did most of the saving, you were obviously taking orders from someone else. We're glad you're better."
My health improved and the days passed more quietly. I convalesced from my ordeals and attempted to finalize plans for dismissal from the hospital. January ended with my health much improved. I anticipated new challenges and a renewal in my life. In an effort to remain close to my family, I chose to live at the nursing home where I had stayed when Dad and Mom vacationed in Florida. While bidding farewell to Robert Long Hospital, I reviewed various adventures of the past two and one-half months. Thinking of a naïve` medical student's ludicrous guarantee of a

short and uneventful stay brought a smile to my face. Though still in possession of numerous kidney stones, I weighed less after sacrificing part of my hip to medical science. After encountering repeated physical insults, my body and emotions needed, and I sought rest and recuperation.

A second admission to Park Riley, courtesy of Dad and Mom, was the beginning of a totally new adventure. After an exhausting and life-threatening hospital stay my goal was uninterrupted rest. Previous weeks at Park Riley during the summer of '68 had been much different than the atmosphere greeting me today and I immediately doubted my decision to become a resident. Winter weather curtailed remembered extracurricular activities such as trips to Anita and Jim's home for outdoor cookouts, and with the school hiatus over, young attractive aides working summer jobs had been replaced by new, and fewer, permanent employees.

I found myself among a census of forty people mostly eighty years or older anticipating nutritious diets of bland noodles and cottage cheese - favorites on the menu. I discovered the food preparation motto in the kitchen was: "flavor is nice, but spice is vice". The present staff at my new, but temporary home provided excellent care while adequately assisting with housing for elderly citizens no longer able to maintain a private dwelling. I learned many families would prefer to personally care for relatives; however situations are invariably altered by circumstantial reality.

After regaining my strength I wanted to accomplish the goals Kaye and I had previously established for our lives. I hoped to utilize my wheelchair, type, and read, but sadly OT and PT were nonexistent. Instead, old warriors competed in daily checker games; ladies knitted scarves; all worked crossword puzzles while breathlessly viewing soap operas. Watching cars whiz by in front of Park Riley was a cherished activity and everyone talked of "the good ol' days". Wise or unwise, temporarily residing in a nursing home had been my choice, but after two monotonous weeks I realized I had relegated myself to a facility lacking personnel or programs needed to provide more than just custodial care. I recalled advice given me by social workers at IUMC before discharge: you must establish a permanent residence elsewhere for six months if you wish to live independently from your parents. The thought of languishing much longer at Park Riley was too depressing, so visiting with Anita and Jim I coaxed, "Please find a convalescent center in Indianapolis where I can get OT and PT. Moving here was a mistake and if I'm ever to gain any independence, I need more support."

My sister and brother-in-law diligently sought another facility willing to accept my respirators and provide OT and PT. While age was not a factor in my decision to reside at a nursing home, physical disability and breathing difficulty demanded proficiency in care and medical expertise. Finding people suitable to accept this responsibility, as my parents had for many years, was a struggle in itself. However, much searching provided the answer and I again awaited transfer to my new home. Ambulance attendants lifted me inside the vehicle as snowflakes kissed my cheeks, today I'd begin another venture in quest of a dream.

Shady Acres Pavilion* (SAP), my new residence, immediately assured me this move would definitely be successful. With awe I observed my new surroundings as attendants pushed the stretcher through imitation marble doorways. Six gleaming chandeliers illuminating massive columns and ultra-expensive decor in the lobby greeted me. The stretcher's casters sank deep into plush royal blue carpeting and I noticed portraits by famous artists accentuating corridors and impressing visitors and new residents. Joe, an older, courteous Administrator, and his Director of Nursing, Sarah, attired in a crisp white uniform, extended their personal welcome. After a warm introduction by the welcoming committee I was escorted to C wing, room 373 as staff nodded and waved. The halcyon atmosphere exploded when an elderly man burst from his room screaming obscenities at an obviously embarrassed nurse's aide galloping in hot pursuit. The poor girl ordered, and then begged him to return for his clothes. He was dressed only in his birthday suit. "Well if nothing else," I murmured, "life certainly won't be dull as a SAP."

"Look at this!" I exclaimed to Mom and my sisters. "A personal color TV in my room with remote control. Electric hospital beds, carpeting, wallpaper. Think, for weeks I've been existing in solitude without radio or TV. I wonder if the food will taste as good as this place looks. Who knows, maybe I'll even be able to read again."

"Danny," Mom cautioned, "the cup outside is beautiful, pray the inside is as spotless."

Mom, Anita, and Judy left then I got acquainted with my roommate and adjusted to new surroundings. Shadows created designs midst the room's flowered wallpaper and I envisioned a fresh beginning tomorrow as I contemplated Mom's warning. Watching late news on my color television, I summarily dismissed any foreboding of possible conflict. The evening grew late, my eyes drooped, and I slept soundly.

*Shady Acres Pavilion is a pseudonym.

23

SOWING THE WIND

My first morning at SAP I awakened to clattering dishes and glasses competing with sounds of jingling silverware. I vaguely observed the outline of a female attendant entering the shadows of our darkened room, nonchalantly approaching my bed and stealthily sliding her hand under the covers. In shock at this unanticipated invasion of privacy as icy cold fingers touched my bare buttocks I gasped, "Just what in the heck are you doing? Granted I'm new here, but this sure is a new kind of proposition. Get out of my pajamas!"

Stunned at my outburst she backed away whimpering, "Oh, Mr. Williams, I didn't realize you were alert. We're told to check for wet beds. Please forgive me."

Anger quickly turned to amusement and I instructed the bewildered nurse's aide, "Forget it, but next time I'll tell you when I have to perform bodily functions. Who are you?"

Morning excitement over, Marti belatedly flipped on the room lights and we became formally acquainted while awaiting delivery of trays. Mouth-watering aromas wafted beneath my nose as we discussed a possible breakfast menu. Eating in hospitals and nursing homes had prepared me for watery eggs, fatty bacon, and cold hard toast. I'd conditioned myself to accept cold coffee and hot orange juice, but was ecstatic as I observed my tray. Food was served in accordance with many federal and state government standards and gourmet cooking was certainly not priority in institutions. However, SAP not only met; but also surpassed all requirements. With salivary glands working overtime, I could already taste the fabulous cuisine placed before my eyes. As Marti gave me a drink of coffee the emergency buzzer sounded and she apologetically excused herself for a few minutes. Although four times the census of Park Riley, SAP unfortunately employed a similar number of staff that obviously couldn't be in two places at once. The tempting tray sat at my bedside until steamy hot eggs were encrusted with a cold, watery surface, crisp bacon assumed a definite limp, and toast could've been substituted for roofing shingles. Gluttony would not be a problem.

Anita and Jim appeared at noon on Sunday, shocked at my evident lack of nursing care. Although the staff and I had eliminated some glitches with my feeding, apparent problems still remained. My angry sister demanded, "Why haven't you been shaved? Danny your shirt is dirty too!"

"Actually," I replied, "they've neither shaved me, nor given me a bath."

"This is ridiculous!" charged Anita. "Mother and Daddy will be here later. Jim, please shave him."

Relocating to SAP was my own choice, but Anita and Jim felt responsible for the situation. They vociferously expressed displeasure at my unkempt appearance and demanded an explanation from the charge nurse. Concern for SAP's capabilities provoked an immediate discussion with supervision, and errors were soon corrected. I thought, "The staff must have been intimidated by my age and their unfamiliarity with respirators. Regardless, all's well now."

The staff's realization of my comparable youth, mental alertness, and humor encouraged increased accommodation. In an atmosphere established for people of greater longevity, days and nights filled with rules and regimentation produce dreaded routines detrimental to staff and residents, but they are standard in all nursing homes. One's bath, bodily functions, meals, sleep, visitation, and TV viewing are all arbitrarily scheduled. Thankfully I was paired with Tim, a young roommate recovering from work-related injuries, and excitedly observed his PT and OT, eagerly contemplating the day my therapy would begin.

The weekend passed quickly and two days later I still awaited a visit from Dr. Alberto, my admitting physician. As nurse's aides pushed a strange looking gurney into my room Della and Jane bubbled, "Dan do we have a surprise for you! Today you're getting a tub bath!"

"No way!" I declared. "Just who's bright idea was this?"

Laughing, Della said, "We have standing orders at SAP for personal hygiene if the patient is physically able. But don't worry; it's not a regular tub. We have a new portable bathtub on wheels. First we transfer you to this stretcher, then the collapsing sides are raised and fastened. After a drain is connected to the sink, we use a hand-held sprayer for your shower. Have you ever been in water since you had Polio?"

Fifteen minutes later I soaked in luxury as they sprayed my body while I enjoyed sensations of soothing, warm water. Memories of what seemed like ancient history flooded my mind as I thought about times in the pool at Columbus. "Soaking in warm water reminds me of my first time in rehab, if only it was deep enough for buoyancy." I sighed.

"Would you tell us about rehab?" Jane asked.

I briefly responded with my life's history, including a vivid description of excursions in the rehab therapy pool. I explained how Drs. Salk and Sabin had made Respo Centers, thankfully, irrelevant. With the bath completed I was returned to my bed and advised I required doctor's orders to sit in a wheelchair. At least progress is in view.

Dr. Alberto's orders authorized use of my wheelchair and participation in activities requiring mobility, PT exercises and strengthening programs, and daily OT assistance. After I consented, PT began exercising my limbs, and for the first time since rehab days I stood on a tilt table. Unlike large stationary units at Respo Centers, this device resembled the portable tilt table Mary shackled George to in Ann Arbor. I was transferred from bed to table by Lars and Mabel (PT's), who detailed utilization of this therapeutic aid. Once Lars secured me to the table, Mabel, operating a ratchet control, slowly inclined my body. The same technique was applied in rehab centers, but following years of absence from vertical exercise, distress was immediately evident. I incrementally reached thirty degrees when blood rushed to my feet, leaving a vacuum in my brain, which some people say still remains. Colorful circles, swirling dots, engulfing darkness, and hollow sounding voices demanded immediate cessation of PT. Remembering rehab days, standing would require more time.

Kaye was unable to leave college for several weeks, so Valentine's Day was celebrated by postal delivery. Our special day was arriving soon, Kaye's visit and birthday. I asked Anita, "Will you take my money and buy Kaye a birthday present? We haven't seen each other for six weeks and this is the first break in exams and winter weather. Last time I saw her I had pneumonia and our future was iffy, but prayers for healing were answered. Distance and time still separate us even from temporary happiness and hospital rules forbid student nurses from wearing engagement rings on duty, but I'll surprise Kaye with something different."

Returning from her shopping expedition Anita inquired, "Well brother, is this necklace what you wanted for Kaye?"

"Thanks Sis." I responded. "It's exactly what I had in mind, now one more favor. Sunday is a special day for us so please encourage other people to go elsewhere this weekend."

Kaye's appearance following an unavoidable, nearly two month absence brought joy and smiles to our faces. Hugging each other was both thrilling and frightening. Recalling the last time she left my bedside, both of us had been skeptical of reunion in this life. Clinging to hope and faith with a belief our love was predestined had provided us patience to endure another separation. Presenting Kaye with my birthday and engagement gift I said passionately, "I will always love you. For now, this is a symbol of commitment, some day I'll place a gold band on your finger."

Wiping tears from her eyes Kaye responded, "Thank you. It's beautiful! I'll wear this pearl necklace until we are married. At least now I faintly hear wedding bells."

I described the surroundings at SAP; especially high on my list of praises were portable bathtub and tilt table. I said, "This place is wonderful. Not only will I be able to sit in my wheelchair, they'll assist me with reading and typing. My previously discussed column may now be more than a dream. Emphasis on PT and OT won't only be healthy; it encourages full participation in life. They even mentioned experiments with electrical muscle stimulation on my hands."

"Dan, this sounds too good to be true." Kaye hesitantly said. "The key word was 'experiments', be careful. All of the therapy will be beneficial, but will it help you to use your feeder? The one you refused to talk about."

Somberly I stared in her direction and said, "I didn't come here for rehab. Let's talk about something else. I'm so glad you came today, can you stay all afternoon?"

A shadow of disappointment covered Kaye's face, as she mumbled, "No, I'm sorry. My girlfriend and I left college after church and she's waiting in the lobby. We can't stay long. Sue grew up on a farm near Huntington and I know you two will like each other, shall I invite her to join us?"

Following an hour visit I commented, "SAP's menu isn't bad, but sandwiches sound good. Would you two mind going to a drive-in and getting us something for dinner? Kaye, get some money from my wallet, I'm buying."

After gorging ourselves on carryout food Kaye groaned, "I hate to eat and run, but Sue and I must return to campus for more study and work. You and I haven't seen each other for so long, even a hurried trip is special. Your move to SAP made our relationship long distance, but someday neither illness, miles, nor circumstance will separate us."

Euphoria following Kaye's visit evaporated. The bubble of excitement burst when family notified me that Grandmother Williams had passed away. I was aware arteriosclerosis had necessitated her move to Heritage House Convalescent Center, the new nursing home in New Castle, where Dr.Heilman Jr. had eighteen months earlier assured me of admission. Sad news left me restless all night, thinking, if only she could've survived long enough to attend the wedding of a grandson who wasn't supposed to be alive. Thankfully, Grandma had earlier met Kaye at a mother-daughter church banquet when introduced by my Aunt Zella, Kaye's Sunday School teacher.

Therapy continued midweek as Lars inserted electrical impulse needles into my fingers. "Watch the response, Dan." he instructed. "As I increase micro-voltage they'll move and once you become accustomed to the tingling I'll augment power, enabling you to strengthen your muscles. We'll begin treatment on your left hand to determine feasibility, but as time progresses I'll initiate procedures on your right hand. We should achieve greater success on that hand since it received rehabilitation surgery."

Enthused by success I eagerly agreed Lars could expand the treatment and allowed needles attached to electrodes to be inserted into my fingers and toes. Electromyographics (EMG) performed on me soon after diagnosed with Polio were similar in nature, so I wasn't alarmed by the procedure. Blinded by hope I chose to ignore a major difference - now electrical stimulation entered my body rather than the machine recording existing nerve viability. As Lars predicted, more success was visible on my right hand where muscles and tendons had been transplanted during surgery at Columbus. Minute evidence promoted a cascade of false hope.

Following increasingly progressive discomfort I began asking myself if the decision to participate in this caper had been correct. Subsequent to voicing concern I was told failure to avail myself of therapeutic procedures would most certainly limit any insurance coverage at SAP. Hesitantly submitting, I unwisely chose "toughing it out".

One day after Lars and Randy the orderly, positioned me on the tilt table I was standing before my doorway watching two visitors pass in the hallway when Lars directed, "Randy keep an eye on him, I'll return in half an hour."

Randy leaned back against the foot of my empty bed and took a cigarette break. Inhaling a couple of times he began relaxing when we heard the DON's voice calling, "Randall, I need assistance, where are you? Come quickly, help us with the patient in 368."

"Oh no!" Randy moaned. "If she catches me smoking on duty I'll get fired. Here, open your mouth, hold this!"

I was now standing at ninety degrees, strapped to the tilt table looking out my room's open doorway with a lighted cigarette drooping from my lips as smoky gray columns curled upward surrounding my head and engulfing me in a thick haze. My brother-in-law Kenny appeared at the door startling both of us. He hadn't seen me standing since I had Polio, never nervously puffing a cigarette! His mouth agape and staring in utter disbelief he muttered, "Do I have the right room? Uhh, Danny? Man, I'd better sit down." Later that evening I smiled at the memory while observing nature's concert from my window. Tree branches swayed and fluttering leaves bowed in response to gentle spring breezes. Colorful tulips arrayed themselves at attention, their quiet demeanor illuminated by beams of light emanating from the building. I found solace in their peaceful appreciation of God's sigh, influencing my desire for a good night's rest.

During the next few days I gleefully repeated the story about the tilt table. After one of my comical reports Randy laughed, "Have a cigarette. Today ol' buddy, you'll smoke one of your own."

Progressively, I sank into a life of self-centered, bad behavior. Ignoring my health problems, I chose to affix my actions to the temptations of a more base nature. Randy, by placing a cigarette in my mouth, had introduced me to smoking and my room soon became a break room for disgruntled staff. Marti, one of the regulars rationalized, "Hey, 'long as you smoke in your room they won't object to our presence for the same reason. Our new break room even has TV!" Dr. Alberto and others voiced concern over my changed behavior, justifying their objections while pointing to the respirator.

Summer passed with Kaye visiting every third Saturday. Working her way through college severely limited the already scarce time we could spend together. Kaye walked in one day just as Marti finished holding my cigarette. Staring at me, she silently put her umbrella in my closet. Embarrassed and ashamed I said to Marti, "I think you better leave."

Though our visit proceeded with uneasiness, Kaye didn't lecture me about my irresponsible behavior; however, tension made me miserably uncomfortable and I felt sick inside. One can reason away any bad choice, and like Marti, I also found rationalization handy. Promised activities at SAP had not materialized, so I convinced myself any escape was deserved. Reading, typing, and writing opportunities were infrequent, but happily PT still included standing on the tilt table. I dreaded the other PT treatment consisting of sitting in my chair while submitting to many painful, experimental, and I think, simply fanciful therapeutic theories. Summarizing the problems being encountered at SAP I attempted to justify my actions explaining to Kaye, "Sharp pains shoot through my fingers and toes after each procedure and I'm now alarmed by an eerie numbness. I tried to end any further participation in the program, but Lars, my PT who conducts these sessions, warned me without measurable proof of progress my insurance benefits are in jeopardy. Pondering his words, I'm sure he wasn't threatening me, but advised I be careful in my choice because remaining at SAP may well depend on this project. I considered all alternatives and decided tolerating a little pain was preferable to possessive suffocation at home."

Kaye shook her head replying, "Dan you can try to sell that to other people, but I think you're just searching for an avenue of vindication for repeated harmful behavior. I wish you'd be honest with yourself and me..."

Interrupting a very disconcerting conversation I heard, "Hi Danny." as Mike reentered my life for the first time in eighteen months. "I got your letter several weeks ago, but rarely visit Indianapolis. My meeting ended early allowing me to visit before leaving central Indiana. How are you my friend? Well, well, who's this lovely young lady?"

"It's good to see you Mike." I responded. "I'm fine. Allow me to introduce Kaye, my wife-to-be. Don't ask when, but it will happen after she graduates from nursing school. I guess you went back to college after leaving the Air Force? Hey, is Mary Lou well?"

"We're both in excellent health," Mike replied, "she's teaching school, and I'm in school. Kaye, I'm happy to meet you, but I don't understand how Danny captured you."

"Hold it!" I interjected. "She peeked behind my paper, and that's how Kaye captured me."

"Oh you big jerk!" Kaye teased. "Now tell the truth."

Amidst glares from my fiancé, and laughter from Mike, I hesitantly explained our differing opinions.

Later after dinner, Kaye prepared to leave, admonishing me with these simple words, "I love you Dan, regardless your choices. Only please, don't send our lives up in smoke."

In finding myself willingly blinded by an atmosphere of temporal influences, I chose the wrong path to fulfillment. I disregarded Rev.Kerschner's biblical teachings and with an arrogant impunity continued engaging in behavior detrimental to the temple of God. Only grace assured eternal security. My love for Kaye and the desire to please her had also taken second place to common sense, resulting in near destruction of my life, and our relationship.

On Sunday, 10:56 PM, EDT, staff members, friends, and I watched history in progress on TV while smoking, drinking coffee, and joking.

ONE SMALL STEP FOR MAN, ONE GIANT LEAP FOR MANKIND
NEIL ARMSTRONG, FIRST MAN TO WALK ON MOON
JULY 20, 1969

As JFK said, "We will go any place, pay any price."

I decried the necessity of submitting to what I thought were apparently inappropriate treatments while endeavoring to retain my insurance benefits. Discussions with various authorities reaffirmed additional financial assistance would not be available while I received insurance coverage via my father's policy. In effect not only was I still legally his dependent at twenty-six, he was also financially responsible because of insurance. My benefits would soon be expended so I knew a choice at this juncture in life would determine the future - either independence with Kaye, or existing wholly dependent on other people's decisions. These pressures of reality were weighing heavily on my mind when Joe the Administrator requested, "Daniel, may I please speak to you?"

"Certainly Joe." I responded, sensing urgency.

"I've received notice you are reaching the cap on your insurance." he informed me. "We must arrange a new mode of payment if you are to remain a resident of Shady Acres. I have Medicaid application forms; your respirator and obvious quadriplegia should qualify you for all possible benefits. Once insurance is depleted, requesting assistance is sure to present fewer problems. Your address will remain the same assuming of course, you are satisfied with our facility."

Daniel R. Williams

I nodded, "Referring to my respirator and Polio, once Medicaid assumes financial liability The March of Dimes will suspend coverage for my medical equipment. After Kaye and I marry we'll confront a major dilemma unless you can obtain assurance they'll resume coverage at that time. I'm fearful difficulty may arise in the future, but I've been a client since 1957 so perhaps the question is academic. Would you phone The March of Dimes, explaining the situation? It would give me peace of mind to know they do understand fully the dilemma I could face some day. Please keep me posted."

Later in the week Joe informed me, "Daniel I called The March of Dimes headquarters in White Plains, New York. They assured me of their support with no anticipated problems for your future coverage. They say your Polio, respirators, and seniority guarantee successful and immediate reinstatement of benefits if Medicaid suspends coverage."

"Can't ask for more." I grinned. "Joe, before signing these papers I must be certain of one fact: I forbid my parent's signatures any place on the form. Any benefits I receive are to be in my name only! I'm a twenty-six year old adult, competent, and no longer wish to be dependent. I will not permit power of attorney papers, and all decisions must come from me personally. Understand?"

"Absolutely." Joe affirmed. "The only stipulation, as you can see, a medical emergency involving unconsciousness. In that event, next of kin must be consulted for decisions."

"Under those conditions I'll sign the application. Joe just place the pen in my mouth and hold the paper firmly on your clipboard before my face." Reaffirming my admonition, I continued, "All decisions are mine. Anita is next of kin. Eventually, Kaye will be my power of attorney."

I celebrated my birthday in a nursing home, honored now as a full-fledged SAP. Kaye presented me with a bathrobe to alleviate drafts while I was standing on the tilt table for thirty minutes during weekday therapy sessions. Along with other activities PT occupied much of my day. Repeated UTI's resulting from kidney stones and pain from PT forced me to use the self-hypnosis I learned at Columbus. Regardless its effectiveness, my ordeal at times became nearly unbearable. Fortunately these repeated episodes responded to medication and their ill effects subsided, eliminating need for hospitalization.

Kaye was at her parent's home for Thanksgiving break, planning to visit me Friday and I forlornly contemplated the holiday alone. I realized fellowship this year would be celebrated away from family by choice, exchanging traditional feasts for dreamed of "independent living". My brother and sisters would enjoy an afternoon with each other while I envisioned family life centered around Kaye. Although her summer quarter transfer to Ball State University School of Nursing in Muncie brought us closer in miles, distance still continued to intimidate. My family communed together, Kaye spent the holiday with her parents, and I ate Thanksgiving dinner with "SAPs".

The brief interlude before Christmas was spent watching snowflakes falling outside my window. They camouflaged ugly barren branches with white purity, anticipating a season of love, compassion, and giving. Mike's visit surprised me and he bemoaned the cold, snowy, windy weather. "It's difficult to believe," he said, "but Mary Lou and I will be commuting to her parent's home in New York for the holiday. Curiously she isn't satisfied with Indiana's snow, we have to travel to Syracuse. One snowball is as cold as another."

"Now, now," I teased, "'tis the season to be jolly."

"You're right." he confided. "To be honest, I've been looking forward to our trip. Before leaving Indy, I wanted to stop by to offer season's greetings and our best wishes for a Merry Christmas. Suppose you'll ever get out of here?"

"Yes, I'm gone when Kaye graduates from nursing school. Hopefully we'll have a home of our own. Waiting around gets old, but for two more years, patience is the key word."

Christmas music filled the air at SAP and everyone was excited with the season. Kaye entered my room with a small tree in one hand and a sack of decorations in the other. A wall shelf holding supplies was cleared, and then transformed to beautifully display our first Christmas tree. Lighting was not permissible, but iridescent trim and miniature ornaments sparkled merrily, reflecting light from room illumination. Visions of sugarplums danced in our heads.

Christmas carolers crowded the corridors of Shady Acres Pavilion. Local school children and many churches fulfilled God's commandment to "love thy neighbor", communing with us and singing of Christmas joy. Organizations played Santa's helpers presenting us with gifts, candy, and fruit. A civic group brought their children and pets to SAP allowing those who wished, to pet their family friends; thus, initiating a new and favorite activity between Christmas and New Years. I was especially impressed with two large dogs - Twinkles, a Siberian Husky, and a German Shepherd named Prince, who was reserved and much too sophisticated for such foolishness. I must say, Twinkles was another story. I mistakenly clicked my tongue to show friendship, and talked to her. She stood on hind legs, put her forelegs and paws on my shoulder, fondly licking my ear. Twinkle's owner, concerned I might be injured, ordered, "Down, girl!" Lowering her ears in guilt, Twinkles dragged her paws across my bare arm, scraping claws into my flesh. The owner, aghast and obviously embarrassed, thunderously corrected my blood-sister and apologized to me. Teasing I said, "If I get rabies, she gets Polio."

Taking advantage of Christmas break, and days off work, Kaye spoiled us with another trip to Indianapolis. Ignoring snow, she assured her mother driving to Indy was necessary. We reminisced about our first New Year's Eve, and her church solo after reading my letter of intent. Realizing today was our last visit for several weeks made time more precious to us, but as she left my room I reluctantly instructed, "Honey it's best if you don't phone, the aides are too busy to hold the receiver to my ear. I'll call you when they have time to assist me. I've heard the situation will be much better here next year; promises of more help are forthcoming. Drive carefully, build me a snowman, and Happy New Year."

Nurses and aides toasted the stroke of midnight with me as we celebrated a New Year, 1970. While compromising principles with a friendly facade, I forgot the most important fact of life. Though still being graced with opportunity to receive God's blessings, I once again ignored subtle warnings from a small voice continually crying in my head. Conscience!

A new year began with high expectations for everyone as word spread that changes were underway. Staff dreamed of salary increases and additional personnel; I fervently hoped some more people would enable me to begin anew with OT activities long denied. I lingered in bed most days, sitting in my wheelchair only long enough for haircuts. Frightening numbness in my hands and feet worsened and I now experienced new weakness from prolonged electrical muscle stimulation. Disgusted and angered, I at last demanded Lars terminate my participation in this experiment, at which time as he'd so prophetically promised, PT quickly vanished. The right hand on which I'd endured agonizing pain prior to rehab surgery became useless as my fingers contracted. Regardless all my emotional stoicism, I anguished over needless losses.

While contemplating my stupidity of surrendering future goals for immediate, but feared irreconcilable consequences, Joe entered my room escorting a short, heavy set, middle aged man with steely blue eyes staring through thick glasses, a balding head accentuating his granite-cold countenance. Joe nervously announced, "Daniel meet SAP's new administrator."

Keep Smiling and Never Give Up!

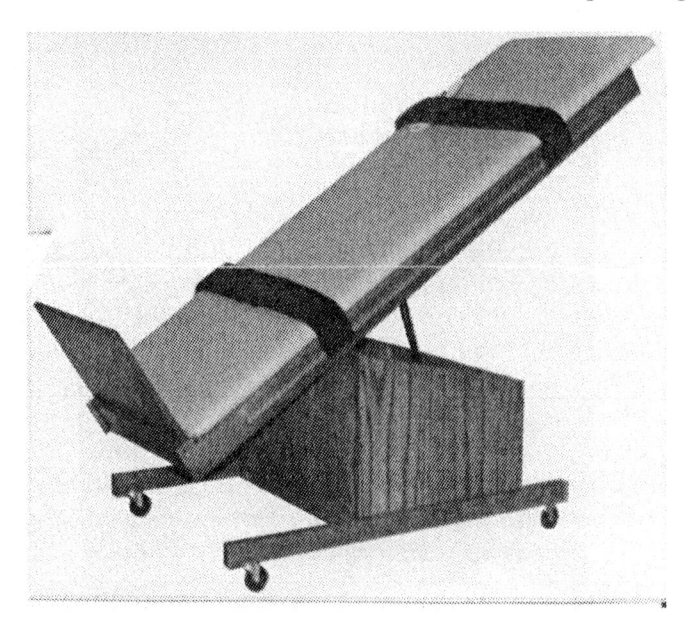

Photo Courtesy: Indianapolis Rehabilitation Agency.
Tilt table used to incrementally and slowly learn to stand after being bedfast for a lengthy period of time.

24

QUICKSAND OF EVIL

An inviting place with great potential became for me a destiny fraught with discouragement and danger. Resident's anticipation of better days and brighter tomorrows dimmed as disillusioning changes began immediately. Enthusiasm faded as menus quickly deteriorated and hoped-for progress failed to materialize. Myriad detrimental modifications occurred, repeatedly thwarting dreamed-of expectations. Not only did residents and staff experience disappointment, new managers affirmed we would remain the same old SAP's.

The early weeks of a happy new year groaned slowly by as each of us at Shady Acres adjusted to unexpected change. Therapy was nearly nonexistent, haircuts were infrequent since I seldom sat in my wheelchair, and portable tub baths were no longer possible. Television, visitors, mail, and a dream of future happiness helped maintain sanity, but vices of smoking and self-pity predestined self-destruction. Anticipation of Kaye's visits reinforced hope, which had been incrementally denied by circumstance. Days of monotony in the grip of sin were exacerbated by pain as an old nemesis – kidney stones and infections reentered my life.

As Kaye arrived I averted her eyes and sighed despondently, "My hand and fingers are now contracted, thanks to experimental therapy. Both feet and hands have numbness and weakness and unless time reverses these problems I'll never benefit from those years of suffering and hard work. In the future, only a mouthstick will replace my needlessly damaged hand."

"Oh no!" she exclaimed. "Dan, you don't mean it! I've been so afraid this would happen. Now I understand why you stopped using your hand to operate the TV remote control."

I was suddenly stricken with pain, hematuria, and nausea, eliminating our lunch. Kaye provided many glasses of water, the nurse's aides frequently repositioned me, and nurses delivered pain medication, all which proved ineffective against this agony. My staid remedy of self-hypnosis was useless, as concentration became an impossibility. After Kaye departed I requested Marti, the aide who emptied my bloody urinal, "I'm in trouble, please inform the nurse I need Dr. Alberto."

"I phoned Dr. Alberto and he increased the dosage so you should feel better shortly." the Director of Nursing stated.

Nodding groggily I muttered as she walked briskly from my room after administering the medicine, "Thank you."

February passed and Kaye belatedly surprised me with a personally catered, heart-shaped, triple-layered homemade Valentine's Day cake. After exchanging greetings and cards we enjoyed carry-in food while Kaye pumped me with questions about my health and circumstances at SAP. Frustration with a situation for which I was largely responsible burst forth and I bluntly answered, "Nursing care, therapy, and simple activities have progressively disappeared. I feel terrible, so maybe my views are slanted, but physical ills don't have any bearing on the resignation of many staff. To be honest, life at SAP stinks! Shortage of assistants and autocratic leadership have ensured infamy for this place. The reasons I came here have sunk into oblivion and I now simply count the days before leaving. Don't worry though, I'll be fine."

As Kaye prepared to depart Marti entered exhibiting her pack of cigarettes asking, "Ready for a smoke?"

The woman I loved, the one for whom I chose living at this place, left the room with tears brimming her eyes and my shame thundered. Inwardly I attempted to reconcile a sad lifestyle of concealed guilt, but conscience cried, "My God, what am I doing?" With heart aching and mind seared by acts of cruelty I shook my head no to Marti, asking her to leave. Cold loneliness engulfed me as I stared at the ceiling while searching for perceived justification. Angered by thoughts of any personal culpability, I rendered judgment on self by deciding the pain in my abdomen requiring strong medication and social indignity, provided me an avenue for escape from responsibility. Conscience however, refused to be ignored and I reacted with appropriate sadness. Unbelievably, I'd traded love of reading and writing for visits from staff as I mutually participated in cigarette breaks. Edgy malaise reigned and independence became a distant dream. My vile choices led to grief and a dreary maze of bewilderment.

Sunday and Monday proceeded with dreariness of spirit as events surrounding Kaye's departure Saturday were frozen in my mind. Traumatized by the reality of my actions, life had degenerated into vapors of indifference. The TV blared, attempting to drown my silent screams for help, and I sought relief thinking of what might be - some day.

Staring bleakly out my window at midwinter's snowy assault I cried, "How did I get into this mess?" With my head spinning and stomach in knots I gazed upward seeking answers to the agonizing dilemma in which I found myself.

Mom's warning to beware had gone unheeded and my goal to live independently was slowly evaporating. "What have I done to myself? Can't go home, most nursing homes say no to my respirator, and SAP is stealing my hope. I'm perilously trapped in a quicksand of evil while my disastrously unwise choices are effectively sucking me deeper and deeper into a living hell, an inferno of cataclysmic proportions."

March winds whistled outside the window in a last gasp refusal to loosen their grip on Indiana's winter. Undaunted by snow accumulation, and rejecting her mom's advisory about driving in inclement weather, Kaye traveled to Indianapolis where we celebrated her twentieth birthday. The worsening weather wasn't conducive to journeying outside for our food, forcing me to eat nursing home cuisine.

Midway through her package of peanut butter crackers Kaye narrowed her eyes asking, "Are you going to tell me what's wrong? We can't be considering a life together without honesty."

Shame overcame my desire to withhold facts from her, so quietly I recounted the situation at Shady Acres, "I've got to get away from here soon."

Between anger and fear Kaye pleaded, "Dan, let me talk to your sisters about what's happening, they need to know."

"No! They'll insist I move back to New Castle. Keep searching for a facility in Muncie to accept my respirators and someday this will all be over. Now drive carefully going back to BSU. I love you."

The scourge of kidney problems worsened and I asked Dr. Alberto to prescribe stronger pain medication. To my chagrin, the new medicine proved ineffective and I asked to be hospitalized at IUMC for evaluation, blood tests, and X-rays. My request was denied and hoped-for relief vanished as I plunged deeper into a vortex of swirling terror. I endured daily repeated bouts of agony. Frightfully, each time when I swallowed pills or was given a shot, confusion, doubt, and suspicion pierced my mind. I experienced intensified cycles of nausea and dizziness with days of lucidity interrupted by attacks of virulent hallucinations. A maelstrom assaulted my mind and body, pain increased along with the anxiety of taking medicine. Terrifying days and nights crept by as I attempted to combat moments of dread, striving unsuccessfully to isolate mind from body. Repeated shards of pain defeated my resolve.

Kaye brought me an Easter basket with a chocolate bunny and candy eggs. Spring break occurred Easter week, allowing her to visit me twice within six days. I joked, "This could be habit forming. I understand rapid behavioral changes can be quite disruptive to the psyche and sudden withdrawal from established emotional patterns is dangerous. It's possible we might be forced into a lifelong situation."

Answering with a smile Kaye said, "Soon I hope."

Vivian and Kenny came to visit later in the afternoon, entering my room just as I refused to eat any food. "Here let me try to feed him." Vivian requested, taking the tray from Kaye. "Come on Hon, take a few bites of Jello for your big sister."

"Danny, you better eat some of that Jello." Kenny said.

"I wanted to go buy his favorite sandwich from the café, down the street," said Kaye, "but he's too sick to eat."

"Get that snake off my bed!" I screamed. "There! It's on my foot! Oh No! Don't let that big spider crawl on me! Kill it Kenny! See it? See it? Oh my gosh!"

"Tell me where Dan," Kaye directed, "I'll knock it off your bed. Do you see it? Is it gone now?"

"Here folks this piece of candy will quiet him down." said Thomas, Dan's roommate. "Sometimes after they give him medicine or Jello he yells about seeing bugs and animals."

Silence permeated the room and looking puzzled, Vivian patted my arm assuring, "It's all right Danny. You're going to be all right. Kaye maybe we should tell him they're not real. Why is he doing this? Has he been drugged?"

"They're real! They're real!" I screamed.

Attempting to calm me, Kenny insisted, "Don't worry, I killed him Danny, he won't be back. Viv, we better leave."

My sister leaned over kissing me on the cheek assuring, "Hon, you'll be alright. Everyone's praying for you. We'll be back soon." Vivian and Kenny exited my room, their faces clouded with worry and uncertainty.

After they left I looked at Kaye befuddled saying, "I'm fine. What did she mean? Do you think Viv's okay?"

Darkness reclaimed the last vestiges of daylight while reality interrupted my haze of confusion. Wistfully looking in my direction as she left, Kaye returned to college and I was alone in a vacuum of precarious existence.

Sunday, Dad, Mom, Andy, and Millie stepped hesitantly through the doorway approaching my bed. "Hi stranger." They chorused. "Vivian told us you had a bad day yesterday. Do you feel better now?"

"I'm feeling fine." I insisted. "Is Vivian okay?"

"Son," said Dad, "what's wrong? Tell us the truth."

Looking at Millie I inquired, "Heard from Malcolm? Has he left for Nam? Remember Travis, Kaye's brother-in-law, he got his orders to serve in that undeclared war which is now a political travesty. Patty's living in New Castle awaiting birth of their third child."

"Malcolm is getting along just fine." Millie answered. "Stop changing the subject, answer Dad's question."

"Hmmm! Are we grouchy today! All right," I yielded, "here it is. Judging from past experience, I have a kidney stone lodged in my urinary tract causing severe pain requiring constant medication. I've bled twice with this stone, and requested hospitalization, but have been denied admission. After each dose of medicine I quickly become nauseated and confused. Some staff members think I'm receiving the wrong medicine, and are convinced sedatives are being mixed with my food before it's served."

"Oh Danny, nothing like that's happening." my parents declared. "Why don't you just snap out of it?"

"Here Danny." said Millie. "This card containing money for you arrived at home, should I put it in your wallet?"

"Wait just a minute Sis, the nurse is bringing me some medicine." I instructed.

Jackisue, an LPN, requested everyone wait in the hall while she administered a shot. Upon return to my room, Mom challenged, "If you're sure they're doing something wrong, why do you continue taking medicine from them?"

"Do you have any ideas Mom?" I asked. "This stone and infection are debilitating my system, the pain doesn't stop. I either take the medicine or moan with agony. My symptoms are different from previous bouts of kidney stones. I feel like my bladder and abdomen are being ripped apart."

"Danny I'll put your money in the stand." said Millie, opening the drawer. "Uh oh."

"What in the world are you doing with cigarettes?" Mom shouted. "No wonder you're sick. See Ray, now we know why he wanted to leave home. You need a good smacking young man."

"Be reasonable Mom, don't you think I'm just a bit old for a 'smacking'?" I charged. "Mistake or not, I smoke by choice with my friends' help."

"Well, your daddy and I are going to talk to the nurse." Mom announced.

Millie interjected, "Mom, he is twenty-seven."

"You be quiet little lady." directed Mom. "This matter doesn't concern you. Ray, do something."

"Velma if he wants to act like this I can't stop him." Dad frowned. "Come on. We'll wait outside while he visits with Andy and Millie."

Andy rolled his eyes and shook his head. Cupping hands around her mouth Millie whispered, "I didn't know cigarettes were in the drawer."

"Forget it Sis, enjoy your trip home. The conversation should be thought provoking. If you wouldn't mind, could I speak to Andy alone? Incidentally, are you getting warm?"

"Andy are you doing well in school?" I asked. "I hope your football team is winning. Did you see that spider?"

"Uuhh, Danny, football season was over five months ago. I just finished wrestling. What spider?" he asked, looking frightened. "Are you feeling okay? I'll call a nurse."

"Sure I'm fine, just a bit strange." I yawned. "Andy! Andy! Do you have your knife? Kill that rabbit on my bed! Oh No! Oh No! That snake's here again!"

My fifteen-year-old brother left the room in tears. I, meanwhile, confronted my demons alone. The weeks dragged on and I spun between lucidity and confusion; hope and despair.

On many occasions over the next few weeks I phoned Kaye long distance informing her of my situation at Shady Acres. The subject of kidney stone pain was overshadowed by doubts associated with my staying at SAP. She'd investigated many facilities in close proximity to BSU, sadly discovering they all refused to accept respirator-dependent patients. Thankfully, Kaye had witnessed my unusual behavior during periodic all day visits; so importuning her for belief in the unsafe situation at SAP wasn't necessary. She was aware I was in pain most of the time and held hostage to a dilemma, but I withheld these onerous facts from my parents and siblings. I was certain they'd react by insisting I return to New Castle and be admitted to a local nursing home. At best they would reason, "How can anything be wrong, Danny asks for and takes medicine from the very people he views with suspicion?" As pain became seemingly unbearable I would relive the anguish of six-year-old Cindy, her terror, and the valiant effort she displayed to not complain. Reproved and encouraged, I chose renewing my response to "How are you?" with, "I'm fine". Kaye, my rock of stability, returned three weeks later bringing to me a spiritual reality I seemed unable to grasp by myself. The presence of someone whom I could trust eliminated previous reservations of bravado and upon seeing her I smiled, "Honey, am I ever glad to see you!"

Kaye grinned, "Dan you're really looking better, I hope things are changing here at SAP. I'm counting on spring to help the situation. Tell me what's happening."

Nearly an hour passed while I discussed the disturbing events taking place at SAP. After quietly listening to my dread and anger Kaye encouraged, "Enough about them, tell me about you. I can hear in your voice something is wrong."

I sighed, "Each day is like a roller-coaster. Some are good and I feel fine, but others are bad. The pain is never gone and there are inexplicable moments of terror."

Kaye declared, "Kidney stones cause pain, but 'terror'? Do you mean the snakes and spiders are back?"

"Sometimes." I replied. "The agony eases and my confusion ends, then stabbing pains resume and I ask for more pain medication. After I get a shot weird things begin happening. It's really frightening. Like I was saying before, the atmosphere here is changing. Many people have already quit and, while the remaining friendly staff brings me food from a drive-in, even eating out doesn't seem to change the way I feel. I'm always nauseated, hurting, and suffer repeated nightmares. I know it's wrong trusting the nurses to give me injections, but what choice do I have? If only a nursing home near Muncie or BSU would accept my respirators, I could leave Shady Acres. I can't stand it much longer."

The lunch tray arrived and Kaye volunteered, "Why don't I go out and get us something for lunch?"

Before I could answer Marti signaled from the doorway, beckoning Kaye to the corridor. Returning momentarily, Kaye excused herself as Marti exchanged places with her, offering to keep me company. "You go on to the little girl's room." she commented. "I'll feed Dan some of this Jello and then we'll have a cigarette break."

After what seemed a long time Kaye returned ashen faced and visibly shaken. I demanded, "Where did you go? Why are you upset? Is something wrong? Marti would you excuse us please? Cigarette break is over. I couldn't eat much Jello, but thanks for trying to feed me."

"Dan you won't believe what the DON ordered me to do." Kaye gasped, her voice trembling.

"The DON?" I questioned. "Is that where you went? Did Marti know where you were? What's going on?"

"Yes, she knew." Kaye sighed. "Marti was sent by the DON to get me and keep you occupied. That woman is vicious! She said we would never be married and I'm not supposed to come see you ever again. She said, 'Just look how sick he is, besides he's paralyzed.' She warned me 'Don't come back'. Can you believe it? Dan? Dan? Please don't leave me now. Honey, wake up!"

"Oh no! Help me!" I screamed. "Help me! The spiders are all over my bed! Hurry Kaye, kill that snake! Oww, I hurt so bad. Hurry! Call the nurse."

After receiving an injection of pain medicine I drifted into a restless sleep most of the afternoon. I awakened on occasion to gain comfort from Kaye's presence at my bedside. Sunlight dissipated and shadows appeared on the wall, signs ending one more day of confusion and terror. The pain eased and my thoughts again cleared. Kaye announced, "I'm going out for food. Please tell me what sounds good."

My appetite was nonexistent, but in efforts to placate her fears I agreed to try drinking a milkshake. I recalled an incident earlier in the day and

Keep Smiling and Never Give Up!

asked, "Kaye, why did you leave this afternoon? Marti tried feeding me Jello, but I couldn't eat much. How long were you gone? Please forgive me, I couldn't stay awake today, when you return we have to talk. Drive carefully, but don't take long."

After drinking a portion of the milkshake and watching Kaye nibble at her sandwich, I realized something was wrong. "Tell me what's going on. Why are you so quiet tonight?"

Kaye shakily replied, "I'm frightened. The DON warned me not to return. She says we'll never be married."

"The DON? What has she got to say about us?"

"I don't know." said Kaye. "Her words were cutting and it was like she knew something's going to happen. How can I leave you here by yourself, they could do anything. I'm so scared! If the aides and orderly are right, there's trouble ahead. I'm glad you have some friends on staff."

"Marti and Tammy are the only friendly aides remaining. Randy quit last week." I informed Kaye. "Have any of those other nursing homes called you with their decision regarding my admission? Surely there's a place near Ball State."

"Dan I've investigated every facility in Muncie." Kaye responded. "So far they all refuse to accept respirator-dependent residents. The last hope, Parkview Nursing home should let me know next week."

I lamented, "If only I could get out of here, maybe my nightmares would stop and some lucidity return. Don't worry though; we've endured more in the past. Everything will be okay if we just stay strong. Besides, I'm fine anyway."

Frightened, I headed the car toward home remembering a similar night we had parted foreseeing nothing but darkness in our future. I aimlessly sipped a Coke to unwind; the day had left my nerves in knots. Leaving SAP, The DON's vitriolic words flooded my mind, "He's sick, paralyzed, and it's absurd for you to consider marrying him. You'll find another man. He won't be here long, so leave and don't return." Wonder what she meant? Dear God, why is this happening to us? Maybe I'll quit school and stay with Dan. I can't quit I promised Mom and Dad I'd graduate. Decisions, decisions. My head throbbed with many tumultuous questions. "Oh please God help me find the answers." I prayed. Torrents of spring rain blew across the highway, illuminated by headlights of oncoming cars. As wipers cleared the windshield of nature's weeping, I brushed hot salty tears from my cheeks. Nothing could erase the anger and fear instilled in my heart today by SAP's cruel and vicious DON. Searching for strength I thought of a time two years ago, our lives already entwined, when I left Dan near death at Robert Long Hospital. Words echoed in my mind as he'd encouraged, "Kaye always remember, faith, love, patience, hope, and keep smiling."

Daniel R. Williams

Flashes of so many recent unwise choices flooded my soul with guilt and an intolerable burden of shame shook my fragile existence. As the medicine dulled my senses, the Lord's Prayer manifested itself on my lips and I began, "Our Father who art in heaven...uhhh...uhhh...HELP! Thy will be done...Oh God...forgive me...forgive me......."

Keep Smiling and Never Give Up!

25

REAPING THE WHIRLWIND

Tuesday I awakened adrift in an endless sea of opaque silence, peering through bleary eyes at two obtuse figures floating in my twilight zone of convoluted images. Della and Hazel, friends and dear aides who'd previously been so kind, were sitting me in my wheelchair. "Noooo, please," gulp, gulp, "don't," gulp, gulp. "I need my," gulp, gulp, "respirator." Gulp, gulp, gulp, "Help me," gulp, "I can't breathe." Gulp, gulp, "Why are you," gulp, gulp, "hurting me?" I gasped for air, "Oohh my stomach." gulp, gulp, gulp, gulp.

"We're sorry Dan. We have orders that you sit in the wheelchair. Please forgive us."

I frog breathed trying desperately to stay alive while crying out in pain. Kaleidoscopic dots and swirling yellow circles attacked my senses and an enveloping veil of black descended around me. As the door slowly opened, daggers of light knifed across my room ripping open the enshrouding maze of darkness. Through clouded eyes struggling to recognize a prayed-for saviour, I discerned Mom and Judy. Alarmed, they shouted, "What's going on? Get him to bed now!"

"Mom...help!" I cried before fainting.

Dizzily succumbing to a dungeon of terrifying demons, I screamed repeatedly to whoever would listen, "Help! I can't breathe!" Frantic, I vainly tried to explain my chest shell wasn't fastened properly. "The seal is broken!" gulp, gulp. "No vacuum!" gulp, gulp. A raging fire seared my lungs as I slipped into a fog of unconsciousness. I was jostled partly awake by the uniformed arms of two people when transporting me from bed to ambulance stretcher. Struggling to breathe, I threw my head from side to side, gasping for air. Someone in the room yelled, "Grab the oxygen, bag him, bag him!"

Earsplitting sounds from motorcycles, trucks, and cars assaulted my mind, numbing cold assailed my body, and harsh blinding light intensified my fears. I groggily heard deep echoing voices arguing, "Sure there's a risk, his breathing during anesthesia will be a problem, but he needs immediate surgery to stop the bleeding."

"Breathing him during surgery is not the problem, what are we doing to do while he's recovering?" asked one figure cloaked in white.

"We'll keep him breathing with his chest respirator and hope it works. We can always trach him." someone else said. "Either way, I'm not sure he'll survive."

Anguished cries as if from hell permeated my senses and blurred images of old style hospital beds floated before me. Turning my head toward a deep voice I pleaded, "Dad, Dad..."

I confronted a dilemma. I wanted to honor Dan's earlier plea to not phone his room; therefore my only recourse to sanity was prayer. Separated by seventy-five miles, attempting to concentrate on critical quarterly exams, and struggling with the unknown left me feeling overwhelmed and helpless. My stomach tied in knots; I fervently prayed someone would soon call. Three days passed with no news. Dread consumed every thought and unable to wait any longer, early Friday morning I dialed Dan's number. His phone rang, and rang, and rang. Immobilizing fear gripped my heart. Clutching the receiver I called SAP's office and was curtly informed, "I'm sorry, Dan no longer resides at Shady Acres Pavilion."

Stunned, I slowly turned to face our housemother, Mrs. Bell, stammering, "He's not there!"

She calmly asked, "Who would know what happened? Call them to find the answer so you can stop worrying."

As I reached for the phone, it rang. Vivian, Dan's sister, called to say he was at University Hospital (IUMC), advising me, "Don't visit until Sunday at noon. We'll bring Mother and Daddy about 1:30 PM. Danny doesn't need to be involved in another argument." When I asked what happened she only sighed, "Kaye, the doctors don't know yet, just be there."

I drove to Indianapolis as directed and found Dan in a private room with blinds drawn. A drainage bag containing minute amounts of dark amber urine hung at the bedside, and an IV pole stood at the foot of his bed. University Hospital had just recently opened and I was stricken by the starkness of his room. Expectantly I called Dan's name, but he didn't respond and my heart sank. His nurse took me to the chart room and spoke confidentially, nurse to student nurse. She stated, "Legally I shouldn't talk to you, but after hearing bits about the situation I won't withhold vital information. Your fiancé, is gravely ill. Since he's unconscious he won't be able to see you or respond to your voice, the doctors are amazed he's still alive. The trapped stones were removed, but it's important you understand a more serious problem is complicating his ability to awaken or recover. Mr. Williams's bloodstream was laced with five foreign chemicals. Our lab is still trying to isolate the substances.

"The past few weeks he has insisted people at the nursing home have been giving him the wrong medicines. Has Dan been alert since admission to the hospital?"

The nurse cautiously responded, "Friday night after his admission, Diane, a Respiratory Therapist, was monitoring the respirator when he struggled to speak crying out, "Diane help me!" She said they knew each other at Robert Long when he was a patient. Except for that one incident, he's been totally unresponsive."

Returning fearfully to Dan's room, I cried when looking at his lifeless form. I whispered "Oh Dan," and kissed his icy lips. He didn't respond. I grasped the bed rails for support, trembling as my knees and legs began to buckle. He was shivering, and his arms felt so cold to touch. With the nurse's help, I covered Dan's trembling body with additional blankets then rubbed his freezing arms and hands, trying to comfort him with warmth and love. "Honey, your parents are coming so I must leave. Please be strong." After trying to soothe him for a brief hour while I prayed and awaited some semblance of life, I wrenched myself away, hesitantly moving toward the door. Through inward sobs of anguish I vowed to return soon. "Dan remember, God willing, we will always be together." Brushing by Anita and Jim, I wiped tears from my eyes and left, confronting visions of our death for a third time. Foreboding waves of impending nausea rushed upward as I relived moments of past crises, my throat clutched by the throes of grief. Exiting the hospital I walked numbly to my car, brisk spring air merging with steamy hot tears flowing down my cheeks. Looking upward to Heaven I prayed, "Please God, don't let him die. Bring him back to me. Give him strength. Lord, give us strength."

Upon dismissal from University Hospital, May 21, 1970 I was admitted to a nursing home in New Castle. I was unaware of the journey, people, or event, but retain vivid memories of being escorted through a long dark hallway, hearing loud shrieking voices and cries for help. Moments of terror attacked my debilitated spirit overloading a frangible nervous system, ensuring repeated nightmares and destroying any chance for rest or recovery. Suffocating darkness and fear of the unseen will forever be indelibly etched within my being.

Reassuring, calm voices greeted me as attendants pushed my stretcher through lonely corridors. I was gingerly transferred to bed, listening to fragments of conversation as Dad instructed those present about my chest shell and respirator. Excruciating pain surged through my body and I cried out, "Give me some medicine, help me."

One of the people patted my head assuring me everything would be fine, "Dr.Heilman has been called, we are awaiting his orders. Try to rest."

"Are they crazy?" I thought. "Dr.Heilman? Where am I? I'm waiting for Dr.Alberto. Oh, I'm hurting so bad." My body felt as though razor blades were peeling away skin and cutting my body from reality. Overhead lights glared beyond the gray blanket of fog surrounding my head, and the mirror effect created larger-than-life images. "You have to help me." I screamed at the voices beside my bed. "You said the doc would come, why doesn't he?" Fleeting reflections of Kaye's face flashed through my mind and I yelled, "Kaye!"

Daniel R. Williams

Soothing voices tried reassuring me all would be well, but the stabbing pain shooting throughout my body negated all their kind words. Searing fire crossed my abdomen and I cried out in agony, "Please get me some medicine!" Sensing they weren't going to help I reverted to the only solace I had found in this turmoil. Trying to internally visualize her face and encouraging eyes I listened intently for sounds of a comforting voice. In my tortured memory I saw Kaye and began calling her name. "Kaayyyee! Kaayyyee! Kaayyyee! I need you! Where are you? Help me please!"

Ruby the nurse encouraged, "Danny, you must drink some milkshake. You aren't eating anything and we won't let you starve. Come on now, take another sip. That's good."

"I can't eat! I'm so cold! Who are you? Please call Kaye. Where am I? What happened? I'm so cold! Kaayyyee!"

Following a phone call from Vivian, I anxiously drove twenty-five miles from Muncie to New Castle. Entering the nursing home's front door I was startled by Dan's loud and incessant cries as he screamed my name. Totally unaware of any improvement in his condition since last seeing him five days ago when he was in a coma, I silently, but exuberantly thanked God to once again hear his voice. Walking quickly to the nurse's station I asked for Dan's room number. The nurse requested my name then reported, "Danny can't have any visitors. Kaye I'm sorry, but we have our orders."

Remaining calm, I listened as Dan repeatedly called my name before exclaiming, "Orders?! Do you hear that cry? I am 'Kaayyyee'? Where is he?!" Drawn by sounds of his voice I began walking toward Dan's screams, ignoring the nurse's befuddled and feeble protests. Shortly I stood in front of his door scanning beds for recognition of Dan's location. I watched another nurse encouraging him to drink a milkshake, my heart breaking as he pleaded for help, "Where's Kaayyee? Ooohhh I'm so cold. Kaayyyee! Kaayyee!" Stepping to the foot of his bed I prayed for and anticipated an enthusiastic greeting. Looking warily toward me the nurse shook her head side to side as he again called my name, "Kaayyyee, Kaayyee, where are you?"

With joy pounding in my heart, knees shaking, and body trembling I answered, "Dan, I'm here."

"Kaye, I can't see! Touch me." I cried. "I'm scared! I'm so cold! Please don't ever leave me."

Pressing her tear stained cheek to mine Kaye whispered, "I love you Dan. You're safe now. I'll never leave you."

Our tears of joy and relief mingled as we silently gave thanks for one more moment of grace. "Thank you God."

"Excuse me." said the nurse. "I'm Ruby. Are you Kaye? I hope so, he's been calling her name constantly and nothing we do helps. For the first time in two days Danny's stopped screaming. I don't know the entire story, but please dear, don't leave. I'm going to get him another blanket."

Kaye replied, "I'm not leaving his side for anyone. When did he begin waking up? If I may ask, how long has he been here?"

Ruby answered, "Danny was admitted Thursday and he has shown steady improvement. Periodically rousing from a drug-induced stupor, he screams and yells for Kaye."

"I'm Kaye. We're engaged to be married."

Assuming Dan's feeding, I held a straw to his mouth and encouraged him to drink some hot soup and coffee. However, when I placed a spoonful of Jello in his mouth he jerked his head sideways yelling, "Don't give me that, it's full of bad medicine. I don't want it! No! Get away! Get away!"

"Okay Dan, okay, calm down." I soothed. "I won't feed you anything bad. You're not at Shady Acres anymore."

"They tried to kill me!" I shrieked. "Why? Dear God, why can't I see? My head hurts. Kaye don't leave. I gotta sleep, so tired..."

I awakened to hear my parents demanding, "Why are you here? Only family is permitted in Danny's room. Our son is home again and we're in charge. Now you go home."

Listening to their threatening words I sensed our lives being torn apart. Shocked awake by the commotion I angrily responded, "Kaye, don't move! I can't see or understand why you are doing this Dad and Mom, but Kaye isn't leaving."

After they left Kaye sighed, "Dan, will it ever change? You've been resting peacefully all day, why can't they see we are good for each other and accept our love?"

As Sherry the evening nurse prepared to check my blood pressure she commented to Kaye, "Don't be overly concerned about visiting, we can all see how important your presence is to Danny."

Someone brought me another milkshake and handed it to Kaye greeting, "Hi, I'm Betty. Maybe this will help."

Our time together was over much too quickly as evening became night. Daylight changing to dark wasn't significant to me, but for Kaye who could see, it meant parting again. Quietly she said, "Dan I promise to be back tomorrow after church, I'm staying in town tonight with my parents. Meanwhile, please relax, rest, and leave your fears with God. Pray and never forget, faith, love, patience, hope, and always keep smiling."

Kaye fed me Sunday dinner before returning to college, thankfully, this time she'd be just twenty-some miles away. Exhaustion and semi-consciousness once again overwhelmed my being, but I was vaguely aware of frequent family visitors. During those fleeting moments of lucidity I remember asking, "Why am I hurting so much? Am I still bleeding? Do I have a catheter? I can't ask Kaye, so will someone please talk to me? What happened?"

The first full week at my new home began with a visit from Dr. Heilman Jr. "Good morning Danny," he greeted, "are you feeling better today? I see by the chart you didn't eat well this morning."

"Why can't I see? I'm so cold. Do I have a catheter? Why do I hurt so much? Why are you my doctor?" I demanded.

"Danny, your parents requested I resume responsibility. I promise to take care of everything." he assured me. "You are safe near family and friends."

"Safe? Near friends? What do you mean, I was near my friends before coming to this place. What happened, I can't see. Oooh, just get me some glasses." I demanded.

"Give yourself time to heal Danny." he replied. "When you're feeling better we'll talk. Right now you need rest."

Following Dr. Heilman's departure a shadowy figure near my bed cheerfully spoke, "Hi Danny, my name is Connie your nurse's aide this week. I understand you came from another nursing home by way of an Indianapolis hospital. Did they give you good care? It looks like they didn't care at all. Hey what's the turtle shell on your chest? Marilyn, one of the nurses taking care of you this weekend, said you wore a respirator. Will you tell me how it works? Can you breathe any on your own? Danny...Danny...?"

Her words faded as I slipped behind my curtain of fog.

"Uhhh...what do you want?" I mumbled as someone shook my arm. "I wanna' sleep."

"Danny, it's Marilyn." voiced the blur before my face. "Do you remember me? I'm the Head Nurse at Heritage House. Come on now, wake up."

Traces of their conversation filtered through the drug-induced netting which enshrouded my fragile existence. As I struggled to listen Connie remarked, "I was talking and next thing I know he's asleep again. Guess he's tired."

Marilyn replied, "Yes, he's tired all right. I can't tell you much about the situation, but his kidneys continue to work overtime trying to strain dangerous toxins from his system. Let's discuss the respirator. If he fully awakens I'm sure Danny can tell us more about his equipment than any other person, but until then we'll rely on family advice."

"Don't be afraid of my respirators." I urged drowsily. "Give me a few minutes, I'll tell you what's going on."

Marilyn patted my shoulder and said, "Danny we aren't afraid of your respirators. I'm trying to sound smart."

"No offense Danny," Connie smirked, "but it looks like it'll take you more than a few minutes to get it together."

I smiled as Marilyn attempted once more to sound smart. "Danny does need rest."

"Speaking of rest," I grumbled, "are you through?"

Laughing, Marilyn said, "Almost. Connie as you heard, Danny's already asserting himself and taking limited control of his surroundings. He was admitted just four days ago, and every day he's a little better. Did you know Danny's engaged to be married?"

Connie nodded, "Is that who you were screaming for when they brought you in on the stretcher? The name Kaye is very familiar around these halls, she must be special."

Endless days became weeks as my health slowly improved. I continued asking for an eye specialist, but my request was deferred until I could remain awake with a longer attention span. During this time my family brought me homemade foods and many, many milkshakes. Kaye visited two to three times a week, always bringing food or driving to the nearest fast food establishment for our dinner. Strength slowly returned to mind and body, but blindness remained unabated. Visions and dreams were interrupted by nightmares. Much needed rest was destroyed by the images of past terrors.

Marilyn, Connie, and Frances trouped flippantly into my room pushing a wheelchair, mission bound. "Today, my dear, you arise." announced Connie. "Any questions?"

"Just one." I mumbled. "How do I breathe?"

"Easy," said Marilyn, "we'll sit you in the wheelchair wearing your chest shell. It's that or mouth to mouth, and Kaye would object. Ready?"

"This reminds me of the Respo Center." I remarked. "We either worked or got out. Push, push, push. Marilyn, since I'm better, how about that eye doctor?"

Dr. Heilman came into my room while I was sitting up, "Doc, enough stalling. I demand you call Dr.Burnett." He agreed at last and as he walked from my room I reentered a lost world of outlines and shadows.

Two days later Dr.Burnett shined a bright light into my eyes, quietly concluding his diagnostic examination. "Dan, it would be of no value to either of us for me to delude you as to the facts or give you false hopes. Multiple doses of unknown drugs and hypoxia severely weakened optic nerves and the damage may well be irreversible. This factor, combined with retinal scarring sustained during the storm in Michigan, presents a disappointing prognosis of limited return. I've searched through all the lenses I brought in hopes I could find one to minimally aid your vision, but I honestly think you must adjust your perspectives for the near future. Focusing on small objects or distant images, watching TV, and most especially reading will be improbable, if not impossible. Don't give up, be strong, and I'll return with your glasses in two weeks."

For days I inwardly trembled each time I thought of my life without sight. What can I possibly do, no more reading or typing and TV's the only way I can participate in sports. "Dear God, what about Kaye and our future?"

"Danny, Hi Hon. Remember me?" asked the voice. "It's Aunt Vera."

"Of course I remember you, Aunt Vera." I answered. "It is good to uuhh, uuhh - I can't see. We can talk though, my voice and ears are in good shape."

Squeezing my arm Aunt Vera continued, "Your mom told me you couldn't see, but the Lord is watching over you. Every time our church holds services we pray for your recovery."

I could feel tears streaming down my cheeks as I said, "I haven't been very good lately, Jesus might not like me."

"Shhh, Danny you know better." Aunt Vera corrected. "I promise, Jesus won't forget you. Would you want my minister and some of our members to visit? They're young and I know you would like them, can I tell them it's okay to come over occasionally?"

"Sure, please tell your pastor and friends they're very welcome, as long as they read to me. It's been a long time since I heard the Bible or any devotions."

That evening Rev. Shaw and Ray from Bible Covenant Church entered my room carrying workbooks, devotional tracts, and their Bibles. "Hi Danny, we came prepared." said Rev. Shaw. "I understand your eyes are dim, but I'm told your ears are in perfect condition. We'll read until you tire, or we do. Don't forget visiting hours are over at 9 PM."

I deeply appreciated the precious times these men dedicated to reading, bringing back memories of those days after Polio when Rev. Kerschner read to me from the Bible, books, and magazines. Once again I heard words of wisdom so long denied me by my tragically unwise choices. Moving from my parent's home had been necessary, but abandoning the Word of God and His commandments proved nearly irreconcilable.

While trying to force my eyes to focus on ceiling tiles one morning, two friendly people entered the room. Giggling and talking they introduced themselves, "Hi Mr. Williams," greeted the serious one, "I'm Lynn, recreational intern, and meet Donna, my assistant. The nurses said you have vision problems, so would you enjoy having us read to you? We have a great collection of books with us and the city library can supply any material you request."

"That's right." agreed Donna, the giggling one. "But if you prefer, I'll read to you from the newspaper."

"Whoa!" I protested. "Take a breath. First of all my name is Dan. Yes, I would like being read to and I'm sure the books you have will be sufficient for now. Donna, I'd enjoy hearing the newspaper, thanks for the offer. Actually I would prefer reading by myself, but...problem is..."

Lynn suggested, "Perhaps you can read by listening to Talking Books. Written material is transferred to records and available without charge to disabled or blind people. If you're interested I'll prepare and submit an application to the State Library. In turn, they'll contact the Library of Congress. The answer will be forthcoming shortly."

"Please do." I agreed. "I'm certain you've noticed my qualifications are superb."

Donna interjected, "I'd rather not read books. If you don't mind, I'll just read aloud from *The Courier-Times* and *News Republican*."

Several weeks after being admitted to the nursing home in New Castle I had made excellent progress in my recovery. The long journey from bed to chair and learning to identify people by the sound of their voice and footsteps became much easier with time and patience. It's amazing how quickly one can acclimate to new habits, and the wonderful people at my new home were intent on renewing hope. Early one morning Connie, Jackie, and Mayme lifted me into my wheelchair then Connie positioned me outside the door. Happily I joined the world for the first time since my arrival. I habitually sat with my eyes closed, eliminating questions or conversation from people I couldn't see. Not since my early days after Polio at the OSU Respo Center had I been so self-conscious. While sitting in the hall I listened intently to approaching footsteps as Marilyn's familiar voice teased, "Well who have we here? Antisocial huh? Perhaps you'd prefer moving near the nurse's station. I won't converse long distance."

"Don't forget to turn my respirator off before you pull the plug." I cautioned. "The alarm is deafening."

"I'm sure glad you're using a portable respirator." She declared. "I still don't understand how you can eat a meal or drink anything with so much pressure on your stomach."

All lucid wheelchair occupants chose the hall adjacent to a nurse's station as their favorite meeting place. Until I regained some of my sight it remained insignificant that at twenty-seven I was much younger than my companions whose average age was eighty. While talking with other residents Dr.Burnett entered, saw me, and immediately offered to push my wheelchair back to the room for more privacy. Somberly he began, "Dan these are your glasses, but don't expect any miracles. Maybe we should just be content if you can see." I anxiously waited for swimming, fuzzy, images to focus, but instead of clarity, my vision remained blurred with cascades illuminated by frightening shadows of despair.

"Oh no!" I cried. "Please God, not my eyes too!"

"Dan if only I could bring you better news," Dr.Burnett lamented, "but you cried out to the only solution."

Stunned, I sat quietly trying to absorb the enormity of this revelation. The doctor's warnings had been sufficient, but because of my inward optimism, I expected a more positive prognosis. The world around me was collapsing. I needed privacy and solitude. "Dr.Burnett, I refuse to allow release of any medical information. Only Dr.Heilman is to know. Tell the nurse I need to lie down." Back in bed my mind became a cacophony of despondent voices telling me what to do, and what I couldn't expect any longer. How could I confront Kaye with these facts? How could she marry me now, not only am I paralyzed, I can't see to read or write. With a pandemonium of intimidating doom the hours passed quickly, and at noon Judy brought me home-cooked food. The sickening news about my vision obliterated any appetite or possibility for lunch. My quiet demeanor upset Sis and she repeatedly questioned, "What's wrong? You've been doing so well, are you feeling OK? Maybe you're tired? Should I tell Mother and Daddy? Well, since you don't want to talk, I'll leave."

Judy apparently reported my depressed attitude because Dad, Mom, and other family members visited later attempting to "cheer me up". I remained silent concerning Dr.Burnett's devastating evaluation of my eyes, not wishing to hear more excuses why I shouldn't consider involvement with Kaye. The reason for my blindness kept hammering away and I exploded in anger, bitterness, and resentment. I implored, "Dad will you help me uncover facts proving SAP's guilt? Regardless what you and some people choose to believe, they did hurt me and it's wrong if they aren't held responsible."

"Danny, we don't believe that." he responded. "Doctors said it was because of drugs. They said you would probably not live, so just be grateful you are alive. Please don't let the nurses hear you say these things. I don't ever want to hear you talk about crazy things again."

"Dad, the records speak for themselves. Did you ever ask the doctors **why** all those drugs are in my body? Don't you wonder **how** they got there? Hospital records will prove what happened to me, so why cover it up? My fingers, toes, and feet are mostly numb, the hand on which I had surgery is useless, and I'm blind, but never mind you don't believe any of those things happened anyway! I vaguely remember Mom and Judy coming into my room witnessing them forcing me to sit in my wheelchair without a respirator. What does that tell you? Oh well, it's obvious you won't help me uncover facts, so believe me I'll never mention it to you or family again!" Exhausted and emotionally drained I mumbled, "My life's over anyway. Thinking about the situation maybe you're right, it really doesn't matter. Nothing does!"

"Danny, today's the third day you've refused to sit in your wheelchair." said Marilyn. "What's going on? Unless I miscalculated, you haven't been up since Dr.Burnett was here. Shall we talk? Isn't Kaye supposed to visit today? Don't you want to be sitting up when she gets here? Ahh, the old silent treatment. I'll leave, let me know if you change your mind and want to talk."

Kaye walked into my room announcing, "I brought corned beef with dill pickles, your favorite sandwich, and a milkshake from the drive-in. Why aren't you up? Don't I even rate a 'Hi'?"

"Sorry hon, my mind was elsewhere." I said. "I'm not hungry, but I'll sip some of the milkshake."

"Don't say that, I made your sandwich with my very own fingers, but I can't guarantee the milkshake since I picked it up on the way. Hey sourpuss, smile, that was supposed to be funny. What's wrong?"

My silent desolation erupted against the very person who'd been my earthly guardian angel, "Forget the food!" I ordered. "Dr. Burnett brought my glasses Wednesday, they're in the bedside stand drawer. They don't help. We have to talk. He says my optic nerves have been severely damaged and there is nothing medical science can do. If improvement occurs only God can give it. Bluntly, I can no longer read, type, watch television, or clearly see your face. Basically I'm in trouble, or should I say, we're in trouble."

Our lunch remained on the table as Kaye slumped to the bedside chair. "Dan, doctors don't know everything. Those at IUMC said you wouldn't live. Even if it is true, this isn't the end. Many people have vision problems. Look at me, I wear glasses. Come on honey, it could be worse. I bet your parents were upset, what did they say?"

Ignoring her comments I stated, "Kaye, listen closely. I'm not like other people, I'm paralyzed. Reading Braille is impossible so the written word is gone forever. There is no typewriter with Braille keys because a mouthstick simply isn't that sensitive. My dream of writing has ended. I've asked you to accept many of my previous problems, but I would never hinder your happiness. This is undoubtedly the most painful decision I've ever made, but I want you to leave and forget us. I will always love you, but please go."

"NO!"

"Kaye, I've thought about this continuously night and day since Dr.Burnett's visit. When I asked you to marry me things were different. I was only paralyzed. History tells of many happily married people confronting simple handicaps, traveling, raising families, and enjoying life's pleasures, but there's no way I can live with the fact my love for you burdened your life with insurmountable obstacles. My life at SAP has scarred me forever and the consequences continue to unfold daily. Rev. Kerschner once told me everyone must reap what they sow. I now understand why choices, good or bad, undoubtedly determine the direction of one's life. I want you to never forget I love you, and your well-being is always foremost in my mind. Regardless what you think now, I'm concerned someday you will resent me and, my darling, that would be the ultimate devastation. Chances for us to be married have ended, but we gave it a great try. Please walk away before we both suffer more heartache."

"No! I'm not leaving. Now is not the time to make a major decision." Kaye sobbed. "Loving someone means having faith and trust in them. You just said good or bad choices determine a person's future. This is a very bad choice, so don't ask me to leave."

"For both our sanities," I cried, "I'm not asking you to leave, I'm telling you. It has to be over."

Trembling with helplessness Kaye leaned down and kissed my cheek. Our tears of parting mingled and she sobbed, "Dan think it over. I'll be at Mom and Dad's. Please call."

I walked past the nurse's station with tears streaming down my face wanting only to reach the fresh air outside. I hurried to my car carrying the sack full of cold lunch I'd brought for us today. "How dumb! Why didn't I leave his food?" Not wanting my parents to see red eyes and tear-stained cheeks, I drove around town then out through Memorial Park. I stopped beside the lake, watching ripples of water travel aimlessly from bank to bank. "How did this happen?" I wondered. "The other times pain was inflicted by outside forces, but now Dan is surrendering to adversity. I know he must be dying inside by allowing this catastrophe to destroy our lives. In the past he said, 'Faith, love, hope, patience, and always keep smiling'. Dan is forgetting his instructions to me. Could our love be like the wind-blown waves on this lake, with each ripple it becomes weaker? No! It can't be true! Our love's too strong; we've been through too much to let this destroy our future. He'll call. I'd better go home and wait. Oh dear God, please don't let him throw us away."

26

HERITAGE HOUSE

I listened to the fading sound of Kaye's footsteps and the agony of complete loneliness swept through my being. I had not felt this forlorn since those endless nights in my iron lung following the diagnosis of acute Polio. Tears welled in my eyes and I tried forcefully willing myself to think of better times, but recent horror-filled days only encouraged thoughts of nightmarish tomorrows. Aides and nurses peeked hesitantly around the doorway, knowing something was wrong. Kaye's untimely departure caused considerable concern, but everyone waited for someone else to ask, "What happened?" "How could I have been so dumb? So I'm blind, big deal. We could have made it work couldn't we?" my mind twisted with doubt. "No, it has to be this way because I love her too much." I argued with myself. Only those days when I'd watched my body die from Polio could be compared with the vulnerability and helplessness consuming my life today. John Greenleaf Whittier's poem entitled "Maud Muller" flashed in my mind, "For of all sad words of tongue or pen, The saddest of these: 'It might have been!'"

Thankfully by midafternoon Vivian and daughter Kennetha appeared at my bedside. "Why are you crying?" Vivian asked. "Are you hurting some place? We brought you a milkshake."

Shaking my head no, I said, "Forget it, I'm not hungry. I'm fine. Would you please wipe my eyes?"

Vivian continued to question me, ignoring my silence. "You may as well tell me, I won't leave until I know what's wrong. Do you want me to call Mother and Daddy?"

"Vivian, please leave me alone." I pleaded. "This time it's personal."

"Bet I know." said Kennetha. "It's Kaye, isn't it?"

"Drop it Kennetha!" I demanded.

Lowering her head my niece whispered, "I'm sorry."

"Don't be sorry." I apologized. "It's been a bad day."

"Well, is she right?" asked Vivian. "What happened?"

"Aww Sis, I'm ashamed, sick, and scared. I did a dumb thing." I confessed. "This mess in my life got to me and I told Kaye to leave and not come back."

"You did what! After the love and devotion she's shown you? It isn't only your eyes that need help Danny; you've got a big problem with your brain! How smart - here you are alone crying, Kaye's some place drying her tears, trying to understand, and you're both miserable. I know things seem

Keep Smiling and Never Give Up!

awful right now, but you've been through tough times before, always managing to come back with a smile. I remember many years ago when you returned to Riley Hospital. I guess life must have looked pretty bleak at that time, but when you and Rev. Kerschner spoke on the speaker phone before leaving he said, 'Don't forget Danny, all things work together for good to them that love God, to them who are the called according to His purpose.' Big brother, you're here for some reason."

I turned my head muttering, "Only reason I can think of would be to make other people feel better about their little problems. You got any better ideas?"

Disgusted by my shallow thoughts and self-pity, Vivian shot back, "No! But then I'm not God!"

Duly reprimanded by my big sister I turned my head in embarrassment as tears began flowing again. Holding a thin dime between thumb and finger Vivian sagely remarked, "This is all that stands between you and NO future. Is she home, or at Muncie? Shall I phone and tell her you're sorry?"

Looking sheepish and ashamed I weakened, "Yes, please talk to her at Ben and Myra's. Don't tell her I'm sorry, I can eat crow by myself."

Vivian returned from placing the call with a wide grin on her face, "I spoke to Kaye, she'll be right here. Come on Kennetha, they'll need some privacy. Hon, I understand life seems like a tragedy right now, but everything will get better in time. I've been there too, but thank goodness the good Lord always has a plan in mind. Be patient and wait!"

I passed the tension filled afternoon hoping my stomach would stop churning. I stared at the soap operas my mother watched, dreading her questions, "Why are you home? Doesn't Dan feel good today? Is he sick?" Interrupted by a ringing phone, my heart beat faster as Mom announced, "Kaye, this is for you, it's Vivian."

Walking past the nurse's station I saw smiles of relief and heard, "It's a good thing." Standing outside Dan's door I couldn't decide whether to assault him or hug him. So on trembling legs I entered his room sighing, "Thank you God."

As when sunlight warms a cold lonely place and the glow of its presence eliminates shadows of despair, my anguished heart leaped with joy when Kaye walked back into my life. A comforting peace descended on me and I prayed insurmountable problems would become minor bumps in the road. Leaning over me, touching my cheek Kaye whispered, "Shall we start this day over?"

"Forgive me," I pleaded, "it will never happen again."

Struggling to remain calm and collected, Kaye eased the tension with her remark, "Don't ever do something like this again or next time you'll apologize on your knees."

"Maybe I should practice," I frowned, "Kaye you know we are confronting more than the usual number of obstacles."

Kaye acknowledged, "Aren't you the one who told me only through adversity came worthwhile opportunities?"

Shaking my head I said to the air, "Brother, not even married and already she's throwing words back at me!"

After our mutual agreement to confront future troubles together with strength reinforced by faith, we spoke of more mundane matters. Kaye said, "I'm hungry. I haven't eaten anything today, have you? Will you eat something? Suppose we celebrate with a giant tenderloin, fries, and milkshake?"

"I'm so relieved," I assured her, "not only will I try some sandwich and milkshake, I'll even eat Jello."

Our evening concluded after we reminisced about all the tribulations that had taken place in our lives. I told Kaye about Rev. Kerschner and Dr. Walcher's anecdotes, comparing life's problems to polishing a rough diamond. "It's true, but I didn't realize there would be so many jagged edges."

Kaye laughed, "At this rate we'll both be valuable gems before long. Seriously, the Bible says the Lord chasteneth those He loves. Now don't you feel special?"

I smiled, "Yeah, He must really love me."

"We both do." Kaye affirmed. "You mentioned what Rev. Kerschner and Dr. Walcher said about diamonds in the rough. Remember, a diamond begins as peat and a lump of coal under tremendous pressure for many years. It must endure nature's molding before it can be mined, cut, and then edges smoothed to make it valuable. Multiple pressures in your life create a diamond as rough edges are continually ground away. God predestined our lives together, now with courage and trust we must both undergo pressure and polishing to become one. Like a diamond, our love and lives must be tested to ensure strength and endurance. In the letters I wrote while in my sophomore year at Marion College I summarized bits about my childhood history concerning rheumatic fever, Dad carrying me everyplace, and going to handicapped school. I neglected to tell you when I was twenty-four months old our family doctor told my parents I probably wouldn't ever recover, attend public school, or run and play like other kids. They were warned, 'It's quite possible your daughter will die'. A search for consolation led my parents to complete dependence on God for health and the life of their baby. Elders at Christian Missionary Alliance church anointed me with oil then everyone prayed for my survival and healing. You know the rest, my health returned, I went to public school, ran and played almost like most children, and in time I'll be a nurse - a graduate of BSU's School of

Nursing. Then God willing, I'll become your wife. Believe, trust, be patient. Honey it's getting late and so I'll leave you with the words I know you've heard from many ministers, doctors, nurses, and friends. Never give up! As Aunt Zella always reminds you, keep smiling."

Marilyn was working an unusual evening shift and after Kaye left she came into my room and said, "Let's talk."

No longer wishing to be Mr. Silent, I explained to her Dr.Burnett's opinion of my vision problems. "Apparently the radio will be my avenue to information and entertainment."

"I would imagine," she said, "one of the first lessons you learned after paralysis was to accept, then adjust. Why don't we explore the possibilities? You can't see to read, so listen. You can't use a Braille typewriter, so dictate. Muscles in your eyes need exercise and stimulation, why not try watching television? I'm sure at first it will just be a blur, but work at this as you did rehab. You know better than I there's no gain without pain, or should I say strain? I suggest a new motto for your mind, 'use it or lose it'. Ask your parents to bring a table model TV. At least try."

Much to my surprise, Dad and Mom entered the room next day carrying a portable television. "I don't understand how the nurse thinks this will help," Dad puzzled, "but here's your TV. Maybe you can listen to the programs."

"Set the television on this." Marilyn directed, pushing a bedside table into my room. "Let's try various locations until you can best view the screen. How about it Danny, can you see any of the baseball players?"

"No!" I responded glumly, my initial excitement stolen by reality. "They resemble sticks floating in a dirty fish aquarium. Try another channel, maybe news. Marilyn changed channels where panelists discussed the recent invasion into Cambodia, which resulted in protests and killings by National Guard troops at Kent State, a small university in Ohio. I asked incredulously, "When did that happen? Apparently I've missed a few major events."

Rather than sitting in my wheelchair I lay in bed for several days, my eyes glued to murky TV pictures as I tried to regain some of the life I'd lost. News programs helped realign my memory with current events; game programs such as *"JEOPARDY!"* aided me in establishing lost thought processes; and struggling with sports programs became my entertainment. I refer to this exercise as a struggle; it was impossible to focus on thrown baseballs, kicked footballs, or basketballs being bounced by puppet-like figures. Fortunately, in years before Polio I had participated in sports, so I visualized sights by listening to play-by-play announcers. Some memories can be wonderful! Scheduled programs enabled me to devise some semblance of time awareness, becoming an important element in the restructuring of my life. I concentrated intently on blurry pictures, desperately seeking to regain my sight.

Rev. Shaw visited on Saturday evening, reading parts of the Bible as we discussed problems confronting Kaye and I in an uncertain future. I confided the misgivings experienced recently and my situation involving loss of vision. After praying he counseled, "The Bible says we are to give thanks in all things, for all things. I'm sure you've heard this before, but be wise in the choices you make now. From what I understand, Heritage House (HH) is an excellent place for starting a journey down a new road. Give thanks every day you are no longer a, what did you say, 'sap'?"

As he spoke, memories of times past flashed through my mind and with a broken heart I again pleaded, "God forgive me! Please help me choose the right path. I can't see with my eyes, but may Your will be done in my life."

Rev. Shaw patted my arm before leaving saying, "Amen."

Sunday after the usual morning routine I was attempting to focus on ceiling tiles when a strange sensation occurred in my head - an unsettling pressure behind my eyes. Fearful of another disaster occurring in my body, I called for a nurse. Turning my head sideways I peered toward sounds in the hall, shocked to realize that for the first time since my arrival at Heritage House, I could SEE! Like adjusting a camera's zoom lens, my surroundings came into focus. They were still blurry, fuzzy, and distant, but with distinguishing lines at last. Awestruck, I couldn't believe it! Staring longingly out my window I saw beautiful blue sky above trees and green grass. "I must be dreaming." I thought. "If somebody walks in I'll ask them to pinch me." Carolyn, a nurse's aide, brought a bouquet of homegrown flowers into the room placing them on the table across from my bed. "Give me my glasses." I said then casually remarked, "Those flowers are beautiful. The red ones really accentuate your long blond hair."

"Thank you Danny." she said. "Just a little something to brighten your room." Then turning slowly she stared at me demanding, "How did you know these are red flowers? Long blond hair?! Wait right here, I'm getting the nurse!"

Although I'd never told family members about the extent of my visual problems or Dr. Burnett's limited prognosis, they were obviously aware my sight had suffered some type of trauma. Wishing to surprise them and Kaye, I secured a promise from the staff to join my conspiracy. Vivian arrived to feed me dinner and I told her to observe the beautiful red bouquet. Crossing the room to admire the flowers Viv said, "Oh these are pretty." Doing a double take she turned asking, "How do you know these flowers are red?"

Anita and Jim visited later and I asked her to hold up a driver's license or Social Security card. It was then my pleasure to startle them by reading the large print. Anita ignored my pleas to remain quiet so I could surprise

Keep Smiling and Never Give Up!

Dad and Mom declaring, "No! I'm calling them now. They'll be happy too." Silently reviewing the past three months, it was easy to understand everyone's joy. For months my weakened eyes couldn't fathom life around me, but now I can see. God surely did bless me with another miracle.

Two days after the limited return of my eyesight, Kaye entered my room, unaware of happenings prior to her visit. Interrupting her greeting I said, "Wow! That white ruffled blouse and green skirt look great on you. Honey why are you wearing a sweater today? No one mentioned it was cold. Let me see, doesn't that lunch sack say The Trojan Drive-In?"

The forgotten sack fell to the floor as she quickly ran to the side of my bed saying, "Thank God." Kaye leaned over me, cradled my face in her hands and we kissed.

Although I could focus on larger objects I was unable to read small print. Talking Books remained a window to the world outside my room. Weekdays, Donna and Lynn still read to me from newspapers and magazines; then evenings Rev. Shaw and parishioners read Aunt Vera's devotional books, helping to re-acquaint me with divine scriptural promises.

During one of his many visits to my room since I became a resident at HH, I asked the Administrator, Jim, to remove all names relating to guardianship from my admission forms. "My vision, though impaired, is more than sufficient and as you are aware; I'm no longer incompetent. Would you please initiate reinstatement of Medicaid benefits in my name?"

"Of course, Danny. There is no doubt in anyone's mind you've regained a measure of independence. Maybe I should begin addressing you as Dan." he laughed. "I'll be back in a minute with the form and witnesses."

***

"No! No! Don't give me that shot! I can't eat Jello! I'm cold! Don't close the door! Somebody help me!"

"Danny, Danny, wake up. It's all right." said Beverly the nurse. "You just had a nightmare. You're at Heritage House, it's okay. Here, drink some water, then I'll get a cold cloth and wipe your forehead."

***

The day after my midnight rendezvous with terror I bid greetings to Millie, and husband Malcolm just home from Nam. He grinned, "Danny you really look better than I expected. Reading my wife's letters I thought you were almost dead and sure didn't think I'd find you smiling or watching TV."

"I'm fine." I laughed. "We both dodged a bullet."

"Well big brother this is goodbye for a while." Millie said preparing to leave. "With Malcolm's safe return from Nam we're moving to Albany, Georgia, his next duty station."

"Sorry to see you go Sis." I answered. "Take care of Krissy, I'm glad Malcolm's home and you're family of three is together."

Happily my eyesight steadily improved, but tiny objects were still blurred and it was impossible to see baseballs in the World Series between Baltimore and Cincinnati. Every TV picture revealed views of fuzzy images, but thankfully I now deciphered many words and numbers appearing on the screen. Reading, previously my favorite activity, became a distinct future possibility. One afternoon Marilyn waltzed into my room announcing, "Guess what! You're getting a new address. Soon we'll be moving you to a room off the main hall where you'll temporarily be by yourself. Danny, you'll like the new room, it's much warmer around the corner. Winter's cold winds will soon be here and maybe changing location will end your need for so many blankets. Considering all the drugs in your body, I guess you essentially went cold turkey, but I just don't understand why you stay so cold. Don't smirk, and don't tell me it's because you're cool."

Chuckling I said, "Perhaps it's from the trauma my body suffered while I was a SAP."

"What did you say?" she asked. "A sap?"

I explained my previous residence was named Shady Acres Pavilion. "We referred to ourselves as SAP's. Never mind, you had to be there. Thanks for moving me before winter sets in, the ward is cold and drafty."

Two gentlemen visited HH one day registering new voters for the upcoming 1970 congressional election. I explained how I'd recently returned to New Castle, related my vision difficulties and they replied, "We'll witness your signature and reinstate legal residence in Henry County. On election day two people will assist you in marking the ballots."

I celebrated Halloween with a move to Room 16B. Kaye entered my new abode voicing pleasure with the relocation. I enjoyed new perspectives with my bed next to a window that looked out over the hilly tree-lined countryside. Several days later political representatives visited me providing opportunity to vote. "Incredible!" I mused. "I'm alive, can see a little again, and now I'm legally franchised in my home county. Mysterious ways for sure."

November 10th Kaye brought cake and ice cream to celebrate my twenty-eight year odyssey on earth. "Happy Birthday." she sang, while presenting me with a game of Scrabble. "Focusing on these letters will help you strengthen your weak eyes and challenge our brains. You, of course, have a winning handicap."

"Thank you honey." I said. "Don't worry, if Scrabble becomes too difficult for you I'll remove my glasses."

My eyesight continued improving and from the window I saw a rainbow of color disappear as days rapidly sped by. A contrasting hue of browns, reds, golds, and silver modestly shielding barren limbs, fell in submission to God's seasons. The trees lost their clothing of autumnal leaves revealing stark nakedness. A lonely forlorn appearance awaited cold, blustery winter winds promising to freeze every defenseless branch with impunity. From the warmth of my room I watched as pristine snow blanketed Mother Nature's glorious coppice.

Kaye and I planned to eat Thanksgiving dinner together so we ordered a 'companion tray'. Obviously neither of us considered HH a "normal" home, but following two traumatic years of indescribable horror, it was a beginning.

"Hi my name is Pat," said an attractive brunette. "I'm the new Activities Director making get-acquainted rounds and asking for suggestions of how I can assist you. Who's the young lady in this photo?" indicating Kaye's Christmas gift from two years ago. "She's really cute, I'm impressed." As Pat studied the picture intently she exclaimed, "Kaye! You won't believe it, but I know this person. I attended high school with her big sister Patty."

"You're right on both accounts," I responded, "Kaye is cute and her sister is Patty. Kaye will be here tomorrow, you two can have a reunion."

"Great." she replied. "Now about my question, would you enjoy some reading material, or perhaps I might provide some stationery so you could write letters."

"Pat, did anyone tell you about my situation?" I asked. "Apparently not, please have a seat and listen." During my brief review of the past year I watched Pat's eyes widen as the enormity of my words provoked shocked realization. "One day I'll get hospital records which will corroborate what I just recounted. In case you're not sure whether to believe me, you must talk to Kaye about last year."

"Danny I believe you." Pat replied. "Now about leaving you some stationery, perhaps it would be better if I helped you write letters. I bet you'd like writing to Kaye. Hey, I just realized you might enjoy talking to another guy your age. You know, man-to-man stuff. Would you mind if Dennis, my husband came to meet you? Who knows, maybe you two have something in common, sports, checkers, cards?"

"Conversation with someone my age would be fantastic." I remarked. "I don't know about checkers or cards though, I have trouble focusing clearly on lines or figures. I like to play chess, but these days the men would be camouflaged."

Daniel R. Williams

"I'm not sure he plays well enough for any competition, but you guys decide when you meet." Pat advised. "I'll talk to you tomorrow when Patty's sister visits."

Next day Kaye walked through my doorway carrying a big shopping bag. After appropriate greetings I intoned, "My, are you ever hungry! It's sad when the drive-in can't give one a large enough container for lunch."

"Well aren't you feeling good today!" Kaye responded. "For your information I have a surprise, so cool it. This bag's contents are guaranteed to brighten your future while establishing my reputation as an interior designer. Viola! Your own miniature Christmas tree! Decorations courtesy of S.S. Kresge and my wallet. Today's project is to transform your room into a warm, comfortable, homey atmosphere."

Joining us later Pat exclaimed, "Your room really looks dressed up. I'm especially envious of artwork on the door. Now I see why Danny wanted me to let you decorate."

"Okay Pat, don't over do it." I cautioned. "She might charge for this operation. Please, just call me Dan."

"Sorry, I thought everyone called you Danny. Ok, Dan it is. Kaye it's been a long time since you were a little kid irritating your sister and me during our gin rummy games and serious teenage talks. I haven't seen Patty for a long time, where is she now?" Pat inquired. "Still in England?"

"Me? Irritating? It has been a long time." Kaye laughed. "Patty's in Ball Memorial Hospital. She just gave birth to Sandi, their third daughter. My sister is living in town while Travis is serving in Viet Nam. Pat, I'll tell her you work here at HH."

Waving goodbye Pat left my room laughing after Kaye had finished telling her how we met. I teased, "Your memory is just short, you really did peek behind my paper."

Kaye playfully retorted, "I trust my memory, after all I'm younger than you."

I smiled while reliving yesterday's visit with Kaye as I listened to the scraappe and squeeaakk of a wheelchair's cold, rubber tires sticking to warm hallway tiles. Slowly, two feet on pedals nosed around the doorway as JJ leaned forward asking, "Hi stranger, remember me? Mother and Kaye's mom sometimes talk at the grocery store so I postponed a visit until you could regain a little strength. By the way, may I come in?"

"Sure JJ." I grinned. "Thanks Pal for rolling by. I'm curious my friend, have you ever traveled in warm weather? Been to Michigan lately?"

"Yuk, yuk." he jeered. "From what I've heard, certain people should be more careful with their words. Seriously, I really hope you're better. Welcome back."

Keep Smiling and Never Give Up!

The Christmas season would have been incomplete without exuberant school children and church choirs singing carols. They brought sparkle to the eyes and joy to the hearts of HH residents. Clubs and civic organizations wrapped gifts and played Santa Claus for everyone.

"Merry Christmas Dan." said Kaye. "Now that your sight has improved enough to see a clock, watch the time and know I'm thinking about you each minute of every day."

"Merry Christmas Kaye." I whispered. "When you wear this sweater close your eyes and imagine the warmth clinging to your body will forever be my arms embracing you in love."

During Christmas week my memory continually returned to three years ago when I first wrote to Kaye. Finally I said to Marilyn, "I have a favor to ask. On New Year's Eve could you please extend visiting hours? It's a special day for us since we've been given a third chance in life. We want to begin the New Year with a celebration."

"Do you realize what you're asking?" Marilyn replied. "If we do that for you, everyone will want extended time."

"Fine." I said. "Others have special memories too. I don't mean all night, only until we say goodbye to 1970."

Smiling, Marilyn responded, "I'm teasing. We've taken steps to modify visiting hours in answer to many resident's requests for flexibility. The administration anticipated a surge of 'Auld Lang Syne'."

Enjoying our precious, but limited time together, Kaye and I snacked on refreshments provided by Freida, a nurse's aide. We spent New Year's Eve reliving events of the past three years: my anonymous courtship cards; flowers; family arguments protesting our engagement; nursing home "vacations"; hospitals; illness; college. "Think, it all began when you peeked behind my newspaper and said, 'Hi I'm Kaye'. That sealed my future." I quipped.

"Humm," Kaye squinted, "Our journey really began when Millie delivered your letter - the one given me just moments before I sang a solo in church. Mysteriously, the song was "Open My Eyes, That I May See", hymnal page number 267. And, you were admitted to this oasis of hope - blind, near death, and Heritage House's 267th resident. Dan, we can't ever forget how blessed we are in the eyes of God."

I sighed, "Sometimes thinking about the past sends icy shivers through my body! Yes, we're truly blessed by God's mysterious ways. As Rev. Kerschner promised me years ago, 'miracles really do happen'."

27

OASIS

Snow blowing against my window signaled passage of another season. Noting elapsed time on the calendar as 1971 droned on I pondered, "Kaye's promise to her parents will soon be fulfilled; perhaps then our future can really begin. Next year, maybe next year."

My eyes continued to improve, although reading remained only a dream. The combination of focusing on TV images and wearing glasses was strengthening my vision. Most everyone, especially family members, was stunned I'd survived such an onslaught to body, mind, and soul; nurses and aides were all justifiably proud of my recovery. Kaye and my family sowed seeds for life, staff watered, and God gracefully reinforced my umbrella of faith.

I watched a young man transport a new resident through the hall to his room, and then walking by my doorway with an empty ambulance stretcher he stopped to introduce himself, "Hello, my name is Dale. I'm surprised to meet such a young person in a nursing home. What brought you to HH? It must be your respirator. Wait a minute! Are you the one Joe brought here from the Med Center last year? Surely not, he was almost a dead duck. Oh, I'm sorry. I didn't mean, uuuhh, uuuhh."

Smirking, I replied, "I was brought here by the wheels on your stretcher. Actually, I'm alive. Quack, quack!"

The week of Kaye's twenty-first birthday was indeed a most pivotal point in our lives. I purchased a unique charm bracelet for her with significant dates engraved on special trinkets. The day was important for Kaye and me, because I'd requested and she hesitantly agreed to be my power of attorney.

"Dan how about another game of Scrabble before I leave?" Kaye asked. "Your eyes must be improving or else you're getting smarter. For some reason, I keep losing."

"Talent, my darling." I responded. "Just talent."

I questioned, "Kaye, before our mental exercises would you help me write a letter to Dr.Walcher? He was working at the National Institutes of Health, but that was prior to SAP time. When you get home contact NIH and request his current professional address. If NIH refuses to release his address send the letter to IUMC and request it be forwarded. I need to gain access of my medical records, then maybe I'll uncover the secret of what happened to me at Shady Acres and University Hospital. I know they can legally deny me these papers, but maybe he knows some doctors who might help."

"Hello Dan. Meet my husband Dennis." announced Pat. "I told him about the chess set and box your brother and sister helped build. Dennis did I tell you Dan won a tournament at the rehabilitation center in Columbus?"

"Pat you're embarrassing me." I remarked. "I'm pleased to meet you Dennis, maybe some time we could play a game."

"Ignore Pat's comments." he said. "She's just nervous. I'd much rather sit and talk. Pat, go to work while Dan and I get acquainted. I hear you're engaged to be married. Hey is this her picture? You have good taste."

I joked, "My eyesight's bad, not my judgment. Dennis, I trust Pat informed you I have trouble seeing. Before we ever play any chess you should be aware my ability to focus quickly is impaired, lines merge and squares mingle. Every day I make progress, but I haven't played chess since...uhh, well, before I was...no problem though, the match will just take longer. Maybe we should stick to checkers."

The following day Pat asked, "Well, did you both enjoy yourselves yesterday? I hope you didn't get too tired."

"Dennis is a nice guy." I said. "Pat, my head is hurting again today, could we talk more later? Maybe I stared too intently at the board."

"Marilyn, these headaches are hitting me every two or three days," I moaned, "think it's still my kidneys? Maybe it's my eyes. Has Dr.Heilman called about the blood test?"

"It might be your kidneys. I think your body is working overtime to filter out all the toxins in your system. Straining your eyes didn't help either." she responded. "Take it easy today."

By midweek my head stopped swimming and while sitting in my usual spot across the corridor from a nurse's station and kitchen door, I observed a gentleman dressed in laborers clothing enter the dining room. Soon thereafter he emerged carrying tools in his grease-covered hands. I nodded and he said, "Hello sir, you've been sitting here most of the day, are you a patient?"

"No I'm a resident." I responded. "Patients are sick."

"Oh, excuse my mistake." he apologized. "Are you happy and satisfied with your life at Heritage House?"

"It's excellent." I stated. "The staff is great and my care is superb. They saved my life! Only one problem. The menu's formulated primarily for older people. Obviously I'm young for a nursing home, but there are middle-aged people living here too and sometimes they'd certainly appreciate foods other than pudding, soup, and noodles. Don't misunderstand, I'm not complaining about administration, just suggesting a more varied menu should be considered."

Walking away the man nodded and remarked, "Hmmm."

The next day I watched three well-dressed businessmen enter the administrator's office. Jim greeted them at the doorway and I recognized my greasy-handed acquaintance. Calling Marilyn to my side I whispered, "Who is that guy?"

"You mean the one you were talking to yesterday? He's one of the owners." she grinned.

A few days later some of the dietary staff waved at me when leaving the HH kitchen. "Boy do we have a surprise for you tomorrow!" Peggy smugly announced.

"Yeah," Blanche grinned, "no more bland food for you."

"Now girls," cautioned Marie, "Theda's the boss, it's supposed to be her surprise. Shush!"

Two days later Judy brought home-cooked food saying, "I thought you might like something spicy for a change. Norman said not to eat too much barbecue chicken."

"Thanks Sis." I responded. "I don't know if I'll have room after yesterday's tenderloin and fries."

"Oh shoot, I bet Kaye was here yesterday." Judy stated.

"No. The HH menu changed at last." I reported.

I received a welcome surprise in the mail a few weeks after writing to Dr. Walcher. Hesitant to trust anyone with this information I told Mayme to hide it in my bedside stand until Kaye returned. Two days later after greeting Kaye, I directed, "Honey, please read Dr. Walcher's letter to me, it's in the stand drawer."

"Already!" she exclaimed. "When NIH didn't give me his address I thought forwarding your letter would take longer. He writes, 'One of three rehab and neuro specialists at IUMC should be able to provide you with this information. I will contact them and forward your letter. Keep me informed. Danny, following so much previous physical devastation, how did this happen?'"

Listening to Dr. Walcher's words as Kaye read his letter to me I could only envision a look of stunned disbelief. He had relentlessly directed the initial survival treatments of my acute Polio, and now he had read of a cruel, inexcusable tragedy. Envisioning his thoughts, they appeared to mirror my own: denial, anger, disbelief, fear, and hope.

After giving me time to recuperate, one day Pat walked into my room stating, "The administrator has been unable to get any agreements for a newspaper column, but wants you to please go ahead with the newsletter idea. What do you say?"

"Okay Pat," I conceded, "tell Jim I'll write the paper if he'll continue seeking cooperation for a column. I guess for now we'll circulate a

Keep Smiling and Never Give Up!

questionnaire to the employees and residents. Remember your promise Pat; you gather all the information on birthdays and anniversaries. I'm glad Jim has an instant camera so photographs can be published along with the articles. Scheduling photo sessions in addition to capturing their stories for posterity will be your task."

"Dan, I know this isn't big time, but at least you'll be writing again." said Pat happily. "Who knows? Maybe soon the paper will accept our concept of community service. I'm certain everyone is anxious for free publicity."

Pat left the room with me considering my agreement. Suppose she quits, this will simply be another understaffed newsletter, and I'll be responsible for the impossible. I was deep in thought when Marilyn walked into my room, sat in the chair, and engaged in small talk. Following a thorough discussion of the weather, and pleasantries aside she said, "Danny, I am leaving soon..."

"You're what?" I groaned. "Why? Just when I get you in focus! You're not making this one of my better days."

Marilyn covered her eyes, "I'm sorry, but you already know my replacement, Elizabeth. She was here when you first arrived. This time you'll be able to see her."

"You've been my main anchor here at HH. I really hate to see you go Marilyn. Your ideas helped me overcome trauma to my body and mind. Words of thanks are not enough. Pat and I agreed to work on a writing project for HH revolving around interviews with staff and residents. Would you be my first newsletter subject?"

"Danny I remember when you were so completely devastated. You cried, 'Marilyn, I'll never write again'. This is great news! I'm so happy! Of course I'll be your first guinea pig, I can't think of anything more appropriate."

Kaye walked in next day and I couldn't wait to tell her the crushing news, "Marilyn's leaving!"

"What! You aren't serious?" Kaye exclaimed. "When? I don't know how you or we could've survived without her wise understanding of the situation when you were so sick. I hope the nurse replacing her has as much insight and compassion."

"Elizabeth's her name, she worked here before leaving to be with her husband in the service. I didn't know her well."

"Want some more news?" Kaye inquired. "Graduation day in August is not official for those of us who transferred from Marion College. I'm not really finished. When Sue and I transferred to BSU School of Nursing we went from semesters to quarters and lost some accumulated credit hours. Although participating in the ceremonies, we can't graduate until November after regaining those lost credits. Please wait until then to spoil me with congratulations."

"Are you sure this isn't a ploy to escape marriage and forever remain nursing home buddies?" I teased.

"Definitely not!" Kaye angrily exclaimed.

The summer sped by, Kaye finishing classes and working while Pat and I created a well-received newsletter every two weeks. Judy surprised me with a birthday gift from Norman and her saying, "With the police scanner you'll be able to keep tabs on your friends. Ready for some birthday cake and ice cream? I hope Kaye didn't get here first."

Chuckling, I said, "No, she's too busy reclaiming lost study time to bake me a cake this year. Thanks Sis. Oh, by the way, tell Norman if I hear his name I'll keep quiet."

Two days later Kaye bounced into my room waving a sheet of parchment proclaiming, "It's over! I kept my promise to Mom and Dad."

"Let me see that sheepskin!" I demanded. "Show me what you've been struggling to attain. Hey, this documents your graduation all right! Does it also mean you're mine soon?"

"Well, actually," Kaye stammered, "I have one more step to freedom - State Boards changing GN to RN. First though, Sue and I are moving to an apartment, providing room for new student boarders at Mrs. Bell's house."

Thanksgiving we partook of the turkey feast offered to all HH residents. I requested a companion tray for Kaye, so we celebrated dinner prior to her leaving for work and home. Our Thanksgiving blessings were many this year.

"Will Kaye be decorating your room for Christmas?" Pat asked. "Do you think she'll have time along with her new job? I was just wondering, now that she has graduated, are you two getting married soon?"

"Unfortunately her transfer to BSU's School of Nursing delayed our wedding. We have to wait for State Registration Board exams in February. I'm sure I've confused you, but despite misgivings from some people, we will be married someday."

Kaye worked many extra hours to repay educational loans, but regardless limited time together we enjoyed those special days. Our visits no longer confined to study or semester breaks; precious moments together became more glorious even though we continued a long distance courtship. Christmas holidays presented us with numerous occasions for exceptional joy. I say numerous, comparing once monthly dates to several visits each week.

JJ rolled by on his annual Christmas pilgrimage and we discussed effects of cold weather on humans. "I've heard numerous comments about your newsletter, many people receive great pleasure in reading about their loved ones at Heritage House. Maybe someday you can progress to articles directed to the entire community." he hinted.

"Thanks JJ." I responded. "My dream is to either write a book about my life, or a newspaper column."

Days passed quickly, Kaye took her registration exam, and when March arrived without knowing results of her efforts, she became more nervous about the future. One day while I pondered our future, Gladys walked into my room inquiring, "Have you chosen a special present for Kaye's birthday?"

"Are you kidding?" I replied in exasperation. "Believe me, I need a second job. Not only her birthday, I want a unique keepsake to commemorate the day Kaye becomes a licensed RN. It would help to combine gifts."

"I have a thought." she said. "My daughter Connie is painting ceramic sculptures. Perhaps she'll have an idea. Think about it and I'll tell her your dilemma."

Entering my room with a wide smile beaming from ear to ear, Kaye waved her license before my face fairly shouting, "Feast your eyes upon this! I'm now officially a Registered Nurse. If you're nice I might let you congratulate me."

I tried to suppress a smile saying, "Just think, your license is a wonderful birthday present. Adhering to your words on saving money, I decided it would be better if I didn't spoil you with so many presents at once. So in quoting an old adage, 'good things come to (s)he who waits'. I think we should celebrate with a special dinner."

Following the festivities I instructed Kaye to retrieve two packages from my closet. "Yesterday I received a carton and I think you may be interested in its contents."

"I thought this package came to you." Kaye remarked. "Why isn't your name on the outside?" Opening the first box she exclaimed, "Oh! A statue of a nurse in a white uniform and cap. Look! My name is on the pocket. Honey where did you find such a wonderful present?"

Contentedly observing satisfaction in her eyes I said, "Gladys's daughter sculptured and painted the statue with your photograph as her model. I'm happy you're pleased, now don't forget to open the other surprise."

"Oh my goodness! A nurse's cap charm for my bracelet." Kaye whispered. "You shouldn't spoil me so much."

Smiling I said, "Happy Birthday Registered Nurse."

We immediately began planning our long awaited wedding, envisioning an early summer ceremony. Sue and Tin prepared for their April wedding and a move to Milwaukee. The only apartment Kaye and Sue could rent the previous fall was not accessible to wheelchairs so Kaye began intensive efforts to convince the landlord terminating her rental agreement would be in his best interest. Unfortunately, he disagreed. Her lease would remain valid until late October.

Undaunted by the landlord's unyielding stubbornness, our fall wedding plans proceeded as Kaye and I refused to allow people with shallow perspectives to control our lives. We convinced ourselves this apparent obstacle provided time and opportunity to save money and plan for the future. As with past difficulties, we relied on faith, love, patience, hope, and tried to keep smiling. Sublimating postponed matrimony; we spent many long hours in my room playing Scrabble.

In one of their visits Dad and Mom informed me, "We're selling our house and buying a mobile home." Dad explained, "I'm retiring soon and we hope to spend winters in Florida."

My parents had often discussed and dreamed about moving south so their announcement was not unexpected. I spoke to Jim, HH's Administrator, requesting he officially designate Kaye my medical sponsor; thus, effectively eliminating any future problems I might encounter with health emergencies. Aware most of my possessions were still at home, I directed Andy and Judy to bring my typewriter, mouthsticks, clothes, and hydraulic bedside lift to Heritage House. Jim permitted storage of some belongings and issued a challenge for me to utilize my skills with the typewriter and mouthstick, "Use them while they still work. Why allow dust to gather?"

Taking advantage of opportunities Jim gave me, I began typing part of "Heritage Happenings", HH's newsletter, in the activities room. "I don't believe it!" Pat marveled. "The typewriter keys aren't very large and we know your eyes aren't the greatest, how do you manage such accuracy?"

"Being modest, I won't say 'talent'." I joked.

Observing my efforts for the first time, Jim remarked, "You want a job in the office? Don't tell Gayle or Wanda, but they make more mistakes with ten fingers. Remember when you write don't give our facility a bad reputation with your first column in *The News Republican*."

"A column?!" I exclaimed. "In *The News Republican*?"

Standing in the doorway Jim chuckled, "Be sure to write something good about us."

"No problem Jim." I assured. "I'll just tell everyone the truth. I'm really glad *The News Republican* agreed to print stories and information about residents. I know the community will be quite interested in these articles and appreciate more fully the contributions of a good nursing home. What more could one ask - employees and residents are recognized, HH receives free publicity, and I'm afforded the privilege of writing? Honestly Jim, we have a win-win situation."

Nodding affirmatively he responded, "I was only teasing about the content of your articles, I can't wait to read the first column. By the way, they'll also publish a photo with every biography and story."

I lay awake that night reviewing the past year and what seemed to be a renewing of my life. Arriving at HH nearly blind, the dimness in my eyes had gradually sought the light and new beginnings flourished all around. I'd dreamed for years of writing a column, but it took the ravages of hell to prepare me for this quest. Spring was blossoming and I now knew dreams come true when visions are fulfilled.

28

HOPE DEFERRED

Marilyn's story in the newsletter was limited to text because arrangements for publishing photographs had not been finalized. My first column accompanied by photos portrayed nurse's aides Connie, Betty, and Frances. Unfortunately, Connie believed one good exposure deserves another, and I was awakened early the next morning to her words echoing in my sleepy ears, "Boy, do I have a big surprise for you today! Danny don't ask me any questions, just say yes to my proposal."

"Oh man, sounds like trouble to me." I grumbled.

"Oh can it!" Connie laughed. "I'm serious."

"OK, tell me what it is." I sighed. "You know I won't agree to just anything anymore."

"Promise you won't say no until I explain everything." she pleaded. Not waiting for an answer Connie proceeded to outline her plans for taking me to the shower. "We'll sit you in a shower chair, drape a sheet around your body, then pull you backwards through the hall while Frances holds your head. You've watched us take other residents to the shower many times. It's no big deal."

"No way!" I protested. "I'm not just another resident. What about my respirator? Breathing has become a habit. I really would like to know, who's brilliant idea was this?"

"Not that it matters," she sniffed, "it was mine. Just think, soothing warm water flowing over your body. Come on, I promise if it doesn't work we won't do it again."

"You got that right! I'm not sure I can frog breathe in steam." I lamely argued.

"Don't be so stubborn, you owe me one." Connie coaxed. "Let us try. Pleeeezzz."

"Oh Brother!" I groaned. "A guilt trip."

"Frances, don't drop my head!" I cautioned. "A broken neck will paralyze me."

Billows of steam poured forth as the shower room doors opened. "Now relax!" Connie encouraged. "With this hand-held shower spray the water will make you feel much better. Now admit it, didn't I have a good idea?"

"No offense," gulp, gulp, "I was doing," gulp, gulp, "fine with a bed bath." Gulp, gulp

Exiting backwards from the shower room into the hall, cold spring breezes gusted under my draped sheet, invading certain personal belongings.

"Ah haa! Constance," gulp, gulp, "we're even lady!" Gulp, "My bed may get wet," gulp, gulp, "during a bath," gulp, gulp, "but at least there are," gulp, gulp, "no blasts of," gulp, gulp, "arctic air. Look Frances!" gulp, gulp, "I've got ice dripping," gulp, gulp, "off my body parts."

Blushing, Frances insisted, "It's warm weather."

Giggling at my situation Connie urged, "Daniel hush!"

"This dear one," gulp, gulp, "is the last time," gulp, gulp, "I write about you." Gulp, "Remember your promise, 'if it doesn't work we won't do it again.' That's right, never again!"

While recovering from my excursion to the steam room I was visited by an old friend. "Hi JJ." I greeted. "So you wised up and decided to travel in sunshine. Those cold and snowy trips were a bit rough, aye?" Another visitor entered the room and I said, "JJ, may I introduce my fiancé, Kaye. Someday we're getting married. No, don't ask when."

"Oh, you're Kaye." he responded. "Our mothers exchange information weekly. Now I know who she's referring to when mentioning your name. Mother told me you were a doll, why would you want to waste your time with this joker?"

"Hmmm, Hmmm," Kaye teased. "Let me think."

The next few weeks contained a flurry of activities. I watched Andy walk from my room after modeling his graduation cap and gown recalling, "It's been so many years since I had Polio and he was just a baby. Graduating from high school my little brother is now a young man, six foot two, over two hundred pounds, sporting a beard." Dad retired after working forty-five years at Perfect Circle/Dana then he and Mom, as planned, sold their house and bought a mobile home. Living in the Sunshine State had long been their dream and I fully understood their determination to travel south. The love and devotion my parents had given to us children, especially me, prompted a fervent hope their future in Florida would be divinely blessed.

"Where do you want this stored?" Andy asked, rolling my hydraulic lift into the room.

"Probably the closet," I responded, "HH doesn't have an attic. Like Dad, they insist on physically transferring us from bed to chair or vice versa. Regardless, I just want it securely in my possession when Kaye and I are married."

"Why don't you two just elope?" smiled Andy. "Oh yeah, Dad said to arrange an outside visit soon for Sunday dinner. They have a surprise for you. Oh by the way, in case you're interested, I've made an appointment with the Marine recruiters next week. I can't let Millie embarrass me, now can I?"

"I'm proud of you little brother." I praised. "A word of advice, prior to your interview, go visit a barber! The beard and long hair must go; otherwise he might think you're an anti-war protestor. After your long overdue grooming, approach Dad and Mom with utmost consideration. A drastic improvement in your appearance could be detrimental to their health."

As Andy left my room Moneva entered remarking, "Danny, I couldn't help overhearing Andy. What he said makes sense, why don't you and Kaye elope?"

Dalene joined the conversation exclaiming, "For sure! Why wait, you're not getting any younger."

"Listen smarty," I quipped, "don't be cute just because you're getting married next month at the age of eighteen. I need to type some announcements, will one of you please take me to the activities room?"

"Interesting." Dale remarked. "I've never seen anyone type with a stick in their mouth. What is it called?"

"Not to be a smart aleck Dale," I wryly remarked, "it's called a mouthstick. We also turn pages, paint, and author signatures this way. It assures one of being ambidextrous."

Attempting to arrange a leave of absence for the Sunday dinner as requested by my parents, I entered the frightening world of bureaucratic red tape and incredible stupidity. I said to Jim the Administrator, "Are you serious? For a few hours away from HH while I break bread with my family, it's necessary for me to get special permission from the state? What do the Medicaid people expect from me in two hours? I wonder if they think I'll abscond with the funds."

"Dan don't complain," he cautioned, "at least you are going. Be sure to return before dark."

Dad and my brothers-in-law Kenny and Jim carried me on a chaise lounge into my parent's new mobile home where Mom greeted, "Welcome! Isn't this nice? I prepared a special meal today; hope you like our going away party. Andy will be here soon."

"This is beautiful Mom. Why leave for Florida now?" I commented. "How did you ever pack everything from the house into such a small place?"

"It wasn't easy Danny," she responded sadly, "we sold and gave away so many sentimental items. Since you kids all moved away your dad and I don't need a big house any more. The girls are married, Andy's talking about joining the Corp (whatever that is!), and you're being taken care of at the nursing home. So, Florida here we come."

Two days later I stared meditatively out my window when startled by, "I did it!" A well-groomed stranger swaggered into my room announcing, "I leave for San Diego Marine Corps Recruiting Depot September 29th. I hope you're satisfied! I'm going to think about you every time somebody yells at me."

"Quick, close the door! Perhaps we can fight off your admirers." I teased. "Seriously, I'm so happy and proud you finally got smart. If it'll make your drills any easier, imagine my picture on the bull's eye during weapons training and think about me each time you toss a grenade. Four years to learn responsibility and discipline. I know signing away part of your life doesn't seem wise right now, but in a few years you'll be happy with this decision. Are you sorry?"

"No, not really." he snidely replied. "After listening to your lectures, the DI will be a relief. Anyway, cutting my gorgeous long hair was the worst part of all."

"I wish he hadn't enlisted." murmured Nina, Andy's girl friend. "I want him here, I'm only a junior this year."

Sharon, a nurse's aide, delivering ice water remarked, "Why Andy, you look so cute!"

Kaye's search for our ground-level apartment in Muncie proved futile and we combated problems of wheelchair access from another direction. For months she toured model mobile homes looking for the correct room and door dimensions. At last finding a solution to our housing dilemma, Kaye signed mortgage papers for purchase of a mobile home. With no time to spare on the apartment lease, she moved into new quarters expecting this to be an answer for our lives. Predictably, increased debt ensured continued overtime work.

Unable to sleep, I passed the night listening to Nancy, nurse's aide on nights. "I understand Phyllis is leaving HH in the near future." she said. "Elizabeth will become DON. It probably won't change much around here, just thought you would appreciate hearing some of the news - although you've probably already written the story."

"In the best traditions of investigative reporting, no comment." I snickered. "Have you met Connie, our new Head Nurse, she graduated one year ahead of Kaye at BSU."

Nancy groaned, "I thought I had some news. Well, why don't you just go to sleep? I'll see you in the morning."

I chuckled, sleepily bid Nancy good night, and slept.

***

"No! No! Don't give me that shot! I can't eat Jello! Stay away! Somebody help me! Please don't hurt me again!"

"Wake up Danny!" insisted Nancy. "You must be having a nightmare again. Let me get Marietta the nurse."

***

Anticipated changes triggered unexpected events. After another nighttime intrusion of memories of hidden terror, Kaye thankfully appeared the next day. While telling her about last night's episode of "twilight zone" I grimaced, "This has to stop! I refuse to tolerate fear and anguish resulting from these nightmares any longer. Surely somebody will help me find out what happened at SAP."

Kaye agreed and I subsequently contacted an attorney, asking him to try again to have my medical records released from SAP and IUMC. We agreed all information should be sent to Kaye's address in Muncie. Three days of my life had been summarily destroyed, and I desperately yearned for answers affording me peace of mind. My attorney's efforts were soon thwarted and I learned prevailing law prevented all private access to medical records, even though they were mine. The obvious ethical violations and threats to my life remained sealed within bureaucratic secrecy. The darkness of night would remain resplendent with occasional terror.

"For your birthday I want you to see our intended home and I'll fix your favorite meal." said Kaye. "Ask Jim for another leave of absence pass."

Naively expecting unopposed cooperation from the powers that be, I became anxious when no answer was forthcoming. I accosted the Administrator, "Jim, it's been two weeks since submitting my request for LOA. Why didn't someone tell me Medicaid came complete with a prison sentence?"

Shrugging helplessly, Jim said, "I'm doing my best."

A few days later my beleaguered friend entered the room waving a letter. "It just arrived and you may travel outside HH one time per month. The only restriction, you must be home by 9 PM. Permit me to point out the only reason the State agreed to your unusual visit is because Kaye is a Registered Nurse. Otherwise, traveling to another county wouldn't be possible."

"A curfew at my age!" I ridiculed. "These people are not ridiculous, they're cruel."

Anita and Jim drove us to Muncie in their station wagon while I frog breathed because the car was not wired for my respirator. Kaye remarked,

"This is the first dinner I've cooked for Dan. Thanks for helping us with a special evening, even if it is brief."

For ninety minutes I enjoyed privacy and solitude while we ate dinner and toured our home-to-be. With every passing minute I dreadfully anticipated my humble return to HH. The thought continually seared my mind, "What utter humiliation! Thirty years old today, with a nine o'clock curfew."

Familiar side effects associated with bouncing along on a stretcher in the rear of a station wagon were immediately evident. Kidney stones and infection brought recollections of previous journeys. "Don't tell anyone." I stated firmly to Kaye. "Anita and Jim will feel they're responsible, and my parents will be most unhappy. Besides, I'm fine. Simply ask the nurse."

Sherry looked at Kaye, rolled her eyes and said to me, "She's a nurse, why involve me in your conversation?"

"Guess this means companion trays for Thanksgiving." I weakly joked. "Oh well, it doesn't matter, I'm only allowed one mental health sabbatical per month. Maybe Christmas."

"The holidays are not my main concern." Kaye charged. "What about our wedding plans? Postponed again? This time it's not college or apartments. It's kidney stones!"

After Kaye's visit I couldn't help remembering sounds of her voiced anger and frustration. The following morning I accosted Dr. Heilman during his weekly rounds, "Doc, these kidney infections are simply not responding to antibiotics you ordered, don't you think we should try controlling the situation now before I'm too weak? It's been nearly three years since I've undergone thorough examinations, I want to be hospitalized for blood tests and X-rays."

"Take it easy Danny." he responded. "Once you pass the stone you'll feel better. We've coped with this before."

The combination of pain, drugs, immobility, and general disgust inhibited any possibility of sitting in a wheelchair or using my mouthstick for composing the column. Strolling into my room Pat received an unsuspecting challenge from me, "Ever been a secretary? In case you haven't been monitoring the paper, I haven't typed "Heritage Happenings" for nearly a month. Don't you think your taking dictation and directing the office staff to type my words would be a magnanimous gesture? I know Jim would be more than appreciative to see HH's name in public again."

After my cajoling (begging) Pat replied, "I wouldn't do it for just anyone, but I promised to help you organize the paper so I'll type it as a going away present."

I screamed, "What! Did you say going away? You can't be serious! I can't believe it, I'm being abandoned again!"

"I feel like a rat deserting the ship." she confessed. "Dennis landed a good job in Florida and we're leaving soon. Administration hasn't hired a new Activities Director yet but I'm sure when they do, she will certainly help. We know the column is important to Heritage House."

"It's not the position Pat, it's the people." I said. With all the flourishes I could muster I relived the strife I'd endured at Respo Centers writing newsletters. I told her about unfulfilled promises from people agreeing to help produce the paper. When I thought a proper amount of guilt had been laid at her doorstep I ventured, "Without getting maudlin, I'll miss your smile and the happiness you exude. Congratulate Dennis for me and tell him we could play chess by mail."

The Christmas season drew nigh accompanied by a notable occasion honoring Jim as Administrator, and HH for service to elderly and convalescing citizens of Raintree County. As Mayor Scott Bouslog presented a commemorative plaque, guests and residents assembled for the ceremony applauded, registering approval of the honor. All were aware living at HH promised many unique opportunities such as birthday parties, special meals, article/pictorial stories, along with staff and resident's recognition. More important, under Jim's leadership and devotion to excellence, HH residents received care, respect, and love. After the congratulatory dinner, Jim watched as the Mayor and I laughed while reminiscing about yesteryear. Joining us, Jim learned we'd been friends for years - growing up I'd delivered newspapers for him and he and Dad worked together at Perfect Circle.

In early December I received notice from Andy his plane would be arriving in Indianapolis about midnight. Beckoning the Head Nurse to my side I explained the situation and then requested, "Connie, if possible could I arrange for someone to let Andy come to my room when he arrives? I know 2:00 AM is an unusually early visiting hour, but he's getting home from boot camp and I want to personally witness the pride and satisfaction on his face. Not to mention I've missed him."

In the wee morning hours Andy appeared at my bedside in his well-fitted uniform, sporting a "slightly" short haircut. Beaming with accomplishment he reported, "Well big brother, I did it! I'm now a United States Marine!"

Decorations glistened, carols resounded in the hallways, and residents greeting family members visiting from far away places lifted everyone's spirits. The holiday season ended, but my nemesis - kidney stones - and snowy cold weather had prevented any journey to Muncie for three months. In February, Anita and Jim provided transportation to the mobile home, giving Kaye and I an opportunity to celebrate Valentine's Day in private. I apologized, "Sorry no candy, but celebrating lover's holiday alone is much more important."

"Yes." agreed Kaye. "I wish we could have more time to plan our future, but these short visits and your government curfew limit our options. At least we're together."

I sighed, "Don't forget I also have a deadline to meet for Heritage Happenings. You did volunteer to help since the new Activities Director says assisting with the newsletter is not in her job description."

Kaye responded, "I don't mind helping you write these columns, but isn't it HH responsibility?"

As usual the ride inflicted violence upon my kidneys and I spent several days immobilized. The following month, when we planned to celebrate Kaye's birthday in Muncie, I wasn't healthy enough to travel. Sprinkles of rain and warm breezes signaled the start of spring and I sought a new source of transportation so Kaye and I could travel to Muncie for our occasional breather from institutional restrictions. My dear friends at HH commiserated with me on this problem, offering many different solutions. "Of course I appreciate your concern Sharon, I'm just not sure. So you have a station wagon, that's only part of the problem. Kaye will help, but without your husband we still must enlist one more person. I wish John didn't have other plans."

"Don't worry." she said. "I've got the car, now I'll find someone to help. You two plan on a trip to Muncie."

Sharon rushed into my room next day announcing, "I've found someone to lift. Look who volunteered!"

"Moneva!" I exclaimed. "No offense friend, but at only five feet tall do you think you're strong enough to carry a stretcher plus my weight?"

"Well that'sa fine how do you do!" she scolded in her southern drawl. "I try to help and get bad mouthed! Mister you better be careful. I might accidentally let go."

"I'm sorry." I humbly apologized. "OK, assuming you girls can lift me into the wagon, Kaye's next door neighbor might meet us at the mobile home to assist unloading the precious cargo - me. We'll find a way. Thanks Sharon and Moneva."

The day of our trip arrived. Amidst huffing, puffing, and obvious strain Kaye, Sharon, and Moneva lifted stretcher and me into John and Sharon's station wagon. Our sunny day began smoothly with thumbs up from everyone - except me. We left New Castle without difficulty, zipping along for nearly ten miles when our afternoon jaunt was rudely interrupted. Less than midway between HH and Muncie the car tilted to one side, my stretcher slipped sideways, and our bodies bounced to rhythmic thumps and bumps. Sharon maneuvered her car off the busy highway and quickly assessed the situation. "I'm sorry Danny," she announced apologetically, "we have a flat tire."

"Great! All right, get me out." I ordered. "Be sure my stretcher's back off the berm so I won't collide with any passing autos. Man, a flat tire today of all days. Sharon, does John do preventive maintenance?"

Returning in time for curfew, my two weight lifters lamented, "Do you realize we didn't just lift you and that stretcher four times as promised? Thanks to the rotten flat tire and those steps you failed to mention, we picked you up eight times today! No wonder John found a way to be busy."

I grimaced, "Stop complaining, the neighbor did help."

Expectations of brighter days were darkened when kidney problems recurred after our springtime trip. "Doc, I don't understand your position." I protested. "When I was covered by private insurance you insisted on urology exams, X-rays, and blood tests at the first sign of kidney trouble. Now that I'm on Medicaid, you've curiously adopted this wait and see attitude about everything. How many more months do I wait before you order hospitalization for answers? You also know I've been corresponding with Dr.King at IUMC to participate in phrenic nerve stimulation research. I'll need a diaphragmatic fluoroscopy to determine my eligibility for the procedure. I have an opportunity to enhance my breathing and ensure a more stable life after marriage, possibly without respirators. Both matters could be resolved at the same time."

"Be patient Danny." he replied. "The antibiotics will eventually be effective, and as at home, we'll continue to assist with pain medication. Your body's been through some tough times; perhaps you shouldn't engage in research again. Your present respirators are more than adequate."

Our April excursion to Muncie was canceled because of my continued illness; thus, Easter was celebrated with a now familiar 'companion tray'. Kaye and I finished eating and I sighed, "I'm getting weaker. I think relocating would eliminate the problem. In a major city with advanced medical facilities the doctors might discover and then eliminate the cause of these recurrent kidney infections. Certainly you'd be employed at a larger hospital paying higher wages and we could get married sooner. Think about my suggestion, our future will soon be behind us. Meanwhile, I'll attempt to find transportation for another day of escape."

Following weeks of nursing home confinement, I observed activity in the corridor and shouted, "Dale! Let's talk. I have a question for you. Suppose someone requested a round trip ambulance ride to Muncie. What would it cost?"

"You don't want to know." he responded. "Why?"

Keep Smiling and Never Give Up!

"I was just curious. Kaye and I need transportation to Muncie for an occasional date. I fear your pessimistic expression gave me the answer. We can't afford it."

"Well..." he hesitated, "maybe for two friends I could arrange something. I'll get back to you in a few days."

"Look!" announced Kaye, entering my room. "Connie gave me another letter from Dr.King. Opening it she read, "My experiences with the phrenic nerve stimulator have been limited, and I advise you to contact Yale Med School for more information."

"Hold on that letter to Yale." I instructed. "For now I'm not well enough for any medical research."

"Guess what?" announced Jeri while passing my medicine. "I received a letter from Pat today. Because they live near Disney World at Kissimmee, Florida they've visited Mickey on numerous occasions. She says they really enjoy warm weather but miss Indiana and all their friends."

"I sure wish she was here, I miss her." I said. "Tell Pat I said 'hi', and ask if she'll send Mickey or Minnie to assist me with the column. Especially since it was her idea."

Kaye interjected, "Forget another rat, send Pat!"

In the days following Jeri's recital of Pat's letter I contemplated the demise of Heritage Happenings, and decided one last attempt to salvage the column was necessary, so I asked to speak with the Activities Director.

Fortifying myself for an anticipated confrontation that evening, I watched for Jim as he left for home. I certainly didn't wish to disappoint him, but my choices were narrowed considerably by the indifferent attitude displayed earlier by the AD. As he walked by my room I yelled his name. Stopping, he inquired, "Problems? I'm in sort of a hurry."

"Bluntly, I'm through writing the column." I declared.

"What!? You aren't serious. What's wrong?" Jim asked.

I sighed, "The AD won't help, and it isn't Kaye's job."

He frowned, "What do you mean? Maybe we should talk it over tomorrow, you don't want to act impulsively."

Realizing without resolution of the problem I wouldn't sleep tonight I quickly summarized my situation declaring, "We've missed a month of columns about HH and the residents because the AD refuses to assist me with paperwork. On many occasions Kaye has collected questionnaires from residents and taken dictation during our limited time together. It's impossible to continue writing without a change in attitude. I don't want to create problems for you or HH, but following days of deliberation I've decided to call it quits."

Jim nodded, "I'm sorry, but maybe it's for the best."

All staff members and residents were disappointed with the cancellation of their column. Many residents expressed regret for the column's demise because absence of Heritage Happenings would increase isolation; they'd lose acknowledgement of their presence at HH; and their families and friends couldn't be comforted by these words. Employees would likewise be deprived of recognition for service, and Heritage House lost its written connection to the community.

I thought, "Hope it isn't a harbinger of the future."

Warm weather brought spring flowers and Kaye and I planned a date. Providing a friendly discount, Dale agreed to become our chauffeur to Muncie. Exiting the door, I couldn't believe the waiting vehicle. I sarcastically remarked, "Oh wow! Dale, why did you commandeer a hearse with black window drapes for Kaye's and my date? You promised an ambulance."

"Listen Mr. Williams!" he responded. "Beggars can't be choosy. Reduced rate, reduced expectations."

I grumbled, "Just remember, don't take a detour through the cemetery! I'm restricted to a nine o'clock curfew."

Dale and his assistant backed the hearse to Kaye's door and unloaded me. Clang! Slip! Squish! "Oh *½%%$#@!" Dale exclaimed. "Kaye why didn't you move this garbage can? These steps aren't wide enough for two men."

Saturday afternoon I was recovering from our jaunt to Muncie, staring aimlessly out my window at trees swaying in the wind, and listening to birds singing songs of love. The sound of visitors walking by my door directed attention to the fuzzy, but familiar, image of a tall brunette. Shocked by the revelation before my still-fuzzy eyes I uttered, "Diane! Is that you?"

Equally stunned by my voice and appearance she stopped at the doorway gasping, "Danny? I thought you died!"

"Diane, you're about the last person I expected to see at HH." I said, shaking my head in amazement.

After an extended conversation between two rediscovered friends who'd weathered difficult times together, I learned my former respiratory therapist from IUMC had married and was now living at Knightstown, near New Castle. Diane said, "It was bad enough when you had pneumonia at Robert Long, but I really thought you were a goner after they brought you to University Hospital from that nursing home in a coma. I was just here visiting a friend, now thank God; I've found an old friend. I'll bring my husband to meet you; he had Polio too. I can't wait to tell him about today."

I grinned, "Well if he had Polio, he's all right."

A few days later the Administrator walked into my room inquiring about the baseball game appearing on TV. Quietly watching play between mediocre teams he asked, "If you have a few minutes, may I interrupt?"

"Of course." I replied. "The game just started."

Solemnly he began, "Dan, we've been through many trying times together, so this announcement is difficult. Bluntly, I've accepted another position in Marion, Indiana."

Stunned by his news I looked at him, my mouth agape.

Jim resumed, "I've attempted to create a secure, happy, and healthy atmosphere for everyone at Heritage House. My intent was to always provide a stable environment. I hope to continue this approach at Bradner Village."

Unnerved by his announcement and receiving two setbacks in quick succession my only thought was, "Oh no, not again!" Suddenly realizing selfish reactions didn't offer support, I rephrased my response, "Excuse me. I didn't mean to sound unhappy about your new responsibility; my regret is you're leaving. I don't suppose your wife would consider remaining on the staff? No offense, it's bad enough to lose a friend and administrator, but HH will also be losing a good nurse."

"I'm not offended Dan." he responded then chuckled, "No, Nancy will obviously move to Marion with me and the children. She is an excellent nurse and it's comforting to know other people respect her talents. Your reaction is understandable considering how sick you were on admission. Dan, informing everyone of our imminent departure is difficult, but we want you to know we'll be leaving Heritage House soon."

"What now?" I thought, watching him walk from my room. I recalled the last time a new Administrator took charge, and dread burdened my soul as I dozed off to sleep, a blanket of cold fear exposing me to the past.

"Danny, Danny." said Ann, jostling me awake. "Should I get the nurse? Are you okay? You mumbled something about a shot and Jello. Here, drink some water."

"It's not important Ann." I answered. "I'm fine."

Ann frowned, "Didn't sound fine. You want to talk?"

I sighed, "Bad times, you wouldn't understand."

Ann closed her eyes, "Maybe I'm young, but I've had bad times in my life too. My husband died shortly after we were married. A ruptured appendix, can you believe it?"

I shook my head, "Forgive me. Sometimes our own lives seem more important. Ann, maybe we both need to talk."

After completing their work in the kitchen, Peggy, Blanche, Marie, and sometimes Eva dropped by to say goodnight. Peggy and her great sense of humor left everyone in good spirits, even when we felt terrible. Peggy asked, "I heard you were having a rough time. Are you OK?"

"Sure, I'm fine." I grinned. "Just a bad memory."

I took advantage of the moment to describe Dale's foot slipping into the garbage can when he drove Kaye and I to Muncie. Blanche said, "I'm surprised you got away from here so easily, how did you swing that agreement?"

"Only because Kaye's an RN." I explained. "Even then I promise to be home before nine o'clock. I told Dale not to drive his hearse through the cemetery, I was on curfew and couldn't stay."

Cracking up with laughter Peggy chortled, "From the sad look you had on your face when we came in, I'd say you both got lost. It must be terrible to court Kaye in a hearse, why don't you two just get married and get away from here?"

"Why Peggy," I protested, "you want me to leave?"

The precious days Kaye and I sublimated our dreams with games of Scrabble were monotonous, wasted hours. Each time she brought food from a restaurant we determined, "Some day, our situation will change." Kaye often pushed my wheelchair on the sidewalk around HH while we planned our future. One day I charged, "We can't keep living a make believe life! I know if our dreams are ever going to be fulfilled, we must step out on faith. Look at us, I'm a thirty-year-old man, you're a college graduate, RN, and we're both adults. It's humiliating and degrading to realize our emotional stability is dependent on ludicrous curfews or limited expansion of 'visiting hours'. Let's get married and leave this mess."

"I'm hesitant to move away from family." Kaye responded. "A pediatric position I previously requested is available. If I accept it with a pay increase, perhaps we could get married and stay in this area. September 13th is near. Let's plan for a new beginning. I agree, we need our own home."

29

BE PATIENT

A monotonously slow and at times excruciatingly painful five years had passed since Kaye and I embarked on a romance beset with unexpected storms. The wedding we envisioned one day was seemingly thwarted at every turn. Only undying love and determination, commitment strengthened by our faith, and patience in tribulation provided hope for the future.

Observing friends traveling the highway of matrimonial bliss we asked ourselves, "Why not us?" When family members were married and began raising their families we beseeched the Heavens with our prayer, "When God, when?"

My favorite place to sit in the corridor was dictated by the nearest electrical outlet for my respirator. One day I was shocked to see my dear friend Dr.Heilman Sr. escorted before me in a wheelchair. Dr.Heilman Jr. smiled wanly in my direction, sadly shaking his head as he admitted his dad to Heritage House. "Age and illness." he whispered.

The heart-wrenching emotions of this event encouraged return to my room while awaiting Kaye's arrival. During our visit she coughed a confession, "Aack, Aack, Ahuh. I think my new boyfriend has given me adult croup. I'd better stop his advances, especially those good night hugs and kisses."

"Boyfriend huh?" I asked cautiously. "Tell me more."

"Well," she joked, "he's blue-eyed, blond, and quite a lover. He won't keep his hands off me. Are you jealous?"

"Puh-leeze! Are you referring to that three year old on your Pediatric ward?" I laughed. "No darling, believe me I'm not worried."

"Mail call." announced Donna, laying some letters and a card on my bed. "Hmmm, these look important. Letters from doctors at IUMC and Yale addressed c/o Connie, Head Nurse."

"Right Donna." I teased. "I'm going to med school."

"Oohh for crying out loud! You're always the smart mouth." she moaned leaving my room.

"These must be answers to the letters Connie helped me write concerning phrenic nerve research." I commented.

Nervously opening one letter Kaye read, "...essentially Mr. Williams, this type procedure is experimental and we at IU have not perfected the operation. My suggestion, discuss this thoroughly with physicians at Yale. Even though they have performed this surgery for a few years, its success is still questionable."

"Dr. King's letter was not encouraging." Kaye declared. "Let's see what Dr. Glenn at Yale has to say, "...Mr. Williams your enthusiasm for contributions to knowledge gained from this surgery is commendable. While I have performed numerous procedures involving (EPNS) electrical phrenic nerve stimulation, any success is a direct result of nerve tissue viability. You are aware this surgery requires placing an electrode around the phrenic nerve. This cuff is then connected to a radio transmitter placed subcutaneously near the 5th and 6th ribs; thus stimulating the diaphragm in a prescribed cyclical pattern. This ventilatory support is obviously an extremely delicate operation. If satisfactory, the patient achieves greater reliability in ventilation and freedom from bulky respiratory equipment. If failure occurs during this surgery the phrenic nerve can be damaged and any existing diaphragmatic potential is compromised. One should use extreme caution in approaching a decision to participate in this program. Please contact me again if you desire any further investigation in this area."

"Now it isn't just discouragement, it's fear." Kaye said, shaking her head side to side as she folded the letter. "Maybe it would be better to drop this idea."

"Not yet." I said. "There's one man in my past I trust to give me an informed evaluation. At last report he was in Washington, D.C. at NIH. Actually, the same location as Dr. Walcher. Dr. Oliver is a pulmonary specialist and I know he will give me an honest appraisal. Now the challenge will be finding him, shall we write a letter? If he isn't there NIH might also forward his correspondence."

"Now that we have completed writing, do you suppose we could play a game of Scrabble?" asked Kaye.

"Another game of sublimation?" I responded resignedly. "Why don't we try a new game? Next time you go shopping at the mall search for a game that will afford both of us more mental stimulation. Since my eyes have gotten better you're not presenting much of a challenge."

"Boy, you just wait!" charged Kaye. "If I didn't know you were teasing I'd turn your respirator off. Rest assured when I return next week, you'll be sorry."

Connie, HH's present Nursing Supervisor, became shall I say, in a family way. Her husband decided it would be best if she began supervising their home, so Pat, a dry witted lovable middle-aged lady with a rare personality cultivated by experience with tragedy became HH's new nursing supervisor. Pat had suffered a slight stroke, but returned to nursing. Each day I listened impressively to her common sense conversation with certain arrogant doctors. Invariably, she instigated a universal irritation when addressing these learned gentlemen by their first name. Much like a condescending mother to an unruly son, she would place her arm around their shoulders and calmly confer wisdom. Not once did I observe an angry reaction from any of them, they were obviously respectful and more than a little cowered.

One day while sitting in the hall, Gussie, a wheelchair-bound resident, was escorted to my side. Beaming with pride she said, "Meet my grandson Ken."

My gaze settled on a young man with glasses, sporting a crew cut. Although fifteen years had passed since seeing my coffee-drinking buddy, but I knew him immediately and exclaimed, "I hope you don't expect me to stand. Hi stranger!"

"Danny? Grandma didn't tell me your name," he gasped, "just that she wanted me to meet a nice young man. I can't believe it! You don't look the same without the iron lung. How long have you been here at the nursing home?"

"I've lived here three years." I answered. "Your dear grandmother has certainly retained her judge of character, hasn't she? I'm happy to know you're still around. If you have time today, maybe we should take a coffee break."

After kindly chauffeuring Kaye and me to Muncie on many occasions, Dale's skill in climbing narrow mobile home steps without falling into the garbage can dramatically increased. Cold hard rains of reality washed away our bridge to sanity when Dale announced, "I hate telling you this, but I'm going to move back home. The situation at work has progressively worsened so I've decided to pursue my career as a mortician in Lafayette, my hometown. Dad and Mom also need my help. I know you're depending on me for travel to Muncie, but this spring journey will be the last time I'll be able to assist. Dating and brief escapes from HH are a must, so I'll speak to Joe my boss, but being understaffed he probably won't show any concern. What can I say? I'm terribly sorry."

Dale's disconcerting news regarding his imminent move captivated our thoughts and we confronted a recurring dilemma, transportation from HH to Muncie. We nibbled at the food on our plates, stomachs in turmoil following Dale's depressing news and I angrily asserted, "Being dependent on other people's good will or spending our meager funds for a ride in a hearse is ridiculous! Kaye, is there any possible way we can buy some wheels? I think the money we're applying to these trips might be more wisely spent on a station wagon. Let's analyze the situation." After a distressing conversation involving our lack of financial freedom we agreed to shop for a needed vehicle. As Dale's black hearse returned my body to the nursing home, September 13th once again became an elusive mirage.

Walking happily into my room Kaye sat a shopping bag on my bedside table and said, "When I'm finished feeding you, a new game of sublimation awaits your approval, dear one."

After losing my fifth game of Score Four I moaned, "I'm not sure this is good for my well being. Obviously, these losses can be attributed to my eyesight. Wouldn't you much prefer Scrabble? I don't understand how you win so often."

"Talent, my darling." replied Kaye joyfully. "Talent."

Pain, hematuria, fever, kidney stones, de`ja` vu. "Oohh, Oohhh, I'm sick Pat. Did you phone Dr.Heilman?" I groaned. "I don't understand why he won't hospitalize me for X-rays and tests."

"Danny, here's an antibiotic Dr.Heilman prescribed over the phone." said Madeline RN. "I know you've taken this med before, but maybe it will help this time."

***

"No! No! Don't give me that shot! I can't breathe! Stay away! Somebody help! Please don't hurt me again!"

"Danny, Danny, wake up!" said Granny, my nurse's aide. "You must have dozed off after your roommate died. Are you okay? You haven't had a nightmare for ages. Let me get a nurse."

"No, no I'm fine, just some bad memories that continue coming back. Maybe some day I'll forget." I sighed.

***

While waiting for Kaye I stared out my window, mesmerized as the swaying leaf-covered branches responded to soft summer breezes. I was startled by her appearance when she said, "Watch outside, I'll drive by to show you our car. It isn't new, but we have a station wagon."

Returning to the room she asked my opinion. "Actually, it looks like a well kept automobile." I remarked. "You're right, it is a station wagon. I noticed a rusty trailer hitch. If the car has towed very often it sometimes leads to brake and transmission problems. We'll deal with those difficulties when they happen, for now, you did good. I'm curious, did your father help you select the car?"

"No. I did this all by myself." Kaye proudly replied. "It isn't a Chrysler product so Dad wasn't thrilled. When he saw the trailer hitch he too was skeptical of the car's longevity. After searching for weeks, it was the only station wagon I could find."

"Did you haggle for a good price?" I inquired.

Keep Smiling and Never Give Up!

"The window sticker listed the price." She stated.

"Did you ever accompany your dad when he purchased a car?" I asked, amazed at my sweetheart's trust. "I'm sure he haggled or negotiated."

Kaye puzzled, "I didn't have a trade-in, so what was I supposed to negotiate?"

"Oh boy!" I sighed. "Changing subjects, it's becoming lonely at HH. Sharon moved to Indianapolis, Gayle left, now Vicky and Sherry enlisted in the Marines. The loss of all these caring people following administrative changes has me alarmed. Thank goodness you aren't seventy miles away like the last time a similar occurrence happened."

Kaye trudged solemnly into my room one October morning announcing, "My grandma died. I'm driving our station wagon taking family to Tennessee, and we're leaving in a couple hours. I'll have time to feed you lunch before going, then we'll be home in three days. We knew Grandma Ollie was ill, but it was still a shock. I can't forget my summer vacations, she..."

"Sometimes words are inadequate." I whispered softly. "Take comfort knowing your grandmother is with Jesus."

During Kaye's absence the aides and nurses attempted to compensate for my loneliness. When delivering mail Adeline, an aide asked, "Shall I read this mail to you or put it in the drawer until Kaye returns? Most look like cards, but one is a business letter from a Dr.Oliver."

"I'll look at the cards now, but yes, put the letter in my stand drawer." I instructed.

I counted the hours until Kaye arrived at my door, back from her unhappy pilgrimage to Oneida. While staring out my window I thought, "You're acting like a teenager. Remember how many times you didn't see each other for months, and now you're being a nervous ninny after three days. Pitiful!" I finished castigating myself for being a wimp moments before Kaye walked in the door. Coolly I inquired, "Did you have a safe trip? Is your dad coping well with his mom's death? I hope the car ran smoothly. I'm curious, were the brakes OK for those Tennessee mountains? Oh yeah, how many miles to the gallon? I trust you didn't have a flat tire."

"Hold it!" declared Kaye. "I'm happy to see you too! Yes, yes, yes, mostly, sixteen mph, and no! Anything else?"

"Sorry I'm hyper." I apologized. "I'm glad you're home safely honey. Wish I could have met your grandmother. Once we've chatted about your trip please check the stand drawer, Dr. Oliver answered my letter."

Kaye read Dr.Oliver's message to me, "Dan, your letter traveled many places before arriving in my mailbox. I am just now answering after many weeks, so if you're still interested here are my thoughts. I've only had limited, but 50/50 success with electrical phrenic nerve stimulators. I have referred two patients to Dr.Glenn at Yale. It might be possible for this procedure to be performed at IUMC, but for something this delicate and experimental I think it best to attain services most familiar with the surgery ...If you are still interested, contact me please, and I will be a willing intermediary for you to Dr.Glenn. Tell Kaye I said hello."

Laying the letter aside, we finalized next week's plans.

The days prior to Saturday, November 10th took forever to pass, a week fraught with anticipation of journeying to Muncie without being shielded by black curtains. HH staff, Kaye, and Faye lifted me into the back of our station wagon and our adventure began. I marveled, "Imagine, three great presents. A date, and a trip in our first car, alone!"

"What do you mean 'alone'?" Faye charged. "My sister may be driving the car, but I'm here too."

Chuckling at our remarks Kaye asked, "How does the ride compare to Dale's hearse? If you miss the window curtains I'll buy some black crepe paper. Isn't it wonderful to have our own transportation?"

"Yes! Not being confronted by that headache is such a pleasure." I answered. "The shocks are level, springs don't squeak, acceleration is smooth, and the ride is comfortable. Kaye, for your first used car you did a fine job. You sure the neighbor will be available to help carry me up those big steps on my stretcher? I hope you cautioned him about that infamous garbage can. Remember Dale?"

"Don't worry." Kaye laughed. "With Faye and I lifting one side, Jack and his son can handle the other. They live in a mobile home too, so he knows the steps are narrow."

Glorious memories of an unforgettable birthday were not long without competition from my traditional nemesis. "Oh no, not again!" I moaned. "Why me? Every time I ride on a stretcher my kidneys react in horror. Dr.Heilman, don't you think some routine diagnostic procedures are in order such as X-rays and a cystoscopy? Surely there's a problem other than just kidney stones again. I repeatedly take the same medicine, but the problem simply recurs. Many more bouts of this and I might as well stop thinking about EPNS."

"Danny," he responded, "the medicine I'm prescribing is helping. Just be patient. As I said before, I don't think you should continue pursuing this idea of medical research."

Thanksgiving arrived and Kaye and I celebrated with our companion trays. Looking glumly at a banquet of food before us I remarked, "Dinner reminds me of the present situation. I'm beginning to feel like that turkey." Speaking to Pat later I pleaded, "I don't know what to do. Dr.Heilman Sr. brought me into the world then provided care day and night when I came home in an iron lung after I had Polio. When Doc Sr. retired, Dr.Heilman Jr.

Keep Smiling and Never Give Up!

took over and continued treating me with compassion and superb medical support. Now I'm confronted by a situation keeping me awake at night. I know Dr.Heilman must be sick at heart because of his dad's health, and my own problems seem insignificant. I hate having to accost him when he comes here to visit his father, but it's the best opportunity I'll have to seek advice or a listening ear from my doctor. They've both been great to me and my family, so contemplating change is upsetting. I have a dilemma. Maybe relocating to another city and a new doctor would be the answer."

Kaye volunteered to work New Year's Eve, so we planned to welcome 1974 watching football bowl games. Lunch arrived complete with a companion tray, and while eating we admired many beautiful floats in the Tournament of Roses parade. As halftime began at the Cotton Bowl Kaye suggested we try our luck at a game of Score Four. Sighing reluctantly I agreed, "If you insist, but when the ballgame resumes, I have to coach!"

Seven rapid losses later Kaye remarked, "Dan, why can't we play another game? The Cotton Bowl isn't exactly living up to all the hype. I think your stubborn refusal to play is suspiciously linked to forty-four consecutive losses. You told me to find a game to replace Scrabble, and now you say 'it's not any fun.' Do you realize how much that hurts me? You're neglecting to show proper appreciation for my success. It surely couldn't be darling, but do you have a problem with me winning?"

"No smarty." I begrudgingly replied. "After all, you won my affections didn't you? You're just too lucky at Score Four!"

Kaye sniffed, "Luck huh! Talent, darling, talent!"

A welcome interruption occurred when Loretta brought the mail. "Danny here's a letter from some doctor." she said. "Kaye, make yourself useful, read it to him."

I frowned, "Loretta, there wasn't any mail today, where did you pick this up?"

Loretta answered, "I found it at the nurse's station, guess they forgot to deliver it yesterday."

Opening the letter from Dr.Oliver Kaye read, "Dan, I've unsuccessfully tried telephoning Kaye for several weeks. I spoke to Dr. Glenn and he informed me you must go to IUMC for a cine fluoroscopy exam of your diaphragm during spontaneous breathing. If IUMC is unable to evaluate their film, send it to Dr.Glenn for a decision...Keep in touch."

Pursing my lips I remarked in exasperation, "What could I possibly accomplish? Considering my questionable health and the intractable resistance I'm incurring, maybe participating in advanced pulmonary research is not a good idea. I haven't been able to convince anyone hospitalizing me for evaluation of my kidney problems is important, how on earth can I approach the subject of a trip to Yale medical school for research? I guess until we relocate to a larger city, any effort to pursue phrenic nerve stimulation must be postponed indefinitely."

Unable to conceal her glee at my decision to wait, Kaye remarked, "I'm happy you've chosen to give consideration of our future dreams a more important role than a trip to Yale. By the way, I have a surprise. Look! Our wedding rings are back from the engraver. Aren't they beautiful? See, inside the gold bands is etched, 'MTY/LTT'."

Winter months proceeded without unusual developments. No travel, better health. A young man walked into my room and I greeted, "Hi David, are you visiting someone?"

"Danny? I didn't know you were here." he said. "I'm checking out nursing home facilities. Dad's suffering from ALS, Lou Gehrig's disease. His muscles are deteriorating and he's paralyzed. Man, last time I saw you there was a stack of evening papers on your bicycle. Remember? Maybe Dad will recognize our old paperboy. When they told me Mr. Williams would be Dad's roommate I didn't make a connection. Danny, did your parents retire to Florida? If not, I'm sure when they visit you Dad will recognize a man he worked with for years. Maybe seeing an old buddy will cheer him up."

"It's good to see you again, unfortunately this isn't a great place for a reunion. David, I'm so sorry to hear the terrible news about your dad." I confided. "My parents are spending winters in Florida, they'll be back in a week. I know Dad will be surprised and devastated when he sees your dad, my new roommate. I'm waiting for Kaye, my fiancé, but when they admit your dad I promise to help any way I can. I hope he still likes baseball. We can share my TV."

David raised his fist in the air declaring, "All right! Yes, Dad's still a sports fan and it's great you have a TV. Mention the word baseball and his eyes sparkle, especially the Cincinnati Reds. I remember years ago he really got a big kick out of ribbing your dad about his Dodgers. Danny, I can't begin to tell you how many tears we've shed lately, this is such a relief. You've taken a big load off my mind, now we won't have such a heavy burden on our hearts. Admitting my dad to a nursing home won't give us nightmares after all."

***

"No! No! Don't give me that shot! I can't breathe! It's cold! Somebody help! Please don't hurt me again!"

***

Keep Smiling and Never Give Up!

"Dan, Dan, wake up." whispered Kaye. "Why did you cry out for help? Why didn't you tell me you're still having these terrifying nightmares? Sorry I'm late honey, but the surprise spring snowstorm made driving on slick roads a bit tricky. Now tell me what's happening!"

"Uuhhh." I murmured drowsily. "Guess I must've fallen asleep watching minutes tick slowly by. Sorry you heard my recital of the distant past, can't a guy have any privacy? Actually, I usually only do this when I'm asleep."

"Don't joke about it." Kaye scolded. "I'm afraid living in a nursing home will just continue to reawaken those horrible memories. Marriage is the only answer, we need our home. I guess moving away is the solution. Next week I'll search for a job in Indianapolis. Going back over there gives me nightmares too!"

I grinned, "We'll keep each other company at night."

30

FEAR TO JOY

The days following Kaye's critical decision were filled with apprehension; nights consumed by restless dreams. Our news, although exciting for us, promised to be disconcerting to HH staff. I tried concealing my hoped-for departure from nurses and aides, but after four years of deciphering moods and thoughts such efforts became futile. Word of my leaving spread and people were both supportive and disappointed. I understood the ambivalence; they'd brought me back from the brink of death. Divine predestination forever entwined our lives with bonds of memory and love never to be broken.

My parents returned from their winter hiatus in Florida looking healthy and tanned. "Danny, you would really enjoy fishing from my boat." said Dad. "Our excursions even have your mother enthused. I see you have a new roommate. Who is he? What happened to Mr. Jerritt?"

"Mr. Jerritt died." I answered quietly. "Look closely, you'll recognize an old friend. Remember Fred?"

After receiving minimal response from his greetings to Fred, Dad turned away in stunned silence. "I feel guilty." he lamented. "You're in a nursing home, my old friend has been attacked by an evil disease and is dying, and I'm talking about fishing and a wonderful life in Florida. I remember when you had Polio. Like that, this just isn't fair."

Mom said, "Seems like everybody has troubles."

I stated, "Dad, Mom, please don't ever let yourselves feel guilty about enjoying life's blessings. You've waited a lot of years for a home in Florida, be thankful your dream came true. If you're happy, your children are happy."

Dad shook his head saying, "Those are nice words, but we know going to Florida has been your dream too."

"I will," I assured them, "after Kaye and I marry. Who knows, we might even live there someday. Just remember, it was my decision to live in a nursing home. Fred's suffering and imminent death is a mystery to all human reasoning, which makes everyone feel sad and vulnerable. Only God knows the answer for debilitating diseases, in time we'll know why."

While sitting in my usual location by the nurse's desk Monday I received a call from Kaye, informing me she had scheduled an interview with a mysterious hospital, the name of which she was saving for a surprise. A few minutes passed before I realized this was probably her first step in seeking employment in another area. Suddenly shivers of joy and trepidation engulfed me and I understood my fiancé's hesitation to make such a move. Certainly we'd be separated from our network of family and friends, but the advantages of medical facilities and better job compensation provided necessary incentives for future security. Despite my inward arguments, I couldn't stop fearful imaginings.

Searching for a job in a larger city I learned about a pediatric nursing vacancy at Methodist Hospital in Indianapolis and made an appointment for an interview. When I arrived at Methodist the Personnel Department's apologetic Nurse Recruiter shook my hand announcing, "I'm so sorry Miss Williams, the advertised pediatric nurse position was filled yesterday. Could we possibly entice you to consider another department? We have a vacancy in Medical Research, do you have any experience in this area?"

I explained, "Just limited exposure from correspondence with IUMC and Yale concerning my fiancé's personal inquiries into phrenic nerve stimulator implantations."

"Hmmm, sounds complicated." the recruiter reacted. "If the Nursing Director for Medical Research is available I'll set up an appointment now. Since there's a evening vacancy, I know Judy will be quite interested to meet you."

Completing my interview with Judy, she escorted me to Medical Research and introduced staff that might soon become colleagues. Leaving the unit I commented, "Judy, I'm very impressed with Methodist's personnel and equipment, friendly atmosphere, and the professionalism of everyone I met today. Let me consider your offer overnight, I'll telephone you in the morning with my decision."

Judy responded, "I know you'll be more than satisfied working with us, I'll expect an affirmative answer when you call me tomorrow."

I waited patiently and expectantly all week for Kaye's interview, eagerly anticipating her visit Friday with a possible answer to our future. As she walked into my room I exclaimed, "Welcome back to HH! When do we move? Or maybe I should ask where?"

Kaye teased, "I've never worked nights before, but if you insist."

"NIGHTS!" I exclaimed. "No way, that's my time."

"Dan! Shh!" Kaye declared. "Now for my report. I met with the Nurse Recruiter at Methodist Hospital in Indianapolis inquiring about a pediatric position. That position unfortunately was filled Wednesday, but she offered me another job. What do you think about Medical Research? The positives are: Evening shift, a major medical facility, opportunity for advancement, excellent salary, and a superb ancillary staff. The hospital is huge and the equipment is more advanced than I've ever seen. Now the negatives: This is not a pediatric job, I would have to sell my mobile home, we wouldn't have family or friends nearby, and you would be required to, temporarily, live in another nursing home."

"Are you serious?" I squinted, confounded by her announcement.

Kaye sighed, "One thing we neglected to consider, all new employees must undergo six weeks orientation on days. I will have to live in Indianapolis by myself until we find a place for you or until we get married. I know neither of us counted on this dilemma. Dan, do you realize how alone and vulnerable we'll both be?"

"Loneliness is a state of mind reflected by emptiness in one's heart." I stoically remarked. "Our hearts are full of love for each other and the grace of God will protect us. Kaye, if this is really meant to be then fears are irrelevant."

Kaye reflected, "I'll keep reminding myself of those thoughts, but it's easier said than done."

I responded, "Many times in Respo Centers, hospitals, and nursing homes I would wonder why I was destined to live apart from family. Eventually I realized my loneliness wasn't determined by environment so long as family and the Lord remained in my heart. I learned to accept and adjust my attitude, emotion, and thoughts to any given situation. During my life, places where I enjoyed the most contentment were the very places where most people thought I should have been the loneliest. Honey I'm certain pangs of separation will plague both of us, but this move is necessary to lay a solid foundation. In his book, *As A Man Thinketh,* James Allen wrote, 'Dream lofty dreams...Your Vision is the promise of what you shall one day be...' I see this move as an opportunity, not an obstacle. As I recall, the Bible says, 'Fret not thyself...Lo, I am with you always.'"

I concluded a phone call accepting the position when my new boss Judy summarized, "I'm sure you will have a career in Medical Research which is both exciting and challenging. I'll see you Monday, May 6th at 8:00 AM. The interim will give you time to move and get acquainted with Indianapolis."

Predictably, when awaiting change or events, time passes much too quickly. The six weeks prior to Kaye's departure sped by incredibly fast and we approached a major crossroads in our lives. As my wife-to-be prepared to leave for Indianapolis we stared into each other's eyes seeing a reflection of horrible memories when we were last separated by distance and circumstance. Kaye and I prayed for safety and strength then I sadly watched her walk forlornly from my room. Our love reinforced by faith and prayers for the future gave us hope all would be well. Gazing out my window, I tried blocking from my mind thoughts and fears of unknown terrors confronting her in a city where I'd suffered so much devastating trauma. Kaye would be coping with employment, unfamiliar surroundings, and searching for reliable nursing homes without benefit of support from family or friends. I struggled daily with bad memories, but was comforted by a surrogate family of caring people; obviously the advantage was mine. When Kaye left my side I whispered, "Always think about the words we've lived by: Faith, love, patience, hope, and always keep smiling. Never forget Joshua's words: 'be strong and of good courage.'"

Once more our eternal commitment to each other incurred severe testing. During the next few weeks the loneliness I minimized to Kaye became unexpected despair in my life. It was as though the forces of evil had been challenged by my bravado as they raised their ugly heads. Turmoil reigned even though staff, other residents, and my immediate family filled every waking hour. I envisioned Kaye returning from work entering a lonely apartment thinking to herself, "Why am I doing this? I hate being here by myself." I decided maybe I'd asked her to do the wrong thing and prayed nothing would happen to make us regret our choice.

One day a flurry of activity took place around the bed next to me, indicating a crisis in Fred's health. Sue, an aide, tried vainly to comfort him, but her limited skills in coping with terminal illness were profoundly apparent. She summoned Becky, an LPN who assumed his bedside care while a hush fell over the room. Hands on the clock moved slowly as family kept an hour-by-hour vigil beside their husband and father. Evening approached as Fred labored to remain alive, inevitably losing the battle to a cruel unyielding foe. An RN, Carol, closed the privacy curtains between our beds and I heard David utter one last sob, "Dad."

***

"No! No! Don't give me that shot! I can't breathe! Stay away! Somebody help! Please don't hurt me! Oh no!"

"Danny, Danny, wake up! That was over a long time ago. It's okay now." Betty soothed.

***

Escaping the quiet surroundings of a now private room I assumed my official position in the main corridor at HH. I observed Pat consoling Dr.Heilman Sr. as he emerged from the dining room. Leaning down on one knee, she patted his arm reassuring, "Now Bill, calm down. You know the food will be better next time." I heard her say, "Hello Dr.Rector. I'll wheel Dan to his room so you can examine his eyes."

Pat pushed my chair back to the room and connected the respirator to an outlet then left me in George's care. "I'm glad you gave me such a quick appointment." I smiled. "Only a short time remains before I move to Indianapolis - say you wouldn't by any chance make long distance house calls? Oh, give Sandy my thanks for delivering the message I wanted an appointment before leaving town."

"It's good my wife told me you were relocating," George replied. "Examining your eyes is a pleasure now, especially since your progress has been so remarkable. I remember the first time I checked your eyes after Dr.Burnett retired, as the records reveal, prognosis was poor."

I nodded agreement, "The future looked sort of dim at that time, no pun intended. Thank God I'm much better now, my eyesight is really improving. So's the future."

George repacked his instruments and was in the process of leaving when JJ's attendant wheeled his chair through my door. "Thought I'd better check things out before you left our fair city." he remarked jovially.

"Glad you rolled by." I responded. "JJ, I'm curious, can you manage New Castle all by yourself in my absence?"

"Yuk, yuk!" JJ laughed. "Actually, with you gone I'll be able to concentrate on more substantive issues. I'm also curious concerning a number of things, what happened to your typewriter? What about your lift, you know you'll need it later. Tell me about some of the nurse's aides."

"JJ you're really behind on current events." I replied. "The subject of my typewriter is old news. I asked Kaye to take it home nearly a year ago when the opportunity to write a column for HH became nonexistent. Kaye is transporting my Hoyer lift to her Indianapolis apartment for use after our wedding. Nurse's aides? Are you planning to steal my people?"

"Relax friend!" he declared. "You're leaving town so at least I'm waiting until you're gone. In a gesture of our close friendship, please give me names of the ten best aides at HH. In your opinion, what chance do I have for employing these ladies as home health attendants?"

"Well...," I teased, "as long as I don't tell the truth about you, chances are good. These women are compassionate, loving people who care. Of course they'll be interested."

JJ smiled as he rolled from my room, his words trailing behind, "We might not see each other again until eternity. Mother said 'tell you bye'."

For some reason a large lump formed in my throat as he bid me farewell and good luck. After JJ departed I accosted the first available assistants, "Holly, Dot, Jo! Would one of you take me back to the corridor? My visitors are gone and I'm in need of socialization."

"Come on Danny Boy." Margaret quipped. "They're really busy right now, but I have a few minutes."

Moments after I resumed my position as hall monitor, in walked a delightful surprise. "Well, today is filled with unscheduled appearances, some of them lovely." I exclaimed. I'm not complaining, but you weren't

Keep Smiling and Never Give Up!

supposed to be here for two weeks. I guess orientation classes finished early."

"Yes, I've been reeducated." replied Kaye. "I received my six-week schedule then decided to come home for a visit. Dan, you won't believe the enormity of Methodist Hospital. I work on a 54-bed research unit and love every minute. You said another unexpected visitor? Who else was here? I hope everything's all right at HH. Honey, I personally inspected five nursing homes and found two that seem to be receptive to your respirators and needs. Want to hear about them?"

"Slow down!" I grinned. "My unscheduled visitors beside you were Dr.Rector and JJ. Suppose we take a stroll around the building and discuss today's events, my room is too eerily silent, reminiscent of a recent death."

"Oh, did Fred die?" Kaye frowned.

"Yes." I answered quickly, not wishing to discuss the matter further. "It's getting late, let's walk."

Attempting to ease tension Kaye replied, "I'll walk, you ride. I think you should take a load off your feet."

"Look at this," I cracked, "not married and already I'm getting shoved around. Oh well, let's get going."

Kaye walked and I rolled slowly around the grounds at HH as I received a picturesque verbal tour of Methodist and a new apartment in Indianapolis. Excitement resounded from her voice as she described a fascinating new job, but a pall of bleak countenance appeared when she spoke of hours alone. "Dan, you wouldn't believe the last four weeks! I remember you said loneliness could be overcome by directing one's thoughts toward those you love and miss, but it didn't help much. Thankfully I didn't have a lot of time to think because each day after work and on weekends I searched for a nursing home. I couldn't eliminate the feeling something bad was waiting for me around the corner. Walking to and from my car, shopping, driving around the city, everywhere, I sensed an evil unseen force lurking in the shadows. It was awful!"

I shuddered, "Same thing happened here. Our guardian angels have been dueling with the demons of darkness."

Kaye grasped my hand and quietly whispered, "On those long lonely nights when every creak and sound seemed to be coming from my apartment I read the Bible for strength. A special passage was Psalm 91:2,5, 'I will say of the Lord, He is my refuge and my fortress: my God; in Him will I trust Thou shalt not be afraid for the terror by night.'"

Impressed by her courage and faith I readily agreed. A drop of moisture hit my forehead and I muttered, "Well, that was either a wayward bird or it's beginning to sprinkle. I think perhaps we should continue this conversation inside. Odd, last time I moved to Indianapolis it was raining, but I'm sure sunny skies are just beyond the horizon."

Sitting comfortably in my dry, quiet room we watched as droplets of water slithered down the windowpane. Returning to our interrupted conversation Kaye continued, "I brought with me information about the two nursing homes which seem acceptable."

Kaye showed me brochures and her inspection report and I considered pros and cons of each nursing home. I sighed deeply and made a decision, "When you return to the big city initiate my admission to Northwest Manor (NM). If all goes well in the immediate future, schedule it for June 20th."

Following our get re-acquainted meal, Kaye spent much of her four-day Memorial Day weekend at home in fellowship with family. I listened distractedly to the Indianapolis 500 from my bed at HH, visualizing a new beginning at another convalescent center. Accustomed to the superb care, trustworthy administration, and loving people at HH who'd become family, I dreaded the unknown. Only four years ago I'd found myself floundering in a situation which nearly resulted in my death and I prayed, "Please God, not again." It's difficult to express my emotions leaving a staff and facility that had given succor to my life.

My thoughts rambling, I heard Beth lament, "Hey Danny! After you leave HH we won't have a radio on this hall."

"Radio? What radio?" I joked. "I've been singing."

"Oh man!" she moaned. "Want something to drink? You should be thirsty after racing 150 laps."

Kaye fed me Sunday dinner and then my partner-to-be in life left my side returning to Indy, a new job and lonely apartment. The moment seemed very reminiscent of recent times past as she walked hesitantly from my room, heading resolutely to what we both agreed was our future.

Following Andy's return from Okinawa he and Nina began preparing for their wedding on June 11th. Walking into my room I commented to him, "You certainly are looking handsome and tanned. Do you two have any plans for a honeymoon?"

"No plans." said Nina. "This long-distance romance is ridiculous. Maybe now we won't be separated any longer."

Final days at Heritage House were chaotic. My time was consumed approving discharge papers, bidding farewell to old friends, and completing last minute moving details. Wanda, HH's Business Office Manager, prepared transfer papers for Kaye's signature as my power of attorney. Velma, Director of Personnel and Records, dropped by to offer best wishes. When I was first admitted to HH, Marilyn, the Head Nurse, had directed Ralph our Maintenance Supervisor to build me a footboard. Elizabeth, one

Keep Smiling and Never Give Up!

of my many visitors and present DON stated, "The footboard should go with you to Indy. It was made for you, let's call it a Heritage House memory."

June19th Judy brought my last sandwich from her kitchen commenting, "I hope you realize leaving isn't fair, noontime will never be the same. Norman will probably have to remove wheels from our car since it heads this way everyday at lunch."

Dad and Mom visited that evening to express last minute farewells and admonished, "We hope your insistence on moving back to Indianapolis doesn't become a tragic mistake again. After all, you won't have family and friends nearby. Danny are you sure this is a good idea?"

"Yes! I'm positive for Kaye and me it's a great idea. Remember, send me a postcard from Florida."

Vivian promised, "Jeff, Kennetha, and Richard will be here in the morning. They'll follow Kaye, Main and Frame's ambulance and you to Indy bringing your possessions. Have a safe trip. I love you hon. Be strong. See ya' later."

During a mini going-away party Wednesday evening Betty, Irma, and dear Moneva shared potato chips, peanuts, Cokes, and best wishes - our lives forever connected by memories of tears, struggle, and laughter. Prior to departing Thursday morning Connie, an important person in my survival, along with Frances, Mayme, Jackie, and Gladys offered last minute wishes for Kaye's and my happiness.

While getting me ready for the journey to another home, Mossie and Anna, my aides for the morning said, "Danny, we hope you don't forget us. Maybe someday you could write a story about this nursing home and your friends."

"Bye! Bye!" my Heritage House family chorused, waving as the ambulance doors closed and I left the last four years of my life behind, bound for a strange, new, and presumably temporary quarters at another nursing home.

My journey to Indianapolis revived many memories – some ancient, others recent. I remembered traveling west nearly seventeen years ago as part of my introduction to Polio. A Christmas trip home in my iron lung via moving van occurring shortly after, still brings happiness to my heart. Sadly my joy was submersed in despair when I returned to New Castle four years ago, a physical disaster following two years in an Indianapolis nursing home. The effects of this terrible tragedy will probably forever inflict horrible nightmares. I vowed never again, my choices would be different now. Very soon Kaye and I would marry and begin our lives together.

After entering the city we meandered along tree-lined Kessler Boulevard marveling at many gorgeous homes holding court among acres of plush, spectacularly manicured lawns. Following multiple changes in direction

Daniel R. Williams

Mark, ambulance driver, announced, "Dan I must say, there's a bit more traffic in this city, but we made it at last. The sign reads, Northwest Manor Convalescent Center."

"Welcome Dan," said the Director of Nurses, "you missed lunch, but if you're hungry we'll prepare a snack. My name is Jennifer. I'll let everyone introduce himself or herself. Jerry our Administrator and I informed Kaye we have another young resident. I'll ask Nila to visit later after you have time to get settled and recuperate from your trip."

Everyone spoke at once. Introductions of roommate and staff, minimal explanation of my visual problems, location of bureau for the TV, and cursory directions to convenient fast food establishments (one must be prepared) simultaneously occurred. Added to the confusion we heard, whirrr, click, click. "Hello." greeted a young woman in an electric wheelchair. "My name is Nila, welcome to a good nursing home. I came to offer my assistance in acquainting you with facility and staff, but it seems I'm late. Forgive my interruption."

"You aren't interrupting. Hello, my name is Kaye. I'm Dan's fiancé. Nila, we're planning to have a pizza, would you care to join us?"

"I haven't had pizza for a long time." Nila hesitantly replied. "It sounds great if you're sure I'm not imposing. Be careful driving Kaye. I don't want to lose a new friend immediately after accepting a dinner invitation."

After Kaye left I again resumed center stage smiling, "Hi, I'm Dan. Thanks for welcoming me to NM. How long have you lived here? More importantly, why do you live at a convalescent center?"

Nila answered, "I've been at this facility less than a year. I transferred from another nursing home after, shall we say, 'inadequate care'. I'm quadriplegic as a result of an auto accident. Our car made an indentation in a tree and disrupted a fence line in an attempt to plant vehicle parts in the ditch. I'm sorry to report, my body didn't respond well to bouncing off the dashboard. Following many months in the hospital, I've lived in nursing homes."

"In other words, you're spinal. Am I mistaken, or did you mention, 'our car'? I trust no one was killed."

"My husband was driving, but he wasn't injured. We divorced after the wreck. Yes, someone died." she answered sadly. "I was pregnant."

In the process of briefly telling Nila my life story concerning Polio, Kaye returned with our pizza. After enjoying a meal we participated in a game of Scrabble. Sighing wistfully I summarized our mini-progress of four years, "Please take note of the advances we've made in our lives Kaye. Despite moving some seventy miles, getting a new job and apartment, and my transfer to another nursing home, sublimating our dreams in board game competition still rules our world. Look at us! We're still playing Scrabble! Well at least we found a new friend and teammate."

Following my journey from New Castle to Indy the usual revenge of kidney stone displacement, fever, and UTI plagued me for nearly one month. My admission to NM triggered hopes of resolving a problem that had been debilitating my body for quite some time. I was again advised to, "give the medicine time, and just be patient."

I passed Judy in the corridor at work and she inquired, "How is Dan? Have they begun any new medicine?"

"Nothing has changed," I replied, "Dan's fever and pain continue, but his temporary doctor refuses hospitalization to diagnose the problem. Medicaid policy appears to be the same in Indy as New Castle. I don't understand."

Judy stated, "It's time Dr.Lloyd and I admit him to our facility for X-rays and evaluation by Methodist specialists. As you know your floor 8B, and 7B are designated for nursing research, but 5A, our special eleven-bed unit is equipped to monitor his respirator. My nurses can provide him excellent care and we'll try to put an end to this problem. Dan's obviously receptive to the idea; more advanced medical facilities were one reason for moving to Indy. Discuss it with him tomorrow and let me know."

I gratefully accepted Judy's suggestion and within days a nurse greeted me as I was ushered onto 5A where she had pre-arranged my admission. "Hello Dan, I'm Cathy, RN and I understand you need a thorough medical work up. Before we report off to the evening shift, let me introduce the staff. Meet Krilla, Head Nurse, Vicki and Sue, RN's, Bessie, NA, and Holly, GN. Ron, our orderly works days and he'll help settle you in bed, then Holly will take your medical history."

After only three days of intensive examinations, X-rays and blood tests by specialists in nephrology and urology, a hidden culprit responsible for inflicting years of needless pain and infection was diagnosed. Andrea, day RN approached my bed with a syringe and needle poised for action saying, "Gentamicin is a powerful antibiotic and will eliminate the bug precipitating all those UTI's following each episode of kidney stones."

I nodded, "Doc didn't inform me how many shots I would need to solve the problem. What is it, two or three doses? Imagine the years of unnecessary suffering that could have been prevented with just a few sticks."

"Get ready for a surprise!" laughed Gloria, LPN, while turning me on my side. "A course of injections is scheduled every twelve hours over the next ten days."

I soon discovered daily blood tests were necessary when receiving such potent medicine. Regardless my misgivings, I could envision an end to this vicious cycle. Nineteen shots later I'm not sure my body felt any cleaner inside, but it certainly was more sore. With my spirits and health better than they'd been for quite some time, I enjoyed her humor as the night RN, Helene, told jokes and laughed prior to injecting my twentieth shot. Alberta, LPN teased, "After receiving so much of this bug killer, you shouldn't be harboring any bad things in your blood. Matter of fact, when you finally do get married, Kaye should be safe."

"Alberta!" exclaimed Helene.

Chuckling I said, "It's okay Helene, We understand each other."

Every midnight after Kaye's shift ended she had stopped by my room to say good night. During her last visit tonight I commented, "Everyone should have a good friend like Judy who's always willing to help when other people turn away. I don't think you could hope for a better boss."

After discharge from Methodist I returned triumphantly to NM full of holes and weak, but rapidly regaining stamina. "Do you believe it Kaye?" I marveled. "Only fourteen days at Methodist, back to NM less than a week, and believe it or not I feel like a new person. It's time we finalized wedding plans!"

31

MTY/LTT

F A I T H and L O V E

    The Bible says, "Ask, and it shall be given you; seek, and ye shall find; knock, and it shall be opened unto you." Kaye and I had prayed this on numerous occasions. We'd often been counseled, God answers prayers in His will: no, wait, or yes. "No" occurred prior to Kaye's graduation from college and my dependence on others. "Wait" is what we had been doing for six long years because of my chronic and life-threatening illnesses, and the inability to resolve our financial problems. "Yes" followed my divine recovery and Kaye's recently secured employment, affording us opportunity to establish our dreamed-of home. God was now granting our petition as He answered our fervent, unceasing prayers.

    After finalizing plans for our wedding date, I notified Medicaid of our impending marriage, receiving assurance they would inform The March of Dimes. Anticipating resumption of financial responsibility for my respiratory equipment a mere formality, as per promises given me while a resident of SAP, I was disheartened when reality invaded my naivety again. Though an inexplicable delay in response once more threatened our day, Kaye and I continued planning the wedding ceremony. We dreamed of grasping the golden rings in our future.

    I needed to view the apartment Kaye had rented where we expected to establish residence. Conkle's mortuary in Speedway loaned a stretcher, then Jerry and Alma, NA's drove with us for inspection of Oak Brook Village. Once entering the door I became painfully aware our planned home was entirely too small to accommodate three respirators, hydraulic life, hospital bed, and my wheelchair. A cursory look at available space was discouraging, prompting discussion about release from the contract. Looking upward we both murmured at once, "Oh no, not again!" Suddenly a smooth transition to marriage seemed impossible as Kaye and I recalled past difficulties. "I'll speak to the apartment manager in the morning." Kaye assured. "I can't believe we've waited patiently for another postponement!"

    While Kaye was appealing to a leasing agent for relief from our present dilemma, I was honored with a visit from my social worker who informed me, "Mr. Williams, I've contacted my superior about your respirators and home nursing. Should you marry, the state won't provide money to rent respiratory equipment, pay for nursing, or medicine. I advise against marriage and strongly urge that the State retain responsibility for your care.

I'm sure your girlfriend will understand, maybe you should discuss a more practical approach."

"There's nothing to discuss!" I charged staring at her. "We will be married! Kaye and I haven't endured six years of horror only to be patronized by someone who's supposedly working on my behalf. Our determination is bolstered by faith and love. We will succeed. Your support for my quest of an independent life is humbling, thank you. This unpleasant conversation is over, please leave."

After a wearying day of emotional anguish I restlessly drifted to sleep, hoping tomorrow would be better.

***

"No! No! You don't understand! Someday I will marry! Don't close the door! Don't hurt me again! Oh God, no!"

"Dan, Dan, it's all right." soothed Brenda, NA. "No one will hurt you. You're just having a nightmare."

***

I spent a restless night and morning dreading telling Kaye of the complications we now confronted. When I finished talking Kaye sighed, "Dan, what can we do? No respirators, medicines, or aides, what is wrong with these people! Can't they understand, living at home with minimal assistance is the best answer? Surely it's apparent a nursing home would cost thousands of dollars more, and you'd remain confined like a prisoner. My salary will not cover the cost of both nursing and respirators. If we fast a lot, we only need support for one or the other. I can't believe the state laws are so rigid. Wait a minute! Didn't The March of Dimes promise to reinstate coverage of your respirators after we marry?"

I nodded, "They most certainly did."

Kaye raised her hands in disgust, "What happened?"

"Who knows!" I exclaimed. "The only disruption in my coverage occurred with their knowledge, and they purportedly promised resumption of support upon our marriage. I'm convinced the problem doesn't stem from The March of Dimes. Since I contracted Polio in 1957 I've depended on respirator and medical assistance from them, so my seniority is firmly established with MOD. Since it's unlikely the social worker is serious in assisting my transfer from Medicaid to MOD, I'll personally contact The March of Dimes headquarters in White Plains, NY. Regardless their response, we'll continue planning our wedding. Certainly the financial woes are great right now, but there will be an answer. Whether it be the money

Keep Smiling and Never Give Up!

tree needed, or manna from heaven, we will be successful this time. During a long sleepless night I happened to remember, John and Sharon relocated near Indy, so let's ask them to be our witnesses. Well, those are my news flashes; it's your turn. What happened when you approached the manager about cancellation of your lease? Are we faced with the possibility of living in a tent?"

"Tent, huh? First the good news." Kaye replied. "If I pay two extra days through September 15th, we're free. Now the bad news. Oak Brook doesn't have larger apartments, and my search for more affordable space has been fruitless. We are in trouble without assistance for your respirators. I need an immediate salary increase."

"Kaye," I chuckled, "I was joking about a money tree! We're getting married! God didn't provide us strength and will to survive an endless six years of anguish only to be thwarted again by small minds or tiny apartments. Somehow, September 13th will be our special day. Suppose we contact your minister in New Castle for advice. Perhaps you should also speak with the Methodist Chaplain you met at work. I guess Moneva and Andy were correct - we should've eloped!"

Frustrated and bewildered I phoned my minister seeking guidance through this maze of confusion, "Hello Rev. Hollen, I'm calling to update you about Dan's health and our current situation as you requested when we left New Castle. Thanks to Methodist Hospital's excellent doctors and nursing staff, Dan's problem was diagnosed and correct antibiotics stopped the infections. He's quickly regaining strength and we're now planning our wedding. Alarming new obstacles stand in our way and we need help turning them into opportunities."

After explaining the difficulty confronting us Rev. Hollen responded, "Remember, the government is not in control - God is."

I finished my lunch and tried concentrating on the TV when Nila whirred and clicked her electric wheelchair into my room complaining, "So many preparations are necessary for a wedding, I just wish there was something I could do."

Taking my eyes off the baseball game I jumped at Nila's offer, "Hey friend, if you're really serious, you can! We need announcements typed and envelopes addressed in a way as they say, economically. Are you interested?"

"You better believe it!" she exclaimed. "Two things at which I'm excellent: talking, and typing announcements in a way as I say, cheap!"

Dr. McElroy made rounds and we discussed my forthcoming marriage to Kaye. He suggested we both have our blood tests drawn under his orders at the nursing home. I agreed, since his kind offer would eliminate one more problem.

Daniel R. Williams

Summer days were eclipsed by autumn's cooling breezes and plans for NM's annual Labor Day picnic proceeded. "Will you and Kaye be attending our patio cookout?" asked Betty. The nurse's aide with whom we had developed rapport beamed, "Each year we have festivities in the courtyard for all NM residents. It's great! Our convalescent center provides a special event for everyone who lives here. Not many places care as much. Northwest Manor is one of a kind."

Ambulatory residents, wheelchair jockeys, and beds for those lying down on the job assembled to celebrate work and togetherness. I remarked to Kaye, "This picnic brings back great memories of Respo Centers and supportive staff showing love and respect to residents. Honey, did I tell you about the fishing trips Lee, NM's Activities Director, and Rene`, a volunteer, organized for the men, or women, if they don't mind baiting their own hook? Not only that, she takes the ladies, and guys if they wish, shopping at the mall. Their willingness to provide opportunities for others' happiness and contentment is impressive. After the horrors I incurred as a SAP, I've been so blessed with stays at Heritage House and my present summer vacation spot. I'm certain God's grace must surely adorn NM and HH."

Kaye agreed, quietly reviewed the past and said, "Dan, the picnic's wonderful and I wish I could stay. However, if I want Friday the 13th off duty to attend a wedding, it's necessary for me to work extra days. I'm sorry, but Methodist is calling."

Nila quickly assured, "Don't worry, I'll keep him busy after dinner by playing non-stop games of Scrabble."

Kaye pointed her finger at me and cautioned, "Stay in your chair. I'll see you tomorrow."

All our plans seemed to be progressing without trouble, but we should've known "best laid plans of mice and men". A reality check erupted when Kaye hurried into my room, burst out in tears, and sobbed, "The minister scheduled to preside at our wedding just got word his mother died and he's going out of town for the next ten days! The church phoned with the bad news, only events for members will be honored. I'm beginning to wonder, will it ever get better? Now what?"

"Remember, 'pressure forms the diamond'. Only one more jagged edge is being smoothed." I assured. "First we pray." "In the morning continue looking for an apartment. John and Sharon agreed to meet with us in a few days to finalize plans. On Friday September 13th, we become Mr.& Mrs. Daniel Williams."

Keep Smiling and Never Give Up!

I submersed my worry in work, praying for an answer to our latest dilemma. Passing Judy in the hall at Methodist she asked, "What's happening with Dan and his respirators? Are we still hoping for plan A concerning the wedding?"

"No Judy," I confided, "Nothing's going right. The State refuses to cover the respirators after we marry and denied any assistance for home nursing. Dan hasn't heard from The March of Dimes. Things were looking bleak, but today we've been informed the pastor's mother died, he's leaving town, and since we're not members, no wedding ceremony. The only good thing, Dan's getting better. We can't thank you or the doctors at Methodist enough for solving that problem."

Judy shook her head telling me, "Go back to work. I'll contact Chaplaincy for ideas and information. I think it's time to institute plan B. See you before I leave."

Judy phoned, "On your supper break take your sandwich and go to the Chaplaincy office."

As instructed I went to Chaplaincy. "Thank you Chaplain Filbey for meeting me on such short notice. I guess my boss told you about the problems, any ideas?"

"You're quite welcome Kaye." Chaplain Filbey responded. "Yes, Judy and I had quite a discussion about you and Dan. Let's see what can be arranged regarding the chapel. Tell me about your relationship and why you want to get married."

Thursday Kaye entered my room with a new countenance. She bubbled, "I found it! A ground floor apartment with two bedrooms and more than enough space for both of us, and it's affordable. Now if The March of Dimes will resume coverage of respiratory equipment, we'll manage the nursing. Judy's interest in us led to my meeting yesterday evening with Rev. Filbey, a Methodist Chaplain. He's concerned and hopes to reserve a hospital chapel for our marriage ceremony. Honey, he needs to meet and talk with you before the wedding. What a busy day tomorrow, I must go shopping then to New Castle for a visit with Mom and Dad. I promise to be back in time for our session with John and Sharon."

I smiled, "You sound excited! I'm teasing, really, it's great you found an apartment. I can't believe we've found a friend like Judy; maybe at last plans for our future are coming together. Rev. Filbey sounds like a special person too, I'm looking forward to meeting him and our wedding is beginning to look possible. Kaye, we could get married at home if a Methodist chapel isn't available. John and Sharon need directions to the apartment, so where is our palace?"

Kaye smiled, "We'll live at Village Square Apartments."

Friday I contemplated the enormity of our decisions and sought courage for our convictions. Kaye walked through my door slumping exhaustedly to the chair sighing, "I promised to return from New Castle before John and Sharon arrived and I'm here! All plans are in motion: Wedding dress is being altered; your suit is being pressed; Mom and I even located drapes

Daniel R. Williams

with the correct dimensions; and Faye, Patty, and Mom will help move me on Tuesday while you and Chaplain Filbey have your little talk."

Amazingly, the next four days moved like clockwork, our tentative plans for Friday the 13th appeared increasingly feasible. Tuesday afternoon I was greeted by a sandy-haired man with gentle, penetrating eyes, "Hello Dan, I'm Chaplain Filbey. Following Judy's encouragement, and my conversation with Kaye, I feel we've already become acquainted. Learning more about you two is important to me, is there somewhere we could speak privately?"

"Pleased to meet you." I welcomed. "Yes, the patio has electrical outlets for my respirator if you will please push my wheelchair to the courtyard."

"What an inviting spot for a meeting." Chaplain Filbey declared. "Now explain why you are in such a hurry to get married. Kaye mentioned September 13th, Friday?"

"Are you kidding?" I exclaimed. "I'm sure she informed you we've been engaged six years. Perhaps I'm missing your intended humor, but after so many disappointments it's most difficult to find levity within despair."

"I'm sorry." he replied. "I should have realized this subject for you two has ceased to be a joking matter. Kaye referred to financial problems concerning coverage for your respirators. I understand you also have a dilemma locating a chapel or church. Most people getting married confront a few last minute difficulties, but this is a bit unusual. I assume the majority of problems have been solved, but fill me in."

"Today, Kaye and family are moving her possessions into a new apartment then later Jim, my brother-in-law and nephew Kent will accompany Kaye to pickup a hospital bed. Thursday they will transfer my belongings to our home. Medicaid has paid the rental for my respirators and provided care through nursing homes, but law forbids such financial support once we're married. The March of Dimes had previously agreed to resume coverage of my respirators after our marriage, but an apparent misunderstanding is delaying approval. After MOD reinstates me, one problem will be solved. We'll find our own solution to home nursing while Kaye works. We'd found a local church for our wedding, but it was cancelled because of a death in the pastor's family, and schedules are being honored for members only. Kaye's pastor from New Castle has agreed to marry us, but it's necessary we know if Methodist has a chapel available Friday afternoon. Also, we would be honored if you would join Rev. Hollen in performing the ceremony. Kaye and I fervently seek God's blessing and sanctification of our marriage and lives. As Kaye indicated to Rev. Hollen, we don't understand why all these problems arose, but we hope you two are the answer."

Keep Smiling and Never Give Up!

Chaplain Filbey responded, "It certainly seems you're approaching life responsibly. In Mark 12:17 Jesus teaches, 'render to Caesar what is Caesar's, to God what is God's'. I'm especially touched by the commitment you've honored during the past six years. Many times people are under the illusion all will be well in marriage because they love each other, but as I've counseled, be prepared for those troubles that await all of us. To be sure, I think you and Kaye have already successfully battled many storms. I need to pray for guidance, make several inquiries, and see if your schedule can be accommodated, Friday is closer with each tick of the clock. As I leave shall I escort you back inside?"

"I would really prefer solitude right now. Please ask the aides to remember me in about an hour." I requested.

"I'll leave a message." he smiled. "I'll inform Kaye of chapel availability in time for any last minute arrangements."

I nodded understanding as he left me with my thoughts.

Wednesday arrived with no news, I sat quietly staring at a blank TV screen when I heard whirrr, click, click and Nila breathlessly exclaimed, "Dan, tell me quick! Where are you getting married? Stan's phoning and he wants to know in what direction he's taking you Friday. My friend's worried there might be an emergency during the time he's supposed to provide you transportation in the ambulance. Any news?"

"Nila, I really appreciate your wedding gift of a ride to our ceremony and home," I said, "but tell Stan, I haven't been told where to go yet. Just pick me up here."

Lee and Rene` came into my room with secretive smiles on their faces. Lee said, "I've arranged for wedding flowers, a cake, and purchased the gift you requested."

"I hope you like it." said Ren,. "Remember, have a door key ready for us and we'll take these gifts to the apartment while you're getting married. We've ordered table flowers, and I'll wrap the present."

"Excuse us." said Norman and Judy, surprising me with a visit. "What's all the excitement? Danny are you getting married? Do Mother and Daddy know?"

"Hi!" I exclaimed. "Yes, Kaye and I are finally tying the knot. Judy you know the folks, they aren't interested."

"Oh Danny," Judy said shaking her head, "yes they are."

Norman smiled, "Well I certainly am, can we help?"

I pursed my lips, "I think the only thing left is for me to memorize 'I do'."

Ending a relaxing afternoon they left saying, "Tomorrow we'll be back with wine for your wedding reception."

Kaye left early for work Thursday afternoon hoping to meet Chaplain Filbey, we still had no response. Norman and Judy walked into my room carrying a bottle of wine as promised. Judy and I reminisced about past times, memories of growing up on the farm; Norman and I fondly recalled many fishing trips and waxing his car. When leaving Judy pointed her finger at me charging, "Call Mother and Daddy."

Thursday evening I phoned Dad and Mom, wishing her happy birthday and informing them of our wedding next day. The conversation became distressing as I answered numerous questions. "No...we aren't sure where, either a chapel at Methodist Hospital or our apartment. We'll be married somewhere...Oh Dad...no, it isn't a big mistake. Considering all Kaye and I have successfully endured for six years, of course it will last...I'm really not concerned...sixty days, six months, six years, or with God's blessing a life time...Well Dad, regardless your misgivings, it will happen. Oh yes, call and cancel my Social Security as of tomorrow. I tried, but they insisted since it is on your record, you have to initiate cancellation procedures. I love you and Mom. Maybe someday you'll understand."

My nurse Arlene again held the phone to my ear, "Hello John...No, I'm sorry, I still don't know where we're going. I know it's tomorrow...Of course I'll be there...Please be here at 12:00 noon...Thanks buddy...I'll know by then."

Knock, knock, ring, ring, ring. "What is the problem?" demanded Jackie, RN. "It's 2:00 AM, why are you so late?"

"I'm sorry for the delay," said Kaye, "but I just left work. Please let me speak to Dan. We have a chapel!"

"You might as well visit, he's still wide awake. Maybe he's nervous, what do you think?" she teased, patting me on the back.

"Dan," Kaye whispered, "Chaplain Filbey made a decision. The chapel is ours today at 2:30 PM. He spoke to Rev. Hollen, and together they will officiate the ceremony. I'll take the remainder of these boxes with me tonight. Oh, did you talk to John or Sharon? What about Betty?"

"Darling relax! Everything's under control." I smiled.

"You're something else!" said Kaye shaking her head. "Didn't Jackie just tell me you were so nervous you couldn't sleep? I repeat, what about Betty?"

"We're very fortunate." I replied. "Betty will come to work for us, it's also an answer to her problems. She needs evening hours for personal reasons and I promised her while Dan-sitting she could keep Stacey, her grandbaby. John and Sharon will be here at noon. Kaye, write directions to the apartment from NM, then place them under my telephone. I'll need John with me, but Sharon can't get lost trying to find you. I trust John inflates the

Keep Smiling and Never Give Up!

tires enough this time! At last, we're 'goin' to the chapel'. Our prayers are finally being answered yes! Go home and get some rest."

Kaye waved bye, tiptoeing quietly past my roommate.

"Dan, you better get some sleep." encouraged Pam, NA. "Morning will be here before you know it, turn your thoughts off friend."

"Soon." I whispered. "Soon..."

Morning dawned with Norma, NA shouting, "Wake up Dan! Leisure time is over, it's your wedding day!"

Following a restless night I forced my bloodshot eyes open, groggily focusing on the breakfast tray sitting beside my bed. The kitchen staff provided a festive array of eggs, bacon, toast, fruit, coffee, and tomato juice. "Norma, with a stomach full of butterflies there's no way I can eat this much food. What if I just drink my coffee or juice?"

"Consider it your last meal." she joked. "You must eat to replenish the energy you expended in thought last night. Pam said you didn't get to sleep until 6:00 AM."

I sat in my wheelchair nervously looking out the window at a gloomy day. "September 13th was supposed to be sunny like Tuesday, but just look at that cold, blowing rain. What a day for pneumonia." I thought. While bemoaning the unusual weather, John and Sharon arrived about noon.

"Well, look at Dan!" Sharon appraised while observing me clad in suit and tie. "Will Kaye ever be impressed!"

"Sharon cool it!" I implored. "You're embarrassing me. Anyway, you see John in a suit all the time, surely you've become accustomed to viewing handsome gentlemen."

"Sure, but he's already married." she grinned.

John asked, "Dan, do you know where we're going? It's important you get married and become a member of Henpecked Husbands Anonymous. Well, has Kaye told you where to go? Which map shall I use?"

"You won't need a map." I laughed. "You'll ride in the ambulance with me to Methodist. Sharon, under my phone is a paper with directions to our apartment. Would you deliver this beautiful centerpiece? Tell Kaye it's a wedding gift from the staff at Northwest Manor. Your husband and I will meet you at Methodist Hospital's Mary Hansen Chapel."

"If you get lost from those directions call us." Teased John. "Don't leave me standing at the altar!"

"Or me either!" I snickered. "Village Square is only a half mile away, she'll be fine. Don't have a flat tire."

Whirrr, click, click, screech. "Dan do you know where you're going yet?" Nila demanded. "I need your classified itinerary to type announcements. Oh, meet Stan your driver. If you don't mind I'll listen as

337

you tell him the destination. I've heard of last minute details, but this is ridiculous!"

"Now let me get this straight." Stan verified. "I take you and your best man to Methodist Children's Pavilion; cool my heels for about an hour; then transport you and your new wife home. Got it! Let's go."

"Dan don't forget we need a key to enter your apartment and deliver wedding gifts." Lee urgently reminded. "We have surprises all planned."

"Oh yes!" I exclaimed. "Thank goodness I needed a key yesterday evening so family could move some personal items. Kaye didn't question my request, she totally depended on my assertion I was just moving a chest of drawers."

"Dan! Dan!" Nila shouted from the hallway. "I'll have your announcements completed economically by Sunday."

Jennifer asked, "Dan do you want to hold a pen in your mouth and sign the release, or shall John witness an 'X'?"

"As a final farewell to dependence I want to hold the pen in my mouth and sign my name, but nerves have induced a form of palsy in my neck." I quipped. "I'll 'X' and grant John the honor of endorsing my freedom."

"Freedom? Ha!" said John as he signed papers.

"Are you warm enough back there Dan?" yelled Stan from his driver's seat in the ambulance. "This weather is weird. Can you believe it was sunny and warm Tuesday? Only an hour ago it was cold, blustery, and raining. Now look! Snow and sleet are hitting our windshield!"

"What do you expect?" John responded. "It's Friday the 13th. Oh, sorry Dan I forgot today's your wedding day."

Upon arriving at Methodist Stan unloaded my chair from the ambulance, motioning for John to assume command. "Okay you guys, I'll return in an hour." said Stan. "The chapel's just inside to the left. Did you receive directions?"

"No." I replied. "I still don't know where I'm going."

"Don't look at me." John said. "I'm just along for the ride. As best man I shouldn't be pushing the groom around."

"Pitiful! Pitiful!" exclaimed Stan shaking his head. "All right, I'll escort you inside, but I won't go all the way to the altar without threat of bodily harm."

Sitting inside the open chapel door John said to Stan, "I'll take over. Surely I won't get lost now."

"Wait! Let me look one more time at a free man. Dan, you're so brave." Stan heckled. "Any last wishes?"

Chaplain Filbey walked to my side, and to negate Stan's snide remark I introduced John. "Meet my best man and long time friend. Is everything set?

Have you studied the vows Kaye and I wrote? What about taped music? Oh no, where is Rev. Hollen?"

"Dan, calm down." insisted Chaplain Filbey. "I'm happy to meet you John. Now in succession, yes, yes, hopefully, Rev. Hollen has yet to arrive. Methodist is a big hospital and confusing at times, but don't worry Rev. Hollen's been here before, and he has God on his side. One minor detail you didn't mention, is the bride coming? I don't see her."

"Oh brother!" I exclaimed.

At that instant Sharon walked through the chapel doors announcing, "We're here. We'll be ready in a few minutes."

Brushing by Sharon on her way out the door, Rev. Hollen rushed in out of breath, "No one told me there was more than one Mary Hansen chapel. Never mind, I'm here now."

Chuckling, Chaplain Filbey said, "I think we had better rehearse the ceremony. Dan, have you advised John how best to position Kaye's ring in your hand so you can place it on her finger? Rev. Hollen, you recite the vows Dan and Kaye have written, then I'll perform the traditional ceremony."

During our brief rehearsal, minus bride and matron of honor, Sharon reappeared at the chapel door. Responding to her discreet signal, a recording of the wedding march began. After walking slowly down the aisle Sharon stood before the ministers, turning to await the bride. Within seconds Kaye appeared, proceeding to the altar adorned in a street length satiny white wedding gown, her head and face concealed under a delicate white lace veil, hands tightly clasping a bridal bouquet of yellow rosebuds and baby's breath, my soon-to-be wife, a classic portrait of angelic beauty encompassed in an aura of innocence and love.

I closely observed as she carefully cadenced her steps in time with, "Here Comes The Bride". My pounding heartbeat became deafening and it provoked suave, but nervous glances toward our friends whom I hoped would ignore such jittery anticipation. With eyes tearing I silently offered thanks for the devotion shown me by this wonderful, loving woman. With Kaye beside me, John turned my wheelchair to the altar, locked its brakes and whispered, "You can't run now!"

Friday, September thirteenth, nineteen hundred seventy four at two thirty in the afternoon, Daniel Ray Williams and Myra Kaye Williams were united in Holy Matrimony at the Mary Hansen chapel, Methodist Hospital. The double ring ceremony was performed by two divinely chosen men of God and witnessed by three close friends. Chaplain Filbey lovingly enunciated a phrase we had longed to hear through years of tribulation, "Dan and Kaye, I now pronounce you husband and wife."

Rev. Hollen prayed for faith, love, patience, hope, and read Matthew 19:5, "'For this cause shall a man leave father and mother, and shall cleave to his wife: and they twain shall be one flesh. Wherefore they are no more twain, but one flesh. What therefore God hath joined together let not man put asunder.'" Closing the Bible he addressed those gathered, "May this Holy union be blessed in the name of God: the Father, the Son, and the Holy Spirit. Amen."

Chaplain Filbey smiled, "Dan, you may kiss your bride."

Kaye raised her veil revealing a radiant glow emanating from the eyes of my God-given wife. I returned her gaze and at Chaplain Filbey's invitation, Kaye and I eternally sealed the sanctity of our wedding vows with a kiss.

"Sharon, take several pictures for our family album." I instructed. "Today culminates a struggle of six long years. We definitely want memories of today's ceremony for family and friends who couldn't be here to share in our happiness."

Click, click, flash. As she photographed the wedding party Sharon directed, "Kaye, both ministers, stand by Dan."

"That's enough pictures of us." said Rev. Hollen. "The best man and matron of honor gather around the newlyweds and I'll take pictures."

"Excuse me." Stan interrupted. "Apparently the wedding is over. Mr. & Mrs. Williams, are you ready for the ride to your new home? I have a big red and white limousine waiting outside, and for a little extra, I'll use lights and siren. Ha! Just kidding. Really, congratulations."

I don't remember much conversation on our trip between chapel and home; my attention was passionately focused on a lady in white - Mrs. Williams, my new bride. One teasing comment I do remember from Stan, "Atmospheric conditions are terrible, the windows are all steamed. I can hardly see!"

We arrived home preparing to enter the apartment door, when Kaye sat on my lap and Stan hurriedly wheeled us across the threshold to our new life. Snow flurries driven by raw, blustery winds prevented photographs of his thoughtful act.

Once inside, Kaye began an exercise that will continue for a lifetime, pushing me around! Leaving a life of degradation and despair accentuated by occasional peaks of glory, bride and groom embarked on a voyage of contentment and happiness. Peace and joy filled our hearts, lives eternally together.

"Surprise! Say Cheese! Smile!" With flashes blinding our eyes we heard, "Congratulations! Welcome home!"

"Who are Lee and Rene`?" John inquired. "They prepared a table with goodies, plus a card and gift from Dan to Kaye. Here's the remaining roll of toilet paper someone used while decorating your apartment. Including the birdcage! I guess whoever's responsible apparently thought inexperience would hinder consummation of your marriage. If you have problems, follow the giant arrow of TP all the way to the bedroom."

"John hush!" ordered Sharon. "The ministers are here."

"Now I know what people mean when they refer to the new blushing bride. Look at Kaye!" I teased.

"Blushing nothing!" Kaye exclaimed. "How did they get into our apartment? All right Daniel! What other surprises can I expect today? Where's that key?"

Avoiding the subject I gasped, "Would you connect," gulp "my respirator? Whew, thank you. Now check out the table."

"Aaahh, how wonderful!" exclaimed Kaye. "Look at our beautifully decorated wedding cake and flowers. I'll open my gift later when we're alone."

"Who are Lee and Rene`?" John repeated. "Speak up!"

Realizing I couldn't escape an explanation I confessed, "Lee is Activities Director at Northwest Manor, my temporary summer home, and Rene` volunteers, assisting residents with recreational opportunities and services. Family transferred some of my possessions from NM to the apartment last night, after which I conveniently made the key available to Lee and Rene`, so they could deliver these items during the ceremony. I wasn't aware they planned to TP the apartment."

"Cut the wedding cake." Rev. Hollen urged. "I have to find my way through Methodist and locate a missing car some place in the parking garage."

"Kaye, you do the honors." advised Sharon. "Remember, Dan gets the first messy bite."

"Cool it Mrs. Williams! I can't reciprocate." I warned.

"I knooww!" Kaye laughed.

"The cake is delicious." Chaplain Filbey praised. "Are you responsible for this Dan?"

"Absolutely! I baked it myself." I quipped.

"Okay everybody, gather around." Sharon coached. "It's time for more pictures commemorating the wedding reception."

The camaraderie existing between friends who'd traveled the highway of love with us added joy to our celebration. Fellowship with dear friends while creating indelible memories came to an abrupt end as Chaplain Filbey remarked, "I must return to the hospital."

Prior to leaving Rev. Hollen directed, "Let us pray for God's continued strength and fulfillment."

We and the ministers exchanged farewells, with promises of visiting each other soon. Following their hurried exit I breathed aromas drifting from the kitchen, "Mmmm, does the food ever smell delicious! It's been tantalizing my taste buds since arriving from the chapel. I didn't eat breakfast and I'm starved! How soon can we eat?"

John and Sharon were previously invited to our post-nuptial dinner. John agreed with me exclaiming, "Yes! I'm hungry. Let's relax and eat."

After enjoying Kaye's delicious oven-cooked dinner, we reminisced about events preceding our wedding ceremony. "I don't want to be too personal," Sharon apologized, "but will you please explain those letters engraved inside your rings? I couldn't help noticing, 'MTY/LTT'."

"Yeah." John interrupted. "Kaye's ring also had those letters, 'MTY/LTT'. I spent most of your ceremony wondering what they signified. Come on, you can tell us."

Looking furtively at Kaye and blushing from embarrassed silence, I responded, "In 1968, on the day we were engaged, our avowed promise was to have faith and love in each other, 'MORE THAN YESTERDAY, LESS THAN TOMORROW!'"

"I've often remembered the way you two were so devoted to each other." Sharon confided. "At Heritage House we were all touched by your closeness and the love you demonstrated. We used to remark, 'how much longer must they wait'?"

"Enough melodrama!" declared John. "I remember the day Sharon radioed on my CB, 'Help, our tire is flat!'. I still don't understand how I was supposed to repair the car from twenty miles away. I should have come along."

I glanced at the wall clock then back at John who must have thought I wanted them to go away because he suggested, "Sharon, let's get out of here, the newlyweds need to be by themselves. I remember the night we were married..."

Sharon blushed, "John be quiet!"

"Good idea John." I hurriedly agreed. "Before leaving, would you lift me into bed? I want to end my old life, then begin independence tomorrow when Kaye uses my hydraulic lift transferring me from bed to wheelchair." After putting me to bed they waved goodbye motioning thumbs up. I choked on the giant lump filling my throat, "Thank you dear friends."

The apartment door shut behind John and Sharon, leaving us alone in our new home. Kaye nervously collected soiled dishes and headed for the kitchen. "One thing you'll learn about me," she said, "I hate waking up to a messy kitchen."

"Uumm hummm." I sighed.

Keep Smiling and Never Give Up!

Patiently awaiting Kaye's reappearance in our bedroom I quickly reviewed past events - great happiness sandwiched by intolerance, pain, and suffering. Our lives had been shaped by personal tribulation; our destiny fashioned in heaven. I knew together we could not only overcome any difficulty, but, through faith, enhance our diamond-like marriage. Glancing sideways I looked longingly at the elegant pink negligee lying on the bed, my birthday gift to Kaye six months ago – no longer in the box. Unable to contain any longer I beckoned, "Honey if you continue washing and drying those dishes and pans, they won't survive our first dinner." Ignoring my feeble protests, Kaye still procrastinated. She washed and dried the dishes, dried the pans, and endlessly polished the cabinets. Weary of staring helplessly at blank walls I suggested, "Mrs. Williams, it's time you follow the arrow of TP! Sublimation is over my darling."

Years of unfulfilled dreams were consummated behind our bedroom door, twain became one. Married at last!!!

> We, Dan and Kaye Williams, announce with pleasure that on the afternoon of Friday, September 13, 1974, at 2:30 P.M., celebrated our ceremony of Holy Matrimony.
>
> This announcement is made in the hope that you share in our love, joy and happiness which we pray will endure for eternity.
>
> Our home is at 3650 D North Mission Drive, Indianapolis, Indiana 46224. You are welcome to visit us in our new home.
>
> Mr. & Mrs. Dan Williams

Personal Photos: Our Wedding Day
(Top) Our Wedding Announcement.
(Left) Wedding Party:
Front Row: Groom, Dan, Bride, Kaye, and Matron of Honor, Sharon.
Back Row: Best Man, John, Rev. Hollen, Chaplain Filbey.

(Right): Bride and Groom in their first home, about to cut the wedding cake.

ABOUT THE AUTHOR

In October 1957, Daniel Ray Williams, a healthy fourteen-year old member of his high school football team and band member, contracted Polio. His was the first case of the last Polio attacks in New Castle, Indiana. Suddenly, without warning, he was paralyzed and dependent on an iron lung for every breath. With intense rehabilitative efforts he escaped the iron lung though remaining paralyzed and breathing with portable respirators. He wrote many short stories and three books. His life is a testimony to his favorite scripture, II Corinthians 12:9 "My grace is sufficient for thee: for my strength is made perfect in weakness." This is his first book published. He died in June 2001.